The Eternal Future

The Eternal Future of the 1950s

Essays on the Lasting Influence of the Decade's Science Fiction Films

Edited by DENNIS R. CUTCHINS
and DENNIS R. PERRY

Afterword by Thomas Leitch

McFarland & Company, Inc., Publishers
Jefferson, North Carolina

LIBRARY OF CONGRESS CATALOGUING-IN-PUBLICATION DATA

Names: Cutchins, Dennis R. (Dennis Ray), 1963– editor. | Perry, Dennis R., editor. |
Leitch, Thomas M., writer of afterword.
Title: The eternal future of the 1950s : essays on the lasting influence of the decade's
science fiction films / edited by Dennis R. Cutchins and Dennis R. Perry ;
afterword by Thomas Leitch.
Description: Jefferson, North Carolina : McFarland & Company, Inc., Publishers, 2023 |
Includes bibliographical references and index.
Identifiers: LCCN 2023017486 | ISBN 9781476687858 (paperback : acid free paper) ∞
ISBN 9781476649276 (ebook)
Subjects: LCSH: Science fiction films—United States—History and criticism. |
Motion pictures—United States—History—20th century. | Nineteen fifties.
Classification: LCC PN1995.9.S26 E79 2023 | DDC 791.43/615—dc23/eng/20230606
LC record available at https://lccn.loc.gov/2023017486

BRITISH LIBRARY CATALOGUING DATA ARE AVAILABLE

ISBN (print) 978-1-4766-8785-8
ISBN (ebook) 978-1-4766-4927-6

Front cover: Poster art from the 1951 film *Flight to Mars*
(Monogram Pictures/Photofest)

Printed in the United States of America

*McFarland & Company, Inc., Publishers
Box 611, Jefferson, North Carolina 28640
www.mcfarlandpub.com*

To all lovers of science fiction movies from the glorious fifties,
and to Mary Lyn and Marianne for their tireless support.

Table of Contents

Introduction: The Past and Present Future
DENNIS R. CUTCHINS *and* DENNIS R. PERRY · 1

Part I: Adapting a 1950s Science Fiction Aesthetic

Presenting Frank Darabont's *The Mist* (2007) in Glorious Black & White:
The Remaking of a 1950s Sci-Fi Aesthetic
GREG SEMENZA · 11

Retro Reboots: Adapting 1950s Science Fiction in *Bioshock, Fallout,*
and *Wolfenstein*
DANIEL SINGLETON · 25

The Truth Is Out There: 1950s Science Fiction, *The X-Files*, and the Shifting
Dynamics of National Anxiety
JESSICA METZLER · 43

Part II: Monsters Within and Without

Extinction Panic: Prehistoric Creatures of the Anthropocene
ZAK BRONSON · 61

"Forget the world and hang on to the people you care about the most":
Giant Monster Movies from the 1950s and Their
Twenty-First-Century Counterparts
ROBIN JEREMY LAND · 75

"Something's lost in the translation!" Hemimetabolic Adaptation
(or Incomplete Metamorphosis) in David Cronenberg's *The Fly*
RICHARD BERGER · 95

Adapting the Monstrous Other: del Toro Re-Shapes
Creature from the Black Lagoon
GLENN JELLENIK · 110

Part III: Alien Invasions

The Day the Earth Stood Still, The Thing from Another World,
and the Creation of Two Archetypes
DENNIS R. CUTCHINS · 127

Queer Anxieties and Perverse Desires in the Alien Infiltration Film
   MICA A. HILSON   148

The War of the Worlds: Masculine Heroism and Symbolic Spaces
   in Invasion Narratives
   JOAN ORMROD   162

The Space Children and the Alien: Magic and Paranoia at World's End
   DENNIS R. PERRY   182

The Alien in the Graveyard: Extraterrestrial Reanimation in Ed Wood's
   Plan 9 from Outer Space and Walter Mosley's *The Wave*
   PAUL PIATKOWSKI   195

Double Trouble: Martin Guerre, *Invaders from Mars*, and the Body
   Snatchers Films
   SAM UMLAND   210

Part IV: Other Worlds and Dystopian Visions

Escaping Earth: The Uninhabitable Home in *Rocketship X-M*, *Interstellar*,
   and *Ad Astra*
   CHRISTOPHER LOVE   223

From the Promise of the 1950s to the Uncertainty of the 1960s: The Surety
   of *Forbidden Planet* Against the Empty Center of *Solaris*
   ROBERT MAYER   237

New Maps of Hell: Racebending and *Fahrenheit 451*
   WILLIAM HART   251

Still Captive? The Maternal Body in 1950s Science Fiction Disaster Films
   and *Mad Max: Fury Road*
   REBECCA JOHINKE   267

*Afterword: Yesterday's Tomorrows: The Double Consciousness
   of Science Fiction*
   THOMAS LEITCH   285

About the Contributors   297

Index   299

Introduction

The Past and Present Future

DENNIS R. CUTCHINS *and* DENNIS R. PERRY

> In these troubling times, the urgency to trouble time, to shake it to its core, to produce collective imaginaries that undo pervasive conceptions of temporality that take progress as inevitable and the past as something that has passed and is no longer with us is something so tangible, so visceral, there is a sense in which it can be felt in our individual and collective bodies—Barad 306

Near the end of *Rocketship X-M* (1950), discussed at some length by Christopher Love in this collection, Colonel Floyd Graham (Lloyd Bridges) and Dr. Lisa Van Horn (Osa Massen) are preparing for a fiery death. Their spaceship has run out of fuel and they have no way of slowing their re-entry into Earth's atmosphere. Having discovered that Mars is a post-atomic wasteland, in their final moments of life they radio a desperate warning about the dangers of nuclear weapons to the people of Earth. They also confess their long-hidden love for each other. Van Horn pleads for Graham to hold her tightly, and Graham comforts her.[1] He notes that they don't have much time but suggests that "time isn't so important." And then, voicing the central message of the film, he quickly adds, "there's not that much difference between the future and the past." The notion that there isn't much difference between the future and the past is one of the premises of this book. Speaking specifically of renewed fears of nuclear war in the twenty-first century, Karan Barad suggests "the twentieth century is anything by past/passed" (306). The relevance of both the fears and the hopes of the 1950s may be witnessed in the fact that the plots, themes, and aesthetics of 1950s sci-fi films are so thoroughly embedded in more recent films that sometimes it is difficult to see the individual trees for the forest of influence. Indeed, the central conceit of this book is that the sci-fi films of the 1950s play a key role in understanding not just the past of sci-fi but both its present and its future.

Sci-fi films have been around almost as long as the film industry. Georges Méliès' *Le Voyage dans la Lune* (1902) occupies an important place in early film history, and Fritz Lang's *Metropolis* (1927) is a classic in anyone's book. But it should not be surprising that the *modern* sci-fi film was invented in the 1950s. There are any number of possible reasons for this. In addition to the higher profile of science and scientists after World War II, the elusive and exciting future seemed closer than ever

Figure 1. From left: Dr. Lisa Van Horn (Osa Massen), Dr. Karl Eckstrom (John Emery), Harry Chamberlain (Hugh O'Brian), and Colonel Floyd Graham (Lloyd Bridges) discover the retrograde state of the Martian natives in *Rocketship X-M* (1950) (Lippert Pictures Inc./Photofest).

in the '50s. Credit cards, super glue, computer hard disks, and Ford Thunderbirds, all invented in the 1950s and all still around today, gave a taste of the promise of the future. More practically, newly invented transistors and semi-conductors ushered in the electronic age. Human organ transplantation became a reality in 1954 and revolutionized the medical world. And in the 1950s humans stood on the edge of outer space, peering into the void. Paranoid, post-war space competition with the USSR was brought on by the Cold War and spurred by the success of Sputnik. Americans realized that they were being left behind in the Space Race, and that realization led to unprecedented scientific advances in the relatively new field of space travel. The field quickly moved from fantasy to scientific pursuit to reality. Thus no one blinked in the late '40s and early '50s when kid-oriented sci-fi like *Captain Video* (1949–1955) and *Superman and the Mole Men* (1951) or more sophisticated, thoughtful, and adult films like *The Day the Earth Stood Still* (1951) appeared. Sci-fi, at this point a major cultural development, became the only language that could express our mingled fear, concern, and excitement about the future in an era of constant change, scientific breakthroughs, and cultural uncertainty.

It would be easy to dismiss any set of films, especially any set of genre films, as products of a given moment and not particularly relevant to other ages. Bryan Vizzini may fall into this trap in "Cold War Fears, Cold War Passions: Conservatives and Liberals Square Off in 1950s Science Fiction." Despite beginning his article by warning his readers, and presumably himself, that "forming meaningful generalizations about American culture in the 1950s is a tricky affair," Vizzini concludes his treatment of 1950s sci-fi by suggesting that

> Hollywood's science-fiction output in the 1950s reflected the tensions, conflicts, and debates playing out in the broader American political landscape. Just as Republicans proved ascendant in the beginning of the decade, so too did studios increase production of films justifying the agenda that both McCarthyists and liberation advocates laid out. The political opposition, though, did not disappear—it continued to wage its battles onscreen and off ... eventually eclipsing its opponents in the 1960s [38].[2]

This generalization does not mar the insightful analysis of the films Vizzini treats in his article, but it does have the unfortunate tendency to limit the perception of 1950s sci-fi films to one-dimensional artifacts of a particular period rather than vibrant texts that continue to resonate with contemporary audiences and filmmakers. Indeed, despite the intense scrutiny of sci-fi films from the 1950s, contemporary scholars have largely ignored the ongoing influence of these films. It is possible that the kind of study you hold in your hands has not yet been attempted because readers and critics often consider sci-fi either as inextricably mired in a particular historical moment or as a monolithic genre. These approaches are both problematic, the first because it ignores the massive and ongoing influence of the 1950s and the second because it runs the risk of missing the ways sci-fi has evolved over the decades. In *Invasions USA: The Essential Science Fiction Films of the 1950s*, Michael Bliss explores the broader significance and popularity of 1950s sci-fi films when he argues "the very real anxieties dramatized in these films involve fears that come from a region more personal than political. They come from the depths of human psychology. And what they tell us is that the supposedly placid 1950s were haunted by the stuff of nightmares" (x). The notion that a handful of genre films might reflect "the depths of human psychology" is an apt enough place to begin to understand the roles these films continue to play.

Many of these 1950s sci-fi films were powerful and popular because they addressed both our make-believe and our very real fears. These included fears of invasion; fears about the long-term effects of nuclear testing; fears about seemingly imminent world wars; fears about the dangers of space travel; and fears about dehumanization.[3] These films were sometimes brilliant: *War of the Worlds* (1953); *Them!* (1954); *Forbidden Planet* (1956)[4]; and *Invasion of the Body Snatchers* (1956)[5]; and sometimes less so: *Lost Continent* (1951); *Captive Women* (1952); and *Cat-Women of the Moon* (1953). In a single year they ranged along a continuum of insightful speculation in films like *It Came from Outer Space* (1953) to the entertaining nonsense of *Abbott and Costello Go to Mars* (1953), and from the breakthrough special effects of *The Beast from 20,000 Fathoms* (1953) to absurdly inept cheapies like *Mesa of Lost Women* (1953).

The 1950s also saw the development of new audiences for sci-fi both in and out of the United States. Films made about teens and starring them became common fare at local drive-ins. *The Blob* (1958) and *Teenagers from Outer Space* (1959) represent sci-fi films that catered to this emerging audience and helped to influence cars, clothing styles, and music. The striking rise in sci-fi films, and later sci-fi television, was not strictly an American phenomenon. The Japanese *Gojira* (1954) reflected the horrors of atomic war with a surprisingly apt monstrous metaphor and started a franchise that is newly rejuvenated. The Italian *The Day the Sky Exploded* (1958) also warned, less metaphorically, of the dangers of atomic energy as well as the unintended consequences of space travel.

Perhaps the most incredible aspect of this 1950s phenomenon is that the influence of these sci-fi films has continued over the decades from the 1960s into the twenty-first century. As movie-making technology has developed, recent films have re-visited 1950s themes such as space travel in much more realistic and believable ways. *Rocketship X-M* (1950), *Destination Moon* (1950), and *Flight to Mars* (1951) have all been reimagined in terms of our ever-growing space technology in such films as *2001: A Space Odyssey* (1968), *Interstellar* (2014), and *Ad Astra* (2019).[6] Meanwhile, 1950s classics have been remade and re-envisioned by important contemporary directors. Howard Hawks' *The Thing from Another World* (1951) was remade as *The Thing* (1982) by John Carpenter, and the new film soon become a cult classic. Closer in terms of plot to the original short story, Carpenter's film is darker, grittier, and perhaps more serious than the earlier film.[7] The same might be said of David Cronenberg's *The Fly* (1986).[8] Both films used improved special effects technology not just to create more visually striking films but to force audiences to viscerally consider the bounds of the human. Steven Spielberg's *War of the Worlds* (2005) and Tyler Bates' *The Day the Earth Stood Still* (2008) may not have eclipsed their originals in the same way, but both updated the cultural and political contexts of their cinematic predecessors in creative and meaningful ways.

There are any number of reasons that the plots, themes, characters, aesthetic, and "spirit," if you will, of 1950s sci-fi lives on in more recent films. For one thing, the film industry in Hollywood, though it is often identified as politically liberal, is at least in some ways one of the most conservative businesses in the world. The proliferation of zombie movies or teenagers-fighting-a-repressive-government movies released in the early twenty-first century clearly illustrate that point. If one sci-fi film does well at the box office you can bet on a second one being released in short order. This certainly accounts for films like *Stranger from Venus* (1954) and *Laserblast* (1978). *Stranger from Venus* bears more than a passing resemblance to *The Day the Earth Stood Still*, released two years earlier in 1951, and *Laserblast* appeared months after the release of *Star Wars* (1977) and seemed calculated to cash in on George Lucas's success. But in many cases the influence of an earlier film or genre seems to project many decades into the future. The relatively recent rebirth of Kaiju films offers a perfect example. This genre seemed played out by the mid–1960s, but the release of *Godzilla vs. Kong* (2021) is more than the result of a filmmaker attempting to cash in on a trend. The surprising comeback of giant monster films suggests that the genre actually has become meaningful for viewers again, though perhaps for very different reasons.[9]

Giant monsters are hard to miss, but in a much less flashy manner, two recent films offer more subtle homages to sci-fi films of the 1950s. *The Midnight Sky* (2020), directed by and starring George Clooney, was released directly to Netflix. The film follows the final days of Augustine Lofthouse (Clooney), one of the few survivors of a nuclear holocaust. Lofthouse spends most of the film traveling through the Arctic to reach a transmitter that might allow him to contact and warn off a spaceship on its way back to Earth after exploring one of Jupiter's habitable moons. Clooney himself calls the film "dreamlike," and it certainly has the quality of a sort of banal nightmare where the problems are inescapably there but just barely out of sight. The film is based on Lily Brooks-Dalton's 2016 novel *Good Morning, Midnight*, but its post-nuclear war setting, hope for postponement of inevitable death at the poles, and melancholic tone were all foreshadowed by Stanley Kramer's *On the Beach* (1957) and, to some extent, by the film mentioned at the beginning of this introduction—*Rocketship X-M*.

A second film, Andrew Patterson's *The Vast of Night* (2020), depends even more on atmosphere. It follows Everett (Jake Horowitz), a charismatic small-town radio announcer, and Fay (Sierra McCormick), a teenage telephone switchboard operator, as they struggle to come to grips with an apparent alien invasion. Patterson made *The Vast of Night* with a dramatically smaller budget than *The Midnight Sky*, and the film doesn't appear to have been influenced by any particular predecessors. Indeed, when asked about inspiration Patterson cites nineteenth-century novels *War and Peace* and *Moby Dick* ("*The Vast of Night*: Interview"). But *Vast of Night*'s aesthetic, including its meticulously created 1950s small town setting, muted colors (the entire film takes place at night), and ominous tone make it kin to any number of 1950s alien invasion films.[10]

At the other end of the subtlety spectrum are the films of directors like Larry Blamire and Christopher Mihm. Blamire's *The Lost Skeleton of Cadavra* (2001) is a loving parody of 1950s sci-fi/horror films. It was shot on videotape and made with a budget under $50,000. The convoluted plot is reminiscent of films like *Plan 9 from Outer Space* (1959), *The Magnetic Monster* (1953), and *Robot Monster* (1953). Blamire apparently worked to incorporate as many B-movie tropes as possible, including alien invaders, psychic powers, mutants, and an evil scientist. The film inspired a number of similar efforts, including Mihm's *Cave Women on Mars* (2008), Neal McLaughlin's *I Was a Teenage Wereskunk* (2016), and our favorite, Ted Newsom's *The Naked Monster* (2005). In that parody Kenneth Tobey reprises his role as Captain Patrick Hendry from *The Thing from Another World*. Now promoted to colonel, Hendry organizes the defense against the gigantic "naked monster." In a series of inside jokes, Newsom also creates cameos for long-time sci-fi editor Forrest Ackerman and B-movie star John Agar and includes a character named "Lieutenant Nyby," named after 1950s director Christian Nyby.[11]

This abbreviated list of remakes, sequels, homages, and parodies begs the question: what is it about 1950s sci-fi that continues to inspire contemporary filmmakers? J.P. Telotte sums up several assessments of 1950s sci-fi film in the first chapter of his aptly named *Science Fiction Film*, and in so doing he suggests one possible core reason for its continuing influence—its simultaneous embrace and rejection of the world as it now exists. He cites David Hartwell who writes, "science fiction has been an umbrella under which any kind of estrangement from reality is welcome" (Telotte 4). Darko Suvin, also cited by Telotte, seems to agree, calling sci-fi a "literature of cognitive estrangement—a form intent on defamiliarizing reality" (4). Telotte himself, focusing on the formal elements of sci-fi rather than its driving philosophies, argues that "especially in its cinematic form ... science fiction often seems to appeal precisely because it lends itself to the greatest imaginative capacities of the film medium: to its ability, through what we very broadly term 'special effects,' to give shape and being to the imagination" (3). To be clear, none of these appraisals focuses on the element sci-fi shares with all fiction: an effort to portray that which is imaginary. Rather, Hartwell, Suvin, and Telotte identify the more exclusive role sci-fi has carved for itself to actively defy reality while at the same time to engage deeply with it. This position has allowed sci-fi to tackle divisive topics such as race, war, and religion in ways that more realistic fiction and films often can't.[12] Susan Sontag hints at this seeming paradox when she describes her own love/hate relationship with sci-fi, particularly the sci-fi films of the 1950s. Near the end of her famous 1965 essay "The Imagination of Disaster," she writes, "The interest of the films, aside from their considerable amount of cinematic charm, consists in this intersection between a naively and largely debased commercial art product and the most profound dilemmas of the contemporary situation" (130). As Emily Dickinson might have summed up the notions of Telotte and Sontag, sci-fi allows filmmakers to tell the truth but tell it slant.

Certainly one of the truths that sci-fi nearly always tells is about science itself. The widely divergent portrayals of science in sci-fi films of the 1950s may be due in part to the public's often contradictory perceptions of science during the period. Scientists achieved a newly elevated public status in the 1950s, but that status was often countered by the recognition that science had ushered in the incredibly frightening nuclear age. As Robert Oppenheimer suggested in words borrowed from the *Bhagavad Gita*, scientists had "become Death, the destroyer of worlds" (Oppenheimer). This tension regarding science and scientists is reflected in many films of the '50s. For every kind, humble, selfless (and attractive) Dr. Harold or Pat Medford (Edmund Gwenn and Joan Weldon) from *Them!* (1954), there's a selfish, obsessed, and hubristic Morbius (Walter Pidgeon) from *Forbidden Planet* (1956). Indeed, scientists are cast as villains in many films in the 1950s. *Neanderthal Man* (1953), *Fiend Without a Face* (1958), *Monster on the Campus* (1958), *The Thing from Another World* (1951), and *The Cosmic Man* (1959) all feature scientists who are careless, short-sighted, or downright evil. More recently, the seemingly endless public debates over the safety of vaccines suggest that attitudes toward science have not changed as much as one might have hoped over the last 60 or 70 years.

The sci-fi films of the 1950s put the apocalyptic end of the world, space travel, outer space aliens, giant monsters, dehumanization, lost worlds, and body snatchers on the big screen—and there they've stayed.[13] The specific reasons for this sticking power are varied, as the essays herein demonstrate, but likely include the two basic reasons discussed above. The first has to do with the power of sci-fi to reject contemporary reality while simultaneously engaging with it. In the words of Michael Bliss, aliens and robots "start to unhinge us from the usual way of viewing ourselves and move us toward a vantage point distant enough from the norm so that, perhaps for the first time in a long while, we see ourselves as though from the perspective of something unusual, something strange—in other words, something alien" (xii).

That has always been the potential gift of sci-fi, and it is a gift appreciated equally by artists, viewers, and scholars. The second reason is that "the depths of human psychology" and the anxieties spawned there are largely unchanging. They remain mostly untouched by politics and current events. To paraphrase Colonel Graham, there really isn't that much difference between the future and the past.

Notes

1. The gender stereotypes embodied in this scene are laughable in retrospect. For more on gender in the films of the '50s and in more recent films, see the essays of Rebecca Johinke, Joan Ormrod, and Mica A. Hilson in this collection.

2. Dennis R. Perry's essay in this collection analyzes a film that reflects part of the trend Vizzini describes here.

3. For more on the notion of dehumanization, see Glenn Jellenik's essay in this collection.

4. For more on *Forbidden Planet*, see Robert Mayer's essay in this collection.

5. For more on *Invasion of the Body Snatchers*, see Sam Umland's essay in this collection.

6. For more on the relationship between *Rocketship X-M*, *Interstellar*, and *Ad Astra*, see Christopher Love's essay in this collection.

7. For more on these films, see Dennis R. Cutchins' essay in this collection.

8. For more on *The Fly*, see Richard Berger's essay in this collection.

9. For more on the reasons for the resurgence of kaiju films, see Zak Bronson's and Robin Jeremy Land's essays in this collection.

10. For more on the adaptation of a 1950s sci-fi aesthetic, see Greg Semenza's, Daniel Singleton's, and Jessica Metzler's essays in this collection.

11. Other filmmakers have also managed to get actors from the 1950s involved. In Blamire's *Trail of the Screaming Forehead* (2007), for instance, Kevin McCarthy has a cameo.

12. For more on race in sci-fi, see William Hart's essay in this collection.

13. Perhaps the major difference between the sci-fi of the '50s and that of today is that many such films were originally pegged as B movies, while films like *Interstellar* (2014) and *Arrival* (2016) are most certainly A films, with major stars and huge budgets.

Works Cited

Barad, Karen. "Troubling Time/s and Ecologies of Nothingness." *Through Post-Atomic Eyes*, edited by Claudette Lauzon and John O'Brian. McGill-Queen's University Press, 2020, pp. 306–32.

Bliss, Michael. *Invasions USA: The Essential Science Fiction Films of the 1950s*. Rowman & Littlefield, 2014.

Hirschberg, Lynn. "George Clooney Does It All." *Wmagazine.com*, W Magazine, 23 Feb. 2021, https://www.wmagazine.com/culture/george-clooney-interview-midnight-sky. Accessed 27 Dec. 2021.

Oppenheimer, Robert. "I Am Become Death, the Destroyer of Worlds." YouTube, uploaded by Plenilune-Pictures, 6 Aug. 2011, https://www.youtube.com/watch?v=lb13ynu3Iac. Accessed 27 Dec. 2021.

Sontag, Susan. "The Imagination of Disaster." *Science Fiction: A Collection of Critical Essays*, edited by Mark Rose. Prentice-Hall, 1976, pp. 116–31.

Telotte, J.P., and Barry Keith Grant. *Science Fiction Film*. 2001. Cambridge University Press, 2004.

"*The Vast of Night*: Interview with Director Andrew Patterson." *Slamdance*, Sundance Film Festival, 16 June 2020, https://slamdance.com/the-vast-of-night-interview-with-director-andrew-patterson/. Accessed 28 Oct. 2021.

Vizzini, Bryan E. "Cold War Fears, Cold War Passions: Conservatives and Liberals Square Off in 1950s Science Fiction." *Quarterly Review of Film and Video* 26.1 (2008): 28–39.

Filmography

Abbott and Costello Go to Mars. Dir. Charles Lamont. Universal-International, 1953. Film.

Ad Astra. Dir. James Gray. 20th Century Fox, 2019. Film.

The Beast from 20,000 Fathoms. Dir. Eugène Lourié. Warner Bros., 1953. Film.

The Blob. Dir. Irvin Yeaworth. Paramount Pictures, 1958. Film.

Captain Video: Master of the Stratosphere. Dir. Spencer Gordon Bennet and Wallace Grissell. Columbia Pictures, 1951. Film.

Captive Women. Dir Stuart Gilmore. RKO Radio Pictures Inc., 1952. Film.

Cat-Women of the Moon. Dir. Arthur Hilton. Astor Pictures, 1953. Film.

Cave Women on Mars. Dir. Christopher R. Mihm. 2008. Film.

The Cosmic Man. Dir. Herbert S. Greene. Futura Productions, 1959. Film.

The Day the Earth Stood Still. Dir. Robert Wise. 20th Century Fox, 1951. Film.

The Day the Earth Stood Still. Dir. Scott Derrickson. 20th Century Fox, 2008. Film.

The Day the Sky Exploded. Dir. Paolo Heusch and Mario Bava. Lux Film, 1958. Film.

Destination Moon. Dir. Irving Pichel. George Pal Productions, 1950. Film.

Fiend Without a Face. Dir. Arthur Crabtree. MGM, 1958. Film.

Flight to Mars. Dir. Lesley Selander. Monogram Distributing Corp, 1951. Film.

The Fly. Dir. David Cronenberg. 20th Century Fox, 1986. Film.

Forbidden Planet. Dir. Fred M. Wilcox. MGM, 1956. Film.

Godzilla vs. Kong. Dir. Adam Wingard. Warner Bros., 2021. Film.

Gojira. Dir. Ishiro Honda. Toho, 1954. Film.

I Was a Teenage Wereskunk. Dir. Neal McLaughlin. 2016. Film.

Interstellar. Dir. Christopher Nolan. Warner Bros., 2014. Film.

Invasion of the Body Snatchers. Dir. Don Siegel. Allied Artists Pictures, 1956. Film.

It Came from Outer Space. Dir. Jack Arnold. Universal Pictures, 1953. Film.

Laserblast. Dir. Michael Rae. Irwin Yablans Company, 1978. Film.

Lost Continent. Dir. Sam Newfield. Lippert Pictures, 1951. Film.

The Lost Skeleton of Cadavra. Dir. Larry Blamaire. TriStar Pictures, 2001. Film.

The Magnetic Monster. Curt Siodmak and Herbert L. Strock. United Artists, 1953. Film.

Mesa of Lost Women. Dir. Herbert Tevos and Ron Ormond. Ron Ormond Productions, 1953. Film.

Metropolis. Dir. Fritz Lang. Parufamet, 1927. Film.

The Midnight Sky. Dir. George Clooney. Smokehouse Pictures, 2020. Film.

Monster on the Campus. Dir. Jack Arnold. Universal-International. 1958. Film.

The Naked Monster. Dir. Ted Newsom and Wayne Berwick. Heidelberg Films, 2005. Film.

Neanderthal Man. Dir. Ewald André Dupont. United Artists, 1953. Film.

Plan 9 from Outer Space. Dir. Ed Wood. Valiant Pictures, 1959. Film.

Robot Monster. Dir. Phil Tucker. Astor Pictures, 1953. Film.

Rocketship X-M. Dir. Kurt Neumann. Lippert Pictures, 1950. Film.

Star Wars. Dir. George Lucas. 20th Century Fox, 1977. Film.

Stranger from Venus. Dir. Burt Balaban. Princess Pictures Inc., 1954. Film.

Superman and the Mole Men. Dir. Lee Sholem. Warner Bros., 1951. Film.

Teenagers from Outer Space. Dir. Tom Graeff. Warner Bros., 1959. Film.

Them! Dir. Gordon Douglas. Warner Bros., 1954. Film.

Thing from Another World, The. Dir. Christian Nyby. RKO Radio Pictures, 1951. Film.

The Thing. Dir. John Carpenter. Universal Pictures, 1982. Film.

2001: A Space Odyssey. Dir. Stanley Kubrick. MGM, 1968. Film.

The Vast of Night. Dir. Andrew Patterson. Amazon Studios, 2020. Film.

Le Voyage dans la Lune. Dir. Georges Méliès. Star Film Company, 1902. Film.

War of the Worlds. Dir. Byron Haskin. Paramount Pictures, 1953. Film.

War of the Worlds. Dir. Steven Spielberg. Paramount Pictures, 2005. Film.

PART I

Adapting a 1950s Science Fiction Aesthetic

Presenting Frank Darabont's *The Mist* (2007) in Glorious Black & White

The Remaking of a 1950s Sci-Fi Aesthetic

Greg Semenza

The Genius Products Collector's Edition of Frank Darabont's *The Mist* (2007), which was filmed in color, includes an extra DVD version of the film in black & white (B&W).[1] Darabont refers to this version as his "preferred.... Director's cut," acknowledging his original desire to film Stephen King's novella in B&W, which derived from a comment King himself once made about his story being "inspired by those old grainy Black & White Bert I. Gordon monster movies of his youth" ("Frank Darabont Introduces *The Mist* in Black & White"). King was referring to such B sci-fi/horror films as *Beginning of the End* (1957), *The Cyclops* (1957), and *Earth vs. the Spider* (1958). Darabont extends the legacy of those 1950s "grainy Black & Whites" to include such mid–1960s Gordon follow-ups as *Village of the Giants* (1965) and considerably more influential non–Gordon films such as *Night of the Living Dead* (1968); *The Mist*, he explains, was always conceived as a "throwback" of sorts, belonging to what he describes generally as the "pre-color, Ray Harryhausen era of film" ("Frank Darabont Introduces").

Like Stephen King, whose works he has adapted for the screen on four occasions,[2] Darabont has always been preoccupied in certain ways with the legacy of 1950s sci-fi and horror. In addition to directing three feature film King adaptations, all of which partly take place in, or reflect the massive influence of, that pre-color movie era of which he speaks so fondly, Darabont also wrote or co-wrote the screenplays for the 1988 remake of *The Blob* and the 1989 sequel to David Cronenberg's remake of *The Fly*, as well as two episodes of the *Tales from the Crypt* television series that aired on HBO between 1989 and 1996—based of course on the famous early 1950s E.C. horror comics. Darabont's love for this "Harryhausen era" of film pervades even those stories set in recent eras such as Season 1 of AMC's throwback *The Walking Dead*—which he adapted from another famous comic series[3]—and *The Mist*, which deliberately obscures the time period setting in ways that enhance the story's relevance and universality.[4]

The B&W cut of the film, though, goes furthest in separating an earlier tradition of sci-fi/horror from a later 1960s and '70s one, whose rich color palettes marked an important aesthetic shift. As opposed to the '70s films' presentations of their sci-fi worlds as "heightened recreations of reality," the earlier films were powerful, according to Darabont, precisely because of their relative nonreferentiality: "the only place you can see *that* representation of the world is in a black and white movie" ("Frank Darabont Introduces"). The statement is provocative, to say the least, especially in light of the evaluations of previous critics and this very collection, which emphasize how frequently '50s sci-fi films "strongly reflect [the] concerns of the moment" ("Frank Darabont Introduces"). In what ways did the grainy, sometimes semi-documentary black-and-white aesthetic of the '50s films impact their allegorical potential and power? How might the two versions of *The Mist* shed light on the peculiar influence of this aesthetic on subsequent eras of sci-fi filmmaking and reception?

In what follows, I seek answers to these and other questions about *The Mist*'s 1950s sci-fi provenance by focusing on what the B&W version achieves in relation to the color version. To manage this goal, I've sub-divided this essay into three discrete subsections. In the first of these, I discuss King's own obsession with the "Harryhausen era" films and his novella's particular engagement of them. As we shall see, *The Mist*'s story and themes, its structure, and even its hypothetical "appearance" all are influenced by the '50s genre films. Moreover, the novella introduces a self-reflexive subtext, subsequently adapted by the film, which replaces the sciences favored by 1950s sci-fi—physics, evolutionary biology, epidemiology, et cetera—with the modern science of movie-making specifically; in this way it demands that the story itself be analyzed in terms of its relationship to film history specifically. In the second subsection, I turn to Darabont's film, especially its adaptation and/or translation of King's direct and indirect references to '50s sci-fi and moviemaking more generally. Whereas King's novella reveals its position in a complex intertextual system whose most vital element is the '50s sci-fi or monster movie, Darabont's film expands this system by contributing a specifically stylistic and visual language capable of communicating the story's cinematic influences. In the final section, I turn directly to the B&W cut of the film, analyzing how its emphatic embrace of a 1950s sci-fi aesthetic deepens and alters our experience of *The Mist* and perhaps our sense of its relevance to the current moment.

King's The Mist

One summer, in a small lakefront community in rural Maine, a mysterious fog slowly enshrouds the town. Our narrator is David, who writes the story down in a frenzy and, in the novella's final scene, leaves it behind for someone, anyone, to find. At the start, David is at the lake house with his wife Steffy and their son, Billy. Unsettled by an uncanny, escalating storm, he and Billy head off to town to gather supplies at the local supermarket. That's when the mist really rolls in, and the shoppers shut the doors to the outside world, hoping it soon will pass. Rumors circulate that the mist has something to do with the Arrowhead Project, a mysterious science experiment taking place at a nearby military base. Soon the shoppers discover there are monsters in the mist, hungry to tear apart anyone foolish enough to venture outside. Though the supplies are seemingly endless, the crisis escalates when the shoppers discover there are monsters inside the store too—of the human variety. A group of the weak and scared begin gathering around Mrs. Carmody, an Old Testament literalist secretly thrilled that the end of days finally has arrived, thrilled that an angry god is exacting revenge on the wicked.[5] As the monsters terrorize the shoppers from outside, Mrs. Carmody becomes increasingly threatening to those who refuse to join her. After she begins calling for a human sacrifice, David decides he's had enough, and he, Billy, and several trusted allies decide it is time to make a run for the International Scout parked just outside the store entrance. Four of them survive, and they begin their journey south, through more fog, tormented the whole way by monsters of every size and shape. At a Howard Johnson's, where the group has stopped for the night, David writes down everything. Then, hearing a single word through the static of a hotel radio—"Hartford"—he decides that they must keep driving south, away from the mist and toward an uncertain destiny.

The basic setup of King's novella first came to him while storm shopping in the summer of 1976. Imagining "a story about all these people trapped in a supermarket surrounded by prehistoric animals," he thought it might be what "*The Alamo* would have been like if directed by Bert I. Gordon."[6] If the anecdote is true, then King's first vision of this fictional world happened to be filtered through a Hollywood lens—John Wayne meets 1950s B-picture sci-fi—and in a way that would never stop mattering to him. Having already published the story twice, first in the 1980 horror anthology *Dark Forces* and again in his own 1985 short story collection *Skeleton Crew*, King could happily advise his reader, "you're supposed to see this one in black-and-white, with your arm around your girl's shoulders (or your guy's), and a

Figure 2. One of the Throwback Monsters of Frank Darabont's black & white *The Mist* (2007). The black & white format was envisioned by Stephen King himself (Darkwoods Productions/ MGM [2007]).

big speaker stuck in the window. *You* make up the second feature" (King, *The Mist* 568–69). King has always been a movie nut, but if there's another of his stories whose conception is more inseparable from Hollywood fantasy, I don't know what it is. Nor has King been shy about discussing some of the (other) specific cinematic influences on the story. A significant one, for example, was Quentin Lawrence's 1958 independent British film *The Trollenberg Terror* (American title, *The Crawling Eye*); this B&W thriller centers on a series of grisly murders inside a mysterious radioactive mist impacting larger mountain ranges across the globe (the film was also an influence on John Carpenter's *The Fog*, which appeared in 1980 and forced King to retitle his story).[7]

The form and content of *The Mist* are further indebted to 1950s sci-fi in at least three general ways. On the simplest level, the '50s references help King, and his protagonist, speak about the causes of these horrific events. Both the eponymous mist and the creatures it contains are vaguely attributable to the Arrowhead Project and whatever scientific experiments are taking place at the nearby military base. In ways, the novella directly establishes this base as a sort of metonymic site of all government-sponsored nuclear experimentation. When David struggles early on to understand the bizarre weather that Maine has been experiencing that summer, he notes that "some people had dragged out that old chestnut about the long-range results of the fifties A-bomb tests again," an idea that begins to seem less crazy to him as events unfold (King, *The Mist* 28). In an interview with Darabont, King admits to being a lousy science student but a good watcher of sci-fi movies: "On the other hand, I saw a lot of movies in the '50s like *The Thing* and *Them!*, and I know that radiation causes monsters, and most important of all I know that if we mess around too much with the unknown something awful will happen" ("Stephen King").[8] Here well-worn ideas made famous in '50s sci-fi cinema serve King as a direct shorthand for whatever incomprehensible events have triggered this apocalyptic nightmare. And even the results of these tests and experiments, the big bugs and gigantic monsters in the mist, seem derived directly from those famous films.

Second, the '50s references seem partly designed to invite allegorical readings of *The Mist*. In *Danse Macabre*, King's non-fiction book about the horror films and books that scared him, he claims that the '50s sci-fi films were synonymous with political allegory: "All the best films of this political type seem to come from that period" (King, *Danse Macabre* 153). King is unsurprisingly complimentary of *Invasion of the Body Snatchers* (1956) and *The Thing From Another World* (1951), both of which he calls "political horror films," and he generalizes that "if horror movies are the nightmares of the mass culture, then many of these fifties horrors express America's coming-to-terms with the possibility of nuclear annihilation over political differences" (King, *Danse Macabre* 153). King's own story tends to bring these political differences to the forefront, so that the human beings trapped inside the store quickly become more terrifying than the monsters outside. King notes, astutely, that the most "hawkish" political horror films of the era, "like *The Thing*, usually extol the virtues of preparedness and deplore the vices of laxness, and achieve a good amount of their horror by positing a society which is politically antithetical to ours and yet possesses a great deal of power" (King, *Danse* 160). In such films as these, the answer always lies in the military response to a particular threat, but *The Mist* rejects such hawkish ideals and posits the equally radical notion that the monsters win when basic civility, compassion, and reason are replaced by tribalism, guns, and a justice mentality. In the wake of Watergate and at the height of the Cold War, the story manages to preserve hope in the possibility of a safer world, beyond Hartford or somewhere else entirely, one uninhabited by either monsters *or* fanatics such as Mrs. Carmody.

Finally, '50s sci-fi film references serve the story's most complex, and under-acknowledged, feature: its self-reflexive meditation on the sci-fi and horror genres—both literary and cinematic—as a kind of practical tool for managing social crisis. One of the more striking absences from *The Mist*, considering its devotedness to '50s sci-fi, is the character of the scientist assigned by either the government, the military, or other well-meaning characters to help destroy the monsters. Epitomized by flawed but fundamentally moral characters such as Dr. Daisuke Serizawa (Akihiki Hirata) in *Gojira* (1954) or Dr. Harold Medford (Edmund Gwenn) in *Them!* (1954), these men often serve as point-of-view characters who help the audience to understand both what has happened to cause the crisis and what needs to happen to stop it. In *The Mist*, David serves as the reader's main point-of-view character; though flawed, he is always slightly calmer, slightly smarter, and slightly tougher than everyone else. He also possesses a highly specialized type of knowledge that sets him apart from others and is shown to keep him one step ahead: he is in the movie business. David, who works mainly on film posters, is a "big-shot artist with connections in New York and Hollywood and all" (King, *The Mist* 68). This shift likely reflects King's comment, cited earlier, about being a poor science student but a good watcher of sci-fi movies.

At several moments in King's novella, David's ability to navigate the crisis—to predict, to describe, or to respond appropriately to what is happening—is related to his love for and familiarity with movies—especially those "Harryhausen era" sci-fi and monster pics. Upon first seeing the mist itself, for instance, David says, "I had the nutty feeling that I was watching some extra-good piece of visual effects, something dreamed up by Willys O'Brian [*sic*] or Douglas Trumbull" (King, *The Mist* 59). What seems like it could be a mere throwaway line suggests the degree to which King conceived the entire event in cinematic terms (like what "*The Alamo* would have been like if directed by Bert I. Gordon") and the degree to which the reader should be doing the same. If you want to know what that mist really looks like, in other words, think of O'Brien's misty swamps in *King Kong* (1933).[9] In the middle of an unthinkable event, the experience of having already seen something similar helps to ground David in the "real" world.

Though such knowledge is useful to him and will prove useful to his allies, David's associations with the movie industry, with movie magic specifically, also cause him problems. Seen by the more provincial townies as that "bigshot" artist, David is even mistrusted by his educated, hyper-rational neighbor, Norton, who refuses to believe that monsters lurk in the mist. Exhausted by Norton's stupidity, David eventually explodes:

> "What are you screaming for?" I said in his ear. "It's just a joke, right? That's why I took you to town when you asked to come and why I trusted you to cross Billy in the parking lot—because

I had this handy fog all manufactured. I rented a fog machine from Hollywood, it cost me fifteen thousand dollars and another eight thousand dollars to ship it, all so I could play a joke on you. Stop bullshitting yourself and open your eyes!" [King, *The Mist* 80]

David's familiarity with movie magic helps him to assimilate to this emergency precisely by providing him a reference point against which he can define reality. Those like Norton who lack such reference points are simply cast adrift at sea.

The references to movies and movie magic pile up over the course of the novella—and the '50s loom large. When David pays out rope tied to a man who's agreed to venture out into the mist, for example, he says he "suddenly remembered my father taking me to see the Gregory Peck film of *Moby Dick* at the Brookside" (King, *The Mist* 101). When the rope is torn from his bloody hands, he hears a sound from the mist "like no sound I've ever heard, but the closest approximation might be a movie set in the African veld or a south American swamp" (King, *The Mist* 101–02). Later, when David and a member of his trusted cohort are debating whether to make a run for the pharmacy, Miller admits that "I want to get out but I don't want to be dinner for some refugee from a grade-B horror picture," speaking a language he's confident David will understand.

As Miller's line suggests, the movies also become a useful filter for characters' attempts to process monstrosity. Toward the end of the novella, for instance, when Mrs. Carmody attempts to stop David's group from leaving the supermarket, he notes that "her hair frizzed out wildly in all directions, reminding me momentarily of Elsa Lanchester in *The Bride of Frankenstein*" (King, *The Mist* 143). Once inside the hotel that serves as the story's final setting, David is haunted by his memories of "all the horror-movie monsters … back at the Federal; when I cracked the window I could hear them in the woods, crashing and blundering around on the steep fall of land they call the ledges around these parts" (King, *The Mist* 148). At times, he is yet more specific, such as when he imagines "Ghidra the Three-headed Monster" coming out of the fog (King, *The Mist* 150), a reference that prepares us for the memorable Godzilla-like moment just seconds later when a creature of unfathomable bulk and height strides right by the Scout:

I don't know how big it actually was, but it passed directly over us. One of its gray, wrinkled legs smashed down right beside my window, and Mrs. Reppler said later she could not see the underside of its body, although she craned her neck up to look. She saw only two Cyclopean legs going up and up into the mist like living towers until they were lost to sight [King, *The Mist* 151].

Whether to understand the denseness of the mist, the wildness in Mrs. Carmody's appearance, or the size of these horror-movie monsters, David constantly returns to the movies for guidance and understanding.

Any reader attuned like David to the usefulness of cinematic horror and sci-fi precedents for the terrors unleashed in *The Mist* will likely begin to see those film connections and influences even when they are not spelled out quite so clearly. When the character Ollie attempts to explain how the mist relates to the Arrowhead Project, for example, his words sound like something right out of a Bert I. Gordon pic:

"That storm," Ollie said in his soft, level voice. "Maybe it knocked something loose up there. Maybe there was an accident. They could have been fooling around with anything. Some people claim they were messing with high-intensity lasers and masers. Sometimes I hear fusion power. And suppose ... suppose they ripped a hole straight through into another dimension" [King, *The Mist* 117].

The casual slippage into vague techno-babble; the sense of uncertainty in the face of just enough probability; even the rhythms of Ollie's composed but hesitant speech patterns: all these will seem all-too-familiar. Such scenes remind us that it is always David's prose we are encountering, for it is his written account of the experience that we are supposedly reading—and this filtering of an event through the eyes of a "big shot artist" with movie connections renders it ever more inevitable that we will see Hollywood everywhere in *The Mist.* Early in the novel, when a woman implores the shoppers to help her leave so that she can go rescue her children and all of them refuse to help, it is *High Noon* (1952) we are meant to remember:

> *"Isn't anyone going to help me?"* she screamed.... No one replied. People shuffled their feet. She looked from face to face with her own broken face. The fat local man took a hesitant half-step forward and his wife jerked him back with one quick tug [King, *The Mist* 63].

And in the novella's hauntingly ambiguous final scene, when flying bugs are pinging off of the hotel windows and the survivors are torn by a despair that the whole world has been overwhelmed and a hope that in Hartford there may be a break from the storm, David lapses into his most self-reflexive authorial voice. Surely it is the haunting final shots of *The Birds* (1963) we are meant to conjure as he apologizes to us for leaving the story unfinished:

> It is, I suppose, what my father always frowningly called "an Alfred Hitchcock ending," by which he meant a conclusion in ambiguity that allowed the reader or viewer to make up his own mind about how things ended [King, *The Mist* 152].

The "reader or viewer." At the end, just as at the beginning, King conceived of *The Mist* in much the same way David does throughout: as a cinematic tale told through writing.

Darabont's *The Mist*

In this relatively brief section, I wish to discuss some of the ways in which Darabont's film—beyond the B&W cut—is nodding to or directly influenced by an earlier era of sci-fi storytelling. In terms of direct references that can accommodate the cinematic awareness of King's own story, Darabont's most important choice is to develop David's (Thomas Jayne) role as a movie poster artist. He does this in part by opening *The Mist* in David's art studio as he's painting a new poster for a (non-existent) film version of King's *The Gunslinger*, the first volume of the beloved *Dark Tower* fantasy series. The room is based on the actual studio of Drew Struzan, the legendary artist responsible for the posters for *Blade Runner, Star Wars, Indiana Jones,* and *Back to the Future,* to mention only a few of his most iconic works. Darabont himself has worked with Struzan multiple times before, including on *The Shawshank Redemption.* In the background, numerous posters are displayed, the most important of which is Struzan's/David's workup for John Carpenter's *The Thing*

Figure 3. David (Thomas Jayne) in his art studio (with real artwork by Drew Struzan) in *The Mist* (2007). Note the poster art for *The Thing* (1982) in the background (Darkwoods Productions/MGM [2007]).

(see Figure 3). As early as the first shot of the film, then, Darabont brings both the concept of the remake into focus and the enduring legacy of the '50s sci-fi/horror film. These themes are compounded by the fact that David's gunslinger is nearly identical to Clint Eastwood's Man with No Name, made famous by films such as *The Good, the Bad, and the Ugly* (1966).

Interestingly, the shots in David's studio replaced an original first scene (never filmed) set in a military lab that Darabont admits was directly "based on an old *Outer Limits* episode because I grew up loving those" ("Feature Commentary"). Darabont ultimately decided to cut the scene because he wished to preserve the mystery surrounding the mist's origins, but the influence of both *The Outer Limits* (1963–65) and *The Twilight Zone* (1959–64) permeates the film. A few examples should suffice. In the scene where David and allies sneak into the pharmacy nearby the supermarket, seeking supplies and survivors, they encounter a terrifying nest of man-eating spiders. Though Darabont has referred to the pharmacy set as a "Twilight Zone space," he credits both Carpenter's *The Thing* and an *Outer Limits* episode starring Bruce Dern, called "The Zanti Misfits," as his main inspiration for the design of the spiders. He also notes how his radical reinterpretation of King's ambiguous ending (see below) reflects "a bit of a Rod Serling touch" ("Feature Commentary").

Darabont's DVD Commentary on *The Mist* is delightful, especially in conveying the director's enthusiasm about having made such a film under B–movie-making conditions. He goes so far as to call the "theme" of the film the "low-budget" techniques he and his crew were forced to employ—but this is at once a source of pride for Darabont and a factor that, in many ways, brings the final version of *The Mist* closer to the '50s sci-fi source material that originally inspired King. Though the film looks great overall, it does so in spite of a relatively limited CGI budget, tons of matte work and other processed shots, the regular use of two-wall sets, and other similar techniques that Darabont lovingly refers to as "very old school." He also admits that the handheld style he chose for the film—notably different than that used in his earlier film work—was designed precisely to accommodate as naturally as possible these budgetary constraints and the creative workarounds they necessitated. The "semi-documentary" style Darabont refers to throughout his Commentary— the film's "grainy, it's happening now texture"—further parallels the style famously associated with such '50s sci-fi and horror masterpieces as *Them!*[10]

Finally, I want to spend a moment on the ending, a radical revision of King's original and arguably one of the most powerful horror finales ever. In Darabont's version, David, Billy, and three other survivors simply run out of gas. The Scout breaks down on the highway in a place where the monsters and the mist still are present. David's gun only has four bullets, and it's agreed he will figure out some way to off himself after he's killed the others. In a brutal scene filmed outside the car from within the mist, we hear four rapid gunshots, beginning with the one that kills Billy. A distraught David pulls himself out of the car and offers himself to whatever monster might be merciful enough to take him up in its claws. But the ominous noises David hears wind up being the sound of a massive military caravan driving up from the south, chasing away the mist and the creatures it harbors. Realizing his tragic mistake, David screams before the credits roll. Darabont has not been shy about how his own influences extend well beyond classic sci-fi and horror, citing, for example, Shirley Jackson's "The Lottery" (1948), William Golding's *The Lord of the Flies* (1954), and John Frankenheimer's *The Manchurian Candidate* (1962; based on the 1959 novel by Richard Condon) as direct influences on individual sequences and shots of his film. The ending seems most influenced, though, by another realist 1950s sci-fi horror film, Stanley Kramer's *On the Beach* (1959; based on the 1957 novel by

Figure 4. As the mist clears in the film's final scene, David (Thomas Jayne) realizes his terrible mistake in *The Mist* (2007) (Darkwoods Productions/MGM [2007]).

Nevil Shute), in which the survivors of a nuclear war, facing painful deaths from radiation poisoning, consume government-issued suicide pills and even give them to their children. Like King's novella, Darabont's film is a mosaic of influences, appropriations, and references to a range of previous sci-fi and horror stories mainly clustered around the important decade of the 1950s.

The B&W Version

Many film historians and scholars of '50s sci-fi note the distinctive "gray, flat and 'realistic' style" of the films; as Bill Warren says, "A 1950s SF movie can usually be identified in ten minutes or less of footage; the look is that distinctive" (1:10). Warren also notes that there were two advantages to the style. The first was cost, of course: "No worry about atmospheric lighting, just light everything more or less the same, and let shadows fall where they will" (10). While such a cost-saving strategy does not adequately describe the excellent lighting of certain films such as *Invasion of the Body Snatchers*, it does well enough for a majority of the films—even some as great as *Them!* The second advantage is "believability," a term that commentators throw around quite a bit. B&W can of course cover up blemishes and flaws that low-budget filmmakers would wish to conceal, but when most commentators speak about the believability of the films, they are nodding to something else: their realism and associations with realist genres and media.

Warren himself, for example, says of *Them!* that "the use of monochrome distinctly helped the documentary aspects of the picture…. It's contradictory to logic, but black and white films seem more real, and … the picture becomes more convincing because it is not in color" (2:767). Victoria O'Donnell cites the same advantages of B&W, adding that the appearance of these films allowed them to effectively channel the Cold War anxieties of their audiences:

> Many science fiction films were low budget, with a visual style that resembled the semi-documentary look of crime and espionage films of the 1940s and 1950s. Although the science fiction films had extravagant stories about sensational events, their style tended to be restrained and visually bland. They were usually shot in black and white with flat lighting that gave them a gray tone [O'Donnell 171].

By tying the gray, flat '50s sci-fi films to the documentary tradition—a move strengthened by the fact that television, and especially television news (not to mention the newsreels of a previous generation), was still B&W in the decade—or other "realist" genres like the crime films, commentators such as Warren and O'Donnell suggest that audiences would have consciously or unconsciously associated B&W with realism.

The experience of watching a B&W film today is of course a fundamentally different experience than it was then and not merely because we experience our news in vivid color or have seen the color version of *Scarface*. Whether on TV, film, or the internet, color has replaced B&W as the norm; B&W asserts itself always as an exception to the rule, a throwback of sorts. Such circumstances help accommodate better than does Warren's theory or Darabont's aforementioned idea that "the only place you can see *that* representation of the world is in a black and white movie." His logic here, very much the opposite of what Warren and O'Donnell say about the '50s filmgoing experience, is explained most effectively by Wheeler Winston Dixon, author of *Black & White Cinema: A Short History*:

> Black-and-white cinematography is a meditation on reality, *a mediation of reality*, offering the viewer a seductive world of shadow, light, textures, and flesh tones, translated into a code system of monochrome glyphs. It has served the primary function of the cinema since its inception, to take us out of ourselves and transport us to another world [220].

Presumably, transporting us to this other world is precisely what King himself wished to do by encouraging us to think of *The Mist* the way we would some low-budget, B&W Bert I. Gordon flick.

But I want to linger a second on the contradictions. On the one hand, B&W is said to achieve its power through associations with reality specifically. On the other hand, it is said to achieve its power by transporting us to another world, dissociated from the real. The single relevant scientific study on the issue, Walter Julius Utz's 1968 dissertation on "The Comparative Effect of Color and Black and White Film Clips on Rated Perception of Reality," does little to resolve these diametrically opposed views. Utz set out to challenge a pilot study which had suggested "black and white may be better than color in communicating reality," but he found that "the hypothesis that color adds reality to film clips was not supported" and that "color alone does not increase the rated perception of reality" (60–61). He also speculates usefully that color may be a distraction in certain ways for an audience used to B&W—an idea that brings us back to the important differences between '50s audiences, which saw color as the novelty, and modern ones, which see B&W as the novelty.

What all of these conflicting views seem to suggest, in other words, is that highly specific contexts will be the crucial determinant of how we process B&W's relationship to the real. In a world like the fifties, where all news coverage, all television, almost all documentaries, and a large percentage of feature films would have been presented in B&W—and where the experience of color on screen would have been both relatively unusual and different from the experience of color in reality (think of the three-strip Technicolor process that ceased to be used after 1954)— it's easy to understand how a film like *Them!* could be described as exhibiting a semi-documentary style. In a world like our own, where nearly all screen experiences are in color, except those presented as historical in nature (think TCM) or as deliberately artistic choices, it's much harder to associate B&W with the real; moreover, it is much easier for us to accept Darabont's and Dixon's claims about monochrome films' ability to "transport us to another world."

Another important truth about the B&W version of *The Mist* is that it will be watched and appreciated only by a small number of viewers for whom the '50s sci-fi/horror links are particularly important and attractive. It may be the film that King wanted us to see, and that Darabont originally intended to make, but like most DVD extras, it's really only there now for cinephiles—such as the good folks contributing to or reading this volume. And yet the experience of the film is remarkably instructive as a gauge of how anxious '50s audiences might have experienced the films in their time, which seem to have straddled in fairly unique ways those hazy lines between fiction and non-fiction, escapism and reality.

Darabont's *The Mist* has been called a post–9/11 film, a moniker I would tie specifically to its extraordinarily bleak ending but also to its central interest in the ways different individuals manage crisis.[11] Whereas the ending has proven divisive, pushing too far for some audiences wishing to escape reality, the core focus of King's story on crisis management may explain its durability. As I sit here writing this essay, I am in the midst of a quarantine following the physical closures of my university and my children's schools due to the outbreak of Covid-19, recently declared a pandemic by the World Health Organization. It is a scenario much like the aftermath of 9/11, in which anxiety becomes both the most natural condition, even the necessary one, and also the most universal condition; it is an extraordinary moment in time when millions of people around the world are focused on the same reasonable fears and yet are responding to those fears in dramatically different ways—with vigilance, with charity, with denial, with a desire to exploit the weak, and so forth. It is a moment when, somewhat counter-intuitively—an absurd Bert I. Gordon–like fantasy such as *The Mist* can seem *more* relevant than ever before.

B&W is not required to experience *The Mist* allegorically, but that format does allow us a better sense of the way a '50s audience—one made anxious about the threat of nuclear war or a communist takeover—might have experienced fantasies such as *Them!* or *The Thing*. Just as those films achieved their distinctive brand of realism through associations with documentary and other B&W film movements and genres, the monochrome version of *The Mist* achieves a distinctively allegorical dimension through its more direct associations with those '50s sci-fi films so often characterized as allegories. At the same time, as a modern novelty item, B&W provides us a safety net lest we fear to venture too far into our own fears and anxieties, precisely by transporting us to a world that we all know is cinematic. As O'Donnell has noted, the '50s sci-fi films remained popular because they managed to negotiate that thin line between escapism and realism: that is, although they contained realist elements that highlighted their relevance, their fantastic plots and limited special effects helped channel audience anxieties much like a safety valve on a steam pipe (171). What the color version of *The Mist* may lose in its hyper-realistic, even nihilistic ending, the B&W version gains back through its reassuring reminder that it's only a movie. In such a way, the B&W version recreates an aesthetic experience closer to the one many 1950s sci-fi fans would have experienced at their local drive-ins. As we have seen, the color version of *The Mist* does nothing to hide its profound indebtedness to the 1950s sci-fi craze, but the B&W version flaunts that indebtedness by inviting us to step back in time.

NOTES

1. The technique used to transform the film into black and white was Digital Intermediate processing (also known as DI).

2. The films include the features *The Shawshank Redemption* (1994), *The Green Mile* (1999), and *The Mist*; Darabont's first film, a 1983 thirty-minute short, was an adaptation of King's short story "The Woman in the Room."

3. The 32-volume Image comics *The Walking Dead* was written by Robert Kirkman and illustrated by Tony Moore between 2004 and 2019.

4. On Darabont's deliberate mixing of time periods, see Edward Douglas, "An Exclusive Interview with Mr. Frank Darabont!" (November 16, 2007), ShockTillYouDrop.com. Accessed March 20, 2020.

5. John Wade mentions "the biblical prophecy come true" as one of the basic "plot stereotype[s]" of fifties sci-fi (*The Golden Age of Science Fiction: A Journey into Space with 1950s Radio, TV, Films, Comics and Books* [Barnsley: Pen & Sword, 2019], 60. Carmody certainly reflects this convention.

6. The story is told in the Notes section of Stephen King, *The Mist*, in *Skeleton Crew*, Signet Paperback ed. (New York: Penguin, 1986), 568.

7. King also directly references *The Crawling Eye* in his famous 1986 novel *It*.

8. Film historian Phil Hardy agrees: "By the end of the decade monsters of all shapes and sizes were introduced with nothing but a muttered comment about radiation as the justification for their appearance" (*The Overlook Film Encyclopedia: Science Fiction*, 3rd ed. [New York: Overlook Press, 1995], xv).

9. Numerous film historians have noted the important influence on fifties sci-fi and horror of *King Kong*'s 1954 theatrical release. See especially Victoria O'Donnell, "Science Fiction Films and Cold War Anxiety," in *The Fifties: Transforming the Screen 1950–59* by Peter Lev (Berkeley: U of California P, 2003), 169–96 (170).

10. Darabont even explains that he originally attempted to shoot the film digitally but thought it "wound up looking too beautiful," and so he shifted to Fuji 400ASA, which offers a specifically "grainier" look to *The Mist* ("Feature Commentary").

11. John Patterson goes so far as to claim that *The Mist* "may one day be seen as America's definitive post–9/11 movie" (Patterson, "The Human Race Is Insane" [June 26, 2008], theguardian.com. Accessed March 1, 2020), and Terence McSweeney rightly notes that the film was "widely interpreted as an allegory of the post-9/11 decade on its release six years after 11 September 2001" (*American Cinema in the Shadow of 9/11* [Edinburgh: Edinburgh UP, 2016], 227–48 [229]).

Works Cited

Dixon, Wheeler Winston. *Black & White Cinema: A Short History*. Rutgers University Press, 2015.
Douglas, Edward. "An Exclusive Interview with Mr. Frank Darabont!" ShockTillYouDrop.com, 16 Nov. 2007. Accessed 20 March 2020.
"Feature Commentary by Writer/Director Frank Darabont." *The Mist*, produced by the Weinstein Company, Disk 1. Genius Products Two-Disk Collector's Edition. DVD.
"Frank Darabont Introduces The *Mist* in Black & White." *The Mist*, produced by the Weinstein Company, Disk 2. Genius Products Two-Disk Collector's Edition. DVD.
Hardy, Phil. *The Overlook Film Encyclopedia: Science Fiction*. Overlook Press, 1995.
King, Stephen. *Danse Macabre*. Gallery, 2010.
———. *The Mist*. Penguin, 1986.
Kirkman, Robert. *The Walking Dead*. Illustrated by Tony Moore, Image Comics, 2004–2019.
McSweeney, Terence. *American Cinema in the Shadow of 9/11*. Edinburgh University Press, 2016.
O'Donnell, Victoria. "Science Fiction Films and Cold War Anxiety." *The Fifties: Transforming the Screen 1950–59*, edited by Peter Lev. University of California Press, 2003, pp. 169–96.
Patterson, John. "The Human Race Is Insane." *The Guardian*, 26. June 2008. Accessed 1 March 2020.
"Stephen King and Director Frank Darabont Talk The Mist." Movieweb.com, 13 Nov. 2007. Accessed March 10, 2020.
Utz, Walter Julius, Jr. "The Comparative Effect of Color and Black and White Film Clips Upon Rated Perception of Reality." 1968. University of Illinois, Ph.D. Dissertation.
Wade, John. *The Golden Age of Science Fiction: A Journey into Space with 1950s Radio, TV, Films, Comics and Books*. Pen & Sword, 2019.
Warren, Bill. *Keep Watching the Skies! American Science Fiction Movies of the Fifties*. McFarland, 2010.

Filmography

Beginning of the End. Dir. Bert I. Gordon. MGM, 1957. Film.
The Birds. Dir. Alfred Hitchcock. Alfred J. Hitchcock Productions, 1963. Film.
The Blob. Dir. Irvin Yeaworth and Russell Doughton. Paramount Pictures, 1988. Film.
The Cyclops. Dir. Bert I. Gordon. B&H Productions, Inc, 1957. Film.
Earth vs. The Spider. Dir. Bert I. Gordon. American International Pictures, 1958. Film.
The Fly. Dir. David Cronenberg. 20th Century Fox, 1989. Film.

The Fog. Dir. John Carpenter. AVCO Embassy Pictures, 1980. Film.

Gojira. Ishiro Honda. Toho Studios, 1954. Film.

The Good, the Bad, and the Ugly. Dir. Sergio Leone. United Artists, 1966. Film.

The Green Mile. Dir. Frank Darabont. Warner Bros., 1999. Film.

High Noon. Dir. Fred Zinnemann. United Artists, 1952. Film.

Invasion of the Body Snatchers. Dir. Don Seigel. Allied Artists Pictures, 1956. Film.

King Kong. Dir. Merian C. Cooper and Ernest B. Schoedsack. Radio Pictures, 1933. Film.

The Manchurian Candidate. Dir. John Frankenheimer. United Artists, 1962. Film.

The Mist. Dir. Frank Darabont. MGM, 2007. Film.

Night of the Living Dead. Dir. George A Romero. Continental Distributing, 1968. Film.

On the Beach. Dir. Stanley Kramer. United Artists, 1959. Film.

The Outer Limits. MGM Television, 1995–2002. TV Series.

The Shawshank Redemption. Dir. Frank Darabont. Columbia Pictures, 1994. Film.

Tales from the Crypt. Warner Bros., 1989–1996. TV Series.

Them! Dir. Gordon Douglas. Warner Bros., 1954. Film.

The Thing from Another World. Dir. Christian Nyby. RKO Radio Pictures, 1951. Film.

The Trollenberg Terror. Dir. Quentin Lawrence. Eros Films Ltd., 1958. Film.

The Twilight Zone. CBS, 1959–1964. TV Series.

Village of the Giants. Dir. Bert I. Gordon. Embassy Pictures, 1965. Film.

The Walking Dead. AMC Studios, 2010-Present. TV Series.

The Woman in the Room. Dir. Frank Darabont. 1983. Short Film.

Retro Reboots

Adapting 1950s Science Fiction in Bioshock, Fallout, *and* Wolfenstein

Daniel Singleton

Video games have embraced sci-fi since *Space Invaders* rocketed into arcades in 1978. Games have been a natural fit for the sci-fi genre because they let players use the futuristic technologies that they have read about in books or seen in movies. As such, many developers have adapted existing material, with Hollywood blockbusters like *Star Wars* (1977), *Aliens* (1986), or *The Matrix* (1999), in particular, generating countless officially licensed game tie-ins and unofficial homages. Bucking this trend, however, three long-running franchises—*BioShock* (2007–2013), *Fallout* (1997–2019), and *Wolfenstein* (1981–2019)—have let players explore the totalitarian dystopias and atomic wastelands from the Golden Age of sci-fi (c. 1940–1960). The massive success of these games raises several questions about how video games adapt other texts. Why do these franchises adapt sci-fi movies which were produced almost three decades before the emergence of video game arcades and which relatively few players will have seen? How have these games revised the popular memory of the Atomic Age in light of contemporary political debates about unregulated capitalism, environmental disaster, and homegrown fascism? How do the allusions to '50s sci-fi contribute to theoretical arguments about medium specificity in games? That is, how do allusions to "old" sci-fi movies reframe unanticipated, unwanted reboots of "old" franchises as nostalgic throwbacks to classic titles? How do retro-futuristic sci-fi technologies imbue outmoded gameplay mechanics with cultural significance? This essay explores how and why recent games have rebooted classic franchises as nostalgic homages to '50s sci-fi. I show how the games underline surprising affinities between disparate sci-fi media, and I discuss how these connections legitimize disreputable media, rebrand floundering companies, position titles within an overcrowded media marketplace, and contribute to the lasting influence of '50s sci-fi on contemporary media.

They Came from Beneath the Sea: Atomic Anxiety in BioShock

Developed by Irrational Games, *BioShock* (2007) reboots a cult PC game, *System Shock 2* (1999), by way of literary dystopias like Aldous Huxley's *Brave New World*

(1932) and Ayn Rand's *Atlas Shrugged* (1957) as well as low-budget exploitation films about atomic monsters like *It Came from Beneath the Sea* (1955). These allusions accomplish several things. First, the literary references legitimize video games, transforming a disreputable toy into an artistic, socially conscious medium for reexamining the legacy of the Cold War. Second, the retro-futuristic aesthetic of '50s sci-fi reframes the outmoded mechanics from the *Shock* games (i.e., cumbersome inventory screens, confusing level design, etc.) as relics from gaming history. In this way, *BioShock* would establish a template for rebooting forgotten video game franchises and revitalizing outmoded genres as nostalgic homages to the retro-futuristic dystopias of '50s sci-fi.

BioShock was conceived as a spiritual successor to two cult sci-fi games, Looking Glass Studios' *System Shock* (1994) and *System Shock 2* (1999). These games take place in abandoned spaceships that have been hijacked by rogue A.I., and they emphasize slow-paced exploration and puzzle-solving over twitchy, fast-paced action. The second game, in particular, lets players choose between fighting enemies using their psionic powers, hacking security systems to clear paths ahead of them, or simply sneaking past obstacles using the ship's many secret passages. The *Shock* series' open-ended gameplay and eerie sci-fi setting, which often recalls the *Nostromo* from *Alien* (1979), impressed critics and spawned a cycle of other "immersive simulations" like Looking Glass's own fantasy-themed *Thief: The Dark Project* (1998) and Ion Storm's cyberpunk *Deus Ex* (2000). But cumbersome mechanics—such as clunky controls and complicated inventory screens—alienated casual gamers. Looking Glass shut down a few months after releasing *System Shock 2* and the immersive sim cycle mostly disappeared from the marketplace by the early 2000s.

One of the developers of *System Shock 2*, Ken Levine, would spend several years pitching reluctant publishers on making another *System Shock* sequel or reviving the immersive simulation genre through a new franchise. The resulting game, *BioShock*, would refine the *Shock* games' slow-paced, open-ended gameplay and relocate the action from a cyberpunk spaceship to an underwater dystopia inspired by the mid-century dystopian fiction of Huxley, Orwell, and Rand.[1] The game opens in 1960. The player character, Jack, has crashed his airplane into the Atlantic Ocean. After swimming to a mysterious lighthouse, Jack rides a small submarine to an underwater city, Rapture, that looks like a Cold War version of Atlantis. Its skyline is filled with art deco skyscrapers which recall the fantastic locations in underwater adventure films like *20,000 Leagues Under the Sea* (1954) and *City Under the Sea* (1965) or the iconic technologies in Arthur Radebaugh's comic strip, *Closer Than We Think!* (1958–1963). As Jack marvels at the city, he watches a short film narrated by the city's megalomaniacal founder, entrepreneur-turned-mad-scientist Andrew Ryan. He extols Rapture as a libertarian haven, a nuclear-powered version of Galt's Gulch from Rand's *Atlas Shrugged*:

> Is not a man entitled to the sweat of his brow? "No," says the man in Washington, "it belongs to the poor!" "No," says the man in the Vatican, "it belongs to God!" "No," says the man in Moscow, "it belongs to everyone!" I rejected those answers.... I chose the impossible. I chose Rapture! A city where the artist would not fear the censor, where the scientist would not be bound by petty morality, where the great would not be constrained by the small!

Figure 5. The underwater city, Rapture, from *Bioshock* (2007) (2K Boston/2K Games [2007]).

But when Jack exits the submarine, he discovers that the city has materially decayed and morally degenerated into Oceania from Orwell's *1984*. In the Welcome Center, banners with doublespeak slogans—"No gods or kings, only man" and "A man chooses, a slave obeys"—hang above monuments to Big Brother Ryan; closed-circuit security monitors and heavy-duty combat drones protect the city's entrances from "CIA jackals" and "KGB wolves."[2]

Audiotapes recorded by the city's inhabitants reveal what happened to Rapture, and the cautionary parable that unfolds recalls '50s sci-fi movies about everything from atomic mutation and nuclear war (e.g., *Gojira* [1954], *Them!* [1954], etc.) to radiation poisoning and drug addiction (e.g., *Invasion of the Body Snatchers* [1956], *The Man with X-Ray Eyes* [1962], etc.). In the early 1950s, Ryan and the scientist Brigid Tenenbaum, who is modeled on the fictional scientists in *This Island Earth* (1955) and *Killers from Space* (1954) as well as real-life figures like Albert Einstein and J. Robert Oppenheimer, discover a mind-altering, strength-enhancing substance called ADAM, a thinly veiled substitute for atomic energy.[3] Although ADAM initially boosts Rapture's economy, its addictive nature slowly reduces users to ADAM-addled "splicers" who resemble the drug-addled denizens of Burroughs' sci-fi-tinged beatnik novel *Naked Lunch*. For example, there is a deranged plastic surgeon, J.S. Steinman, whose deadly scientific experiments on unwitting patients recall how the crazed doctors played by Basil Rathbone and Boris Karloff in *The Black Sheep* (1956) and *Corridors of Blood* (1959) succumb to drug addiction and megalomania. An artist, Sander Cohen, makes statues from hapless neighbors à la the aspiring artist played by Dick Miller in *Bucket of Blood* (1959), who rocks the art world by killing his critics, pouring plaster over their bodies and exhibiting the results in galleries. Soon the gangster Frank Fontaine, whose ruthlessness recalls Lee Marvin and Richard Conte's gangsters in *The Big Heat* (1953) and *The Big Combo* (1955), starts exploiting the public's crippling ADAM addiction for political power.

He goads working class dissidents into overthrowing Ryan's government on New Year's Eve 1958, the same date on which communists seized control of Cuba. He consolidates his power by ingesting enough ADAM to become the spitting image of *The Amazing Colossal Man* (1957).

The references to '50s sci-fi perform a few functions. First, the retro-futuristic setting distinguishes *BioShock* from popular sci-fi franchises like *Halo* (2001–2020), whose space marines are modeled after characters from *Aliens* (1986) and *Starship Troopers* (1997). Second, the references to "classic" sci-fi texts which critique Cold War ideology suggest to skeptical critics how another disreputable form of media—video games—could make artistically adventurous and socially significant statements about art, politics, and culture. An early sequence exemplifies how *BioShock* uses tropes from '50s sci-fi to deconstruct conventions of video games. Upon arriving at Rapture, Jack receives a radio message from a mysterious man named Atlas, who promises to lead Jack out of Rapture if he will "kindly" follow all of Atlas's instructions to the letter. Atlas then asks Jack to inject himself with ADAM. The ensuing sequence thrusts players into a harrowing experiment with atomic energy from a '50s sci-fi film. After sticking the syringe into his arm, Jack's hands start shaking as ADAM rewrites his genetic code. But the painful procedure is well worth enduring, as it gives Jack the ability to shoot lightning bolts, fireballs, cyclones, and insect swarms from his fingertips.

Coming at the beginning of the game, this sequence suggests how *BioShock* will adapt outmoded conventions from *System Shock 2*, which also gave players psionic powers like pyrokinesis and cryokinesis, by way of '50s sci-fi movies about atomic energy. The game initially encourages the player to revel in being an atomic superman. These ADAM-infused powers make *BioShock* addictively re-playable, as experimenting with different abilities will change how combat encounters unfold. But the power fantasy becomes a cautionary tale as Jack starts suffering the effects of ADAM addiction. He is soon tempted to "harvest" more ADAM from "Little Sisters," kidnapped little girls who have been genetically mutated to gather ADAM from the bodies of dead addicts. Later he discovers that ADAM has put him under the control of Atlas. Atlas—who is actually Frank Fontaine—has been using the coded phrase "Would you kindly?" to manipulate Jack into killing Andrew Ryan and consolidating Fontaine's control over Rapture. Once this goal has been accomplished, Fontaine uses more coded phrases to destabilize the ADAM in Jack's blood. For the next several levels, Jack randomly loses health points as well as control over his abilities; the interface cycles between every power in the game until players find the antidote, another vial of ADAM.

This plot twist has provoked more discussion about video game narration than virtually any other element of any other video game title, with many critics seeing Atlas/Fontaine as a surrogate for developers who manipulate players with the illusion of free choice.[4] But few critics have discussed these twists in relation to '50s sci-fi movies, despite the widespread attention that has been paid to the game's literary allusions. For example, Jack's identity as a sleeper agent echoes Cold War paranoia about the linked threats of invisible radiation poisoning and imperceptible ideological subversion by Russians in "body snatching" films such as *Invasion of the Body Snatchers* (1956), *I Married a Monster from Outer Space* (1958), and *The Manchurian*

Candidate (1962).[5] To confront the supercharged Fontaine, Jack then undergoes the irreversible process of becoming a "Big Daddy," a monstrous super-mutant clad in thick metal armor and armed with a gun and a large drill. This transformation casts players as the hulking atomic robot from *The Colossus of New York* (1958) or an abortive science experiment from *The Incredible Shrinking Man* (1956) or *The Fly* (1958). And if players have killed more than one "Little Sister," the game ends with a cutscene in which Jack hijacks a submarine containing more than enough nuclear weapons to destroy the world. The cinematic references and game conventions reinvigorate each other. The stark moralism of '50s sci-fi movies about atomic power reinforces the game's critique of power fantasies in modern games. And the mechanics allow players to interact with atomic energy's important role in both the microcosm of postwar American life and the macrocosm of Cold War ideology.

BioShock's musings on Cold War ideology and metacommentary on the morality of player choice earned the game instant acclaim upon its release in October 2007. The game generated two sequels—*BioShock 2* (2010) sent players back to Rapture as a "Big Daddy," whereas *BioShock Infinite* (2013) sent players into Columbia, a nationalistic city in the clouds circa 1912—as well as a host of ports, remasters, tie-in novelizations, academic articles, and even a Smithsonian exhibit. And its success revived the market for "immersive simulations," leading to the production of more sci-fi-themed games like *Deus Ex: Human Revolution* (2011), *Dishonored* (2012), *Prey* (2017), and *Cyberpunk 2077* (2020) which emphasize player choice and emergent gameplay. But few of these games have been as impactful as *BioShock*. In transforming Randian utopias like Galt's Gulch and totalitarian dystopias like Oceania into the irradiated stomping grounds for atomic monsters and mad scientists, *BioShock* confronts players with the consequential choices about atomic energy faced by the mad scientists in '50s sci-fi movies.

Worlds Without End: Postmodern, Post-Apocalyptic Playgrounds in Fallout

The success of *BioShock* led other reboots to embrace '50s sci-fi. The most notable example, Bethesda Softworks' *Fallout 3* (2008), is both a belated sequel and a complete reboot of another cult PC franchise, Black Isle Studio's *Fallout* (1997) and *Fallout 2* (1998). This franchise has long been celebrated for gamifying '50s sci-fi books and movies about post-apocalyptic American societies, but *Fallout 3* goes farthest in transforming the atomic wastelands from novels like *Star Man's Son, The Long Loud Silence, The Chrysalids*, and *Dr. Bloodmoney*, as well as films like *Day the World Ended* (1955), *On the Beach* (1959), and *Panic in Year Zero!* (1962) into a postmodern playground packed to the brim with underground fallout shelters, mutated monsters, and irradiated junk. The game contains a Bakhtinian profusion of attitudes about atomic annihilation. *Fallout 3* veers between satirizing the naïve fantasies about nuclear war in '50s disaster movies as well as public service announcements on "duck-and-cover" drills and stewing in melancholic nostalgia for the lost innocence of the Atomic Age.

Developed by Bethesda Softworks, *Fallout 3* is a sequel to two computer role-playing games (RPGs) that had been developed by Black Isle Studios more than a decade earlier. The first two games take place on the West Coast about one hundred years after a devastating thermonuclear war over scarce resources like petroleum and uranium destroys most of the world on October 23, 2077. The games have been richly intertextual from the start. For example, *Fallout* is an unofficial sequel to another PC RPG, *Wasteland* (1988), which was produced by the designers of the tabletop RPG *Tunnels and Trolls* (1975), a popular knockoff of *Dungeons & Dragons* (1974). The isometric environments of these games recreate the post-apocalyptic wastelands on display in *Mad Max II/The Road Warrior* (1981) and *The Terminator* (1984), whereas the dense skill system and branching dialogue trees—both of which are adapted from tabletop RPGs—allow players to adopt any sci-fi persona they can imagine. More than one player has created a deadly avenger like Mad Max, a myopic recluse like *The Twilight Zone*'s Henry Bemis, or a ruthless schemer like *Lost in Space*'s Dr. Smith.

Fallout developed a cult following among PC gamers and tabletop RPG fans and led Black Isle to develop several more acclaimed fantasy-themed, tabletop-inspired RPGs for the PC, notably *Baldur's Gate* (1998–2000), *Planescape: Torment* (1999), and *Icewind Dale* (2000–2002). But the niche appeal of these franchises forced the studio to declare bankruptcy and cancel the third *Fallout* game in 2003. The publisher then sold the license to another developer of PC RPGs, Bethesda Game Studios. Their flagship series of fantasy games, the *Elder Scrolls* franchise (1994–2020), differs from Black Isle's games in several ways. The early *Fallout* games are set in a post-apocalyptic sci-fi universe, use a third-person point of view, and emphasize talking and thinking over fighting. By contrast, the *Elder Scrolls* games are set in a Tolkienesque fantasy world, adopt a first-person point of view, and have more dungeons than dialogue. But Bethesda lead developer Todd Howard had little interest in recreating Black Isle's gameplay to please an existing fanbase of tabletop gamers and computer geeks. Rather he aimed to expand the audience for the franchise—and the Bethesda brand—to a larger audience of casual console players by merging its '50s sci-fi iconography with "our style of game" ("History").[6] They reworked *Fallout* using the same proprietary software engine and design principles as the fourth *Elder Scrolls* game, *Oblivion* (2006), with the result that *Fallout 3* often plays like an unofficial *Elder Scrolls* spinoff. For example, it replaces the earlier games' isometric perspective with a subjective point of view, turn-based battles with real-time button-mashing, and complex dialogue trees with binary choices between "good" and "evil" responses. The changes are so profound that many fans dismissed it as "*Oblivion* with guns."

Fallout 3 compensates for revamping its precursors' gameplay by doubling down on the references to '50s sci-fi movies. Notably, the developers relocate the action from the West Coast to Washington, D.C.[7] The earlier games had leaned on late Cold War movies like *WarGames* (1983), *The Day After* (1983), and even *The Atomic Café* (1982), but the Capital Wasteland, as the game dubs it, synthesizes many '50s sci-fi movies. The sight of familiar Washington landmarks being occupied by super-mutants parodies films like *The Day the Earth Stood Still* (1951) and

Earth vs. the Flying Saucers (1956), which displace nightmares about atomic annihilation by Russians onto fantasies about alien invasions by Martians.[8] The ruined schools, stores, museums, and offices scattered across the map recall the atomic wastelands in *The Twilight Zone*'s "Time Enough at Last" (1959) and *The Last Man on Earth* (1964), and they contain the giant insects, atomic mutants, and overreaching robots from films like *Them!* (1954), *Creature from the Black Lagoon* (1954), and *Forbidden Planet* (1956).[9] But whereas many of these films cautiously reassure audiences that thermonuclear war is manageable, survivable, and even winnable, *Fallout 3* often satirizes '50s culture for disavowing the awfulness of atomic annihilation. The game's prerelease trailer establishes the method. It opens by parodying television ads for fallout shelters: "You can secure your family's future by reserving your spot in a state-of-the-art underground vault from Vault-Tec.... In just a few short years, you and your fellow vault dwellers will repopulate our great country!" But the next shot undermines this sales pitch by tracking back from a TV set to reveal the Capital Wasteland, as Bob Crosby's "Dear Hearts and Gentle People" plays over the soundtrack. The game recontextualizes other seemingly innocent songs like the Ink Spots' "I Don't Want to Set the World on Fire" (1941), Danny Kaye and the Andrew Sisters' "Civilization" (1947), and Bob Crosby's "Happy Times" (1950), which are broadcast across the Capital Wasteland from a makeshift radio tower atop the Washington Monument, as ironic portents of disaster. These moments mock Atomic Age pop culture for promoting the fiction that nuclear war was survivable, let alone winnable.

But elsewhere the game's treatment of nuclear weapons recalls how atomic allegories like *20 Million Miles to Earth* (1957) or *The War of the Worlds* (1953) innocently mythologize nuclear weapons as supernatural objects or normalize them as bigger

Figure 6. A nuclear device explodes in the apocalyptic landscape of *Fallout 3* (2008) (Bethesda Game Studios/Bethesda Softworks [2008]).

versions of conventional bombs.[10] Although the narrative of *Fallout 3* purports to warn how nuclear weapons will destroy the world, its mechanics often transform these weapons into gamers' personal toys and encourage players to do whatever they want with the nukes they find lying around the Capital Wasteland. One sequence of quests makes players choose between defusing an unexploded nuclear bomb in the town of Megaton or detonating it to entertain the wealthy owner of a nearby hotel. Most players will detonate the bomb at least once—just to see what a nuclear explosion *really* looks like—and then travel to Megaton to see if anybody survived the explosion. When some townspeople who have mutated into radiated ghouls scold players for destroying their homes, many of these players will reload an older save game to defuse the bomb and collect a hefty reward for their trouble. Another sequence sends players to a virtual reality simulation called Tranquility Lane. Players are trapped inside this greyscale cul-de-sac, which looks like the suburb from *Leave It to Beaver* (1957–1963) or perhaps *The Twilight Zone*'s "The Monsters Are Due on Maple Street," by a German scientist named Braun, who goads players into tormenting the VR simulation's other hapless residents. Braun's increasingly absurd list of tasks—making Timmy cry, ruining the Rockwells' marriage, and rigging Mrs. Henderson's oven to explode—tempts players to have fun destroying a facsimile of postwar American society. And the morality of situation is tempered by the simulation's self-reflexive status as a game-within-the-game. Braun reassures players that victims' deaths are simulated and that they can be resurrected with the push of a button. Like *BioShock*, this sequence mocks '50s pop culture for conjuring artificial utopias but then shifts to deconstructing video games for creating inconsequential virtual realities and enabling all sorts of perverse power fantasies about technologies.[11]

These sequences come strangely close to reproducing rather than repudiating the naïve technological utopianism and black-and-white morality of much '50s sci-fi. The binary choices between destroying or saving the Capital Wasteland recall how '50s sci-fi films distinguish between "good" and "bad" ways to use nuclear bombs, artificial intelligence, and other dangerous technologies.[12] In the main plot, for example, players can choose to help their character's father, James (voiced by Liam Neeson), and the technophilic knights of the Brotherhood of Steel to cleanse the Potomac River of nuclear waste. Or they can help President John Henry Eden, an advanced supercomputer whose A.I. is based upon the personalities of past presidents, flood the Capital Wasteland with even more lethal doses of radiation. The game's uncritical identification with the binary morality of '50s sci-fi can be seen in its reward system, in which "good" decisions almost always give players better equipment or more bottle caps, the wasteland's preferred currency. Individual vignettes may criticize how the Cold War standoff between capitalism and communism led to the reckless proliferation of nuclear weapons, but the gameplay mechanics pin the survival of the human race and the restoration of the United States on resourceful capitalists like the player. In short, the game's postmodern satire of '50s sci-fi belies its affinity for these films' binary conflicts between peace-loving Americans and aggressive aliens from Russia or outer space.

Like *BioShock*, *Fallout 3* was almost universally praised for rebooting cult PC games as homages to '50s sci-fi. Even skeptical fans were captivated by the game's playful pastiche of post-apocalyptic fiction.[13] The game became a cultural phenomenon; its iconography has adorned T-shirts, lunchboxes, and tote bags, and the popularity of its melancholic, nostalgic satire of the Atomic Age has inspired subsequent post-apocalyptic action games. For example, a spinoff called *Fallout: New Vegas* (2010), which was developed by several former programmers from Black Isle, restores older gameplay mechanics from the first two *Fallout* games (i.e., branching dialogue trees, morally ambiguous decisions, etc.) to Bethesda's fully 3D open-world. Players help several archetypes from '50s pop culture to consolidate power over the Mojave Wasteland, the real-life setting of hundreds of atmospheric tests during the early 1950s. For example, Mr. House is a Howard Hughes–like billionaire who lives in a cryogenic tank atop his Vegas penthouse. The centurions and gladiators from Caesar's Legion have recreated the lost worlds of sword-and-sandal films like *Quo Vadis* (1951), *The Robe* (1953), and *Ben-Hur* (1959), not to mention the Romanesque civilizations in sci-fi texts ranging from Isaac Asimov's *Foundation* to *Star Trek* (1966–1969).[14] Bethesda's *Fallout 4* (2015) also extends its precursor's technological utopianism. It opens with a short scene dramatizing how nuclear war destroys the world in 2077—players reach the underground fallout shelter just in time to see a mushroom cloud explode over nearby Boston—that sets up the player's main task for the rest of the game: rebuilding America using assorted prewar junk. By contrast, two post-apocalyptic franchises from the former Soviet bloc, GSC Game World's *S.T.A.L.K.E.R.* (2007–2010) and 4A Games' *Metro* (2010–2019), which are officially based on novels by Arkady and Boris Strugatsky and Dmitry Glukhovsky respectively, have been positioned as "anti–*Fallout*" games whose representations of Chernobyl and Moscow are much dirtier, sadder, and scarier than the Capital Wasteland.

Bethesda's *Fallout 3* has become a touchstone even for gamers with little interest in '50s sci-fi. The game has endured for several reasons. Its sandbox gameplay lets players use the most dangerous weapons in human history. Its postmodern satire about the popular culture of the Atomic Age creates a pleasurable feeling of omnipotence—the Cold War didn't end in nuclear war!—that soothes twenty-first-century anxieties about climate change and terrorism. Its melancholic nostalgia for the innocence of the 1950s resonates with anxieties about the loss of American exceptionalism. In short, the game contains so many conflicting perspectives about the legacy of '50s sci-fi that it becomes a gamified Rorschach test, a strangely comforting power fantasy about the end of the world.

Invasion USA: Anachronistic Antifascism in Wolfenstein

The influence of 2K Games' *BioShock* and Bethesda's *Fallout 3* can also be felt in the next retro reboots that I will discuss: MachineGames' *Wolfenstein: The New Order* (2014) and *Wolfenstein II: The New Colossus* (2017). These two games have revitalized a storied franchise which is often credited—or blamed—for inventing a controversial genre, the first-person shooter (FPS). Following the leads of *BioShock* and *Fallout 3*, they reboot the *Wolfenstein* franchise (1981–2019) as a retro-futuristic homage to Cold War dystopias like Philip K. Dick's *The Man in the High Castle* (1962) as well as low-budget exploitation films about fascist scientists and atomic-powered superheroes. The allusions not only transform outmoded mechanics from older games into relics from computer history; they also provide the developers with cover for addressing political debates about the resurgence of fascism in Europe and the United States.

The complicated history of the *Wolfenstein* franchise has been driven by an array of industrial pressures, legal complications, and technological challenges. The first two games, *Castle Wolfenstein* (1981) and *Beyond Castle Wolfenstein* (1984), which were developed by Muse Software for the Apple II computers, took inspiration from World War II films like *The Guns of Navarone* (1961) and *The Dirty Dozen* (1967). The games cast players as an unnamed Allied soldier who must steal top-secret war documents from a labyrinthine Nazi fortress, the titular Castle Wolfenstein. The rudimentary gameplay consists of sneaking through procedurally generated mazes while avoiding detection from Nazi soldiers, who are represented by yellow stick figures with swastikas on their chests. The games were moderately successful, but Muse still shut down in 1987, and the franchise seemed poised to disappear from the market.

In the early 1990s, the *Wolfenstein* license passed into the hands of an upstart software development company from Austin, Texas, called id Software. Young coders like John Romero, John Carmack, and Tom Hall rebooted Muse's games, which they had played upon release, as a fast-paced, first-person action game called *Wolfenstein 3D* (1992). The developers adapted the software and mechanics from an earlier project, *Catacombs-3D* (1991), a fantasy-themed action game not unlike Bethesda's *Elder Scrolls* wherein players explore 3D dungeons from a first-person point of view, to accommodate the World War II iconography from *Castle Wolfenstein*. They even augmented the formula with a few pulpy touches from comics and sci-fi. For example, the player's character is now identified as William "B.J." Blazkowicz and visualized on menu screens and interfaces as a square-jawed antifascist crusader, a digitized G.I. Joe, and his journey through Castle Wolfenstein even culminates in a "boss" battle with "Mecha-Hitler," the Nazi dictator clad in a fearsome mechanical battle suit.[15]

Wolfenstein 3D has been called the "first" FPS game, but its impact on gaming would pale in comparison to id's next game, *DOOM* (1993), and the long belated sequel to *Wolfenstein 3D*, *Return to Castle Wolfenstein* (2001), would only appear years after *Saving Private Ryan* (1998) renewed public interest in World War II–themed media. Developed by a third-party contractor, Gray Matter Interactive, the game includes more pulpy sci-fi references than its precursor. Its plot revolves around B.J.'s efforts to stop Nazi General Wilhelm "Deaths-head" Strasse from building an army of super mutants for the SS Paranormal Division.[16] But despite *Return*'s positive reception, id's plans for the franchise were scuttled by two changing market trends. First, interest in World War II media would dissipate by the mid–2000s, leading popular FPS franchises like *Call of Duty* (2003–2020) to abandon World War II for more recent conflicts in the Middle East.[17] Second, the success of multiplayer FPS games like Valve's *Counter-Strike* (1999) and id's *Quake III* (1999) pushed many publishers to prioritize multiplayer formats like team deathmatch and capture-the-flag.

These market pressures would lead id to cancel the single-player campaign of the next game, *Wolfenstein: Enemy Territory* (2003), and release the multiplayer component as a standalone game. They would also lead the belated sequel to *Return*, Raven Software's *Wolfenstein* (2009), to streamline the earlier games' labyrinthine levels and punishing difficulty curve for more casual gamers, at the cost of alienating established fans.[18] That game's critical and commercial failure seemed to confirm that the *Wolfenstein* franchise had become a museum relic: a storied and influential footnote in gaming history but an anachronistic oddity in the modern market.

In 2011, id was purchased by ZeniMax Media (which also owns Bethesda). This merger enabled another ZeniMax developer, MachineGames, to retool the franchise as a retro-reboot a la *BioShock* and *Fallout 3*. *The New Order* (2014), which like *Fallout 3* is both a direct sequel and reboot to the last *Wolfenstein* game, sends B.J. to a totalitarian dystopia from '50s sci-fi. The game opens in 1946 as B.J. returns to Castle Wolfenstein to confront General "Deaths-head." But this disastrous mission fails, and B.J. falls into a coma for the next fourteen years. When he wakes up in the year 1960, Nazis are ruling the world. The premise of a comatose visitor waking up in a futuristic dystopia recuperates the game's own unexpected (and for some fans, unwanted) reappearance after five years off the market. B.J.'s anachronistic antifascism reframes outdated mechanics like limited health points and maze-like levels as relics from gaming history. For players like Heather Alexandra, the clunky controls channel B.J.'s disoriented anger: "The clumsiness feels natural for the character you're playing. BJ is the underdog, outmatched by the sea of soldiers and armored monstrosities in his path. It is only through rough, skin of the teeth struggle that he progresses. The gunplay captures that feeling admirably, turning every gunfight into an exciting scramble to survive" (Alexandra).

But *The New Order* also engages with the rich body of speculative fiction about what might have happened if the Nazis had won World War II. In interviews, lead designer Jens Matthies has credited the game's over-the-top violence and postmodern pulpiness to the influence of postindustrial dystopias like *Robocop* (1987) and alternative history films like *Inglorious Basterds* (2009).[19] But the representation of Nazi Europe circa 1960 is closer to the apocalyptic nightmares about Nazi dystopias in postwar speculative fiction like John W. Wall's *The Sound of His Horn* (1952), Cyril M. Kornbluth's "Two Dooms" (1958), and Philip K. Dick's *Man in the High Castle* (1962). (Notably, the pilot of the Amazon TV series based on Dick's book premiered in January 2015, a scant seven months after the release of *The New Order* in May 2014.) Gavriel D. Rosenfeld notes that speculative texts about hypothetical Axis victories from before the mid–1960s are more pessimistic about Nazi totalitarianism than later fiction.[20] Likewise, the Nazis in *The New Order* plan to abolish the English language, colonize the continents of Africa and Asia, build top-secret nuclear bases on the Moon and Venus, and deport political dissidents and ethnic Others to Polish concentration camps.

This dystopian totalitarianism is encoded into the level design through allusions to '50s sci-fi. Nazi Europe circa 1960 is dominated by a homogenous bloc of security checkpoints, political prisons, and research stations, each containing hundreds of Nazi guards and atomic supermen for B.J. to shoot, stab, and strangle. According to Noah Caldwell-Gervais, the architecture distorts the "whiz-pow" technological utopianism of '50s sci-fi to conjure "a bona fide Nazi utopia, a vision of the thousand-year Reich actually getting settled in for a whole millennium." For example, several levels take place in the Nautica, a research laboratory in downtown London which resembles Orwell's Ministry of Truth in *1984*. The allusions are both visual and thematic, underlining how dictatorships distort history for totalitarian ends. The Nazis built the Nautica to punish the British for resisting the occupation, and its imposing monolithic façade—located within spitting distance of Big Ben— underscores the impossibility of restoring England to its prewar glory. The Nautica's décor reinforces the finality of Nazi victory. Since it is also a launchpad for shuttles to Venus and the Moon, its entrance is adorned with a statue of Werner von Braun, the German scientist who built V2 missiles for the Nazis before building Saturn V rockets for NASA. The statue evokes the contingency of history in two ways. First, it underscores the historical probability that Nazis would have sent nuclear weapons to the moon, if one or two things had turned out a little differently. Second, it suggests how even democracies like the United States distort the facts and conceal troublesome alliances with former Nazis for ideological ends.

MachineGames' next entry in the franchise, *Wolfenstein II: The New Colossus* (2017), extends this dialogue with '50s sci-fi by relocating the action from Nazi Europe to an occupied United States. In one early sequence, B.J. travels to the ruins of New York City, which was destroyed with a Nazi atomic bomb in 1948. These levels are more unsettling than *Fallout 3*'s Capital Wasteland; the silly spectacles of *Earth vs. the Flying Saucers* and hopeful optimism of *Day the Earth Stood Still* yield to nightmares about nuked New York in films like *Invasion U.S.A.* (1952), *The World, the Flesh and the Devil* (1959), and *Fail-Safe* (1964), as well as memories of real-life attacks on crowded cities. For example, the seared skyline evokes the 9/11 terrorist attacks, and another character's descriptions of the "howling ghosts … wandering through the smoke" are based on survivors' accounts of the nuclear attacks on Hiroshima and Nagasaki. *Fallout 3* often minimizes atomic anxieties through melancholic nostalgia for the idealized, impossibly innocent fantasy worlds of '50s media. But *New Colossus* acknowledges that nuclear attacks have happened in the past and could happen again in the future, which would have been an unsettling point for a game to make in October 2017. The developers were finishing the game when North Korea tested two nuclear missiles in July 2017, and the game had been out for less than a month when North Korea launched another missile in November 2017. These events renewed fears of nuclear war; more than one writer worried that terrorists could detonate a miniaturized nuke in the United States,[21] and they sapped this nuked NYC of the innocent nostalgia that pervades the Capital Wasteland.

Subsequent levels further connect older retro-reboots and '50s sci-fi films to real-life history. After leaving New York, B.J. is tasked with nuking the top-secret Nazi base at Area 52. B.J. enters the base from an underground tunnel in nearby Roswell, New Mexico. This sequence, one of many in the game to eschew combat in favor of exploration, plays like Philip K. Dick by way of Norman Rockwell. Disguised as a fireman and carrying a small nuclear bomb in his fire extinguisher, B.J. arrives at Roswell on the morning of July 4, 1961, to observe a Nazified celebration of Independence Day. The diners, movie theaters, and storefronts are adorned with red, white, and black flags. Two Klansmen flatter a Nazi stormtrooper, who berates their mangled German. A sweet old lady casually mentions an upcoming slave auction. A mother and son avoid interacting with the chatty Nazi officer in the soda shop. These vignettes echo the critiques of hysterical conformity in *Invasion of the Body Snatchers* or *The Twilight Zone*'s "The Monsters Are Due on Maple Street" (1959). These tours through archetypal '50s communities suggest that most Americans would surrender to authoritarian aliens if their neighbors were doing it too. But Roswell also flips the script on '50s sci-fi movies by finding its hero outside, rather than inside, the community. Many '50s sci-fi movies focus on the ordinary Americans who are expelling the invading aliens; they only occasionally privilege the aliens' perspectives. But *New Colossus* casts players as the destructive alien force—the Nazis cast him as a terrorist monster named "Terror Billy"—out to destroy postwar American life.

Other sequences use the '50s sci-fi tropes of body snatching and atomic mutation to question whether B.J. is an antifascist superhero or a terrorist. Halfway through the game, B.J. is captured by Nazi general Frau Irene Engel, condemned in a public show trial held in the Supreme Court building, and then decapitated on the steps of the Lincoln Memorial. But at the last minute, B.J.'s severed head is seized by robots belonging to the Jewish mad scientist, Set Roth. Set attaches B.J.'s head to the bioengineered body of an atomic Nazi superman, transforming him into an All-American Frankenstein or Cyborg Captain America. This trope is familiar from films like *The Colossus of New York* (1958) as well as retro-reboots like *BioShock*. But whereas these texts warn that transforming people into killer cyborgs will destroy their souls, in *New Colossus* B.J.'s Nazified body is much stronger and faster than his American one; for instance, B.J. gains fifty extra health points and the ability to charge through walls. These mechanical improvements complicate B.J.'s antifascism;

Figure 7. The Nazi version of Roswell, New Mexico, from *Wolfenstein II: The New Colossus* (2017) (Machine Games/Bethesda Softworks [2017]).

he can only express his righteous anger at Nazis by embracing their technologies and methods. Moreover, B.J.'s resemblance to figures like G.I. Joe and Captain America extends these critiques to other archetypal heroes from Cold War culture. It makes players wonder: how many other comic book superheroes and TV space captains have been harboring fascist impulses?

The focus on American fascism was controversial partly because the game was released in October 2017, two months after the Unite the Right rally in Charlottesville, Virginia, which took place August 11–12, 2017. The publishers capitalized on this coincidence with a controversial marketing campaign that urged players to punch Nazis in the face. The game's official Twitter account issued a stark warning: "If you are a Nazi, GTFO." But the publishers also protected themselves from social media backlash by borrowing a page from leftist filmmakers who had also denied that their fantastical stories about alien invaders and atomic mutants had anything to say about the Cold War. Peter Hines, a vice president of marketing at ZeniMax, reiterated that the game was not written "to make specific statements or incite political discussions. We make games that we think are fun, meaningful, and immersive for a mature audience" (qtd. in Batchelor). Yet the game's strategic ambiguity about its politics forces audiences to read its '50s sci-fi iconography askance; like the texts that inspired it, its bloody, over-the-top violence and unsettling commentary on Nazism force audiences to confront the evil within.

Conclusion

These retro reboots underscore the rich legacy of '50s sci-fi and its role in contemporary media culture. Its retro-futuristic aesthetic serves several functions within the games. First, it distinguishes them within a marketplace dominated by official and unofficial adaptations of *Star Wars*, *Aliens*, and *The Matrix*. Second, it reframes outmoded mechanics from cult franchises as historic relics from gaming history. Third, it legitimizes video games by casting them as the successor to classic texts which use the tropes of malfunctioning robots, evil scientists, and atomic mutants to explore Cold War ideology. The retro reboots may not have inspired many gamers to rent a stack of old movies, but they nonetheless suggest how '50s sci-fi tropes can speak to twenty-first-century contexts. Just as '50s sci-fi displaced Cold War threats onto invading aliens and fifty-foot monsters, these retro reboots gamify fears about unrestrained capitalism, fascist dystopias, and environmental disaster by transforming fascist dystopias and atomic wastelands into postmodern playgrounds filled with hidden secrets to collect and irradiated monsters to kill.

NOTES

1. As Levine memorably tells Douglass C. Perry, "I have my useless liberal arts degree, so I've read stuff from Ayn Rand and [George] Orwell, and all the sort of utopian and dystopian writings of the 20th century.... There was a great period in the middle of the last century where there were a lot of people, Huxley,

Orwell, and Rand, writing about utopias and dystopias." For more information about *BioShock*'s production, see Barratt; Busby; Minkley; and Parkin.

2. For more on *BioShock* in relation to utopian literature, see Cook; McKinnon; Nyman and Teten; Packer; Parker; Rose; Shaw; and Yeates.

3. For more on the characterization of atomic scientists in '50s sci-fi, see Hendershot 23–38.

4. For more on *BioShock*'s deconstruction of video game conventions, see Aldred and Greenspan; Pointon; and Tulloch.

5. For more on the "body snatching" cycle, see Hendershot 39–64.

6. For more on the production of *Fallout 3*, see "The History of Bethesda Game Studios."

7. In addition to its thematic advantages, the developers opted for Washington, D.C., because it is located several miles down the road from Bethesda's headquarters in Bethesda, Maryland.

8. For more about alien invasion films, see Hendershot 101–126 and several of the essays in this volume.

9. One memorable side quest called "Those!" tasks players with killing the giant fire ants from the first film, whereas another side quest called "The Superhuman Gambit" introduces the players to the would-be superheroes, the Mechanizer and AntAgonizer.

10. Hendershot argues that these films "ultimately work to make the nuclear threat mythological and even natural. Hence it becomes something outside of the bounds of human time and also outside of the scope of human responsibility" (112).

11. For more on ethical dilemmas within Tranquility Lane, see Devine et al.

12. For more about technology in '50s sci-fi, see Biskind 119.

13. Patricia Hernandez could speak for many fans: "I lament the genre change—there is no shortage of shooters out in the world, and XCOM proved that you can modernize a franchise without turning it into an FPS.... [But] the Capital Wasteland is a great setting, especially for a game all about America."

14. Hendershot discusses how films like *20 Million Miles to Earth* (1957) use the Roman Empire as a metaphor for Cold War policies: "On the one hand, in postwar America the Soviet Union was often metaphorically linked with the decadence and corruption that supposedly defined the Roman Empire. On the other hand, the Manhattan Project and the ensuing Cold War structures of secrecy and McCarthyism were also metaphorically linked with Roman decadence" (109).

15. For more on *Wolfenstein 3D*, see Griliopoulos; Houghton; Kushner; and Caldwell-Gervais.

16. In these games, B.J. is working for the fictional Office of Secret Actions, a fictional version of the Office of Strategic Services that was headed by William Joseph ("Wild Bill") Donovan, the only person in American history to have received all four of the country's highest military honors.

17. According to Wikipedia, approximately three hundred World War II–themed games were released between 2000 and 2009. By contrast, only about one hundred World War II games have come out between 2010 and 2020.

18. For example, many fans disliked how the developers had replaced the existing health mechanic, which gave the player a limited number of health points, with an infinitely regenerating health bar. The former system forces experienced players to carefully plan their routes through maps and periodically stop to search the maps for medical kits. The latter system permits even the most inexperienced player to survive the deadliest combat encounters simply by ducking down behind some wooden boxes. For more information about the negative critical reception and commercial failure of *Wolfenstein* (2009), see Caldwell-Gervais; Capel; and Wilson.

19. As Matthies explains to Dean Takahashi, "I've never read the book, and I haven't seen the show, but the core idea is the same, of course, that the Nazis won the war. I'm in a place now where I try to stay away from that kind of thing because I want our thing to be our thing. I don't want those specific influences."

20. For more on alternative histories of Nazi dystopias, see Rosenfeld.

21. For more on the possibility of nuclear war, see Jabr and Mosher.

Works Cited

Aldred, Jessica, and Brian Greenspan. "A Man Chooses, A Slave Obeys: *BioShock* and the Dystopian Logic of Convergence." *Games and Culture* 6.5 (2011): 479–96.

Alexandra, Heather. "What Makes *Wolfenstein: The New Order* So Great." *Kotaku*, 24 July 2017, https://kotaku.com/what-makes-wolfenstein-the-new-order-so-great-1797195901. Accessed 15 July 2020.

Barratt, Charlie. "*BioShock*—Post-Mortem Interview." *GamesRadar*, 18 Sept. 2007, https://www.gamesradar.com/bioshock-post-mortem-interview/3/. Accessed 13 July 2020.

Batchelor, James. "It's Disturbing that *Wolfenstein* Can Be Considered a Controversial Political Statement." *GamesIndustry.biz*, 6 Oct. 2017, https://www.gamesindustry.biz/articles/2017-10-06-bethesda-were-not-afraid-of-being-openly-anti-nazi. Accessed 15 July 2020.

Biskind, Peter. *Seeing Is Believing: Or How Hollywood Taught Us to Stop Worrying and Love the Fifties*. Bloomsbury, 1983.

Busby, James. "The Making of *BioShock*: A Development Nightmare Turned Success." *All Gamers*, 30 May 2018, https://ag.hyperxgaming.com/article/4285/the-making-of-bioshock-a-development-nightmare-turned-success. Accessed 13 July 2020.

Caldwell-Gervais, Noah. "A Thorough Look at *Wolfenstein*." *YouTube*, 30 March 2016, https://www.youtube.com/watch?v=tzu0AoUxFhk. Accessed 17 July 2020.

Capel, Chris. "Revisiting Raven's *Wolfenstein*." *EuroGamer*, 23 Oct. 2017, https://www.eurogamer.net/articles/2017-10-22-revisiting-ravens-wolfenstein. Accessed 15 July 2020.

Cook, James. "Rapture in a Physical World: Did Andrew Ryan Choose the Impossible?" *BioShock and Philosophy: Irrational Game, Irrational Book*. edited by Luke Cuddy. Wiley-Blackwell, 2015, pp. 51–57.

Devine, Theresa Claire, William Andrew Presnell, and Samuel Miller. "Games as Art and Kant's Moral Dilemma: What Can Ethical Theory Reveal about the Role of the Game Designer as Artist?" *Games and Culture* 9.4 (2014): 277–310.

Ebert, Roger. "Video Games Can Never Be Art." *RogerEbert.com*, 16 April 2010, https://www.rogerebert.com/roger-ebert/video-games-can-never-be-art. Accessed 16 July 2020.

Griliopoulos, Dan. "The Dawn of the FPS: Inside the Making of *Wolfenstein 3D*." *PCGamesN*, 29 May 2014, https://www.pcgamesn.com/dawn-fps-inside-making-wolfenstein-3d. Accessed 15 July 2020.

Hendershot, Cyndy. *Paranoia, the Bomb, and 1950s Science Fiction Films*. Bowling Green State University Popular Press, 1999.

Hernandez, Patricia. "Let's Rank the *Fallout* Games, Best to Worst." *Kotaku*, 28 Feb. 2018, https://kotaku.com/lets-rank-the-fallout-games-best-to-worst-611408965. Accessed 14 July 2020.

"The History of Bethesda Game Studios." Produced by Danny O'Dwyer, *Noclip*, 2 Nov. 2021, https://www.youtube.com/watch?v=QKn9yiLVlMM.

Houghton, David. "The King of FPS—How *Wolfenstein 3D* Changed Video Games Forever." *GamesRadar*, 1 May 2017, https://www.gamesradar.com/8-things-wolfenstein-3d-gave-world/. Accessed 15 July 2020.

Jabr, Ferris. "This Is What a Nuclear Bomb Looks Like." *New York Magazine*, 11 June 2018, https://nymag.com/intelligencer/2018/06/what-a-nuclear-attack-in-new-york-would-look-like.html. Accessed 15 July 2020.

Kushner, David. *Masters of Doom: How Two Guys Created an Empire and Transformed Pop Culture*. Random House, 2004.

Matthies, Jens. "How I Made ... *Wolfenstein: The New Order*." *Stuff*, 21 May 2014, https://www.stuff.tv/features/how-i-made-wolfenstein-new-order. Accessed 15 July 2020.

McKinnon, Rachel. "Propaganda, Lies, and Bullshit in *BioShock*'s Rapture." *BioShock and Philosophy: Irrational Game, Irrational Book*. edited by Luke Cuddy. Wiley-Blackwell, 2015, pp. 107–13.

Minkley, Johnny. "Big Daddy Speaks." *Eurogamer*, 11 June 2007, https://www.eurogamer.net/articles/big-daddy-speaks-interview. Accessed 13 July 2020.

Mosher, Dave. "I Just Nuked Manhattan in a Realistic New VR Simulation, and the Experience Changed How I Understand the Bomb." *Business Insider*, 14 Aug. 2019, https://www.businessinsider.com/nukemap-virtual-reality-nuclear-bomb-explosion-simulator-new-york-city-2019-8. Accessed 15 July 2020.

Nyman, Elizabeth, and Ryan Lee Teten. "Lost and Found and Lost Again: Island Utopias and Dystopias in the *BioShock* series." *Games and Culture* 13.4 (2018): 370–84.

Packer, Joseph. "The Battle for Galt's Gulch: *BioShock* as Critique of Objectivism." *Journal of Gaming and Virtual Worlds* 2.3 (2010): 209–24.

Parker, Felan. "Canonizing *BioShock*: Cultural Value and the Prestige Game." *Games and Culture* 12.7–8 (2017): 739–63.

Parkin, Simon. "Rapture Leaked: The True Story Behind the Making of *BioShock*." *Eurogamer*, 18 Sept. 2016, https://www.eurogamer.net/articles/2014-04-17-the-true-story-of-bioshock. Accessed 13 July 2020.

Perry, Douglass C. "The Influence of Literature and Myth in Videogames." *IGN*, 17 May 2006, https://web.archive.org/web/20090327154040/http://xbox360.ign.com/articles/704/704806p1.html. Accessed 13 July 2020.

Pointon, Collin. "*BioShock*'s Meta-Narrative: What *BioShock* Teaches the Gamer about Gaming." *BioShock and Philosophy: Irrational Game, Irrational Book*, edited by Luke Cuddy. Wiley-Blackwell, 2015, pp. 1–14.

Rose, Jason. "The Value of Art in *BioShock*: Ayn Rand, Emotion, and Choice." *BioShock and Philosophy: Irrational Game, Irrational Book*, edited by Luke Cuddy. Wiley-Blackwell, 2015, pp. 15–26.

Rosenfeld, Gavriel D. *The World Hitler Never Made*. Cambridge University Press, 2005.

Shaw, Daniel Odin. "Ideology in *BioShock*." *Press Start* 5.1 (2019).

Takahashi, Dean. "How MachineGames Envisioned an America Overtaken by Nazis in *Wolfenstein II: The New Colossus*." *GamesBeat*, 19 June 2017, https://venturebeat.com/2017/06/19/how-machine-games-envisioned-an-america-overtaken-by-nazis-in-wolfenstein-ii-the-new-colossus/. Accessed 20 July 2020.

Tulloch, Rowan. "'A Man Chooses, A Slave Obeys': Agency, Interactivity, and Freedom in Video Gaming." *Journal of Gaming and Virtual Worlds* 2.1 (2010): 27–38.

Wilson, Mike. "A Forgotten Gem? 2009's *Wolfenstein* Deserves to Be Revisited." *Bloody Disgusting*, 19 Aug. 2019, https://bloody-disgusting.com/video-games/3579057/forgotten-gem-2009s-wolfenstein-deserves-revisited/. Accessed 15 July 2020.

Yeates, Robert. "*BioShock* and the Uncanny: The City of Rapture as Haunted House." *Foundation: The International Review of Science Fiction* 44.1 (2015): 66–77.

FILMOGRAPHY

Alien. Dir. Ridley Scott. 20th Century Fox, 1979. Film.
Aliens. Dir. James Cameron. 20th Century Fox, 1986. Film.
The Amazing Colossal Man. Dir. Bert I. Gordon. American International Pictures, 1957. Film.
The Atomic Café. Dir. Kevin Rafferty. Libra Films, 1982. Film.
Ben-Hur. Dir. William Wyler. MGM, 1959. Film.
The Big Combo. Dir. Joseph H. Lewis. Allied Artists Pictures, 1955. Film.
The Big Heat. Dir. Fritz Lang. Columbia Pictures, 1953. Film.
The Black Sleep. Dir. Reginald Le Borg. United Artists, 1956. Film.
Bucket of Blood. Dir. Roger Corman. American International Pictures, 1959. Film.
City Under the Sea. Dir. Jacques Tourneur. American International Pictures, 1965. Film.
The Colossus of New York. Dir. Eugène Lourié. Paramount Pictures, 1958. Film.
Corridors of Blood. Dir. Robert Day. MGM, 1959. Film.
Creature from the Black Lagoon. Dir. Jack Arnold. Universal Pictures, 1954. Film.
The Day After. Dir. Edward Hume. ABC Motion Pictures, 1983. Film.
The Day the Earth Stood Still. Dir. Robert Wise. 20th Century Fox, 1951. Film.
Day the World Ended. Dir. Roger Corman. American Releasing Corporation, 1955. Film.
The Dirty Dozen. Dir. Robert Aldrich. MGM, 1967. Film.
Earth vs. The Flying Saucers. Dir. Fred F. Sears. Columbia Pictures, 1956. Film.
Fail-Safe. Dir. Sidney Lumet. Columbia Pictures, 1964. Film.
The Fly. Dir. Kurt Neumann. 20th Century Fox, 1958. Film.
Forbidden Planet. Dir. Fred M. Wilcox. MGM, 1956. Film.
Gojira. Dir. Ishiro Honda. Toho Studios, 1954. Film.
The Guns of Navarone. Dir. J. Le Thompson. Columbia Pictures, 1961. Film.
I Married a Monster from Outer Space. Dir. Gene Fowler, Jr. Paramount Pictures, 1958. Film.
The Incredible Shrinking Man. Dir. Jack Arnold. Universal Pictures, 1956. Film.
Inglorious Basterds. Dir. Quentin Tarantino. Universal Pictures, 2009. Film.
Invasion of the Body Snatchers. Dir. Don Siegel. Allied Artists Pictures, 1956. Film.
Invasion U.S.A. Dir. Alfred E. Green. Columbia Pictures, 1952. Film.
It Came from Beneath the Sea. Dir. Robert Gordon. Columbia Pictures, 1955. Film.
Killers from Space. Dir. W. Lee Wilder. RKO Radio Pictures, 1954. Film.
Mad Max 2: The Road Warrior. Dir. George Miller. Warner Bros., 1981. Film.
The Man with X-Ray Eyes. Dir. Roger Corman. American International Pictures, 1963. Film.
The Manchurian Candidate. Dir. John Frankenheimer. United Artists, 1962. Film.
The Matrix. Dir. The Wachowskis. Warner Bros., 1999. Film.
On the Beach. Dir. Stanely Kramer. United Artists, 1959. Film.
Panic in Year Zero! Dir. Ray Milland. American International Pictures, 1962. Film.
Quo Vadis. Dir. Mervyn LeRoy. MGM, 1951. Film.
The Robe. Dir. Henry Koster. 20th Century Fox, 1953. Film.
Saving Private Ryan. Dir. Steven Spielberg. Paramount Pictures, 1998. Film.
Star Trek. CBS Studios, 1966–1969. TV Series.
Star Wars. Dir. George Lucas. 20th Century Fox, 1977. Film.
The Terminator. Dir. James Cameron. Orion Pictures, 1984. Film.
Them! Dir. Gordon Douglas. Warner Bros., 1954. Film.
This Island Earth. Dir. Joseph M. Newman. Universal-International, 1955. Film.
20 Million Miles to Earth. Dir. Nathan H. Juran. Columbia Pictures, 1957. Film.
20,000 Leagues Under the Sea. Dir. Richard Fleischer. Walt Disney Productions, 1954. Film.
WarGames. Dir. John Badham. United Artists, 1983. Film.
War of the Worlds. Dir. Byron Haskin, Paramount Pictures, 1953. Film.
The World, the Flesh, and the Devil. Dir. Ranald MacDougall. MGM, 1959. Film.

LUDOGRAPHY

Beyond Castle Wolfenstein. Muse Software, 1984.
BioShock. 2K Games, 2007.

Castle Wolfenstein. Muse Software, 1981.
Fallout. Interplay Productions, 1997.
Fallout 4. Bethesda Softworks, 2015.
Fallout 3. Bethesda Softworks, 2008.
Fallout 2. Interplay Productions, 1998.
Fallout: New Vegas. Bethesda Softworks, 2010.
Return to Castle Wolfenstein. id software, 2001.
System Shock 2. Electronic Arts, 1999.
Wolfenstein. id software, 2009.
Wolfenstein: The New Order. Bethesda Softworks, 2014.
Wolfenstein 3D. id software, 1992.
Wolfenstein II: The New Colossus. Bethesda Softworks, 2017.

The Truth Is Out There

1950s Science Fiction, The X-Files, and the Shifting Dynamics of National Anxiety

Jessica Metzler

The initial run of the television series *The X-Files* (1993–2002) adapted and deployed a conscious mash-up of tropes and themes from 1950s science-fiction films to reflect the shifting shape of national anxiety in the 1990s. The TV series heavily references and re-works narratives and imagery from a wide range of '50s sci-fi films including *The Thing from Another World* (1951), *It Came from Outer Space* (1953), and *Invaders from Mars* (1953). These films reflected outward-facing national anxieties about the Soviet Union, communism, and the existence of the atomic bomb. Forty years later, *The X-Files* re-deployed elements from this genre to depict an inward-facing national anxiety over U.S. government surveillance, the military industrial complex, and technological threats to individual privacy. In adapting tropes such as alien invasion and colonization, shape-shifting, and the existence of dangerous new technology, *The X-Files* reflected contemporary concerns over the role of technology in society, government surveillance, and threats to personal privacy. The repurposing of '50s sci-fi genre elements that were already associated with narratives about political and technological anxiety aided the show's popularity, which began with an enthusiastic "cult following" by fans and built into widespread viewership by the mid–'90s. This popularity continues with the recent revival of the series in 2016 and 2018 demonstrating the enduring influence of 1950s sci-fi films on contemporary depictions of national anxiety.

The plot of *The X-Files* focuses on two FBI agents as they investigate cases involving unexplained phenomena, including supernatural, paranormal, or extraterrestrial aspects. These cases are categorized within the FBI as "X-Files." The series begins when Fox Mulder (David Duchovny), a true believer in paranormal phenomena, is partnered with Dana Scully (Gillian Anderson), a medical doctor and skeptic who believes in the primacy of logic and rationality. Scully is originally assigned to work with Mulder in order to debunk his work. She eventually sees things, however, that cannot be rationally explained and becomes a believer in extraordinary phenomena herself. Mulder's interest in the X-Files stems from his obsessive desire to discover the truth about extraterrestrial contact with Earth after witnessing his

Figure 8. Fox Mulder (David Duchovny) and Dana Scully (Gillian Anderson) in a publicity still from *The X-Files* (1993–2002, 2016, 2018) (© Fox Broadcasting/Photofest).

sister Samantha's abduction by aliens when they were both children in the 1970s. The tagline for the show, which was displayed at the end of each episode's opening title credits, read, "The Truth is Out There,"[1] and Mulder's quest for "the truth" about the paranormal motivates much of the action of the series.

In its focus on alien encounters, *The X-Files* adapts and re-works a number of familiar tropes from 1950s sci-fi films. This essay discusses the most prominent of these: plots involving alien threats to bodily integrity (e.g., shape shifting and the use of implants), and plots involving alien invasion and/or colonization. In examining these tropes, I primarily focus on events from *The X-Files* "mythology arc" plotline,[2] which consists of multiple episodes spread over the entire series.[3] These episodes concern the existence of a "shadow government" operating within the U.S. government. This group is eventually dubbed "the Syndicate" in season six. The Syndicate's existence hinges on a fifty-year conspiracy in which members operating within various federal government agencies conspired to hide the existence of an extraterrestrial alien race intent on colonizing Earth and destroying its human inhabitants with an alien biological virus (variously referred to as "black oil" and "purity").[4] The only humans who would be spared in the invasion would be those who had been turned into alien-human hybrids through a series of invasive experiments conducted on abducted and unwilling victims by government scientists and doctors. These alien-human hybrids would become a "slave race" designed to serve the alien colonizers. In a bid to forestall the colonization of Earth, the Syndicate agreed in the 1950s to work to create this group of hybrids, hoping to buy time to develop a vaccine to treat the alien virus. While the plot of the mythology arc is labyrinthine—and, at times, contradictory—it offers us a clear picture of the ways the series adapted 1950s tropes, such as shape-shifting and colonization, and turned them from expressions of Cold War paranoia to reflections of 1990s technological anxiety—including anxiety over government surveillance and bio-terrorism.

Alien threats to bodily integrity were a core feature of many 1950s sci-fi films. *Invaders from Mars* features aliens who embed mind-controlling implants into humans. The aliens in *It Came from Outer Space* are shape-shifters who can alter their external appearance to imitate specific humans.[5] These plot points are often read as reflections of paranoia over the ability of communism to control or "brainwash" minds and a fear of foreigners from outside the United States. Many critics have noted the Cold War symbolism in 1950s sci-fi films, specifically the ways aliens or monsters stand in for a communist threat. As Peter Biskind notes, "The analogy was usually oblique, but so close to the surface [...] as to be just below the level of consciousness. Presenting Reds as ants or aliens served to establish their Otherness" (132). This threat was nearly always foreign in nature—often consisting of aliens invading from outer space.

While the aliens' motives in these films may vary—some intent on colonizing Earth, others attempting to interfere with U.S. technology, and some simply accidental arrivals—they all present an immediate threat to a perceived American way of life due to the manner in which the extraterrestrials execute their plans. The colonizing plant-based alien life-form in *The Thing from Another World* kills for human blood to feed its asexually produced offspring. Left unchecked, this colonization plan would result in the replacement of the human race with an alien one, which can be read as a metaphor for fear about the United States losing the Cold War and being overrun, or colonized, by communists. Unlike the bloodthirsty Thing, the aliens in *Invaders from Mars* are preservationists, not colonizers. They arrive to sabotage U.S. rocket technology in a bid for self-protection. Such noble motives are undercut, however, by their tactics. The aliens abduct humans and implant microchips in their necks that subject them to mind control and can cause death. These implants can easily be read as linked to paranoia about communism's ability to brainwash those exposed to it and the perceived deadly consequences of exposure. While the extraterrestrials in *It Came from Outer Space* are unintentional visitors to Earth after their ship crash lands in the Arizona desert, their mode of repairing their ship involves shape-shifting to impersonate specific humans, reflecting McCarthy-era paranoia over the existence of communists within the United States.

In these three films, the aliens are external. Extraterrestrials are out there and they are coming for you, with the goal of controlling your movements, attitudes, and behaviors—just as people feared the communists associated with foreign governments, particularly the Soviet Union, were attempting to do. As Mark Jancovich notes, "during the 1950s, many American critics claimed that in the Soviet Union people were all the same; that they were forced to deny personal feeling and characteristics, and to become mere functionaries of the social whole" (325). In each of these films we see this cultural belief play out—an alien force that is without emotion (*The Thing*), causes humans to lose their humanity through mind control or brainwashing (*Invaders from Mars*), or creates wooden imposter humans (*It Came from Outer Space*). In *The X-Files*, however, the source of fear is often domestic. The aliens may be coming from outer space, but they're doing so in collaboration with a U.S. government that has been conspiring against its own citizens since the 1950s. Two *X-Files* plotlines that span multiple seasons can be read as adaptations of 1950s tropes associated with alien threats to bodily integrity. The first is Scully's abduction, experimentation, and chip implantation in season two, which draws narratively and visually from the neck implants in *Invaders from Mars*. The second is the shape-shifting alien bounty hunters and rebel aliens (seasons two through nine), which share commonalities with the shape-shifting aliens in *It Came from Outer Space*.

In *Invaders from Mars*, an alien spaceship lands on Earth in order to destroy U.S. military technology that would have threatened the Martians' existence. In service of these plans, humans are abducted and fitted with neck implants that give the aliens the ability to control a person's behavior. Humans become brainwashed robots doing the aliens' bidding. When their services are no longer needed, the humans are expendable—the chip causes an explosion within their brain that kills them. The film's protagonist, a young boy named David (Jimmy Hunt), sees the initial crash in the sandpit behind his house and is horrified to see people he knows, including his parents, come under alien control. His outlandish-sounding story is finally believed by a female doctor with red hair, Dr. Patricia Blake (Helena Carter), and a male astronomer, Dr. Stuart Kelston (Arthur Franz). These authority figures call in the military to deal with the threat, and the audience sees this victorious response through extended footage of tanks and troops arriving in the boy's small town. The film's climax occurs when David and Dr. Blake are abducted and find themselves underground in the aliens' craft. In a vivid scene, Dr. Kelston rescues Dr. Blake from having an implant placed in her neck. Through David's ingenuity and U.S. military might, the aliens are defeated and their ship is destroyed. The film concludes with a controversial "it was all a dream" ending in which David awakes and the film suggests that the preceding events of the plot were his nightmare. The events of the beginning of the film then start to repeat as David once again witnesses the spaceship landing behind his house.[6]

The X-Files adapts the alien implant plot device into a plot arc that sees Scully—a red-headed female doctor—abducted and subjected to experiments, including the implantation of a chip in her neck. The implant operates as a type of tracking device or homing beacon that triggers a fatal form of cancer when removed. Originally, her abduction is depicted as being perpetrated by aliens. However, the viewer later learns that she was taken by humans working in collaboration with aliens and was experimented on using alien technology. The scenes of Scully's abduction experiences owe a clear visual debt to *Invaders*, as does her character's warm attitude toward and interactions with children throughout the series. The specific paranoia behind the implant narrative shifts, however. The implants in *Invaders* speak to a Cold War paranoia about communist mind control and its potentially fatal consequences. David Seed connects the experiences of brainwashed American POWs in Korea to 1950s invasion sci-fi films, noting, "It is significant that *Invaders from Mars*, the most politically explicit of these films, should show an army general being taken over, but as if a compensatory fantasy for Korea, includes footage of a large-scale army mobilization which results in the ejection of the invaders" (133). M. Keith Booker asserts that the mind-control devices in the film "would seem to participate in a particularly obvious way in the McCarthyite paranoia of the early 1950s" (121). And Nora Sayre notes, "All in all, the parallel between Martians and Communists is quite pronounced in this movie, where those who are programmed to be traitors to America are intent on perverting or suppressing the truth" (199). Instead of serving as an allegory for communism, in *The X-Files* this trope represents a different paranoia about "suppressing the truth"—one where the U.S. government is implicated in a conspiracy to surveil and commit crimes against its own citizens. In the series, the chips implanted in abductees, including Scully, reflect a 1990s paranoia about the privacy invasions made possible by the development of increasingly sophisticated technology and surveillance tools.

The early 1990s saw the rise of electronic employee surveillance at work in the guise of everything from keystroke and telephone monitoring to email interception, cameras (CCTV), and even homing beacons on employee badges. New technology paved the way for a panoptic work environment, giving managers the capability to watch employees' every move. A 1995 *Wired Magazine* article on employee monitoring technology recounts the negative effects of this new situation, most notably how it induced high levels of stress. Sociologist Gary Marx attributed this stress to the idea that "employees really never know when they are being watched" (Whalen). Science created a better panopticon through the miracles of modern technology, including the use of the "Active Badge" in the workplace. This badge contained a computer chip that essentially worked as a tracking device, allowing supervisors and co-workers to track and pinpoint the location of the wearer. The existence and implications of implants as tracking and mind-control devices are introduced in the very first episode of *The X-Files*. In *The X-Files* pilot, victims of alien abductions are found to have foreign metal implants in their nasal cavities. Such implants are thought to be responsible for allowing the aliens who inserted them constant access to the location of the abductees, as well as giving the aliens the ability to alter and control the humans' behavior (causing abductees to meet the space craft and kill others). These implants also trigger self-discipline in the abductees. A lack of discretion about discussing their experiences triggers a reminder, in the form of a nosebleed, that they are being monitored. Unlike these abductees, however, Scully's abduction is not random. It is directly connected to her workplace and her assigned work on the X-Files. Her FBI employer is complicit in her assault and subsequent tracking. The implant placed inside Scully's neck causes her to experience nosebleeds like the other abductees, and exercising the agency to have it removed causes her to develop cancer. Scully's work on the X-Files is no longer an external pursuit; she herself has become part of an X-File case. The implant narrative positions aliens and the government in a panoptic position of technological power—able to watch every move and control behavior, a position paralleled by employers in the technologically advanced workplace of the '90s. Scully's unease at this privacy invasion mirrors the unease of contemporary viewers at what was seen as new technologically-mediated threats to their privacy.

In addition to mind-control implants, *The X-Files* adopts another classic sci-fi convention based on an alien threat to bodily integrity: shape-shifting aliens. In *It Came from Outer Space*, aliens crash land on Earth by accident while en route to a different destination. Recognizing that the people of Earth would be hostile to outsiders, the aliens make use of their ability to shape-shift and impersonate humans, thus allowing them to move among the townsfolk undetected to collect the materials needed to repair their spacecraft and leave Earth. The sense of horror or unease created by this ability emerges from the way the aliens imitate specific individuals. They don't just disguise themselves as humans; they disguise themselves as George and Frank, two local telephone linemen, and even Ellen, the protagonist's girlfriend.[7] In this sense, the film can be read as an allegory for the insidiousness of communism—the ways people feared it could infiltrate a community and take over friends and loved ones, turning them into robot shells of themselves and leaving those who remain in the position of not knowing who can be trusted. When discussing the "dehumanization of humans" in 1950s alien invasion films, Vivian Sobchack writes of the way shapeshifting as a plot device works to incite paranoia and active viewership in the audience:

> The familiar characters we see on the screen and to whose roles we respond with complacency are not what they appear to be. And, because the image attempts to deceive us, no familiar person or activity finally escapes our scrutiny and our suspicion. The smallest gesture of the most innocent characters become suspect; nothing and no one can be taken for granted. Mother, father, husband, wife, child, neighbors, civil servants, must be watched for signs that they are, under the surface skin—invaders. We cannot automatically believe what we see. Thus, these films visually—as well as thematically—suggest that to trust and believe in other people [...] is ridiculously naïve and self-destructive; the way we watch the films—suspiciously—is the way we should watch each other, and "healthy" paranoia is made to seem a reasonable and self-preservational alternative to trust [128–29].

Sobchack is referring here to films such as *Invasion of the Body Snatchers* and *It Came from Outer Space*, yet the experience she describes could just as easily apply to *The X-Files*' exhortation to "Trust No One" in general, and more specifically to the episodes involving alien bounty hunters who have the ability to shape-shift and take on the identity of humans. In two particularly chilling episodes, one of these aliens assumes Mulder's identity, leaving Scully in peril ("Colony"; "End Game"). These aliens also murder law enforcement officers and doctors in order to assume their identities and deceive others, including Mulder and Scully ("Colony"; "The Unnatural"). As viewers watch these aliens morph identities before our eyes, we soon learn not to trust our vision and to assume that nothing is as it appears. While the paranoid effects on the viewer are similar in both *It Came from Outer Space* and *The X-Files*, the focus of this paranoia, again, has shifted. Instead of the fear that one's closest friends and family might have been infiltrated by the communist menace that pervades films like *It Came from Outer Space*,[8] *The X-Files* provides the knowledge that these shape-shifting aliens are linked to a broader government conspiracy rooted in deception, manipulation, and surveillance of the public.[9] This shifts the viewer paranoia from local families and communities to the federal government. Our fear moves from those we can watch to those who might be watching us. Shape-shifting is weaponized in *The X-Files* and is connected to the Syndicate's larger plot to develop alien-human hybrids in service of the aliens' plan to colonize the Earth. A plan whose implementation is made possible through decades of surveillance of the American people.[10]

The X-Files traffics heavily in paranoia about government surveillance against a cultural background of unease with the technology that afforded it. The early 1990s saw unprecedented technological growth and the birth of wide-spread internet access. Yet with all the infant Internet had the potential to offer, including communication without boundaries, online shopping, banking, and communities, one major roadblock existed—government regulations prevented the strong encryption of data that would allow info such as credit card numbers and emails to be delivered without being intercepted by a third, unauthorized party. The government initially crippled strong encryption technology through the existence of munitions export laws that prohibited its distribution. Cryptography was considered a threat to national security due to its capability to interfere with the government's ability to conduct surveillance and intercept messages identifying illegal behavior and foreign terrorist plots. These laws dated back to the Cold War when "the NSA [National Security Agency] was created to spy on foreign enemies' communications and to supervise a system of patent and export laws, ensuring that the spread of American cryptography would not complicate the agency's eavesdropping mission" (Cassidy). Public access to cryptology threatened to end the NSA's monopoly on code making and breaking technology.

A lack of available strong encryption seriously compromised the privacy of individuals on the internet—intercepted email, stolen credit card numbers and seized computer accounts were a few of the possible outcomes (*EFF Sues*). If the web was to become commercially viable and personally useful, steps had to be taken to ensure individual privacy. In 1991 Phil Zimmerman created the encryption program "Pretty Good Privacy" (PGP), distributed it for free online and found himself under investigation by the U.S. government in 1993 for munitions export violations as "strong cryptography was at the time considered a weapon under US law" (Garside; "PGP History"). This proved to be a flashpoint in a new culture war. Cypherpunks, academics, and big business joined together to lobby for encryption, which became synonymous with internet privacy. In 1993, the NSA attempted to circumvent debate about encryption law by controlling the market with their "Clipper Chip." The Clipper would make strong encryption legally available for individuals with one small catch—the government would possess a back door key that would allow the NSA, FBI, CIA, and any number of government offices unfettered access to encrypted information (Sykes 175; Markoff D17). Furthermore, the government contracted with AT&T, who was set to market their own encryption devices, to use Clipper instead—eliminating immediate competition. Public outcry and backlash immediately ensued. A 1994 TIME/CNN poll found that 80 percent of Americans opposed the Clipper Chip and two thirds of those surveyed believed that "it was more important to protect the privacy of phone calls than to preserve the ability of police to conduct wiretaps" (Elmer-Dewitt). Whether or not the government actually wanted to spy on American citizens was irrelevant—the public bristled at the suggestion that they should hand over this ability, and the Clipper Chip idea eventually died in the late nineties without ever coming to fruition.[11]

On another front in the cryptowars, academic Daniel Bernstein, with the backing of the EFF (the Electronic Frontier Foundation—a computer privacy watchdog group), sued the state department, the NSA, the Department of Defense, and the Department of Commerce in a 1995 challenge to the constitutionality of U.S. export laws that defined cryptography as illegal munitions. Bernstein filed his lawsuit after the government informed him that he would need a munitions export license to publish his graduate research on cryptography and a crypto program he designed (Cassidy). In 1996, the case against Zimmerman and PGP was dropped by the courts ("PGP History"; Markoff D1). In 1997, Bernstein won a limited victory against the government and the ruling was upheld on appeal in 1999 (*Bernstein*). Bernstein could publish his code, and the government began relaxing its export laws. The public's right to privacy had temporarily won out against the government's appeals to national security.

Against this backdrop of right to privacy battles in the computer age, the popularity of *The X-Files* grew steadily from its 1993 premiere to its peak in the late '90s,[12] thanks in part to the show's vast legions of dedicated internet fans, who dubbed themselves the "X-Philes." *The X-Files* is often heralded as the first television show to attract and build a massive fan base through the internet, causing servers to crash under the weight of real-time chats, discussion boards, and listserves. A documentary on the *X-Files* fandom, *X-Philes*, speculates that the internet actually saved *The X-Files* after disappointing season one ratings. The internet allowed fans in disparate locations to band together in close-knit online communities to create buzz about the show and demand its renewal (*X-Philes*). As the internet grew, so did the show's popularity. Fox executive Mark Stoman called *The X-Files* the "most participatory show on television" and show creator and executive producer Chris Carter relates tales of immediately hopping online to check the fan reaction to an episode after it aired (*X-Philes*). Demographically, *X-Files* fans, like most early 1990s internet users, were an educated group with mid- to high-level incomes who were invested in analyzing and even deconstructing episodes (Clerc). The internet created a feeling of interaction between the fans and the producers with occasional palpable results. The

Figure 9. From left: Frohike (Tom Braidwood), Byers (Bruce Harwood), and Langly (Dean Haglund), the "Lone Gunmen," conspiracy theorists and computer hackers, appear as recurring characters in *The X-Files* (1993–2002, 2016, 2018) (© Fox Broadcasting/Photofest).

Lone Gunmen characters on the show—Frohike (Tom Braidwood), Langly (Dean Haglund), and Byers (Bruce Harwood)—were not originally intended to be recurring characters until producers discovered that they were popular with fans and brought them back (*X-Philes*). The show's computer-savvy fans saw something of themselves in the privacy-conscious, paranoid cypherpunk hackers the Lone Gunmen represented. The Lone Gunmen were television's fictional equivalent of the Phil Zimmermans and Daniel Bernsteins of the computer privacy cryptowars. These characters represented a countercultural "hacker ethic" with which fans identified. Technology journalist Steven Levy describes this "hacker ethic" as adherents to certain beliefs including the cryptic "All information should be free," "Access to computers should be unlimited and total," and "Mistrust authority—promote decentralization" (qtd. in Brand).[13] The distrust of authority and a view of the government as invasive and determined to violate civil liberties and privacy rights that was overtly present in a hacker community could also be found among a broader internet community and the public at large. *The X-Files'* portrayal of mass surveillance techniques undertaken to support a shape-shifting alien invasion reflected audiences' fears of the government's ability to invade the public's privacy.

Related to the threat to bodily integrity posed by aliens is a second trope *The X-Files* adapts from '50s sci-fi films: the threat of alien invasion and colonization. This threat is central to the plot of *The Thing from Another World* and forms the basis of the overarching *X-Files* mythology plot arc. *The Thing from Another World* is set in the harsh conditions of a scientific arctic outpost where an alien spaceship has been found buried beneath the ice near the North Pole. An attempt to recover the craft fails—the men accidentally blow it up instead—but they do find an alien body frozen in ice and bring it back to the camp. When a guard assigned to watch the creature accidentally defrosts it, the alien turns out to be alive and terrorizes the outpost. The resident scientist, Dr. Carrington (Robert Cornthwaite), determines that the alien creature is composed of vegetable matter, feeds on human blood, and reproduces asexually. The group deduces that the alien plans to colonize the planet, killing humans to feed its multiplying offspring. When other modes of stopping it fail, Dr. Carrington's secretary Nikki (Margaret Sheridan) suggests that boiling vegetables is the way to kill them, and the group devises a scheme to electrocute the alien against the protests of Dr. Carrington who seeks to understand it. The plan succeeds in the end, though the viewer is left with the warning "Watch the skies everywhere. Keep looking. Keep watching the skies."[14]

The invasion and colonization threat in *The Thing* speaks to the fear of losing the Cold War and the implications of such a failure—invasion by the Soviets and colonization by communist ideology. The ship and the alien emit radiation measurable by a Geiger counter, thus associating them with a fear of nuclear technology possessed by the Other. Notably, Dr. Carrington is portrayed negatively as siding with the monster against the rest of the group and is visually associated with Soviet markers (he wears a fur hat that resembles a Russian ushanka and sports a Leninesque beard).[15] The negative portrayal of Dr. Carrington harks back, in part, to the "evil scientist" monster movie trope from the 1930s (e.g., James Whale's 1931 film *Frankenstein* starring Boris Karloff), but it departs from the more positive portrayals of scientists and doctors seen in other '50s sci-fi films, such as *Invaders from Mars*. Some critics have read this portrayal as a warning about the devastating consequences science and technology can bring about, including the threat of a nuclear holocaust that underpinned the Cold War. Peter Biskind writes, "Carrington's behavior justifies the soldiers' mistrust of science, even turns them against the bomb itself" (128). In *The X-Files*, the alien invasion and colonization plot represents a related form of technological anxiety updated for '90s audiences—fear over the potential of bio-technology to be weaponized and turned against the public. *The X-Files* reflects 1990s anxieties that genetic bio-engineering—the result of technological advancement—could be used for unethical and horrific ends.

The alien colonization plot in *The X-Files* rests on the introduction of an alien virus via bees meant to kill all humans, sparing only a genetically engineered alien-human hybrid population who will become a "slave race" to serve the alien colonizers. In a three-part episode that aired in 1995 and spanned seasons two and three,[16] Mulder and Scully unearth evidence that the Syndicate has been accessing genetic material from all Americans since the '50s through mandatory smallpox vaccinations as part of the plot to genetically engineer alien-human hybrids. Yet Mulder and Scully do not stumble upon this information by themselves. The trouble begins when a notorious computer hacker known as "The Thinker" penetrates the Department of Defense computer system and steals secret files that outline fifty years of this government conspiracy. He then arranges to meet Mulder (courtesy of the Lone Gunmen—Mulder's link to a computer underground) and give him the stolen files on a DAT tape. When asked the reason for the disclosure, the Thinker replies, "I want the truth. And I want you to promise that those rat bastards answer to the people" ("Anasazi"). Here we see a classic manifestation of the "hacker ethic"—willing power to the people and asserting that information and the truth should be made free. The Thinker is then murdered, execution style, by the Syndicate's assassins—proof that the truth can get you killed. Thus, the first stage in discovering "the truth" of this government conspiracy comes from a computer hacker who breeches technological security with relative ease. The Thinker states that he didn't take any precautions because he "didn't even expect to get inside." Yet technology alone cannot decipher the secrets contained within those files, for they have been encrypted as well, as Mulder and Scully discover—not by any computer code but in the Navajo language.

Scully recognizes the encryption and points out that Navajo was the only code the Japanese couldn't break in World War II. These episodes show history repeating itself: the U.S. government appropriating the language of a marginalized group of people and using it to encrypt information in the name of national security. Scully manages to come in contact with Albert Hosteen (Floyd Red Crow Westerman), who had served as a Navajo code talker in World War II, and who had also recently witnessed his grandson's discovery of an alien corpse in the New Mexico desert at the beginning of the episode. Hosteen decodes the information on the DAT tape—the truth—and, as Assistant Director Skinner (Mitch Pileggi), Mulder and Scully's superior, reveals to the horrified Syndicate member Cigarette Smoking Man (William B. Davis), "in the ancient oral tradition of his people, he's told twenty other men the information on those files. So unless you kill every Navajo living in four states ... that information is available with a simple phone call. Welcome to the wonderful world of high technology" ("Paperclip"). Skinner's ironic reference to "high technology" in Hosteen's "ancient oral tradition" underscores cryptography's connection to ordinary citizens. Part of changing the Navajo language into cipher during World War II involved using words from the natural world to signify military terms. Thus when the Navajo word for "turtle" was used, it signified "tank" ("Codes"). The episode's allusion to a historical corruption of the natural world to meet military ends was indicative of a larger, contemporary fear—that the government was able to use technology to intrude on the public at large and manipulate ways of life. Yet the vision *The X-Files* presents is not hopeless. Even while the government uses technology for nefarious ends, the possibility for resistance lies in the populous. The code talkers can break the code; the hackers can reveal the secrets. The juxtaposition of cryptography's history (Navajo code talkers) with cryptography's future (computer hackers) is a significant one. It offers a model for a continuing resistance to a corrupt military industrial complex.

The connection between these 1995 episodes and the contemporaneous crypto debate is hard to miss. During World War II, the Navajo language amounted to an unbreakable code, which the military appropriated to control the dissemination of its own secrets. However, it was always within the code talker's power to reclaim the encrypted information and spread it. Likewise, cypherpunks created hard-to-break computer encryption in the 1990s and distributed it to the masses, an action the government attempted to appropriate during the Clipper Chip debacle. Like the code talkers, hackers were always able to reclaim their cryptography and, as Philip Zimmerman did, distribute it freely on the web, thus subverting governmental attempts at information control.

The initial series finale of *The X-Files* came in 2002 after nine seasons. While the reasons given for the series' end vary, and star David Duchovny's exit from the show certainly played a part, it was also undoubtedly true that the cultural moment that had given rise to the anxieties manifested in *The X-Files* was shifting from '90s concerns over privacy and surveillance to a post–9/11 world in which the public became more willing to sacrifice privacy in the name of national security. This included measures such as the PATRIOT Act that authorized sweeping expansions in the use of surveillance, including wiretaps and internet monitoring. As Adam Penenberg writes, "The terrorist assault on America shifted the balance between privacy and security. What was considered Orwellian one week seemed perfectly reasonable—even necessary—the next." The public now embraced and found safety, rather than fear and distrust, in a panoptic society. A Harris poll released in October 2001 found "overwhelming public support for increasing [governmental] surveillance powers and, despite concerns about potential abuse, confidence that the powers will be used properly." The poll showed that 86 percent of Americans favored the use of facial-recognition technology to scan for potential terrorists; 81 percent favored closer monitoring of banking and credit card transactions; 63 percent agreed with increased surveillance of public places and monitoring of internet discussions and chat rooms; and 54 percent favored expanded monitoring of cell phones and e-mail (Taylor). The message was clear—cultural anxiety in the United States had shifted from an internal fear of a corrupt government and panoptic society to an external fear of foreign terrorist threats. A series built on paranoia about the former was rapidly losing its audience amid the tremendous popularity of the reality TV boom in the 2000s, which embraced and celebrated constant surveillance.

Our current historical moment, however, has seen the return not only of the distrust of technology (notably regarding social media and the discourse surrounding "fake news") and the government but also the return of film and television that reflects this paranoia—including *The X-Files* itself.[17] The series returned in 2016 for a tenth season with an eleventh following in 2018, Duchovny and Anderson both reprising their roles as Mulder and Scully. This relatively rare return of a TV series 14 years after it left the air with a continuance of plot lines from earlier seasons involving alien invasion and colonization demonstrates the enduring influence of 1950s sci-fi tropes as vehicles for contemporary depictions of national anxieties.[18]

NOTES

1. Occasionally the tagline would change for specific episodes as a way of telegraphing the importance of the episode to the mythology arc narrative (see note 2).

2. The plot of *The X-Files* utilizes dual narrative devices: "monster-of-the-week" stand-alone episodes in which a single case is investigated and solved (to the extent that any X-file can be solved) and "mythology arc" or "myth arc" episodes, which deal with the ongoing plot of a mass, shadowy government conspiracy to deny the existence of extraterrestrial life.

3. *The X-Files* also spawned two movies, which had theatrical releases. The first film, *The X-Files: Fight the Future*, was released in the summer of 1998 and bridges seasons five and six. Its plot focuses on furthering the audience's understanding of the TV series' mythology arc. The second, *The X-Files: I Want to Believe*, was released in 2008, six years after the show's 2002 finale. The 2008 film's stand-alone plot concerns a serial killer and is largely unconnected to previous series episodes.

4. The syndicate has international members, given the global nature of the threat to Earth but is primarily presented as driven by U.S. actors.

5. While I restrict my focus here to these three films, there are many other examples of these tropes in 1950s sci-fi films, including the notable *Invasion of the Body Snatchers* (1956).

6. Later, edited versions of the film omitted this ending and added additional scenes. For a description of the changes to the film after its initial release, see Warren, 114–21. For more on this film see the essays of Mica A. Hilson and Sam Umland in this collection.

7. *The X-Files* makes a number of narrative and visual references to telephone linemen in various episodes, calling attention to the series' sci-fi lineage. *It Came from Outer Space*, in which two linemen appear as central characters, is based on a short story by Ray Bradbury, whose father was a telephone lineman (Warren 121; 125). A telephone lineman is the victim of alien virus-carrying bees in *The X-Files* episode "Herrenvolk," and shots of telephone poles extending along a rural landscape in the episode visually references *It Came*. In one of the series' more humorous episodes, "Jose Chung's from Outer Space," the opening shot appears to show the underside of a UFO (or a *Star Wars*–reminiscent craft), only to pan out to reveal that the close-up was of the underside of a telephone lineman's truck bucket. The lineman soon encounters aliens, recalling this history of linemen in sci-fi narratives from Bradbury to *It Came from Outer Space* to *Close Encounters of the Third Kind* (1977), in which Richard Dreyfuss' main character, a lineman, experiences an alien encounter. *The X-Files*' knowing nods to classic sci-fi films occur throughout the series, acknowledging its participation in the genre. For a comprehensive reading of the "Jose Chung's" episode see Lavery, Hague, and Cartwright, 13–18.

8. Jeff Smith argues that the shape-shifting abilities of the aliens in *It Came from Outer Space* place it in the category of anti-communist film, noting "one of the concerns about Communist Party activity was that Communists could masquerade as ordinary citizens; thus, their apparent familiarity enabled them to dupe average Joes and Janes" (247).

9. While a number of essays have discussed the connections between conspiracies and conspiracy theories from the 1960s and 1970s and the series (e.g., JFK's assassination, Watergate), my focus here is on the 1950s as the origin of many of these sci-fi tropes. For more on conspiracy culture and *The X-Files* see Graham, Delasara, and Knight.

10. It is worth noting Mulder's connection to the Syndicate here. Both the man he believed to be his father, and the man revealed to be his biological father (the character known as Cigarette Smoking Man), held roles within this conspiracy—their involvement within it ultimately causing the alien abduction of Mulder's sister. In this respect, *The X-Files* can be read as connecting a 1950s paranoia about not being able to trust one's family to a 1990s paranoia about not trusting the government. In Mulder's case, they are often one and the same.

11. In one episode of *The X-Files*, "Memento Mori," the Lone Gunmen mention the Clipper Chip directly when discussing intrusive government technology.

12. "'The X-Files,' which was among the most popular programs in Fox history, peaked in its fourth season (1996–97) when it averaged nearly 20 million viewers per episode. Its all-time high in viewership came on Jan. 26, 1997, when the episode titled 'Leonard Betts' averaged 29.1 million viewers" (Kissell).

13. For more on the topic, see Levy, *Hackers* and *Crypto*.

14. While I focus here on the 1951 film, several episodes of *The X-Files* were also heavily influenced by

John Carpenter's 1982 remake, *The Thing*. The first season episode "Ice" is widely considered to be an adaptation of Carpenter's *The Thing*. For more on these two films see Dennis R. Cutchins' essay in this collection.

15. Others have remarked on these visual markers. Biskind notes that "Carrington, as we have seen, is a pluralist mad scientist, but with his beard and Soviet-style fur hat, he is also a Russian, so we have come full circle. This film attacks pluralists by equating them with Reds" (134), while Sayre remarks, "the scientist in *The Thing* [. . .] is almost as villainous as the super-carrot: in his beard and fur hat, he looks downright Russian" (198).

16. These episodes include "Anasazi," "The Blessing Way," and "Paper Clip."

17. Various forms of workplace surveillance have dramatically increased since the 1990s to include apps, virtual online workspaces, and the use of web cams and microphones on personal laptops (Harwell), such new privacy erosions perhaps reflecting the appeal of the return of the series for seasons 10 and 11 in 2016 and 2018, respectively.

18. I am grateful for Leigh Edwards' suggestions on an early version of this essay.

Works Cited

Bernstein v. U.S. Department of Justice. Civil Rights Litigation Clearinghouse, University of Michigan Law School, www.clearinghouse.net/detail.php?id=13683. Accessed 6 May 2020.

Biskind, Peter. *Seeing Is Believing: How Hollywood Taught Us to Stop Worrying and Love the Fifties*. Pantheon Books, 1983.

Booker, M. Keith. *Monsters, Mushroom Clouds, and the Cold War: American Science Fiction and the Roots of Postmodernism, 1946–1964*. Greenwood Press, 2001.

Brand, Stewart. "We Owe It All to the Hippies." *Time*, 1 March 1995, pp. 54–56.

Cassidy, Peter. "Reluctant Hero." *Wired Magazine*, 1 June 1996, www.wired.com/1996/06/esbernstein/. Accessed 6 May 2020.

Clerc, Susan J. "DDEB, GATB, MPPB, and Ratboy: *The X-Files*' Media Fandom, Online and Off." *Deny All Knowledge: Reading* The X-Files, edited by David Lavery, Angela Hague, and Marla Cartwright. Syracuse University Press, 1996, pp. 36–62.

Delasara, Jan. *PopLit, PopCult and* The X-Files: *A Critical Exploration*. McFarland, 2000.

"EEF Sues to Overturn Cryptography Restrictions." *EFFector Online*, 23 Feb. 1995, www.eff.org/press/archives/2008/04/21-42. Accessed 6 May 2020.

Elmer-Dewitt, Philip. "Who Should Keep the Keys?" *Time*, 14 March 1994, http://content.time.com/time/magazine/article/0,9171,980329,00.html. Accessed 6 May 2020.

Garside, Juliette. "Philip Zimmermann: King of Encryption Reveals His Fears for Privacy." *The Guardian*, 25 May 2015, www.theguardian.com/technology/2015/may/25/philip-zimmermann-king-encryption-reveals-fears-privacy. Accessed 6 May 2020.

Graham, Allison. "'Are You Now or Have You Ever Been?' Conspiracy Theory and *The X-Files*." *Deny All Knowledge: Reading* The X-Files, edited by David Lavery, Angela Hague, and Marla Cartwright. Syracuse University Press, 1996, pp. 52–62.

Harwell, Drew. "Managers Turn to Surveillance Software, Always-On Webcams to Rnsure Employees Are (Really) Working from Home." *Washington Post*, 30 April 2020, www.washingtonpost.com/technology/2020/04/30/work-from-home-surveillance/. Accessed 2 May 2020.

Jancovich, Mark. "Re-Examining the 1950s Invasion Narratives." 1996. *Liquid Metal: The Science Fiction Film Reader*, edited by Sean Redmond. Wallflower Press, 2007, pp. 325–36.

Kissell, Rick. "Ratings: 'The X-Files' Premiere Scores for Fox; CBS' Patriots-Broncos Game Draws 53 Million." *Variety*, 25 Jan. 2016, https://variety.com/2016/tv/news/ratings-the-x-files-premiere-patriots-broncos-cbs-1201687791/. Accessed 4 May 2020.

Knight, Peter. *Conspiracy Culture: From Kennedy to "The X-Files."* Routledge, 2000.

Lavery, David, Angela Hague, and Marla Cartwright. Introduction. *Deny All Knowledge: Reading* The X-Files. Edited by Lavery, Hague, and Cartwright. Syracuse University Press, 1996, pp. 1–21.

Levy, Steven. *Crypto: How the Code Rebels Beat the Government: Saving Privacy in the Digital Age*. Viking, 2001.

_____. *Hackers: Heroes of the Computer Revolution*. Anchor Press/Doubleday, 1984.

Markoff, John. "Data-Secrecy Export Case Dropped by U.S." *New York Times*, 12 Jan. 1996, p. D1.

Penenberg, Adam L. "The New Rules of Engagement: The Surveillance Society." *Wired Magazine*, 1 Dec. 2001, www.wired.com/2001/12/surveillance. Accessed 6 May 2020.

"PGP History." *PGP Corporation Website*, 2003, https://web.archive.org/web/20030401235928/http://www.pgp.com/aboutus/history.html. Accessed 6 May 2020.

Sayre, Nora. *Running Time: Films of the Cold War*. Dial Press, 1982.

Seed, David. *American Science Fiction and the Cold War: Literature and Film*. Edinburgh University Press, 1999.

Smith, Jeff. *Film Criticism, the Cold War, and the Blacklist*. University of California Press, 2014.

Sobchack, Vivian. *Screening Space: The American Science Fiction Film*. Ungar, 1988.

Sykes, Charles J. *The End of Privacy*. St. Martin's, 1999.

Taylor, Humphrey. "Most People Are 'Privacy Pragmatists' Who, While Concerned About Privacy, Will Sometimes Trade it Off for Other Benefits." *The Harris Poll* 17, no. 19 March 2003, https://theharrispoll.com/wp-content/uploads/2017/12/Harris-Interactive-Poll-Research-Most-People-Are-Privacy-Pragmatists-Who-While-Conc-2003-03.pdf. Accessed 6 May 2020.

Warren, Bill. *Keep Watching the Skies! American Science Fiction Movies of the Fifties. Vol. I: 1950–1957*. McFarland, 1982.

Whalen, John. "You're Not Paranoid: They Really Are Watching You." *Wired Magazine*, 1 March 1995, www.wired.com/1995/03/security-2/. Accessed 6 May 2020.

Filmography

Close Encounters of the Third Kind. Dir. Steven Spielberg. Columbia Pictures, 1977. Film.

Frankenstein. Directed by James Whale, Universal Pictures, 1931. Film.

Invaders from Mars. Dir. William Cameron Menzies. 20th Century Fox, 1953. Film.

Invasion of the Body Snatchers. Dir. Don Siegel. Allied Artist Pictures, 1956. Film.

It Came from Outer Space. Dir. Jack Arnold. Universal-International, 1953. Film.

The Thing. Dir. John Carpenter. Universal Pictures, 1982. Film.

The Thing from Another World. Dir. Christian Nyby. RKO Radio Pictures, 1951. Film.

The X-Files. 20th Century Fox Television, 1993–2002. TV Series.

———. "Anasazi." Fox, 19 May 1995.

———. "The Blessing Way." Fox, 22 Sept. 1995.

———. "Colony." Fox, 10 Feb. 1995.

———. "End Game." Fox, 17 Feb. 1995.

———. "Ice." Fox, 5 Nov. 1995.

———. "Jose Chung's from Outer Space." Fox, 12 April 1996.

———. "Herrenvolk." Fox, 4 Oct. 1996.

———. "Memento Mori." Fox, 9 Feb. 1997.

———. "Paper Clip." Fox, 29 Sept. 1995.

———. "Pilot." Fox, 10 Sept. 1993.

———. "The Unnatural." Fox, 25 April 1999.

The X-Files: Fight the Future. Dir. Rob Bowman, 20th Century Fox, 1998. Film.

The X-Files: I Want to Believe. Dir. Chris Carter, 20th Century Fox, 2008. Film.

X-Philes. Dir. Maria Bowen and Christopher Clements. X-Act Productions, 1999. Documentary.

PART II

Monsters Within
and Without

Extinction Panic

Prehistoric Creatures of the Anthropocene

Zak Bronson

Since 2010, contemporary sci-fi cinema has witnessed a major revival of the prehistoric "creature features" once popularized in sci-fi B films of the 1950s. The oversized monsters and primeval dinosaurs common to *The Beast from 20,000 Fathoms* (1953) and *Gojira* (1954) have all re-emerged in recent years in films such as *Godzilla* (2014), *Pacific Rim* (2013), and *The Meg* (2018).[1] Each of these new films utilizes the tropes and conventions of the atomic era films through stories of prehistoric beasts awoken from the depths of the earth due to humanity's meddling into the natural world. In the 2014 *Godzilla*, MUTOs ("Massive Unidentified Terrestrial Organisms") hatch underground in response to continued nuclear testing; in *Pacific Rim*, extraterrestrial kaiju arrive through a rift in the Pacific Ocean as part of a plan to colonize the planet; and in *The Meg*, scientific exploration goes too far and unintentionally unleashes a prehistoric megalodon that terrorizes the Pacific Ocean. However, whereas the atomic era films demonstrated significant anxieties around the use of nuclear power and the dangers of radiation, these more recent films reflect broader concerns around global annihilation, climate change, and extinction. In *Godzilla, Pacific Rim,* and *The Meg*, the creatures are bigger and more destructive than in earlier films. They destroy entire cities, homes, and shelters, and threaten to cause catastrophic devastation that could wipe humanity from the face of the planet altogether.

In recent years, geologists and scientists have argued that the planet has entered a new epoch, formally known as the Anthropocene, in which humanity has taken on the role of a geological force that has left a profound imprint on the environmental record. "Climate change ... will also leave behind geologic traces, as will nuclear fallout and river diversion and monoculture farming and ocean acidification" (Kolbert 106–07). All of this has continued up to the present day, resulting in an explosion of environmental damage. According to McNeill and Engelke, this post-war period (commonly referred to as "the Great Acceleration") is "certainly the most anomalous and unrepresentative period in the 200,000-year-long history of relations between our species and the biosphere" (5). It has enabled a significant transformation in humankind's relationship to the natural environment and ultimately led to massive waves of biodiversity loss and rising temperatures, and is currently on track toward what Elizabeth Kolbert terms a "sixth mass extinction" that follows in the footprints of five previous extinction events that have taken place over the last five billion years (3). Certainly, the coining of the term "Anthropocene" marks a moment of recognition that the planet is undergoing a major global environmental transformation that could spell the end of human civilization. As Christophe Bonneuil and Jean-Baptiste Fressoz summarize,

> The double reality that the Anthropocene presents is that, on the one hand, the Earth has seen other epochs in the last 4.5 billion years, and life will continue in one form or another with or without humans. But the new states that we are launching the Earth into will bring with them a disorder, penury and violence that will render it less readily habitable by humans [21].

Emerging amid these ongoing threats, the prehistoric creatures that populate these films reflect a profound cultural anxiety around the threat of mass extinction, climate change, and the erasure of the human species that have become associated with the Anthropocene's environmental transformations. In each of these recent films, oversized creatures emerge from the depths of the earth and threaten to completely undermine human agency and power. Part of my claim here is that the Anthropocene can be understood as a moment that creates a growing awareness around humanity's impact on the natural world at the same time that it decenters the human from the planet. Since so many of these films deal with prehistoric creatures that threaten to displace humanity from the top of a Darwinist hierarchy, their narratives illustrate an *extinction panic*, a growing anxiety around nonhuman nature's power over humankind, and its ability to remove humanity from the top of the teleological ladder. Extinction concerns, particularly around the replacement of humanity at the "top" of the Darwinist ladder, evokes a tremendous fear around the fact that humanity can be erased from the great chain of being. In this same regard, the prehistoric creatures of these films establish a confrontation with "teleological" history by establishing scenarios where scientific and technological progress result in environmental damage and, ultimately, self-destruction. If the Anthropocene can be understood as a moment that troubles the line between humanity and nature, then the presence of these prehistoric creatures can be interpreted as reflecting the anxiety of an out-of-control nature that fundamentally undermines human agency.

However, even as these films engage with extinction threats, they simultaneously work to alleviate these fears by turning toward the powers of science and technology to empower humanity over nonhuman nature. In *The Shock of the Anthropocene*, Bonneuil and Fressoz argue that the Anthropocene represents a moment of cultural crisis by undermining traditional conceptions of humanity's dominion of the natural world. More to the point, they suggest that the idea that humans somehow slipped into this new age unaware of what was happening is patently false. In their words,

> the opposition between a blind past and a clear-sighted present, besides being historically false, depoliticizes the long history of the Anthropocene. It serves above all to credit our own excellence. Its reassuring side is demobilizing. In the twenty years that it has prevailed, there has been a great deal of congratulation, while the Earth has become ever more set on a path of ecological unbalance [12].

Reactionary and nostalgic narratives that attempt to mitigate this environmental crisis through stories of humanity's agential control of the environment potentially make the problem worse. Instead of enabling newfound stories that rethink humanity's dependence on nature, the era of Anthropocene has witnessed a host of narratives about human exceptionalism, human mastery and regulation of nature, and human progress that negotiate with the competing threats of life within a period of significant environmental change. Recent films such as *Godzilla, Pacific Rim,* and *The Meg* reflect this trend with thrilling narratives about nature's threat at the same time that they seek to restore humanity's place at the top of the Darwinist hierarchy. By building on the tropes and conventions of 1950s sci-fi films, these recent prehistoric creature features return to the narratives of the atomic era to symbolize humanity's teleological placement over the natural world. Utilizing tales of prehistoric creatures that threaten humankind's evolutionary place on the earth, these films embody a fundamental faith in the power of techno-scientific and human progress—the same powers that contributed to the rise of the Anthropocene in the first place—to control nature and prevent the extinction threat.

Creatures of the Deep Time

Although prehistoric creature films predate the 1950s—most notably *King Kong* (1933) which was re-released in 1952 to huge financial success—the 1950s witnessed the emergence of a cycle of prehistoric creature features that dealt with the numerous cultural anxieties associated with the use of atomic power. The release of the atomic bombs in Hiroshima and Nagasaki awoke newfound anxieties that humanity had the technical power to unleash utter annihilation, and the continued use of nuclear bomb testing in the Pacific Ocean throughout the 1950s awoke numerous concerns that radioactivity was an invisible threat that could lead to unknown illnesses and diseases.[2] In the sci-fi films of the era, these nuclear anxieties were frequently expressed in the form of gigantic prehistoric beasts that emerged from the depths of the earth in response to radioactive chemicals and sought to destroy human civilization. Cyndy Hendershot argues that the numerous gigantic beasts that populated these films—including gigantic insects and prehistoric monsters—reflected a deep-seated "cultural paranoia" (1) around the use of atomic power and evoked concerns around "the potential eclipsing of the human species brought about by the atomic bomb and its psychological and physiological effects" (75). Situating large-scale beasts awoken from the "deep time" of the earth against an unprepared humanity, these films spoke to the cultural fears associated with nuclear energy and its ability to destroy nature and bring about human extinction in the process. Yet, even as they did so, these films simultaneously exhibited an ambiguity around the powers of science, technology, and the atomic bomb. Just as they illustrated the dangers inherent in the use of nuclear energy, they often concluded with the monsters being destroyed through the creation of a new, more powerful nuclear weapon. As Peter Biskind writes, "Many of the monsters of fifties sci-fi were at least partially attributable to science; nevertheless, where science causes the problem, science often solved it too" (104).

The Beast from 20,000 Fathoms, the first giant, prehistoric monster film to emerge from this era—and the film that would subsequently establish the groundwork for the films to follow—perfectly captures these anxieties around nuclear annihilation and extinction. The narrative centers around a dinosaur released from prehistoric hibernation due to American nuclear testing in the Arctic Circle. The beast travels through the oceans, attacking unsuspecting civilians, before eventually arriving at its original home in New York to wreak havoc on the city. Emerging from the ice as a direct result of atomic bomb testing and subsequently unleashing destruction in its wake, the prehistoric monster captured the numerous extinction anxieties associated with the use of atomic power. In *Beast*, the creature is clearly figured as an embodiment of out-of-control nature that arises from the "deep time" of the earth and threatens to undermine traditional notions of scientific knowledge, reason, and human agency. At the same time, the film's emphasis on the powers of science and technology works to alleviate these anxieties by promising that nuclear power can stave off extinction threats.

The film's concerns around scientific and nuclear testing are indicated in the opening scene, which depicts scientists and military cooperating in a top-secret atomic bomb test in the Arctic. These experiments are conducted with extreme mathematical precision, while an onscreen voiceover announces that "there can be no margin for error" and "there can be no second chance." The bomb explodes exactly on time and ultimately culminates in a colossal nuclear explosion that destroys the Arctic ice and causes countless avalanches. The mission is completed with perfectly calculated accuracy, ultimately revealing what Mark Jancovich identifies as the process of rationalization, "a process in which rational procedures are used to examine and reorganise social, economic and cultural practices in an attempt to produce order and efficiency" (2–3). *Beast* indicates these ideas early on by drawing attention to the ways that science and technology enable new types of scientific and militaristic organization. The imagery of this scene, including the combined power of science and the military to carry out the test with exactitude, illustrates the film's emphasis on the ways that scientific and technical application can enable the mastery of nature. Taking place within an uncharted and unexplored frozen Arctic land, this opening scene illustrates the powers that science appears to hold over the unknown mysteries of a hidden nature.

Despite the surety of this opening scene, the film displays an ambiguity regarding the dangers of scientific dominion. Shortly after the bomb drops, Colonel Evans (Kenneth Tobey) boasts about the success of the military operation. However, Dr. Tom Nesbitt (Paul Hubschmid) raises some doubts by noting that "when energy of that magnitude is released, it's never over. What the cumulative effects of these atomic explosions and tests will be, only time can tell…. The world's been here for millions of years. Man's been walking upright for a comparatively short time. Mentally, we're still crawling." Dr. Ritchie (Ross Elliott) joins these discussions by suggesting that each of these tests could "write the first chapter of a new Genesis," but Nesbitt responds by commenting that he hopes it won't end up "writing the last chapter of the old one." Nesbitt's comments and general suspicions raises numerous questions regarding the use of scientific power, and particularly questions whether

Figure 10. In *The Beast from 20,000 Fathoms* (1953), the rhedosaurus creates havoc that can only be stopped by nuclear power (Warner Bros. Pictures/Photofest).

the use of these bombs could end up causing humankind's destruction. Nesbitt's concerns soon become a reality as researchers detect a mysterious spot on the military radar. Ritchie and Nesbitt go out to investigate and discover a rhedosaurus that has arisen from the collapsed ice. The beast kills Ritchie and knocks Nesbitt unconscious, leaving him unable to recollect his experiences. Waking up in the hospital, Nesbitt attempts to recount his story of the events, but doctors believe that he must have experienced traumatic hallucinations suffered from the landslide. As the doctors and military personnel question Nesbitt's memories, the beast continues to cause trouble around the world in attacks that resemble natural disasters, including wrecking boats, destroying lighthouses, and creating havoc on coastal areas. Leaving no detectable trace of its existence, the emergence of the rhedosaurus demonstrates significant concerns that atomic power could spell the end of human civilization through an overpowering, inhuman force.

Part of the anxiety that the rhedosaurus provokes is that it seems to challenge a sense of scientific comprehension and linear progress. For the scientists, the emergence of the creature undermines all notions of scientific progress and "teleological" history. In an attempt to understand the monster, Dr. Nesbitt visits the paleontologist Dr. Elson (Cecil Kellaway), who almost immediately dismisses Nesbitt's claims. However, Elson's female assistant Lee Hunter (Paula Raymond) overhears the conversations and cooperates with Nesbitt to help identify the monster by confirming its appearance with other survivors who have experienced attacks from the rhedosaurus. Jancovich argues that the film's emphasis on Lee illustrates a counter-force against the notions of scientific rationality (53). As Jancovich notes, Lee's concern with archaeology and the past represents a challenge to the film's overemphasis on scientific and technological progress. Indeed, within the narrative, her knowledge of history provides the key for unlocking the mystery regarding the rhedosaurus, and her subject position directly opposes the overt rationalism of the military and Dr. Elson who dismiss any dangerous repercussions around the use of the bomb. However, once Lee discovers the truth of the rhedosaurus, she is quickly sidetracked as Elson and Nesbitt, along with the military, begin a scientific investigation focused on confronting and destroying the monster. In one scene, Nesbitt and Elson meet with the military where Elson reveals the truth of the rhedosaurus and predicts its future attacks. Looking at a map (one of the most emblematic symbols of scientific and military power in 1950s cinema), Elson charts the rhedosaurus attacks and successfully predicts that creature's plans to invade New York City. Despite its apparent ambiguity over the value of science, the film ultimately restores faith in the power of reason, embodied in the figure of two male scientists who not only predict the monstrous threat but also hold the power to stop it completely.

These tensions between science and nature are foregrounded in the film's ending, as the military tracks the rhedosaurus to Coney Island and corner it at a carnival. The soldiers are unable to kill the beast, however, since it releases toxic blood when it is shot, so they turn once again to the combined power of science and military to be able to control the threat. Hendershot notes that films from the 1950s frequently place scientists in the role of heroes to embody the values of scientific and technological rationality, and a similar issue appears here. In order to stop the creature, Nesbitt collects a radioactive isotope from his office and enlists the help of a military sharpshooter to attach it to a gun barrel. The military sniper attaches the isotope to his gun barrel and shoots the isotope into the creature's open wound. The beast writhes in pain and crashes into a rollercoaster, causing a massive fire which results in the dinosaur's fiery death. As this concluding scene suggests, although science holds the power to unleash terrible destruction, it also holds the power to correct its mistakes.

In the end, *Beast* fits firmly into the conventions of "secure horror" (Tudor 103), narratives which enable film viewers to experience social and cultural anxieties associated with atomic destruction but which simultaneously work to reassure audiences that the government and military will conquer the monsters and restore social order. Notably, this conclusion presents a significant contrast with the somber tone of the conclusions of films such as *Gojira*, which exhibit much more ambiguity around the dangers of atomic power. In *Beast*, the powers over nature that lead to significant cultural anxieties around extinction are the same powers that resolve them. The fact that these monsters appeared again and again throughout the 1950s, however, and have re-emerged again in recent years, suggests that these anxieties cannot be contained for long.

Toward a Global Extinction

The Beast from 20,000 Fathoms' engagement with the powers of science and technology lays the foundation for many of the recent prehistoric creature revival narratives, such as *Godzilla*, *Pacific Rim*, and *The Meg* which each expand on the tropes of the 1950s films through self-reflexive narratives that engage with the cultural anxieties of life in the Anthropocene. Whereas the 1950s films exhibited a nascent extinction anxiety around the geological force of humanity in relation to the atomic bomb, these recent works can be read as engaging with a "terminal crisis" (Davies 5) in ecological threat, stemming from a growing awareness of anthropogenic climate change and an ongoing societal failure to collectively work together toward reducing environmental degradation. As the Anthropocene has become the "new normal," it has simultaneously become opaque in relation to traditional understandings of the natural environment. Timothy Morton argues that the Anthropocene and climate change can be understood as *hyperobjects*, "things that are massively distributed in time and space relative to humans" (1) such that they remain unthinkable and outside of human comprehension. Although we can experience things such as the weather or the sunburn on one's neck, global environmental transformations such as climate change take place at scalar dimensions outside of human agency and comprehension. As Timothy Clark summarizes,

> the Anthropocene enacts the demand to think of human life at much broader scales of space and time, something which alters the way that many once familiar issues appear. Perhaps too big to see or even to think straight about (a "hyperobject," certainly) the Anthropocene challenges us to think counter-intuitive relations of scale, effect, perception, knowledge, representation and calculability [13].

These ideas hold a particular resonance to the films under investigation. All of them directly expand the scale of the extinction threat by utilizing images of large-scale creatures whose vision and concealment are frequently denied to viewers until partway through the narrative where the threat becomes subject to the viewer's (and characters') gaze as they render them objects of knowledge. If, as Barry Grant argues, sci-fi films can be defined by their "outward gaze" that captures a sense of wonder around the powers of the science, then these recent extinction narratives can be understood for their engagement with a sense of panic and anxiety around the gaze—and ultimately around a sense of control—that illustrates a deepening anxiety around perception and knowledge characteristic of the Anthropocene. Since the Anthropocene can be understood as a global event that evades the local experiences of human agency and knowledge, these films can be interpreted as engaging with the scalar dimension of a threat that exceeds human knowledge and capacity. Yet, even as they do so, these films often render these threats down to manageable levels that make them accessible and understandable.

The threat of global extinction and the increasing opacity of climate change is established through many of these recent films which highlight the prehistoric creatures as global threats that operate across the planet and whose comprehension completely exceeds human knowledge and technological systems. The 2014 reboot of *Godzilla* illustrates this tension by repeatedly concealing the monster from complete vision. In fact, when it was released, fans and critics disparaged the film for depriving viewers full images of the monsters—a staple of the "man in suit" traditions of the Shōwa era *Gojira* films. Certainly, this frustration derives from director Gareth Edwards' stylistic approach which frequently obstructs visions of Godzilla by presenting him from "local" standpoints, such as "on the ground" cameras, moving trains, or obscured images that conceal the grandeur of the beast and render him unimaginable. The film repeatedly refuses full scalar view of the creature, an aspect which adds a sense of anxiety to the film's narrative since the creature always remains outside of perceptual control. In line with this, the film clearly presents Godzilla as a figuration of an out-of-control nature that exists outside of human agency. The symbolism of this is brought out in his various attacks which mirror real-world natural disasters: Godzilla emerges in response to a nuclear reactor accident in a fictional Japanese town which resembles the Fukushima Daiichi nuclear disaster of 2011. Subsequent attacks in the Philippines and San Francisco mimic similar recent natural disasters.

The scalar dimensions of the threat are brought forth in the film's ending which provides stark images of Godzilla that emphasize the smallness of humanity in relation to global threat. Shot using a wide-angle lens, the final scene depicts soldiers jumping out of a plane into New York City, but the individuals remain barely visible in relation to the size of Godzilla. Notably, the film presents these issues through an emphasis on the vertical image, which is associated with power and magnitude. These images reveal what Kristen Whissel identifies as "the new verticality" in relation to contemporary special effects, which focus on images of descent and rising in ways that represent the struggle over power. According to her, this "new verticality" reflects a "profound expression of despair over the collapse of twentieth century civilization (defined by global dominance of U.S. military power and capitalism) and into twenty-first-century ruin (defined by global economic crisis, endless war, and political upheaval)" (57). Certainly, *Godzilla*'s reliance on verticality—as well as its deployment of a concealed gaze—follows a similar route by expressing a tremendous anxiety around the threats of global extinction due to the environmental crisis.

The scalar dimension of threat is also apparent in Guillermo del Toro's *Pacific Rim*, an homage to the Japanese *kaiju-eiga* (monster films) popularized with the *Godzilla* franchise. del Toro's film also draws attention to the dangers of complete global extinction. The film takes place in the year 2013 (the same year it was released, suggesting that these events could happen immediately). A fissure emerges between two tectonic plates in the Pacific Ocean and allows gigantic, seemingly prehistoric kaiju to wreak havoc on coastal towns. To combat the kaiju, "the world came together, pooling its resources, and throwing aside old rivalries for the sake of the greater good," as Raleigh (Charlie Hunnam) explains in the opening voiceover. The united government creates Jaegers, gigantic technological robots designed to combat the kaiju and protect the planet. As the kaiju attacks become more advanced and regular, however, the Jaeger fighters coordinate a last-ditch effort to attack the rift in the ocean by dropping a thermo-nuclear bomb into the pathway between the two worlds. The explosion succeeds in destroying the rift and ends the visitations by the kaiju once and for all.[3]

Throughout the film, the kaiju are linked to an ongoing global environmental crisis, and the film illustrates significant anxieties around the ways that humanity has contributed to ecological degradation. Like their cinematic predecessors, these kaiju provide a clear embodiment of nature. The film is distinguished from other prehistoric creature narratives, however, in that it does not focus on single attacks or individual creatures but rather on the routinization of natural disaster indicative of the current terminal crisis. The kaiju unleash mass destruction on a global scale, beginning in San Francisco, then attacking Manila and Cabo, and eventually occurring too frequently to manage. As part of their damage, the kaiju also leave a host of material impacts, including the massive destruction of cities and the release of kaiju blood (known as "kaiju blue") which is toxic waste that produces excessive environmental degradation. Mirroring the rhedosaurus' toxic blood in *Beast*, kaiju blue is a noxious chemical that turns blood spill zones into radioactive wastelands. Such sites mirror what McNeill and Engelke call "sacrifice zones" (19), areas of extreme environmental damage that have become completely uninhabitable, such as atomic testing zones, dumping yards, and e-waste sites. The kaiju's destruction is extended by their particularly rapacious desire to endlessly consume. As we discover, the kaiju are not simply attempting to get revenge but are actually genetically-engineered creatures created by an alien race to eradicate human "vermin" and allow colonization of the planet. In other words, the creatures are not simply attacking to consume its resources but to erase humanity from the face of the earth. Although the plot reveals that the kaiju had previously visited Earth during the Jurassic era, they have returned once again because the planet's depleting ozone levels, increased greenhouse gases, and rising temperatures have made the planet more hospitable for them. Not only do the kaiju threaten to erase humankind but humanity's wanton destruction of the environment has brought this disaster on themselves.

If human progress has made the planet vulnerable to destruction, it also provides the way out. The film is distinguished from other prehistoric creature narratives in that it focuses on the creation of gigantic robots to combat the kaiju. These Jaegers are created based on the most advanced developments of science and technology and utilize advanced developments in DARPA-constructed jet fighter technology. Operators connect to the Jaegers through a "neural link" that syncs the machine to the operator. However, the technology is so advanced that it requires two pilots whose brains "drift" together with one another to coordinate the Jaegers' movements. This technology provides operators with a transhuman power that enables them to dominate nature completely. As Raleigh states of the power the Jaegers provide: "There are things you can't fight. Acts of God. You see a hurricane coming, you get out of the way. But when you're in a Jaeger, suddenly, you can fight the hurricane. You can win." The suggestion here is that the melding of humanity and technology enables the development of a superhuman power that enables the complete dominance over the natural environment.

Because of their ability to stop the kaiju, the Jaeger pilots become heroes. In contrast to the image of the scientist as hero apparent in the 1950s films, these recent prehistoric creature narratives focus on the *veteran*, stoic male individuals who have lived through previous disasters or attacks and have abandoned their own naivety regarding the dangers of the threat. It is important to note that these characters are almost exclusively male, suggesting traditional ideas of masculine heroism and the ability to dominate nature. These ideas are particularly apparent in recent environmental narratives such as *The Day After Tomorrow* and *Elysium* which, as Greta

Gaard notes, frequently "depict white male heroes working to restore life or love against a backdrop of climate change consequences" (176) and "present the problem of climate change from a (masculinist) technological-scientific perspective" (176). Similarly, David Ingram writes that "male heroism in environmental movies is identified with saving as well as conquering nature" (36). *Pacific Rim* follows these ideas by focusing on heroic male veterans who not only are able to control technology but who also lack the emotional connections that would hinder their abilities. One of the features of the Jaegers is that operators need to be emptied of any memories or reactions when connected to the machine since "the drift" causes them to travel through memories. Raleigh partners with the female pilot Mako Mori (Rinko Kikuchi), who holds painful memories of her parents being killed by a kaiju; when she initially locks into the machine she almost causes a nuclear disaster due to these memories. In contrast, experienced veterans like Raleigh and Pentecost are able to rationally engage with the attacks by abandoning their personal emotions or connections. Near the end of the film, the leader of the Jaeger program, Pentecost (Idris Elba), is forced to go into combat with Herc, without testing their drift compatibility. Being an experienced veteran, Pentecost states that "I carry nothing into the drift, no memories, no fear, no rank." Being able to abandon these personal attachments, veterans like Raleigh and Pentecost embody the ideals of masculinity and rationality that the film suggests are necessary to combat the threat.

The film's turn toward rationalization is emphasized in the conclusion, which illustrates the combined strength of science and technology over nature. After three kaiju emerge from the breach, the Jaegers head out into the Pacific Ocean to stop them and to release a bomb to destroy the ocean rift once and for all. The plan falls apart, but Raleigh and Mako are able to reach the rift and use a thermonuclear bomb to destroy the breach. The scene's setting within the Pacific Ocean directly calls to mind the conclusion of *Gojira*. *Pacific Rim* rejects the bleak conclusion of that earlier film, however, by depicting the monsters' destruction in detail and not revealing any negative consequences of this destruction. The use of this thermonuclear bomb provides an overt figuration of the power of human over nonhuman nature and demonstrates a faith in technology and science to save the day. Despite the great harm that thermonuclear bombs have caused, the film shows no side effects of the explosion. Having completely destroyed the rift in the ocean, there is no possibility of the kaiju's return.

If science and technology pave the path for the future in *Pacific Rim*, then a different set of issues emerge in *The Meg*, a *Beast*-meets-*Jaws* style prehistoric creature narrative that deals with scientists exploring the unchartered depths of the ocean. In contrast to the previous films, *The Meg* does not deal with environmental destruction but instead focuses on the unintended consequences of scientific experimentation. The film centers around American billionaire entrepreneur Morris (Rainn Wilson) who hires a group of scientists to investigate the area underneath the deepest part of the Mariana Trench, which is believed to be a thermocline that conceals a deeper, unexplored part of the Pacific Ocean. During the crew's initial exploration of the trench, their underwater vehicle, Mana One, is attacked by a prehistoric megalodon believed to have gone extinct two million years ago. To rescue the crew, the remaining scientists hire retired deep-sea rescue expert Jonas (Jason Statham) to travel beneath the thermocline and bring them back. Jonas' mission is successful, however, the megalodon follows them from its ocean floor hiding spot and escapes into the ocean. In response, the Mana One crew, including Jonas, attempt to capture the beast; however, its size and scale enable it to easily destroy all the tools and weapons meant to catch it. As a result, Jonas and the rest of the crew go on the hunt to stop the beast from getting out into open waters. After trapping the creature, Jonas manages to tear its side apart with a hook and stabs the beast in the eye. In the end, it is not simply the latest developments of science and technology but also human evolutionary progress that enables humanity to stave off the prehistoric creature.

Despite the film's emphasis on science and technology, *The Meg* displays much more ambiguity around the relationship between humanity and nature than this summary suggests. Like *Beast*, the arrival of the megalodon is the direct result of scientific and technological intervention into the natural world and the film raises a number of questions regarding the crossing of certain natural borders and boundaries. After Jonas rescues the crew, their ship creates a heat pocket in the thermocline that enables it to escape into the Pacific Ocean. When Morris comes up with plans to capture the shark for profit, Jonas questions his hubris by commenting, "Do you ever think Mother Nature knows what she's doing? The thermocline might just be there for a reason.... In case what happened down there wasn't clear to you: man versus meg isn't a fight. It's a slaughter." These concerns around the crossing of natural limits are continued later in the film after the Mana One crew capture one of the smaller megalodons that emerged from the ocean trench. After Morris comments that they had a "serious man versus nature moment," Dr. Zhang somberly warns that "we did what people always do. Discover and then destroy." Zhang's solemn comments highlights his serious concerns around science's crossing of "natural" limits and suggests that he seriously regrets the unintended consequences that his actions have caused. These warnings continue as an even larger megalodon emerges and causes a series of catastrophic disasters, including destroying the Mana One ship, attacking nearby boats, and, in an homage to *Jaws*, threatening a group of swimmers on the beach. In its ongoing attacks, the megalodon becomes a symbol for the dangers of crossing of boundaries between humanity and nature and the unforetold disasters that it could cause.

Much of the film's anxiety centers around the ways that the megalodon creates a panic surrounding the visual and perceptual knowledge of the creature. Since the megalodon is gigantic, it cannot be fully grasped or identified through the high-tech tracking tools and devices the crew uses to investigate it. As with Godzilla, the film repeatedly denies viewers visual perception of the creature by using concealed images or point of view shots that obscure the appearance and scale of the beast. Drawing from the point of view shots used in slasher films such as *Psycho* (1960) and *Halloween* (1978), *The Meg* frequently positions viewers in the position of the megalodon's gaze as it stalks the crew. These scenes create a sense of anxiety centering around knowledge of the threat. Tudor argues that the use of point of view shots in horror slasher films turns away from the traditions of secure horror by placing the viewer in a position of an "unpredictable threat" and an "insecurity of inhuman impulse" (186). Since the film's point of view shots deny the viewers complete comprehension of the creature, while at the same time investing the animal with perspective and logic, the megalodon's attack creates anxiety around a threat that defies human reason and logic. These threats are especially significant given the film's thematic connections between the crossing of the lines between humanity and nature indicative of life in the Anthropocene. By investing the creature with a contradictory mix of human reason and unreason, the film creates an anxiety around the power of nonhuman nature over humanity.

Despite Jonas' experiences with the megalodon, the remaining scientists cast serious doubt over Jonas's authority. During a deep-water rescue five years earlier, Jonas experienced an attack with a megalodon that caused him to leave several crew members to die. While Jonas believes that the attack was caused by a megalodon, an on-board psychologist diagnoses Jonas with "pressure-induced psychosis" due to his time underwater.[4] As a result of these personal experiences and the doubt surrounding his belief in the megalodon, Jonas is ridiculed for his claims and is forced to abandon his work. When he is hired by the crew to rescue the trapped underwater explorers there are significant doubts cast by the doctor's belief that Jonas is unable to perform the task. Since the early parts of the film repeatedly deny any clear visions of the creature, viewers are also left suspicious of Jonas's knowledge and understanding. However, it is Jonas's role as White male hero and veteran that holds the key to understanding the creature. Lacking any of the hubris of the scientists who believe their own technology can stop the creature, Jonas's experience with the creature and his masculine position as heroic leader restores his place of authority and, ultimately, leads to his success in stopping the creature.

Just as the film creates an anxiety around nonhuman agency, it simultaneously restores a sense of human agency and strength as the solution to the crisis. Jonas, who was initially disempowered by the threat of the creature, becomes increasingly more strident as the attacks continue. Most of his anxiety centers around his masculine desire to protect Siyun (BingBing Li) and her daughter Meiying. After the megalodon destroys the Mana One, Jonas turns from hunted to hunter by utilizing his knowledge and experience to attack the creature. When one scientist asks how he plans to kill the shark, Jonas pointedly replies, "Evolution," a term that refers to human biological evolution and is also the name of the ship that he uses. Jonas's words suggest the combination of technology, intelligence, and human agency to combat natural disaster. Hence, his hunting of the creature functions as a metaphor for the strength of human ingenuity over the natural world. Indeed, Jonas utilizes the most advanced technologies to stage an attack on the creature, and when those technologies fail, he drives a spear into the shark's eye. The imagery here, including the vision of Jonas with a spear in hand attacking the shark symbolically suggests masculine mastery over nature. Moreover, the injection of the spear into the eye—not to mention the clear phallic imagery associated with it—suggests an undermining of the visual threat that the megalodon posed. Utilizing this image of masculine strength, the film suggests the power of human agency as a restoration to the current environmental crisis.

The ongoing questions around the lines between human and nature addressed in *Godzilla*, *Pacific Rim*, and *The Meg* all illustrate the profound complexities of life in the Anthropocene as well as the cultural desires to restore human agency and combat the threat. Yet, even as they do so, these films simultaneously suggest that these struggles have not been entirely resolved. Prehistoric creatures can never be fully stopped, as the ongoing battles between human and nonhuman agency necessarily precipitate a constant revival of human agency over the natural world through the same sorts of masculine and scientific practices of dominion that contributed to the crisis in the first place. In what can be said to be the relevance of these ongoing concerns, these prehistoric creatures re-emerge again and again, in sequel after sequel. The recent revival of *Godzilla vs Kong*, *Pacific Rim: Uprising*, and the forthcoming *The Meg 2* all suggest that these issues continue. Yet, the declining popularity of these narratives, with each film quietly plunging in the box office numbers, suggests that these fantasies of humanity's dominion and mastery of nature cannot continue forever. In *Learning to Die in the Anthropocene*, Roy Scranton writes that, "in order for us to adapt to this strange new world [called the Anthropocene], we're going to need more than scientific reports and military policy. We're going to need ideas. We're going to need new myths and new stories [that will provide] a new way of thinking [about] our collective existence. We need a new vision of who 'we' are" (19). The issues addressed in these films reveal the longevity of these narratives of human dominion and the limitations that they offer. At the same time, their increasingly over-the-top narratives and dramatic special effects reveal the need to construct alternate visions, narratives, and stories that collectively imagine a new start to this strange new world.

NOTES

1. The *Jurassic Park* and *Jurassic World* films might also be included in this list. In those films DNA manipulation creates increasingly large dinosaurs.
2. The dangers of these threats were also apparent in the growing concerns around the use of chemicals and pesticides on the natural environment, and which were subsequently detailed in Rachel Carson's *Silent Spring* in 1962. In her book, Carson detailed the build-up of dangerous substances and chemicals created during and after the war, namely DDT, which were "silent" killers that could slowly wipe out human existence and cause mass extinctions as they worked their way into the natural ecosystem. For a discussion of the role that the growth of the pesticides played in the films of the 1950s, see William Tsutsui's "Looking Straight at *Them!* Understanding the Big Bug Movies of the 1950s" and Joshua David Bellin's "Us or *Them!* Silent Spring and the 'Big Bug' Films of the 1950s."
3. Or at least until the sequels.
4. This is similar to the situation in *The Beast from 20,000 Fathoms* when the first witness is assumed to be insane.

WORKS CITED

Bellin, Joshua David. "Us or *Them! Silent Spring* and the 'Big Bug' Films of the 1950s." *Extrapolation* 50.1 (2009): 145–68.
Biskind, Peter. *Seeing is Believing: How Hollywood Taught Us to Stop Worrying and Love the Fifties*. Bloomsbury, 2001.
Bonneuil, Christope, and Jean-Baptiste Fressoz. *The Shock of the Anthropocene: The Earth, History and US*. Trans. David Fernbach. Verso, 2017.
Carson, Rachel. *Silent Spring*. Fawcett, 1962.
Clark, Timothy. *Ecocriticism on the Edge: The Anthropocene as a Threshold Concept*. Bloomsbury, 2015.
Davies, Jeremy. *The Birth of the Anthropocene*. University of California Press, 2016.

Gaard, Greta. "From 'Cli-Fi' to Critical Ecofeminism: Narratives of Climate Change and Climate Justice." *Contemporary Perspectives on Ecofeminism*, edited by Mary Phillips and Nick Rumens. Routledge, 2016, pp. 169–92.

Grant, Barry Keith. "'Sensuous Elaboration': Reason and the Visible in the Science Fiction Film." *Alien Zone II: The Spaces of Science Fiction Cinema*, edited by Annette Kuhn. Verso, 1999, pp. 16–30.

Hendershot, Cyndy. *Paranoia, the Bomb, and 1950s Science Fiction Films*. Bowling Green State University Popular Press, 1999.

Ingram, David. *Green Screen: Environmentalism and Hollywood Cinema*. University of Exeter Press, 2000.

Jancovich, Mark. *Rational Fears: American Horror in the 1950s*. Manchester University Press, 1996.

Kolbert, Elizabeth. *The Sixth Extinction: An Unnatural History*. Picador, 2015.

McNeill, J.R., and Peter Engelke. "The Great Acceleration: An Environmental History of the Anthropocene Since 1945." *Global Interdependence: The World Ffter 1945*. Oxford University Press, 2014.

Morton, Timothy. *Hyberobjects: Philosophy and Ecology after the End of the World*. University of Minnesota Press, 2013.

Scranton, Roy. *Learning to Die in the Anthropocene: Reflections on the End of a Civilization*. City Lights, 2015.

Tsutsui, William. "Looking Straight at *Them!* Understanding the Big Bug Movies of the 1950s." *Environmental History* 12 (April 2007): 237–53.

Tudor, Andrew. *Monsters and Mad Scientists: A Cultural History of the Horror Movie*. Blackwell, 1989.

Whissel, Kristen. *Spectacular Digital Effects: CGI and Contemporary Cinema*. Duke University Press, 2014.

Filmography

The Beast from 20,000 Fathoms. Dir. Eugène Lourié. Warner Bros., 1953. Film.

Godzilla. Dir. Gareth Edwards. Warner Bros., 2014. Film.

Gojira. Dir. Ishiro Honda. Toho Studios, 1954. Film.

Halloween. Dir. John Carpenter. Compass International Pictures, 1978. Film.

King Kong. Dir. Merian C. Cooper and Ernest B. Schoedsack. Radio Pictures, 1933. Film.

The Meg. Dir. Jon Turteltaub. Warner Bros., 2018. Film.

Pacific Rim. Dir. Steven S. DeKnight. Universal Pictures, 2013. Film.

Psycho. Dir. Alfred Hitchcock. Paramount Pictures, 1960. Film.

"Forget the world and hang on to the people you care about the most"

Giant Monster Movies from the 1950s
and Their Twenty-First-Century Counterparts

ROBIN JEREMY LAND

The original trailer for *The Beast from 20,000 Fathoms* (1953) thrilled theatergoers with familiar footage of an atomic explosion, followed by a bold typographical question asking, "Are we delving into mysteries we weren't meant to know?" and Merv Griffin's disembodied head warning us that there are things better left unsolved (Trailer). The trailer's sensational opening and ominous warnings were part of a promotional campaign designed by Warner Brothers and the film's producers to capitalize on the commercial success of the 1952 rerelease of *King Kong* (Warren 103). *King Kong*'s theatrical run was a surprise hit for the movie industry, making more in its second run than its original theatrical debut, and studios like Warner Brothers were anxious to exploit audiences and their apparent love of giant monster movies (Warren 102). Not to be outdone by giant prehistoric apes, *Beast*'s producers overtly connected their giant monster's origins and subsequent rampage through New York City to long-held anxieties about atomic weapons and the Cold War. The combination worked, as the film grossed an estimated $1.5–5 million from a $600,000 production and marketing budget.

The Beast from 20,000 Fathoms was soon followed in 1954 by *Them!*, a technically superior film featuring giant ants rampaging through the desert and the city of Los Angeles. What began with the release of *King Kong* quickly became a bonafide trend of sci-fi/horror films both in the United States and overseas featuring giant mutated monsters wreaking havoc on the big screens. Throughout the remainder of the 1950s, theaters and drive-ins across the country featured every variation of this formula from 50-foot-tall women to killer shrews to giant spiders to more radioactive dinosaurs and colossal predatory birds from outer space. Easily the most critically discussed and arguably the best of the films from this period was Ishirō Honda's *Gojira* (1954) or *Godzilla* to American audiences. Inspired by movies like *Them!*, Honda's kaiju film created a monster that embodied many of the problems facing Japan in the post-war/post-occupation era. On-screen, Godzilla became a living breathing embodiment of the Hiroshima and Nagasaki attacks, the environmental disaster that followed, as well as a myriad of other cultural anxieties facing the Japanese people.

Films like *The Beast from 20,000 Fathoms*, *Them!*, *Godzilla*, and its American remake, *Godzilla: King of Monsters* (1956), created a template for films looking either to exploit or comment upon their audience's fears in the early days of the Cold War. In each of these examples, the monster is born of either a nuclear attack or nuclear weapon testing and returns to its creators to wreak havoc upon innocent citizens. While theatergoers were grappling with the complex and, at times, abstract geopolitical realities of the post–World War II world, they could retreat to the movies and see those complexities and abstractions embodied in a 100-foot-tall atomic-fire breathing monster. While it is true that giant monster or kaiju films, as they are known among Japanese film fans, incorporated concerns about the Space Race after the Sputnik launch in 1957, these films still followed many of the genre conventions established with *The Beast from 20,000 Fathoms*, *Them!*, and *Gojira*.

The monsters in these early films and their interactions with the cities they terrorized became transnational symbols for cold war anxieties about America's emergence as a superpower. For Americans, these films represented the cultural debates that ensued immediately after Hiroshima and Nagasaki. For the Japanese, *Godzilla*, in particular, represented a complex symbol of both the American military, the growing influence of Western culture, and uneasiness about the nation's future. As these monsters raged across the silver screen, their destruction and their victim's response to their destruction came to embody globe-spanning problems that were far too complex for a single nation to address.

Although the kaiju genre continued through the 1960s and well into the end of the millennium, the genre's explicit connection to complex international problems largely faded with the Cold War; however, the complex geopolitical realities of post–9/11 America have inspired a new generation of kaiju films, both in the United States and abroad. The films rework genre conventions established in the mid–1950s into monster movies deeply concerned with a new array of problems facing the global community. Gone are the monsters that embodied fears about American nuclear power. This newer generation of kaiju films terrifies audiences with giant creatures that embody problems ranging from global terrorism to environmental disasters and mass migration.

What began in the 1950s as an expression of fears about the atomic bomb and the Cold War is now a metaphor for a variety of problems facing America and its allies in the twenty-first century. To demonstrate the connection between the giant monster movies of the mid–1950s and their twenty-first-century successors, this essay begins by reviewing the theoretical framework for interpreting a monster's role in a work of fiction and the relevant critical discussions surrounding the kaiju genre films before establishing four basic genre conventions found in the giant monster movies and interpreting those conventions within the context of the 1950s and the twenty-first century.

Although this collection is expressly about sci-fi in the 1950s, the films under discussion in this essay tend to share common elements with horror films, namely the presence of giant monsters. As such, it is helpful to consider some of the prevailing critical theories surrounding monsters and their role in fiction, especially those theories that examine the connection between the audience's emotional reaction to these films and the monster's ability to embody an audience's collective fears and anxieties.

In his essay "Nightmare and the Horror Film: The Symbolic Biology of Fantastic Beings,"[1] Noel Carroll argues that horror and sci-fi films "poignantly express the sense of powerlessness and anxiety that correlates with times of depression, recession, Cold War strife, galloping inflation, and national confusion" (16). For Carroll, the monster in horror films is a symbolic formation of conflicting themes that are rooted in a culture's shared concerns ("Nightmare" 19). The horror film is a stylized manifestation of our collective nightmares and audiences are attracted to these films because they function as a release from tensions generated by those anxieties ("Nightmare" 24). Furthermore, this release from our shared social concerns stems from one of the unique characteristics of this genre. Monster movies have an inherent mirroring effect in which the characters on-screen signal an emotional response intended for the audience (Carroll, *Philosophy* 18). As the fictional people of New York or Tokyo look up at their respective terrifying monster with fear and disgust, the audience is supposed to react in a similar manner. Carroll's approach to the horror film is useful in exploring the kaiju film as it provides a framework for understanding how audiences theoretically react to these giant monsters on-screen and why films like *Godzilla*, *The Beast from 20,000 Fathoms*, and *Them!* continue to influence filmmakers decades after their release.

To understand why audiences have these specific reactions and what they should take away from these experiences, it is helpful to review Phillip Tallon and Margaret Tarratt's arguments about the nature of horror and sci-fi. Tallon builds on Carroll's argument by pointing out that "horror can 'illuminate' the way we see ourselves by showing us a much darker picture than we are used to seeing," a process that is ultimately instructive as well as cathartic (36). The sci-fi/horror film, especially those like *Godzilla*, *Them!*, and *The Beast from 20,000 Fathoms*, call into question the idea that human progress is always good and reminds audiences that they live in a corrupt world (Tallon 38). In this way, Tallon echoes Cynthia Freeland's argument that monsters "raise the specter of evil by overturning the natural order, whether it can be an order concerning death, the body, God's laws, natural law, or ordinary human values" (qtd. in Tallon 39). Audiences react with terror because the creature's presence challenges the audience's established beliefs in an ordered, moral society. However, an audience can only experience the destabilizing effects of a horror film if they already possess a strong sense of what is morally correct and what society should be like. Thus, the horror film "terrifies us and gives us a sense of moral, social, and aesthetic stability" (Tallon 39). To put it another way, as much as we like to think sci-fi/horror films are "concerned with the moral state of society, many are more directly involved with an examination of our inner nature" (383). Ideally, audiences come to the kaiju film to see a gigantic representation of their fears and anxieties rampaging on the silver screen but leave with a stronger sense of what is morally right for society. And, as I will argue, this facet of the kaiju film is ultimately what makes these movies such a useful tool for deconstructing divisive, complex, international problems. The monster's presence fosters both a deeply personal experience and shared morality among its viewers.

Ultimately, the monster is key to fostering both a personal experience and moral reflection in the audience, and the monsters that appear in kaiju films are unique among sci-fi and horror films. In his book *The Kaiju Film: A Critical Study of Cinema's Biggest Monsters*, Jason Barr argues that kaiju films may share a kinship with sci-fi and horror films but are nevertheless a distinct genre, marked by both the monster's unique psychological make-up and the embodiment of global anxieties. To distinguish the kaiju film and its monster from other genres, Barr largely relies on Susan Sontag's critique of sci-fi movies from the 1950s and 1960s and Vivian Sobchack's distinction between monsters and creatures. Barr complicates Sontag's argument that sci-fi films are "largely concerned with the aesthetics of destruction" (Sontag 213) by arguing the disasters sown by kaiju serve the film's thematic purpose and leaves the audience "with a deeper understanding of the central anxieties that powered the work" (9). Barr's interpretation of the monster and the disasters it creates accords with Carroll and Tallon's argument that horror films mirror the emotional reactions desired in an audience, but the kaiju film complicates this process in that the monster at the center of the film is distinctly different than the monster in other horror films.

Vivian Sobchack's distinction between monster and creature provides a meaningful lens through which to distinguish the kaiju from other horror and sci-fi films. For Sobchack, the monster in horror films is a deeply personalized figure whose internal motivations fascinate audiences long after they cease to be repulsed by its appearance (Sobchack 30–31). The creature in a sci-fi film "has less of an interior presence than the monster in the horror film [as it] distinctly lacks a psyche" (32). Because the creature lacks any sense of an internal life it never invokes sympathy in an audience. Viewers are not interested in why it destroys, only in its acts of destruction. This void at the center of the creature creates a blank slate on which an audience may, in turn, ascribe their collective psyche to its motivation. For the kaiju film, this ascribed psyche often reflects deeply held anxieties about geopolitical problems.

This very brief theoretical survey of horror and sci-fi films is intended to put forward the argument that giant monster movies are not necessarily about the giant monsters. Despite taking up figuratively gigantic amounts of space on the screen, the creatures in these films are far less important than the people they terrorize and the audience that mirrors that terror. As psychologically barren creatures, the kaiju is a mutable symbol that film directors can use to embody a variety of complex international anxieties and a tool through which audiences can grapple with and potentially find a release from those anxieties. The beauty of the kaiju film ultimately lies in its capacity to engender small, private cathartic moments in its viewers. At their core, kaiju films focus on an intense romantic or familial relationship tested by the creature's arrival. By the nature of these films, audience members are primed to mirror the character's emotional reactions. Just as audience members are likely to reflect the characters' sense of terror or disgust, they are equally likely to find comfort in affirming human relationships. Familial or romantic bonds are at the core of almost every major kaiju film. The creature is mutable and can be adapted to fit a variety of geopolitical processes, but the importance of human connections remains constant. Kaiju films remind audiences that they can confront complex problems by turning to their loved ones. This reminder becomes a comfort for the audience and is why the giant monster movies in the 1950s continue to be remade and to influence films well into the twenty-first century. Through the kaiju, filmmakers have a useful tool for exploring individual human responses to complex global problems.

Considering it is unlikely that many readers have seen all of the films under discussion, or at least have not seen them in a while, it would be worthwhile to take a few moments and briefly summarize their plots, before discussing the common genre conventions found in these movies and how those conventions reflected the audience's anxieties. *Beast from 20,000 Fathoms* was directed by Eugene Lourié, produced by Mutual Films, released by Warner Brothers, and very loosely based on the 1951 short story "The Fog Horn" by Ray Bradbury with special effects by Ray Harryhausen.[2] The film opens on a remote military base near the Arctic Circle during an atomic weapons test. The explosion inadvertently awakens a long-dormant Rhedosaurus, a fictitious dinosaur created for the film's plot. As the gigantic monster makes its way to its original spawning grounds outside New York City, it is up to Tom Nesbitt, played by Paul Hubschmid, and his love interest/paleontologist Lee Hunter, played by Paula Raymond, to convince the government to stop the beast before it arrives in Manhattan. Of course, they are initially unsuccessful, and a block-by-block battle ensues as the military fights the beast, eventually cornering it in a roller coaster on Coney Island. At the film's climax, the beast is killed with the aid of a radioactive isotope and an army sniper.

Beast's plot structure helped to establish a set of common motifs that many subsequent kaiju films from the 1950s adapted. These films usually begin with the initial arrival of the creature, as is the case when Sergeant Ben Peterson discovers a destroyed trailer in *Them!* or the sinking of two separate ships in *Godzilla*. This initial destruction is usually witnessed by the film's male lead who tries to investigate the creature but is usually too late to stop the creature(s) from an additional round of destruction. Sergeant Peterson is too late to stop the giant ants from continuing to destroy parts of his town, and Dr. Yamane and Ogata are caught off guard by Godzilla's attack on Odo Island. The second round of attacks confirms the monster's existence to the larger world, initiates or affirms a romantic bond between a male and female character, and prompts both a political and military response. Yet, those political and military responses are ineffective in stopping the creature. Eventually, society turns to scientists and hopes they can offer a workable solution. It is Dr. Medford's advanced knowledge of ants and ant biology that makes it possible to track the film's escaped ant queens in *Them!* (1954), and it is Serizawa's oxygen-destroying molecule that eventually destroys Godzilla. In the end, the monster is killed, the romantic couple affirms their love, but the whole of society is concerned that the creature(s) may return.[3]

Based on this generalized plot structure, four useful genre conventions develop out of kaiju films. First, the creature(s) is a symbol of complex geopolitical problems. In turn, the political bodies that respond to the creature are inept and unable to stop the creature with political action. The military exists as an extension of the nation's identity and eventually is called upon to defeat the creature but is unable to grapple with the problem. Finally, individual ingenuity and human relationships are necessary for survival. This, in turn, offers the audience a workable solution to the problem(s) embodied in the creature.

As we will see with *Beast from 20,000 Fathoms* (1953), *Them!* (1954), and *Godzilla* (1954), the creature(s) represent fears about nuclear weapons and the general political/cultural debates surrounding their proliferation. Likewise, these early films present us with various political bodies in disbelief and confusion as to what to do about the creature and the symbolic proliferation they represent. Eventually, both the conventional political and military approaches fail and the whole of society becomes dependent upon a handful of people to save them. These genre conventions are the vehicle through which film directors can comment upon an audience's anxieties and simultaneously offer a release from those anxieties by affirming human relationships.

The first of these genre conventions envisions the giant creature as a living symbol for a complex international problem. For the films that started this genre in the 1950s, *Beast from 20,000 Fathoms* (1953), *Them!* (1954), and *Godzilla* (1954), these creatures are linked to the atomic bomb and the debates surrounding nuclear weapons in the late 1940s and early 1950s. The Rhedosaurus from *Beast* is freed from an icy prison by a nuclear test, the giant ants in *Them!* (1954) are mutated because of their exposure to radiation from the original Manhattan Project bomb tests, and Godzilla is an irradiated pre-historic/mythical monster awoken by a hydrogen bomb test off the coast of Japan. Each film makes this fact explicit and wastes no time in letting audiences know that these monsters are the direct result of atomic weapons. However, the characters' attempts to make sense of the creature(s) existence is a far more interesting subject.

In each of these three films, the creature's presence prompts an open debate about atomic technology, radiation, and the respective benefits and drawbacks of each. Usually, this debate is voiced by some representative from the scientific community, and there is a distinct reason many of the monster movies from the mid–1950s feature a scientist or more specifically a nuclear scientist acting as a moral compass for the viewers. Almost immediately after the development of the first nuclear bomb, many prominent Manhattan Project scientists began publicly to caution against the bomb's use and encourage international dialogue about nuclear proliferation. According to historian Paul Boyer, scientists had long been involved in public debates, but the destruction of the trinity test and the devastation at Hiroshima and Nagasaki left many scientists emotionally shaken. The power of the bomb impressed upon them the need to advocate for the control of atomic and nuclear weapons[4] (Boyer 49–50).

By and large the Scientist Movement of the late 1940s and early 1950s wanted nuclear weapons out of the American military's control and regulated by a civilian body, preferably an international organization that could curb nuclear proliferation (Boyer 49–58). To both convince and educate the public, the anti-nuclear arms movement employed a variety of tactics including a nationwide effort to educate the public; however, the most relevant rhetorical technique to the advent of the kaiju film was the movement's appeals to fear. *Life* magazine in 1945 featured "The 36 Hour War," a fictitious report detailing a hypothetical nuclear attack on Washington, D.C., and New York City that ends with the destruction of iconic landmarks and an invading army. In 1945, *Reader's Digest* featured "Mist of Death Over New York" complete with an image of a mushroom cloud over New York City.[5] These "inversions of the history of Hiroshima and Nagasaki" were intended to scare audiences and relied on technical advice from prominent anti-nuclear scientists to heighten the American fears of nuclear weapons (Broderick and Jacobs 2).

For as much as the Scientist Movement tried to scare Americans into rejecting atomic weapons, there was an equally powerful set of voices advocating for the benefits of nuclear technology. Many of the same publications that ran fictional accounts of major cities being destroyed by atomic weapons also ran fantastic accounts of how the lives of the average American might change with the aid of nuclear-based technology (Boyer 109). The most promising technologies were the potential curative powers of radiation therapy and the chance for unlimited power through nuclear fission (Boyer 109–116). The tension between those scientists who cautioned against the use of nuclear weapons and the popular imagination's efforts to envision a better world "produced some interesting ambiguities" in the American public, ambiguities that are ultimately reflected in the kaiju films of the 1950s (Boyer 117).

The Beast from 20,000 Fathoms (1963), *Them!* (1964), and *Godzilla* (1954) all prominently reflect the world's ambiguous relationship with nuclear power. Within the first 10 minutes of *Beast from 20,000 Fathoms*, the protagonist Dr. Tom Nesbitt and his best friend Richie are awaiting the results of a nuclear weapons test in the Arctic Circle when Richie declares,

> Every time one of these things goes off, I feel like we're helping to write the first chapter of a new Genesis … let's hope we don't find ourselves writing the last chapter of the old one [*Beast* 5:56].

In turn, Dr. Medford at the end of the film *Them!* (1964) stands over the remains of the giant ants and speculates that "when man entered the atomic age, he entered into a new world. What we eventually find in that new world, nobody can predict" (1:32:01). These statements are filled with uncertainty, and the audience, by proxy, is unsure of whether this new technology will create a new world or destroy the one they currently inhabit or both.

However, these characters do not always reflect an ominous sense of destruction related to nuclear technology. Just as the debate surrounding nuclear weapons included the potential for positive application for this technology, so do the early kaiju films. Dr. Nesbitt from *Beast* specializes in radioactive isotopes that can potentially cure cancer, a fact that he shares with his love interest to assuage her fears about nuclear weapons. Furthermore, it is Dr. Nesbitt's knowledge of radiotherapy that ultimately defeats the Rhedosaurus as it rampages through Coney Island. In the film's final moments, Tom Nesbitt along with an army sniper ride a roller-coaster through the park and fire a special radioactive bullet into an open wound, thereby killing the beast. As the Rhedosaurus collapses into the burning roller-coaster, audiences are left with a symbolic optimism that suggests the same technology that birthed the atomic bomb can save mankind as well.

Dr. Medford's and Dr. Nesbitt's characters serve a twofold purpose in their respective films. On the one hand, they act as a voice extolling scientific information that lends a sense of verisimilitude to the film. On the other, they embody the ambiguities surrounding nuclear testing and, as such, reflect the uncertainties in the larger public debate. At times these characters voice warnings about a dark and destructive future and, at times, they offer glimpses into the possibilities of a life with the innovated application of nuclear technologies. In a time when many American audience members were struggling with these very same ambiguities, films like *Beast* and *Them!* offered a cathartic means of facing their anxieties and finding an escape from them as well.

What little optimism that accompanies the end of *Beast from 20,000 Fathoms* and *Them!* does not come from the American government or military's ability to kill the creatures but from the human relationships forged in the efforts to understand and conquer the creatures. In both *Beast* and *Them!*, the government is either too slow to understand the complexity of the problem or it fails to successfully contain the creatures until the last minute. Dr. Nesbitt spends a significant portion of *Beast* trying to convince any political or military leader who will listen that the Rhedosaurus is real and moving toward New York. Nesbitt is only taken seriously when his fellow scientist Prof. Elson dies while studying the creature underwater. The delay is costly, and there is little time to evacuate New York as a street-by-street battle

Figure 11. Robert Graham (James Arness) and Dr. Patricia Medford (Joan Weldon) face one of the giant ants in *Them!* (1954) (Warner Bros. Pictures/Photofest).

ensues. The U.S. military cannot kill the creature and cannot contain the radioactive toxin it spreads in the wake of their battles.

In *Them!* the military and the United States government respond much more quickly to the giant ants but are no more effective than their fictional counterparts in *Beast*. With the help of Dr. Medford, Sergeant Ben Peterson convinces the army to act, but their raid is too late to stop a pair of breeding queens from escaping the nest. Eventually, the remaining ants are tracked to Los Angeles and killed before they can continue, but the final scene and any sense of security are undercut by Medford's ominous proclamation that we don't know the consequences of nuclear power or the new world it creates (1:32:01).

In both *Beast* and *Them!* there is a military victory over the gigantic creatures, but it is not a decisive one. Throughout the conflict, there is tension created by a sense that the military could fail, and the creature will continue its rampage. For many Americans, the U.S. military represented the nation's best defense against a communist threat and a potential nuclear attack. Social historian Masuda Hajimu argues that American fears and anxieties about communism constituted a socially constructed reality that placed communism as a central threat to the United States' way of life, and a strong military was central to the nation's defense (86–91). For audience goers, the military's near-disaster in *Beast* and *Them!* represented an alternative reality in which the United States was not guaranteed a victory against its nuclear threats. As such, the films' original audiences were forced to find an alternative to military action to help them confront their fears. Ultimately, this alternative came in the form of affirmative human relationships.

Both *Beast* and *Them!* feature a love affair between two major characters that ends with each respective couple embracing one another. Both of these relationships offer comfort against the creature's threat by leaving open the possibility of human connection and love for the audience. The military may have struggled against the Rhedosaurus but Dr. Nesbitt and Lee's kiss, which bears a striking resemblance to the famous photograph of a U.S. Navy sailor kissing a woman in Times Square on V-J Day, is a victory all its own. Likewise, Sergeant Peterson and Patricia Medford turn to one another as Dr. Medford warns of the dangers of the new world. Given the creatures' blank psychological state, the growth of these relationships is the only psychological development in the films' story arc. The audience knows the creatures only as a force of nature and that the government and military essentially defeat them out of sheer luck. These events are at the core of the audience's anxieties. Their fears about nuclear weapons are embodied in giant destructive creatures and their government and military are barely able to contain them. Just as the audience is intended to mirror these characters' fears and anxieties as they face the uncertainty of a symbolic nuclear disaster, they are also primed to mirror the relief those same characters feel when they turn to their loved ones. Thus, all that is certain in these anxiety-ridden films is the necessity of human connection. The government and military might fail us but our love for each other will not.

For the Japanese, the debates surrounding nuclear weapons and nuclear technology differed from their American counterparts in that they reflected deeply held concerns about western influence in Japan as well as the lingering effects of

Hiroshima and Nagasaki. For many Americans, the *Godzilla* film franchise evokes images of a man in a rubber monster suit leveling a model city. For many, these films are the height of cinematic camp, but in its original incarnation, *Godzilla* (1954) was a masterful take on the complex relationship between Japan and the United States after World War II. While most modern film audiences rightly connect *Godzilla* with the destruction of Hiroshima and Nagasaki, the fate of the *Lucky Dragon* fishing vessel and the international controversy that followed were more immediate inspirations for the film.

Near dawn on March 1, 1954, the United State detonated a 15-megaton hydrogen bomb on the Bikini Atoll. Eighty-five miles away the crew of the *Lucky Dragon* awoke to a bright flash followed by a concussive wave and a cloud of white ash that covered their boat. When they arrived back in Japan, many of the crew members were already showing visible signs of radiation poisoning. Sadly, the United States underestimated the impact of the explosion and did not warn Japanese officials of any testing in the area. The crew of the *Lucky Dragon* were caught unaware and became Japan's newest symbol for American nuclear power (Ryfle 47–48). The fate of the *Lucky Dragon* galvanized both anti-nuclear protest and anti–American sentiment in Japan and became the genesis for *Godzilla*.[6]

The reaction to the *Lucky Dragon* incident was part of a long series of simmering anxieties related to the American occupation, trauma from the war, and shifting cultural realities for the Japanese people that all became source material for *Godzilla* (1954). The Japanese defeat and the subsequent U.S. occupation imposed a great many cultural changes in Japanese society. Close to 1.8 million people were dead. Major Japanese cities were devastated, either by nuclear weapons or systematic carpet bombings. The Emperor was forced to renounce his godhood, undercutting the traditional Shinto religion. The Japanese military and its empire were disbanded, and the government was forced to adopt western democratic values, values that many felt were a threat to the obligation systems upon which traditional Japanese society was founded (Balmain 30).

The film critic Colette Balmain contends much of Japan's post-occupation cinema was marked by a "tension between pre-modern Japanese paternalism and modern Western democratic values" (30). This tension was not about "abandoning traditional Japanese values for seemingly more democratic ones," but co-opting "one in order to re-establish another" (31). Godzilla and the characters who struggle to cope with its destruction embody these tensions. For Americans, the kaiju films of the mid–1950s represented the ongoing debates about the advantages and disadvantages of nuclear technology, but for the Japanese, Godzilla was more about revisiting the trauma of the past and the ambiguities of the future.

Godzilla, the creature, exists both as a representation of the nuclear bomb that reenacts the destruction and trauma of Hiroshima and Nagasaki, as well as an injured kami spirit brought forth by mankind's indifference to the environment (Balmain 41). There are several key moments in the film where Godzilla is overtly connected to the horrors of Hiroshima and Nagasaki. Dying citizens strike horrified poses as they die in the beast's atomic fire; a war widow clutches her children and takes comfort in knowing that they will see their father again; the ground is poisoned with radiation after the creature leaves an area, much like Hiroshima, and video footage of the monster's aftermath evokes damaged cities after an atomic blast.

Yet, the creature's origin offers a more nuanced depiction of the kaiju. Unlike the giant ants or the Rhedosaurus, Godzilla is not a one-dimensional monster. It does lack the complex psyche normally associated with sci-fi creatures; however, it symbolizes more than the wanton destruction of atomic weapons. Originally, Godzilla was not a creature mutated by atomic testing, as is sometimes thought; instead, it was a prehistoric aquatic reptile driven from his underwater environment by a hydrogen bomb test in the Pacific. "Godzilla is effectively a tragic figure, ... of man's tampering with forbidden Promethean knowledge" (Brothers 38). In some ways Godzilla is an animal whose environment has been destroyed and is seeking refuge, only becoming a walking atomic bomb as it flees its original environment. Alternatively, the creature also functions as a symbol for traditional Japanese culture. When it arrives and makes its first kill, the people of Odo Island immediately recognize Godzilla as an angered kami spirit that they try to appease with a series of ritual dances. Thus, the creature exists simultaneously as a powerful symbol of Japan's traditional Shinto culture, a victim of the American military/western cultural presence, and a symbol for atomic destruction. For a Japanese audience still traumatized by the events of World War II and struggling with the societal changes required by the U.S. occupation forces, *Godzilla* became an emotional touchstone that embodied many of their anxieties.[7]

In this way, Godzilla is a multilayered symbol signifying Japan's past traumas and traditional culture and potentially a model for Japan's future. Not all the characters in the film immediately want to destroy Godzilla. Most notably, Professor Kyohei Yamane believes there is a great deal to learn from the creature. In a tense political exchange in which the nation's representatives argue about the proper response to Godzilla's threat, the Professor reminds them that "Godzilla was baptized in the fire of the H-bomb and survived," arguing throughout the film that the creature's resistance to radiation needs to be studied (34:09). His pleas fall on deaf ears, and the military opts to move forwards with plans to assault the creature; however, his description of Godzilla's origins is evocative of Japan's post-war experience. After all, one could argue that post-war Japan is a nation baptized in the fires of atomic weapons as well, and if Godzilla can survive the trauma of a nuclear attack and arise stronger and resistant, so too might Japan.

Ultimately, Godzilla is a complex symbol for original audiences. It exists as a blank slate with little to no psychological development on to which the characters, and the audience by extension, may project any number of anxieties. For those fearful of the loss of traditional Shinto culture and the existence of a living god among them, Godzilla is a gigantic affirmation of that culture. For those still traumatized by the attacks at Hiroshima and Nagasaki, Godzilla is a cathartic tool for addressing that trauma (Stevens 17). Lastly, for those concerned for the nation's future, Godzilla offers the possibility of both surviving and thriving after the impact of an atomic bomb.

As a kaiju, Godzilla is far more complex than his American counterparts; yet Japan's political and military leaders are no better equipped to resolve these symbolic tensions than their American foils. However, there is at least one important deviation from the genre conventions established by *Beast* and *Them!* that is worth noting, because it involves the United States' influence in Japan and illustrates the complexity of dealing with the international problems embodied in Godzilla. When Prof. Yamane confirms Godzilla's existence, the Japanese government does not want the public to know about Godzilla's connection to the hydrogen bomb tests. They are deeply concerned that it may prompt an unwanted response from the United States government, a concern many audience members would have shared given that the occupation had only ended two years earlier.[8] That occupational period was "characterized by continuity as well as change, and by reactionary as well as progressive impulses" (Bailey 66). In other words, Japanese society, during the occupation, was marked by a loss of autonomy and the reassertion of power during a period of intense cultural changes, a reality that I imagine few would want to return. Thus, the fictional Japanese government's inaction is indicative of concerns shared by many in the audience.

Like its American counterparts, *Godzilla* relies on human relationships as a means of coping with the anxieties represented by the kaiju. At the center of the human drama in *Godzilla* is the love triangle between Ogata, Emiko, and Dr. Serizawa. The original script for *Godzilla* didn't feature a love story, but the director Ishiro Honda added the characters to the script to enhance the audience's emotional reaction (Brother 37). This love triangle is important as it represents a solution to the tensions embodied in the creature. Ogata, Emiko, and Dr. Serizawa are representative of shifting gender roles in post-war Japan and, as such, are also emblematic of the nation's overall shifting realities (Balmain 43). Serizawa and Emiko's paternally arranged marriage is representative of the traditional Japanese culture while Emiko and Ogata's love affair is illustrative of the modern approach to relationships.

Among the more positive aspects of the U.S. occupation of Japan were the newer gender roles for women. Although there was resistance to concepts like suffrage, more education for women, and increasingly more open sexuality, the U.S. occupation provided new opportunities for women in the post-war era. Emiko's relationship with Ogata signifies this advancement. However, her unwillingness to immediately break off her arranged engagement with Serizawa is indicative of the tension many young women must have felt as they faced Japan's shifting cultural realities. Her father encourages her relationship with Serizawa, but her heart belongs to Ogata, thus placing Emiko's conflict at the center of a culture transitioning away from a system of familial obligations toward a more democratic society. The conflict is only resolved when, at the close of the film, Serizawa both blesses Emiko's relationship with Ogata and sacrifices himself to kill Godzilla, thereby keeping his doomsday device from the politicians who might exploit it. His death clears the way for Emiko and Ogata's relationship to move forward and in so doing affirms a pro–Western value system; however, his suicide also reaffirms traditional values like self-sacrifice for the communal good. Serizawa "metaphorically signals both the break down of the traditional Japanese value system and the reaffirmation of those same values" at the same time (Balmain 42). The film's final moments give the audience a means through which they can embrace a Western value system while also paying homage to the traditional values that supported Japan for so long. Serizawa's death is heroic enough as to allow for his veneration, an event that happens in the film, and the veneration of traditional Japanese culture by extension. And Emiko and Ogata's newly blessed relationship is a model for how Japanese families might move forward in the post-war years. By mirroring the symbolic meaning in this relationship, the Japanese audience has a model that reconciles the values of the past with the Western culture they are adopting.

While numerous twenty-first-century films continue the legacy of the 1950s giant monster movie, three films demonstrate the ways in which the kaiju film can morph to reflect varying cultural anxieties while still believing that human relationships are the key to solving or surviving those problems. For the remainder of this study, I am focusing on *Cloverfield* (2008), *Monsters* (2010), and *Shin Godzilla* (2016) as representative films from this genre.[9] Taken together, these three films represent a series of transnational problems plaguing the early twenty-first-century global community, including international terrorism, mass migrations, and environmental disaster.

I should note that the remainder of this essay is focused on kaiju films produced after the terrorist attacks on September 11, 2001, and while not all of the films in this section deal directly with 9/11, many critics have noted that sci-fi/horror movies from this period are distinctly different than those from the decades before and, as a result of the shared national trauma, other critics draw a comparison between these films and many of the sci-fi/horror movies from the 1950s. In an interview with the *New York Times* a little over a month after the terrorist attacks, media critic Robert J. Thompson argued,

> The horror movie is just sitting there waiting to deal with this. It is one of the most versatile genres out there, a universal solvent of virtually any news issue. And it is now perfectly positioned to cop some serious attitude, to play a role where it's not simply a date movie but going further back, to the 1950s, where you have the horror movie as a metaphor [qtd. in Lyman].[10]

Critics like Thompson understand that sci-fi/horror films are a versatile genre capable of adapting to a variety of national fears and anxieties. And I contend that those films created in the decade after September 11 were uniquely suited to adapt the genre conventions of their 1950s predecessors to the modern world, as many Americans drew direct comparisons between Pearl Harbor, Hiroshima, and New York as a means to contextualize their confusion and outrage (Dower).

Cloverfield (2008) is one of the clearest spiritual successors to the early giant monster movies from the 1950s and a clear attempt to reconcile the horrors of September 11. Ostensibly, the film is presented as archival footage found in the wreckage of a recent attack on New York. *Cloverfield*'s narrative centers on a group of young New Yorkers celebrating a going away party for the protagonist Rob, who, not so coincidentally, is moving to Japan. His best friend Hud is tasked with being the evening's videographer and preserving the night's events so that Rob can have a memento of his last night in the city. Rob and his love interest, Beth, fight shortly before a massive monster descends upon the city. From that point forward the film becomes a desperate attempt to rescue Beth and escape New York before they are all killed in the ensuing attack, an attempt that culminates with Beth and Rob being crushed in Central Park.

Released seven years after the 9/11 attacks on New York, the destruction in *Cloverfield* (2008) is designed to play on the audience's fears and anxieties about terrorist attacks and the subsequent War on Terror. While the World Trade Center Towers are not directly referenced, the film nevertheless evokes memories of New York on September 11, 2001, so much so that the movie's original working title was simply "1/18/08" (Ebert). As the unnamed creature terrorizes New York, the streets fill with waves of billowing ash that envelope disheveled and confused citizens; famous landmarks, like the severed head of the Statue of Liberty, crush idle taxi cabs, and severely damaged skyscrapers lean on one another as if their internal support systems are collapsing. According to the film's producer, J.J. Abrams, even the film's "shaky cam" or unsteadied camera technique was intended to mirror the war footage coming out of Iraq and Afghanistan (Keegan).

What is even more important than the film's symbolic representation of the war on terror are the filmmakers' intentions for the audience. In an interview with *Time Magazine*, Abrams argues that

> with *Cloverfield,* we were trying to create a film that would be entertaining and, as a by-product of the subject matter, perhaps be a catharsis. We wanted to let people live through their wildest fears but be in a safe place where the enemy is the size of a skyscraper instead of some stateless, unseen cowardly terrorist [Keegan].

Much like *Godzilla, Them!,* and *The Beast from 20,000 Fathoms, Cloverfield's* creators believed the giant monster was an apt symbol for working through the concerns created by complex international problems.

Gareth Edward's *Monsters* (2010) continues this pattern by adopting the very real concerns about the War on Terror and mass migration into the fantastical world of the kaiju film. In many ways, *Monsters* is a departure from the traditional kaiju movie in that it begins six years after the monsters' rampage. Initially, the audience is informed that a NASA space probe crashed on Earth and seeded Northern Mexico with alien spores that perennially grow into giant cephalopod-like creatures that migrate across the Texas/Mexico border looking for mates. The plot centers around photojournalist Andrew and his efforts to escort his employer's daughter, Sam, back across the border into the United State before the border is closed to them.

Much of the protagonists' trip is intended to evoke the ongoing war on terror. Sam and Andrew's journey spans an infected zone strewn with downed planes and relics from an early military confrontation with the alien monsters. In an interview, Edwards concedes that his film was inspired by the war on terror and the post–9/11 world, arguing, "if *Cloverfield* was like September the 11th, the logical progression from there is Afghanistan, so let's do a film that's set a few years later, where it's a war going on somewhere on the other side of the world, and no one cares" (Lambie). Throughout *Monsters,* there is a sense that both the United States and Mexico are caught in an endless war with little to no clear end goal in mind other than stopping the creature's migration, an effort that leaves many civilians trapped in a perpetual war zone.

Despite Edwards's expressed desire to evoke a sense of endless war through *Monsters,* it is hard not to read Sam and Andrew's journey as a metaphor for illegal immigration, as well, even though the director has said that was not his

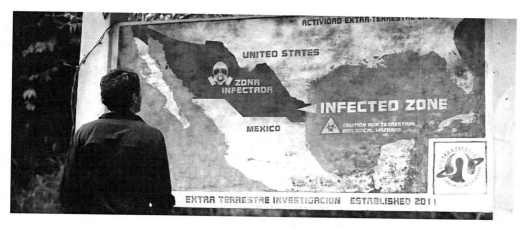

Figure 12. Andrew Kaulder (Scoot McNairy) inspects a map, labeled in both Spanish and English, showing the area of alien "infection" in Gareth Edwards' *Monsters* (2010) (Magnet Releasing/Photofest).

explicit intent (Castillo). Yet film critic Steffen Hantke contends that the massive computer-generated border wall and the militarized border agents are reminiscent of the post–9/11 immigration debates (31). The protagonist at one point even hires coyotes to smuggle them across the border like so many real-life immigrants navigating the U.S./Mexico border. It is even more difficult not to read that migration subtext within the context of post–9/11 U.S. immigration policy given how politicized immigration policy became following the attacks. Both the conservative Center for Immigration Studies and more center leaning Migration Policy Institute cited the terror attacks from 2001 as the impetus for the contemporary immigration debates and policies.

Whether the creatures in *Cloverfield* or *Monsters* represent complex problems like international terrorism, endless wars, or mass migration, each film argues, much like their 1950s counterparts, that military action is ill-suited to solve these problems. Throughout *Cloverfield*, U.S. soldiers fight a running battle, continually retreating from the monster's attack. They do manage to help Rob and Beth escape, only to have their helicopter crash at the last minute, leaving the couple to die in Central Park. Likewise, in *Monsters* the U.S. military is wholly unable to curb the alien creatures' mass migration across the U.S./Mexico border. There is a lot to suggest that the U.S. military is making the problem worse, including graffiti questioning the necessity of constant bombings (26:00) and a coyote's observation that the creatures are only aggressive after U.S. attacks (52:00).

Like their 1950s counterparts, *Cloverfield* and *Monsters* are rooted in overwhelming geopolitical problems and concerns about the military's ability to solve those problems. And while the complexities of global terrorism and the effectiveness of military intervention are distinctly different than those of the atomic age, each of these films suggest a nearly identical means of coping with these problems, as did their 1950s counterparts, namely investing in human connections and relationships. This trope is so apparent in *Cloverfield* that this essay's title is derived from a conversation between Rob, his brother Jason, and best friend Hurd after Rob ends his relationship with Beth seconds before the monster begins its initial attack. In perhaps the film's most expositional scene, Jason reminds his brother Rob that life is "about moments" and to "forget the world and hang on to the people you care about the most" (18:17–18:21).

This juxtaposition between Jason's advice and the monster's attack creates the film's primary tension, becomes the motivation for the protagonists to risk their lives trekking across New York City in the middle of a monster attack, and offers a means through which the audience can find some sense of peace amid so much horror. Rob eventually rescues Beth, but they do not survive. After the couple finally professes their love, they are crushed to death. However, the film's final scene is fragmented footage from Rob and Beth's first date, at Coney Island.[11] *Cloverfield* (2008) is interspersed with fragmented clips from Rob and Beth's relationship each only lasting a few seconds; however, the brevity of the final shot is appropriate for the audience's needs, given Jason's advice. The audience has been told that life is made up of these moments and that is what they should cling to, and just as the film seemingly concludes with the couple's horrific death, that is exactly what the film presents, a single moment in a happy couple's life. It is a hopeful coda to an otherwise sad ending. For an audience for which the outcome of the War on Terror was yet to be determined, the film's final fragment footage suggests a strategy for coping with the ambiguities of complex global problems. In the face of uncertainty and terror, *Cloverfield* (2008) reminds us that we must look to each other for comfort.

Gareth Edward's *Monsters* (2010) deviates from this pattern slightly only in that it attempts to attach a timeless quality to human relationships. Shortly before Sam and Andrew make it across the U.S./Mexico border, they take refuge in a Mesoamerican pyramid surrounded by the jungle and in the shadow of a massive border wall designed to keep the monsters from crossing into the United States. In this brief respite, the couple finally kiss and begin their romantic relationship in earnest. Ultimately, the combination of the ancient pyramid, the gigantic border wall, and the ever-encroaching jungle suggests that despite their great monuments and power, civilizations will fall and be reclaimed by nature. All that can survive, and perhaps flourish, are the human relationships we build in the interim. This is an apt message for a film where the giant monsters are as much a metaphor for mass migration as they are for the forces of nature bent on destroying the United States and Northern Mexico through endless war.

Although there have been numerous remakes and reboots of the *Godzilla* (1954) movie since the original Toho production, including Gareth Edward's *Godzilla* (2014), its sequel *Godzilla: King of Monsters* (2019), and the recent *Godzilla vs. Kong* (2021), the most relevant reboot for this discussion must be Toho Pictures' 2016 film, *Shin Godzilla*. Set-in modern-day Tokyo, this film takes the original Japanese symbol for the nation's collective anxieties about a changing world and the American military presence and reworks it into a lens that examines Japan's place in the modern world and the limitations of its democratic government. In this version, Godzilla is a walking nuclear fission reactor born of toxic waste dumped into the Pacific Ocean. Thus, Godzilla has transformed from a metaphor for the Cold War and the American military presence in Asia into a walking embodiment of the Fukushima

Dai-ichi nuclear power plant's meltdown and subsequent environmental damage. While the film does not directly reference the Fukushima disaster, it was made only three years after the disaster while the nation was still grappling with the fallout from the reactor meltdown; moreover, the characters continually contextualize the monster as if it were a walking nuclear reactor and the realization that the creature was born of nuclear waste released into the ocean mirrors many environmentalist concerns about Fukushima in the years after the meltdown. Even the creature's destructive path across the Japanese islands appears to be a reflection of the toxic waste that drifted away from Japan after the nuclear meltdown.

While the film's reworking of *Godzilla* (1954) is both novel and entertaining, it is the film's response to the giant creature that merits discussion. Like its 1950s counterpart, *Shin Godzilla* ultimately recognizes that a military response to the creature is a fruitless endeavor that only leads to mass causalities; however, in this version, the threat embodied in Godzilla can only be solved through cooperation between the United States and Japanese scientists. Ultimately, this ending reflects the very different geopolitical relationship between the two nations that currently exists, and suggests a very positive solution to global problems. Early in the film, the Japanese government is treated as if it is inept and a hindrance to the solution. Characters openly complain about the governmental red tape one needs to bypass to propose a solution (16:09). It is not until the country's top political officials are killed in a Godzilla attack, thereby literally and figuratively disintegrating the red tape, that one of the film's two main protagonists, Rando Yaguchi (Hiroki Hasegawa), is allowed to assume control and begin to treat the problem less like a military invasion and more like a technical and environmental problem in need of an engineering solution.

From this point forward Yaguchi is aided by his soon-to-be love interest Kayaco Patterson (Satomi Ishihara), a U.S. envoy sent to aid the Japanese government in their response. As Patterson works to stall the United Nations' attempt to drop a third nuclear bomb on Japan, Yaguchi leads a team of scientists looking for a less violent solution; the two become increasingly connected, developing mutual respect and friendship. Eventually, the creature is stopped and the international team is victorious, as least temporarily. However, the most important aspect of this victory is the lasting friendship developed between Yaguchi and Patterson. The film ends with a discussion that suggests they will both one day become powerful political figures in their respective countries and pledge to continue to work together in friendship.

This pledge of fidelity is significant in the development of the Kaiju film in that it conflates the traditional romantic relationship with international political cooperation. While both its 1950s and many of its twenty-first-century counterparts treat human relationships as a last-ditch effort to survive in the face of overwhelming geopolitical problems, *Shin Godzilla* reworks those relationships into a metaphor for healthy multilateral approaches to global crises. The film suggests that the anxieties and fears embodied in the giant creature might be too much for a single nation, but those fears can be overcome through cooperation with other nations so long as that cooperation is grounded in mutual respect and friendship. Thus, Yaguchi and Patterson's relationship is a model for both the audience and the nations of the world to navigate complex international crises.

While we may no longer look at the monsters from *Beast from 20,000 Fathoms*, *Them!*, and *Godzilla* with a sense of fear and dread, because the anxieties they embodied are no longer powerful parts of our collective fears and anxieties, the tropes those films established still influence the ways modern theater-goers work through their concerns. Each of those three films played a crucial role in establishing the giant monster movie genre in the early 1950s, and each one of them placed human relationships at the center of the audience's cathartic experience. Human relationships are an immutable aspect of these films. The creature may be a mutating symbol, adjusting itself to fit the audience's specific anxieties about shifting geopolitical realities, but the film will maintain strong romantic and familial bonds as a means to cope with those realities.

Notes

1. I should note that Carroll does not make much of a distinction between horror and sci-fi in this essay. He argues the "science fiction has evolved as a sub-class of horror" in that "science fiction films are monster films, rather than explorations of grand themes like alternative societies or alternative technologies" (17). While I think this is a bit overstated, it is helpful in this context given that all the films under discussion here feature giant monsters and tend to blend sci-fi with horror.

2. There is a very famous sequence in *The Beast from 20,000 Fathoms* in which the Rhedosaurus rises from the ocean and tears down an isolated lighthouse. This is only scene that bares any resemblance to Bradbury's original short story. It is, however, some of Harryhausen's best animation work in the film.

3. This synopsis of kaiju movie plots is adapted from Susan Sontag's "The Imagination of Disaster."

4. I feel to compelled to note that J. Robert Oppenheimer in an interview in which he recalled the initial trinity test said the explosion reminded him of a passage from the Bhagavad-Gita and the Hindu god Vishnu's declaration "now I am become death, the destroyer of worlds" (Now I Am). Although the original Hindu passage was intended to remind Prince Arjuna that the soul is eternal even if he dies, he will be born again, it is not clear that Oppenheimer shared this belief (Temperton). In the interview where Oppenheimer recalled this memory, he is visibly shaken to the point that he wipes away a tear. This sense of regret and depth of emotion was apparently shared by many of the Manhattan Project scientists.

5. According to historians Broderick and Jacobs, New York was a popular site for fictitious nuclear attacks in the early days of the Cold War. I do not think it is a coincidence then that *Beast from 20,000 Fathoms*, the first of the giant monster movies, shows a creature attacking New York City. By the film's release, New York's destruction via nuclear weapons was a familiar occurrence. By staging the film in New York, the film's producers were playing on an already well-worn convention.

6. While Americans may have forgotten about the *Lucky Dragon* incident, it remains a prominent symbol in Japan. Currently, the fully restored Lucky Dragon is on exhibition in Yumenoshima Park, in Tokyo's Koto Ward where it is "an obligatory stop for school groups visiting Tokyo" and studying the legacy of the atomic weapons (Schreiber).

7. In "The Rhetorical Significance of *Gojira*: Equipment for Living Through Trauma" Shannon Stevens contends that the original Godzilla movie provided a much-needed therapeutic release for the Japanese people still traumatized by the atomic bombs. As part of her evidence she notes the number of people who left the theater crying, emotionally disturbed by the film's scenes of destruction.

8. Interestingly, this section of the original *Godzilla* is used in the 1956 remake, *Godzilla: King of Monsters*, but it is not translated. Instead of a heated political exchange about unwanted American influence in Japanese domestic matters, American audiences are left believing the argument is just panic about the creature. The moment looks like the film makers are trying to shield American audiences from knowing that Japan is not always happy with U.S. involvement.

9. For anyone who has been paying attention to the development of the giant monster movie in the post–9/11 years, this list might appear to be missing a few key titles, namely *The Host* (2006), *Godzilla* (2014), and the sequel *Godzilla: King of Monsters* (2019). While these films are certainly deserving of critical attention and support this essay's thesis, they each have elements in both their plots and production that overlap with the aforementioned films. For example, *Godzilla* (2014) and *Monsters* (2010) are both directed by Garth Edwards and I fear would become a discussion of his film-making. Furthermore, the giant monsters at the heart of *The Host* (2006), *Godzilla* (2014), and *Shin Godzilla* (2016) are all embody fears about environmental disaster, but *Shin Godzilla* complicates the notion of human relationship and international politics in a way that ultimately highlights Japan and the United States interconnected relationship since World War II.

10. I am indebted to Aviva Briefel and Sam J. Miller for drawing my attention to this quotation in the introduction to their excellent anthology *Horror After 9/11*.

11. There are two aspects of this final moment that are worth noting. First, the decision to showcase the couple at Coney Island during a giant monster movie is most likely an allusion to *Beast From 20,000 Fathoms*. Secondly, *Cloverfield*'s director filmed multiple endings to this movie, but each cut concluded with some footage of the Coney Island date.

Works Cited

Bailey, Paul. *Postwar Japan: 1945 to the Present*. Historical Association Studies, Blackwell, 1996.
Balmain, Colette. *Introduction to Japanese Horror Film*. Edinburgh University Press, 2008.
Barr, Jason. *The Kaiju Film: A Critical Study of Cinema's Biggest Monsters*. McFarland, 2016.
Boyer, Paul. *By the Bomb's Early Light: American Thought and Culture at the Dawn of the Atomic Age*. University of North Carolina Press, 1994.
Briefel, Aviva, and Sam J. Miller. "Introduction." *Horror After 9/11: World of Fear, Cinema of Terror*, edited by Aviva Briefel and Sam. J. Miller. University of Texas Press, 2011.
Broderick, Mick, and Robert Jacobs. "Nuke York, New York: Nuclear Holocaust in the American Imagination from Hiroshima to 9/11." *The Asia-Pacific Journal*, 5 March 2012, https://apjjf.org/2012/10/11/Robert-Jacobs/3726/article.html. Accessed 28 Dec. 2021.
Brother, Peter H. "Japan's Nuclear Nightmare: How the Bomb Became a Beast Called Godzilla." *Cineaste*, Summer 2011, pp. 36–40.
Carroll, Noel. "Nightmare and the Horror Film: The Symbolic Biology of Fantastic Beasts." *Film Quarterly* 34, no. 3 Spring 1981, pp. 16–25.
_____. *The Philosophy of Horror or Paradoxes of the Heart*. Routledge, 1990.
Castillo, Michelle. "Filmmaker Gareth Edwards Talks about His Monsters." *Time Magazine*, 18 Oct. 2010, https://techland.time.com/2010/18/filmmaker-gareth-edwards-talks-about-his-monsters/. Accessed 28 Dec. 2021.
Dower, John W. "Cultures of War: Pearl Harbor/Hiroshima/9–11/Iraq." *Pen America*, 2 Nov. 2011, https://pen.org/cultures-of-war-pearl-harbor-hiroshima-9-11-iraq/. Accessed 28 Dec. 2021.
Ebert, Roger. "'Forget I am Legend.' If That Big Lizard Has Its Way, We Are All Legends." *RogerEbert.com*, 17 Jan. 2008, https://www.rogerebert.com/reviews/cloverfield-2008. Accessed 28 Dec. 2021.
Hajimu, Masuda. *Cold War Crucible: The Koran Conflict and the Postwar World*. Harvard University Press, 2015.
Hantke, Steffen. "The State of the State of Emergency: Life Under Alien Occupation in Gareth Edward's *Monsters*." *AAA: Arbeiten aus Anglistik und Amerikanistik* 41, no. 1, 2016, pp. 25–38.
Keegan, Rebecca Winters. "*Cloverfield*: Godzilla Goes 9/11." *Time Magazine Online*, 16 Jan. 2008, http://content.time.com/time/arts/article/0,8599,1704356,00.html. Accessed 28 Dec. 2021.
Lourié, Eugene. "Trailer for 'Beast from 20,000 Fathoms.'" *Beast from 20,000 Fathoms*, Warner Video, 2015, Blu-ray.
Lyman, Rick. "Horrors! Time for an Attack of the Metaphors?; From Bug Movies to Bioterrorism." *New York Times*, 23 Oct. 2011, https://www.nytimes.com/2001/10/23/movies/horrors-time-for-an-attack-of-the-metaphors-from-bug-movies-to-bioterrorism.html. Accessed 28 Dec. 2021.
Mittelstadt, Michelle, Burke Speaker, Doris Meissner, and Muzaffar Chishti. "Through the Prisim of National Security: Major Immigration Policy and Program Changes in the Decade Since 9/11." *Migration Policy Institute*, Aug. 2011, https://www.migrationpolicy.org/news. Accessed 28 Dec. 2021.
"Now I am Become Death." *YouTube*, uploaded by The Atomic Heritage Foundation, 25 Sept. 2018, https://www.youtube.com/watch?v=fa5kA9w7t0Q. Accessed 28 Dec. 2021.
Ryfle, Steve. "Godzilla's Footprint." *The Virginia Quarterly Review*, Vol. 81, No. 1, Winter 2005, pp. 44–63.
Schreiber, Mark. "Lucky Dragon's Lethal Catch." *The Japan Times*, 18 March 2012, https://www.japantimes.co.jp/life/2012/03/18/general/lucky-dragons-lethal catch/#.Xtr_M-d7mUk. Accessed 28 Dec. 2021.
Sobchack, Vivian. *Screening Space: The American Science Fiction Film*. Second Enlarged Edition. Rutgers University Press, 2001.
Sontag, Susan. "The Imagination of Disaster." *Against Interpretation and Other Essays*. Farrar, Straus, and Giroux, 1966, pp. 209–25.
Stevens, Shannon. "The Rhetorical Significance of *Gojira*: Equipment for Living Through Trauma." *The Atomic Bomb and Japanese Cinema*, edited by Mathew Edwards. McFarland, 2015, pp. 17–34.
Tallon, Phillip. "Through a Mirror, Darkly: Art-Horror as a Medium for Moral Reflection." *The Philosophy of Horror*, edited by Thomas Fahy. University Press of Kentucky, 2010, pp. 33–41.
Temperton, James. "'Now I am become Death, the destroyer of world': The Story of Oppenheimer's Famous Quote." *Wired Magazine*, 9 Aug. 2017, https://www.wired.co.uk/article/manhattan-project-robert-oppenheimer. Accessed 28 Dec. 2021.

"The 36 Hour War." *Life*, 19 Nov. 1945, pp. 27–35.
Warren, Bill. *Keep Watching the Skies! American Science Fiction Movies of the Fifties*. McFarland, 1997.

FILMOGRAPHY

The Beast from 20,000 Fathoms. Dir. Eugène Lourié. Warner Bros., 1953. Film.
Cloverfield. Dir. Matt Reeves. Paramount Pictures, 2008. Film.
Godzilla: King of Monsters. Dir. Terry O. Morse and Ishiro Honda. Toho Studios, 1956. Film.
Godzilla vs. King Kong. Dir. Adam Wingard. Warner Bros., 2021. Film.
Gojira. Dir. Ishiro Honda. Toho Studios, 1954. Film.
King Kong. Dir. Merian C. Cooper. RKO Radio Pictures, 1952. Film.
Monsters. Dir. Gareth Edwards. Vertigo Films, 2010. Film.
Shin Godzilla. Dir. Hideaki Anno. Toho Pictures, 2016. Film.
Them! Dir. Gordon Douglas. Warner Bros., 1954. Film.

"Something's lost in the translation!"

Hemimetabolic Adaptation (or Incomplete Metamorphosis) in David Cronenberg's The Fly

Richard Berger

"Yeah, I build bodies; I take them apart and put them back together"
—Seth Brundle, *The Fly* (1986)

This essay foregrounds the idea that adaptation and remaking culture can be conceived of as biological (and therefore "natural") processes of transformation and re-appropriation in popular culture. Indeed, many have argued (e.g., Benjamin, *Illuminations*) that all texts are inherently translatable—within certain conditions; for scholars such as Edmund Chapman, "[t]exts always possess translatability, along with untranslatability. Textuality is the interplay or tension between these two poles" (22). Below I examine David Cronenberg's remake of Kurt Neuman's 1958 sci-fi horror *The Fly*—itself based on a short story by George Langelaan, published in *Playboy* just a year earlier. On the surface, Cronenberg's film uses the original version as a route into examining body dysmorphia and disease, as well as being—as we shall see—a comment on the transformative elements of texts as biological entities. The film can also be viewed as a text that predicts the digital image-obsessed Instagram age. There is some dispute, however, if *The Fly* (1986) is even a remake at all, and if it is, what kind of remake it can be described as: "In the most general terms, film remakes are generally understood as films based on other films. Clear examples of this would be *The Fly* (1986) which is based on the earlier film of the same name" (Herbert 34). For Marty Roth, though, "*Fly* is an original film that has almost nothing in common with the 1958 film of that name" (231).

I will examine the two poles between translatability and untranslatability and sketch out the ways in which both films (and the source story) contemplate biological transformation and metamorphic processes and states. In this analysis, Cronenberg's film stands as a metaphor for the process of adaptation/remaking itself; both films are biologically connected, rather like the twin brothers featured in the movie he would make next, *Dead Ringers* (1988).

Metaphors of biology and flesh have been used before by adaptation critics to describe the process of transforming a text from one medium to another, from Virginia Woolf's famous proclamation that the translation of literary texts into visual ones was akin to a violent sexual assault (269)—a comment perhaps about how her own status as an author alters during the metamorphic process. There have also been the (literal) benign Darwinist principles telegraphed in Spike Jonze's *Adaptation* (2002). In terms of visual-to-visual translation, then surely David Cronenberg's 1986 remake of *The Fly* (1958) is an adaptation that directly deals with the *process* of adaptation (both literally and figuratively) in ways which extend the biological metaphor into new and interesting territories. Though Cronenberg has been a controversial and much scrutinized auteur for some, film critics have nevertheless noted the "fantastic machines" (Clarke 175) of teleportation narrative but missed the biological links. These biological links will be addressed directly below.

The Fly is David Cronenberg's only remake, although he is a filmmaker who has dipped his toe more than once into adaptation waters. Indeed, he is known for his adaptations of seemingly unfilmable works, such as his stagings of William Burroughs' *Naked Lunch* and J.G. Ballard's *Crash*, all novels/films that feature male characters who stand as metaphors for their own creators; *Naked Lunch* deals directly with Burrough's tragic marriage to Joan Vollmer and *Crash*'s central protagonist is even named James Ballard. Both versions of *The Fly* feature a central male scientist, and while both attempt to play God, in the remake Brundle acts as a vehicle for typical Cronenbergian themes of body dysmorphia in ways which suggest that the film could be viewed as his most personal work. Indeed, Cronenberg's film asks us to consider the director as scientist and that the film is his laboratory. For R. Barton Palmer,

> the most useful approach to Cronenberg's filmmaking is through a complex web of literary intertexts, the other works to which his films refer and that they often remake or recycle, ranging from those authors whose works the writer-director has adapted for the screen [175].

Though *The Fly* is ostensibly based on the 1958 movie, the credits cite George Langelaan's 1957 short story as its inspiration. In doing so, I will argue, Cronenberg's version attempts to efface the Kurt Neumann–directed B-movie horror classic and replace it with something more complex and visceral. Indeed, the short story and subsequent filmed versions are about the biological metamorphosis of a human being into something else: the 1958 *Fly* being a complete swap between human and insect (biologically termed a "holometabalous" adaptation) resulting in two entities and Cronenberg's incomplete metamorphosis (the alternative "hemimetabolous" version) into "Brundlefly." Patrick Gonder notes a racial undertone in the original movie:

> When Andre merges with the fly, their union creates two monsters with both insect and human characteristics. The fly parts are black and bestial, the color difference emphasized by Andre's lab coat and his ghostly pale head perched on the fly's body as it screams in the spider's web. Andre and The Fly give birth to racially mixed monsters, twin symbols of the racist fears of miscegenation, and, consequently, both bodies must be destroyed.

As Bruce Clark (2002) astutely notes, "stories of metamorphosis are inherently self-referential: they are always also allegories of the media through which they are communicated."

This essay will further argue that the two (one unseen, one seen) metamorphoses in each film stand as metaphors for the process of adaptation itself—between complete and incomplete versions of texts in initially different and then the same media. While the 1958 adaptation was a signaling perhaps of the high-capitalist tech society to come, Cronenberg's remake concerns itself with the failure of technology to solve global problems, and so re-tools the story to be one about body horror, which some scholars have perhaps lazily ascribed to the HIV/AIDs pandemic of the 1980s.[1] Films are often viewed through their own contextual lens, as Mathijs observes: "[R]eviews of *The Fly* suggest that the film itself is an AIDS metaphor" (2003). However, uncoupling the film from its own time—and its later circulation through the "memescape"—and accounting for the scale and reach of how both versions themselves became source texts for a range of sequels suggest a reappraisal might be worth pursuing. While accepting that "[a]daptation can be a violent process, in either direction" (Milligan), this essay will also cover how previous versions of texts can gain an "afterlife" (Benjamin) through streaming services and their attendant Electronic Program Guide (EPG) preferencing technology—rendering Cronenberg's direct framing of Langelaan's story as source highly problematic. Indeed, the social media channel Looper in 2015 cited Cronenberg's *Fly* as one example in its "Movie Remakes That Were Better Than the Original" YouTube video.

The "Pupa" Phase

Surprisingly, perhaps, *The Fly* (along with its remake) has been overlooked by some key writings on 1950s sci-fi.[2] As Clark notes, "criticism has been focused on cinematic matters, particularly Cronenberg's transformation of Neumann, with little reference to Langelaan" (169). First published in *Playboy* in 1957, and then re-published by *The Magazine of Fantasy and Science Fiction* in its "The Best of 1958" issue, George Langelaan's *The Fly* is a parable, warning readers of the dangers of the new technological world. The focus of this collection is remakes of sci-fi films from the 1950s because it was an era defined both as nostalgic and forward-thinking. This immediate post-war period saw the start of the Space Race (1957), the touch-paper being lit for the later Vietnam War, the development of the hydrogen bomb and the first successful organ transplants (1954). Television went color in 1950 and soon became a mass medium—almost overnight in the UK for the queen's coronation in 1953. In Langelaan's story—itself a blend of horror and sci-fi—television is employed as a metaphor to describe the process of transmission between one form and another, domestic technology here standing in for the biological process. It is clear than that the source story is more interested in the technical apparatus of teleportation than the biological process; the "Fly" here is a terrible (and tragic) mistake, warning audiences about the unintended consequences of rapid technological change.

Set in France, the story is told in the first person, similar to the flashback device used in *Double Indemnity* (1944), as a young woman, Helene, recounts her "crime" to her brother-in-law, François. And like in that film, we begin with a telephoned confession. In this "pupa" text of what would eventually evolve into Cronenberg's *Fly,*

Langelaan uses that domestic technology as the crucible for his teleportation device, the telephone call box—just five years later, on the eve of John F. Kennedy's assassination, that same call box would transport a new kind of mad scientist throughout time and space in the BBC television series *Doctor Who* (1963–). Helene is the wife of a man forged in modernity, the self-proclaimed genius Professor Andre Delambre. In secret, and as a sideline to his classified government work, Andre has created the first teleportation device. Helene's tragic fable recounts to readers how, in incremental stages, her husband is now ready to share his research in classic 1950s sci-fi fashion—that is, in non-peer-reviewed spheres.

After a disastrous attempt to teleport Dandelo (the couple's cat), Andre experiments on himself but does not realize a house fly has also entered the callbox. In a series of tragic events, which cause Helene to be committed to an asylum and eventually lead to her suicide, Andre's experiments produce two new beings: a human with a fly head and hand/arm (fused with what was left of poor Dandelo) and a fly with a human head and hand. Both of these creatures (or versions) presciently predict the two filmed adaptation/remakes.

The Holometabolous Adaptation

The term "holometabolous" describes the development of an insect as a complete biological transformation and is used here as a metaphor to frame Kurt Neumann's transformation of his source material. *The Fly* is an example of a synchronous adaptation, coming just a year after the initial publication of Langelaan's short story in *Playboy* and in the same year the piece was re-published as an example of the best contemporary sci-fi writing. Considering the popularity of *The Magazine of Fantasy and Science Fiction*, it would be fair to say that a sizeable audience would have read the source material either before or immediately after watching the adaptation. Now considered a 1950s B-movie classic, *The Fly* features an actor synonymous with the horror genre, Vincent Price. Staying surprisingly close to the source material, the film also employs a flashback device, as Helene recounts how she came to kill her husband—a type of assisted suicide, we will eventually learn. Brother-in-law François tells the police that that the happily married Andre and Helen "wouldn't harm anything. Not even a fly"—ironic here, the line is used to chilling effect a few years later in the closing scene of Alfred Hitchcock's *Psycho* (1960).

The film opens with non-diegetic "buzz" string effect sounds, and the opening titles resemble a hive, which suggests a level of biological infidelity at least—it seems any buzzing creature will do. The Disintegrator/Integrator device, as it is described, is now rendered as two large metal pods—directly recalling the "pupa" phase of a fly's life cycle. Its instrument panel is pure 1950s sci-fi, with large switches, levers, dials, gauges and the inevitable reel-to-reel computer tape machine. Recognizable to audiences of the era as the new IBM 700/7000 series, mainframe computers were the subject of many news and magazine features from 1952 onward; readers and audiences were confronted with a new technological aesthetic of large rooms full of gray boxes covered in winking lights and reel-to-reel spools whirring away.

Figure 13. Technicians working with an IBM type 704 electronic data processing machine (Wikipedia).

As with the source story, television is again employed as a signature metaphor to explain the teleportation process, and in so doing, reduces a fully biological form to that of an image or radio frequency. As with the source story, early experiments with the teleportation device are not a success, with decorative writing on a transported plate being reversed (in Langelaan's version, the words "Made in Japan" are inverted on a teleported ashtray). Again, Dandelo the cat comes to a sticky end. While directly addressing her anxiety around rapid technological progress, Andre's wife, Helene, confesses her fear of the "suddenness of our age." The ever-present fly (heard but not seen) finally sneaks back into its man-made pupa and is fused with Andre and he attempts to teleport his own body in a grand act of hubristic scientific rationalism.

Teleportation has been used liberally by sci-fi writers since Edward Page Mitchell's 1877 story "The Man Without a Body" to overcome the problem of moving characters through/across large distances in time and space—a trajectory which would eventually result in H.G. Wells' *The Time Machine* a few years later in 1895 and (literally) with the TARDIS[3] in 1963. The genre-defining television serial *Star Trek* (1966–69) would make the most of the storytelling possibilities of teleportation, sometimes adding its own time-travel element in episodes such as "All Our Yesterdays" (1969). *Star Trek* was created in more colorful and optimistic times, however; sci-fi from the more immediate post-war period was far more interested in what could go wrong.

Film scholars such as Michael Bliss estimate that 182 sci-fi films were produced in the United States between 1950 and 1959. Bliss also notes that "the supposedly placid 1950s were haunted by the stuff of nightmares" (8). The political context of the era is often cited as the reason for the themes of technophobia, invasion and paranoia, mobilized by the sci-fi movies of the era: "American science fiction films operated as projections of US anxieties about communist infiltration" (Jones 13). For Melvin E. Matthews,

> Americans became accustomed to living in an atomic world and all that went with it: bomb tests, civil defence messages and drills, maps of the United States showing those places the Russians would likely attack, and maps of New York and other big cities showing the levels of destruction from the center of an atomic blast [79].

The rise of totalitarian powers in the post-war period certainly provided fertile ground for sci-fi writers, and there is no doubt that the 1950s was a grim period for some—in the UK, food rationing did not end until 1954. However, the discovery of DNA in 1953 perhaps was far more influential on *The Fly* and further extends the biological interpretation of its "afterlife" (Benjamin); for the first time, the human body had been reduced to *code*, flesh had been transformed into the helix. The 1950s was a decade defined by medical firsts, as just a year later the first human organ transplant was successfully carried out. For some, these biological advances were terrifying, and, as Gonder reflects, "it should be no surprise that these fears concerning reproduction, mutation, and monstrous disobedient bodies would find expression in the horror film."

By the 1950s, cinema itself was under attack. In 1952, new government legislation forced movie studios to divest themselves of their own cinema chains. While cinema had boomed as a medium during the war years, by the 1950s weekly attendances at picture houses was in steep decline. Indeed, as Martin Halliwell notes, "the fiercest cultural rivalry of the 1950s was between the established film industry and the emerging medium of television" (147). No wonder, then, that *The Fly* was shot on new anamorphic lenses, collectively called Cinemascope, and in DeLuxe Color as a means to offer a new widescreen image and a vibrant color palette to tell its terrifying story as a counter to television's narrow screen and monochrome flicker. Its sequel, *The Return of the Fly* (1959), would be shot on far cheaper black-and-white film.

So while it should not be a surprise that Langelaan's source story paints such a terrible picture of the result of the mixing up of organs and limbs, Andre's transformation in the filmed adaptation is truly horrific. As in the Langelaan source text, the result is two new beings: a human-fly and a fly-human—a complete if unequal exchange between human and insect, a holometabolous adaptation. David Hedison's Andre is left with an insect head and arm, and the fly now sprouts a human head and hand. Andre must now hide in his laboratory, leaving Helene (Patricia Owens) to do the explaining, only appearing to his wife with his head and arm covered by a black cloth. Decades later, another filmmaker interested in deformity, David Lynch, would use a similar black cloth to hide the features of John/Joseph Merrick in his biopic

The Elephant Man (1980). Even with his new features hidden in this way, Hedison's frame is effectively imposing, as he gesticulates with his one good arm and careens about his laboratory. Sound is employed to great effect, particularly when he needs to "feed" from under his cloth. Perhaps the most chilling moment of the whole feature is when Hedison's deep baritone voice is reduced to a tinny shriek coming from the garden—a viscerally unpleasant scene, marking perhaps the moment where horror and sci-fi truly blended to really gruesome effect.

The Hemimetabolous Remake

In biological terms, an incomplete metamorphosis is described as "hemimetabolous" and is here used to describe *The Fly*'s 1986 remake. David Cronenberg's version of *The Fly* directly cites George Langelaan's short story as the source material and so in one sense could be called an adaptation. It is perhaps then worthwhile to spend some time on why this film is a remake, although one with some marked differences from its predecessor. These alterations may have been made for sound narrative reasons, as Thomas Leitch notes: "Kurt Neumann's original version of *The Fly* (1958) was structured as a mystery…. But since such a structure would be less effective for the remake of a well-known story, David Cronenberg's 1986 version of *The Fly* employs a much more linear structure" (42).

First of all, it is not unusual for remakes to attempt to efface other versions in the same media by framing the original film's source material as its inspiration. This is especially the case with American remakes of French cinema (see Mazdon). In this way, "rather than creating new audiences for their source films, remakes typically seek to overshadow or even efface them" (27). So instead of bringing the original film into a circuit of influence, the remake shuts it out—a phenomena rendered pointless when the streaming era a few decades later would loop Neuman's 1958 film into any EPG search for *The Fly*, gaining a new textual afterlife through new models of digital distribution. Second, the original film is so "faithful" to its source material (a biologically complete transformation) that separating the two would be as futile as Helene's misguided attempts to reverse Andre's transformation.

From his debut feature in 1969 with *Stereo*, Cronenberg had always written his own screenplays, based on original ideas—although encompassing many of the same themes of body modification, sexual transgression and the breakdown of social order. For William Beard, "Cronenberg's world has always been characterized by philosophical pessimism, intellectual schizophrenia, and horror and sadness in the emotional sphere." His period of adapting/remaking other works really began just prior to filming *The Fly* with 1983's *The Dead Zone*—based on a Stephen King novel. This era marked a rich sextet of adaptations/remakes, spanning almost two decades, right up until 1999's *Existenz*. Cronenberg's interest in adaptation/remaking should not come as too much of a surprise, because as a filmmaker, he has always been interested in both textual and bodily transition: "David Cronenberg's career of film adaptation then functions as a practical application of his thematic fascination with augmentation, mutating one narrative body into another" (Milligan).

In interviews, Cronenberg would often cite Burroughs and Vladimir Nabokov as his literary heroes (see Beard 287), and this middle period of his work can be viewed as a filmmaker taking stock of a body of work, pressing pause, and reflecting on their earlier career. In 1958, when George Langelaan's short story was re-published and Kurt Neumann's adaptation made its debut in movie theaters, David Cronenberg was fifteen years old and living in Toronto, Canada. Colin McGinn points out that most people feel an aversion to flies and insects, which is gleefully reflected in Cronenberg's film: "*The Fly* is an emblem of our mortal organic condition, our connection to the world of biological process: digestion, dying, the soft and the slimy" (11). But the teenage Cronenberg had a keen interest in lepidopterology and botany, which would later lead him to enrolling in a science program at the University of Toronto in 1963. So it can be stated fairly assuredly that the adolescent future filmmaker (and cinema obsessive) must have a least known of *The Fly*'s existence in one form or another.

The poster for the original version is interesting, as it features a close-up of Patricia Owens (as Helene) screaming—an image more in common with the horror genre than sci-fi and again one which could also have further inspired the poster for Hitchcock's *Psycho* (1960). In examining what Jonathan Gray terms the "paratext"— an "off screen studies … a screen studies that focuses on paratexts' constitutive role in creating textuality" (7)—it is clear that the original movie was marketed in a way to play up its shock qualities. The teenage Cronenberg may even have seen this poster—or a later one featuring David Hedison's malformed hand—while bicycling around 1950s Toronto. The poster for his own remake is a little more ambiguous; at first glance it looks like sci-fi text, with its "pod" and ambient light emanating from it, perhaps reminding audiences of *Cocoon* (1985) from the previous year. However, the infamous tagline "Be afraid. Be very afraid"—spoken by Geena Davis' Ronnie

Figure 14. Shot from the partially transformed Andre's (David Hedison) multi-faceted point of view, Helene Delambre (Patricia Owens) screams as she sees Andre's insect head clearly. The individual image of Helene's screaming face is recreated on the original movie poster for *The Fly* (1958) (Twentieth Century–Fox/Photofest).

Figure 15. The movie poster for *The Fly* (1986) (20th Century–Fox/Photofest).

in the film—and the green tinge of the ambient light puts the film (paratextually, at least) very much in the territory occupied by another movie which effectively blends horror and sci-fi, *Alien* (1979).

Cronenberg's version seems far more interested in flesh and the potential of the human body to remake itself than technology; his "telepods even look like chrysalises—suggesting that his teenage interests in moths and butterflies are still percolating." His protagonist, Seth Brundle, is not here to warn us about a highly technologized future, where men can finally play God, but, as he puts it in the movie, "society's deep fear of the flesh." Cronenberg's film is an asynchronous remake made three decades after the original and exhibited in an era so hungry for the new that audiences would now know Hedison's co-star, Vincent Price, for his chilling voiceover as a coda to Michael Jackson's 1984 song "Thriller" than for his role in *The Fly*. Price, by the way, would later give the view that Cronenberg's version of the story "went a bit too far" (*IMDB*).

The remake is set in contemporary '80s America. Jeff Goldblum's performance of Seth Brundle is as a rather odd and lonely scientist, a counter to Hedison's strident pioneer. In this telling, he is not married but has a love interest (and later girlfriend) in Geena Davis' Ronnie, a crusading journalist firmly in the Lois Lane mold. Their flirting provides many comic moments; at one point Seth attempts to teleport one of Ronnie's stockings. Seth is far more amusing than the straitlaced and suited 1950s Andre: "In *Fly*, Jeff Goldblum performs manic stand-up comedy" (Roth 230). Ronnie is attracted to Seth's genial eccentricity, a counter to her more 1980s corporate incarnate and conventional ex-boyfriend and boss, Stathis Borans (John Getz). For Beard, "Cronenberg's later male protagonists are repeatedly driven from their isolation by the proddings of sexual instinct and the yearning for emotional connection."

There is no cat this time but a monkey (a nod to the early days of the space program, perhaps), which, unlike Dandelo, comes to a very messy *on-screen* end—a deleted scene from the original cut features a cat/baboon hybrid, which was eventually beaten to death by the scientist, a scene which did not work well with test audiences. Seth sticks with metaphors of flesh when describing how his computer "translates and rethinks [meat] … rather than reproducing it," which perfectly encapsulates Cronenberg's own relationship with his source material and his approach to remaking the 1950s version. At one point Seth articulates his ambition to teach his computer to "go crazy" about flesh. Although Cronenberg eschews the cheap tricks of the original—with all of the off-screen buzzing (both diegetic and non-diegetic)—Ronnie does employ insect metaphors to describe her relationships with Stathis: "I still have the residue of another life, you know. I have to get rid of it and scrape it off my shoe."

Seth's transformation, when it comes, is something of an anti-climax; there is no obvious visual clue that the teleportation process has been anything other than a complete success—although the audience has seen the fly enter the pod and presumably knows what is coming. But "what arrives is not what departs but merely a resembling object" (Snowdon 57). Instead, Cronenberg is keen for his audience to watch the slow metamorphosis into "Brundlefly"—something that was off screen in the original movie:

Whereas in Cronenberg's *Fly* of 1986 a fully computerised teleportation creates the fusion of human and fly into one entity—the "Brundlefly"—the transformative catastrophe of the 50s versions yields two metamorphs a fly-headed human and a human-headed fly [Clarke 185].

The first signs of trouble are thick black hairs growing through Seth's skin, seen in gleeful close-up as if viewed through a microscope. In one scene which surely directly references the original movie, Seth shovels sugar into his coffee—the sweetener being used to attract the human-headed fly in the 1958 adaptation. Gradually, Seth's heightened physical abilities become more apparent, as well as his increased sexual appetite. In scenes which could never have been filmed in 1958, Cronenberg's remake depicts extended bouts of lovemaking once Seth and Ronnie finally commit to each other. As Seth's body begins to change, the camera revels in close-ups of flesh and skin—there are no black cloths here to spare audiences of the metamorphosis. If the comic-book hero genre is defined by it characters coming to terms with their abilities, Seth skips a step and dismembers a man in a bar's arm-wrestling contest.

The film's eventual tag line (uttered by Ronnie), "Be afraid. Be very afraid," marks the moment when the exhilaration of Seth's new body gives way to the full horror of his transformation; his skin begins to weep/leak and nails fall off his increasingly elongated fingers—both the 1958 and 1986 versions are interested in limbs and hands. Jeff Goldblum's Seth tries to hide these adaptations with gloves, as does Hedison's Andre. Cronenberg's fly is not a "complete" exchange between two entities but a "fused" being composed of both fly and human—but being neither human *nor* fly. This incomplete (or hemimetabolous) translation between human and insect is described by Seth as being "spliced together." He eventually needs to augment his biology with walking sticks, technology now providing his needed extra limbs, once the biological process has all but played out. Rejected human body parts (such as ears) are kept and curated, as Seth attempts to keep the conceit of scientific discovery alive.

In this last third of the film, Seth begins to describe his condition as an illness or disease: "It wants to turn me into something else," which McGinn also notes: "[T]he story is a metaphor for aging and with it the diseases of aging" (14). Ronnie's pregnancy adds a *Demon Seed* (1977) dimension to the film, and the dream sequence where her graphic abortion procedure results in a pupa being removed from her body foreshadows Cronenberg's next movie *Dead Ringers* (1988) and more directly the sequel *The Fly II*. Like Franz Kafka in his *Metamorphosis*, Cronenberg is much more interested in the aftermath of Seth's transformation into an insect—something which the Langelaan short story and 1958 adaptation only briefly concern themselves with and then only through flashback. Stathis, now in full newsman mode, senses a potential publishing coup but is thoroughly disgusted when he watches a film of Brundlefly feeding—the same scene is mirrored in the original film, but Andre's head remains hooded throughout. Here Cronenberg and Charles David Pogue's screenplay gets closest to Kafka, in having Seth utter surely the movie's most moving lines (to Ronnie): "I'm saying that I'm an insect who dreamt he was a man and loved it. But now the dream is over and the insect is awake…. I'm saying…. I'll hurt you if I stay."

If Mary Shelley's *Frankenstein* gave us both the sci-fi genre and the mad scientist in 1818, then Cronenberg surely remembers that novel's "Modern Prometheus" subtitle in the (uncharacteristically for him) unsubtle staging of his Gothic ending—as Brundlefly looks down from his tower, after capturing Ronnie from a doctor's office where she is seeking an abortion. His desperate "cure" is to first attempt a three-way splice (another stage of holometabolous adaptation), initially with Stathis and then with Ronnie and their unborn child, before finally shedding his skin completely and completing his evolution into a hybrid insectoid human: "*The Fly* features a ... horrific turning away from science and subsequent liberating but ultimately destructive descent into the darker recesses of the self" (Palmer 188).

Brundlefly is finally fused with his own machine—now looking more like a medieval torture device such as an Iron Maiden rather than a technology with limitless possibilities. He asks Ronnie's help in his own assisted suicide, ending this film where the 1958 one began and in doing so predicting a new biological *post*-human (or augmented reality) era. If the 1958 movie warns humanity about the perils of playing God, then the '80s remake presciently predicts this era's social media obsession with transformation, reinvention and body image. While our mobile phones and digital devices use facial recognition technology—marketed to users as a more convenient security protection—*The Fly* becomes a parable, its corollary in George Langelaan's original story. In a hyper-mediated culture of "selfies" and Instagram filters, the scene where Seth's computer fails to recognize Seth Brundle's new augmented reality speaks to the superficiality of our image-conscious era—mirrored in the way Cronenberg's film (deliberately) mis-recognizes the 1958 original.

Fly-Trap

David Cronenberg was a teenager in the 1950s, and his remake of *The Fly* filters the concerns of that decade and maps them onto more contemporary anxieties about disease and post-humanity. The 1950s was also a decade defined by classic sci-fi films, many of them concerned with the future and a fear of technology, dozens being remade in the years to come. Has there been a decade since which provided such fertile ground for remaking, adapting and repurposing—all broadly from the same genre? Both the 1958 and 1986 versions of *The Fly* became themselves source material (or "pupa") for sequels. *The Return of the Fly* (1959) is something of a curio; coming hard on the heels of the original movie, it is shot in black and white and features Vincent Price reprising his role as François, the brother of Andre from the earlier version. *The Curse of the Fly* (1965) marked something of a continuity departure as it was produced in the UK. Still featuring members of the Delambre family (this time, Andre's grandson, Martin), the film was something of a lost text, never getting a VCR release and having to wait until 2007 to be included in a DVD boxset with all its textual relations—including Cronenberg's remake and its sequel.

The unimaginatively titled *The Fly II*, the sequel to Cronenberg's work, mirrors the progeny focus of both *Return* and *Curse of the Fly*; Eric Stoltz is Seth and Ronnie's son, Martin—a reference perhaps to Andre's grandson in *Curse*. Martin's birth scene takes its beat from Ronnie's dream sequence in the Cronenberg version, as he is delivered in a larvae sack. This version of the story amps up the gore but has very little of Cronenberg's finesse, dark humor or body aesthetic. It was unpopular with critics and Cronenberg fans alike, and if it had been conceived in any other period, it may also have become another lost text like *Curse*, but the EPG of the streaming era now acts as a gateway to oft-forgotten versions. Any search for "Fly" on Netflix or Amazon Prime naturally calls back into existence and traps other films with that word in the title. EPG algorithms loop into their searches other work by David Cronenberg, as well as films featuring Jeff Goldblum, Geena Davis, David Hedison, Vincent Price, and Eric Stoltz. The 21st century saw further mutations of the story, with Cronenberg himself directing an operatic version in 2008 and Brandon Siefert and Menton3's 2015 five-part comic book series, *The Fly: Outbreak*, set directly after events in *The Fly II*.

In the streaming era, a remake can no longer efface the original version and now has to live alongside it in ways perhaps not imagined by the creators. This has significant implications for scholars of adaptation and remaking culture, as inevitable comparative strategies will be enacted by audiences. Fans of *Homeland* (2011–2020) and *Euphoria* (2019–) will be directly educated by their television, tablet or laptop that they are in fact watching remakes of Israeli television serials. In *Netflix Nations*, Ramon Lobato describes the ways in which "[t]itles appear and disappear and catalogues shrink and expand, as the platform is accessed from different points of the world" (14).

Figure 16. A meme humorously reappraising *The Return of the Fly* (1959) (Imageflip, https://imgflip.com/i/17643d).

Cronenberg's film now exists in a sphere of influence with all other versions of *The Fly* and attendant paratexts. George Langelaan's short story is very easy to find online and will be out of copyright in 2042. Cronenberg's movie is scattered across *YouTube* in hundreds of fractured eight- to ten-minute clips, with each click calling up dozens of related documentaries which dissect the film, and video reappraisals made by people who were not born in the century both *Fly* movies were created in. These new audiences, used to the promiscuous possibilities of streaming platforms, are entirely comfortable in creating their own commentary films which compare and contrast Cronenberg's film with the original but not in ways bound to any fidelity values. On social media platforms, comparative approaches can be more playful and egalitarian, with some meme creators explicitly referencing what Cronenberg's film has to say about our image-obsessed era. Creators of memes enact almost oppositional fidelity approaches that adaptation and remaking culture scholars could learn a great deal from; Bradley E. Wiggins and G. Bret Bowers have claimed that "people create memes as part of a larger albeit idealized conversation where their contribution might be noticed and remixed further.... Members of participatory digital culture *want* [original italics] their revisions of memetic content to be remixed, iterated, and distributed further as memes."

As a metaphor for remaking culture, Cronenberg's film demonstrates that adaptation is a highly biological—and therefore "natural"—process in popular culture. Now seen as the godfather of body horror by a new generation of filmmakers and audiences, Cronenberg is a filmmaker whose work others are remaking—his 1997 feature *Rabid* was remade in 2019. His remake of *The Fly* also demonstrates how the decade of the 1950s *remade* him, transforming a budding amateur scientist into a celebrated artist; we are all capable of personal transformation, if we dare....

NOTES

1. See Snowdon.
2. See Matthews, Bliss and Jones.
3. Doctor Who's infamous time machine is a "Type 40" TARDIS (Time and Relative Dimension in Space)—forever in the guise of a police call box since its "chameleon circuit" jammed.

WORKS CITED

Beard, William. *The Artist as Monster: The Cinema of David Cronenberg*. University of Toronto Press, 2001.

Beard, William. "Cronenburg, Flyness, and the Other-self." *Cinemas: Journal of Film Studies*, vol. 14, no. 2, 1994, pp. 153–72.

Benjamin, Walter. *Illuminations*. Bodley Head, 2015.

Bliss, Michael. *Invasions USA: The Essential Science Fiction Films of the 1950s*. Rowman & Littlefield, 2014.

Chapman, Edmund. *The Afterlife of Texts in Translation: Understanding the Messianic in Literature*. Palgrave Macmillan, 2019.

Clarke, Bruce. "Mediating *The Fly*: Posthuman Metamorphosis in the 1950s." *Configurations*, no. 10, 2002 pp. 169–91.

Gonder, Patrick. "Like a Monstrous Jigsaw Puzzle: Genetic and Race Horror Films of the 1950s." *Velvet Light Trap*, no. 52, pp. 33–44.

Gray, Jonathan. *Show Sold Separately: Promos, Spoilers and Other Media Paratexts*. New York University Press, 2010.

Halliwell, Martin. *American Culture in the 1950s*. Edinburgh University Press, 2007.

Herbert, Daniel. *Film Remakes and Franchises*. Rutgers University Press, 2017.

Jones, Matthew. *Science Fiction Cinema and 1950s Britain: Recontextualising Cultural Anxiety*. Bloomsbury, 2018.

Leitch, Thomas. "Twice Told Tales: Disavowal and the Rhetoric of the Remake." *Dead Ringers: The Remake in Theory and Practice*, edited by Jennifer Forrest and Leonard R. Koos. State University of New York, 2002, pp. 37–62.

Lobato, Ramon. *Netflix Nations: The Geography of Digital Distribution*. New York University Press, 2019.

Mathijs, Ernest. "AIDS References in the Critical Reception of David Cronenberg: 'It May Not Be Such a Bad Disease after All.'" *Cinema Journal*, vol. 42, no. 4, 2003, pp. 29–45.

Matthews, Melvin, E. *1950s Science Fiction Films and 9/11: Hostile Aliens, Hollywood and Today's News*. Algora, 2007.

Mazdon, Lucy. "Disrupting the Remake: The Girl with the Dragon Tattoo." *Transnational Remakes*, edited by Iain Robert Smith and Constantine Verevis. Edinburgh University Press, 2017, pp. 21–35.

Mazdon, Lucy. *Encore Hollywood: Remaking French Cinema*. British Film Institute. 2000.

McGinn, Colin. "The Fly and the Human: Ironies of Disgust." *The Philosophy of David Cronenberg*, edited by Simon Riches. University Press of Kentucky, 2012, pp. 9–23.

Milligan, Caleb. "Uncomfortable in the New Flesh: Adapting Body Horror in the Cinema of David Cronenberg." *Trespassing Journal*, no. 6, 2017, pp. 28–43.

Palmer, R. Barton. "The Politics of Mad Science in *The Fly* and *Dead Ringers*." *The Philosophy of David Cronenberg*, edited by Simon Riches. University Press of Kentucky, 2012, pp. 175–95.

Roth, Marty. "Twice Two: *The Fly* and *Invasion of the Body Snatchers*." *Dead Ringers: The Remake in Theory and Practice*, edited by Jennifer Forrest and Leonard R. Koos. State University of New York, 2002, pp. 225–41.

Snowdon, Paul, F. "What Happens to Brundle? Problems of Teleportation and Personal Identity in *The Fly*." *The Philosophy of David Cronenberg*, edited by Simon Riches. University Press of Kentucky, 2012, pp. 53–65.

Wiggins, Bradley E., and G. Bret Bowers. "Memes as Genre: A Structurational Analysis of the Memescape." *New Media & Society*, vol. 17, no. 11, 2015, pp. 1886–906.

Woolf, Virginia. "The Cinema," in *Collected Papers* (Volume Two). Hogarth Press, 1966.

Filmography

Adaptation. Dir. Spike Jonze. Colombia Pictures, 2002. Film.

Alien. Dir. Ridley Scott. 20th Century Fox, 1979. Film.

Crash. Dir. David Cronenberg. Alliance Communications, 1996. Film.

The Curse of the Fly. Dir. Don Sharp. 20th Century Fox, 1965. Film.

Dead Ringers. Dir David Cronenberg. 20th Century Fox, 1988. Film.

The Dead Zone. Dir. David Cronenberg. Paramount Pictures, 1983. Film.

Demon Seed. Dir. Donald Cammell. United Artists, 1977. Film.

Doctor Who. BBC, 1963–Present. TV Series.

Double Indemnity. Dir. Billy Wilder. Paramount Pictures, 1944. Film.

The Elephant Man. Dir. David Lynch. Paramount Pictures, 1980. Film.

Euphoria. HBO, 2019–Present. TV Series.

Existenz. Dir. David Cronenberg. Momentum Pictures, 1999. Film.

The Fly. Dir. Kurt Neumann. 20th Century Fox, 1958. Film.

The Fly. Dir. David Cronenberg. 20th Century Fox, 1986. Film.

The Fly II. Dir. Chris Wallas. 20th Century Fox, 1989. Film.

Homeland. 20th Television, 2011–2020. TV Series.

Naked Lunch. Dir. David Cronenberg. 20th Century Fox, 1991. Film.

Psycho. Dir. Alfred Hitchcock. Paramount Pictures, 1960. Film.

The Return of the Fly. Dir. Edward Bernds. 20th Century Fox, 1959. Film.

Star Trek. CBS Studios, 1966–1969. TV Series.

Stereo. Dir. David Cronenberg. Film Canada Presentations, 1969. Film.

Adapting the Monstrous Other

del Toro Re-Shapes Creature from the Black Lagoon

GLENN JELLENIK

"[The Creature from the Black Lagoon] just needed a little affection—
a sense of being loved and needed and wanted."
—Marilyn Monroe, *The Seven Year Itch*

Early in *Creature from the Black Lagoon* (1954), ichthyologist Dr. David Reed (Richard Carlson) describes his professional mission: "By studying [the lungfish] and other species, we add to our knowledge of how life evolved, how it adapted itself to this world. With that knowledge, perhaps we can teach men to adapt themselves to some new world of the future." Right at the outset, then, we see another Cold War–era movie implicitly concerned with negotiating a changing world (due to shifting political landscapes and apocalyptic nuclear fears) and explicitly concerned with biological adaptation. This essay, of course, is concerned with cultural adaptation, but as Gary Bortolotti and Linda Hutcheon point out, "a homology [exists] between biological and cultural adaptation … both kinds of adaptation are understandable as processes of replication. Stories, in a manner parallel to genes, replicate; the adaptations of both evolve with changing environments" (444). Simply put, the idea (and necessity) of adapting to a perpetually changing world is just as applicable to cultural adaptation as it is to biological adaptation, just as inevitable for the stories that make up cultural memories as it is for genes that make up biological organisms.

This essay positions Guillermo del Toro's *The Shape of Water* (2017) as a revisionist adaptation of *Creature from the Black Lagoon* (Arnold, 1954). Leo Braudy calls remakes (and, by extension, adaptations) "meditation[s] on the continuing historical relevance (economic, cultural, psychological) of a particular narrative. A remake is thus always concerned with what its makers and (they hope) its audiences consider to be unfinished cultural business" (331). del Toro's film recycles narrative and mise-en-scenic elements from *Creature from the Black Lagoon* and in doing so conducts unfinished cultural business. In particular, I explore the productive ways that *Shape* reimagines, recasts, and revises cultural concepts of otherness and monstrousness.

The adaptation pivots directly away from *Creature*'s presentation of Gill-man as both Other and monster, ultimately transforming him from a titillating curiosity to a protagonist. In interviews del Toro has described his immediate attraction and affinity for the Creature: "The creature was the most beautiful design I'd ever seen, and I saw him swimming under [actress] Julie Adams, and I loved that the creature was in love with her, and I felt an almost existential desire for them to end up together. Of course, it didn't happen" (Kit). The Creature's tragic fate was prescribed by 1950s sci-fi concepts of otherness and monstrousness, concepts that *The Shape of Water* both questions and revises. But that revision of a classic creature feature narrative does more than offer del Toro's desired happy ending for the Creature; *Shape* also inverts the hero/villain dialectic. It re-thinks concepts of Otherness/monstrousness by de-Othering and centering the Creature (Doug Jones) as a paradigmatic hero and casting the traditional hegemonic power, Colonel Strickland (Michael Shannon), as an Othered avatar of toxic masculinity, a monster bent on destroying love (as well as anything and everything different than himself). By extension, the film also de-Others a set of characters traditionally marginalized by both Hollywood and American society. The adaptation re-fits an old story to a new world. By reading forward—that is, by thinking about the ways that the adaptive changes tap into contemporary socio-political concerns—it becomes possible to use *Shape* as a barometer, to measure changes or "evolutions" in society.

Where its source is a horror-tinged cautionary tale, the adaptation is a fantasy of wish fulfillment, a revisionist adaptation that seeks to "fix" the past. In order to "teach men to adapt themselves to some new world of the future," the period piece replaces tone-deaf 1950s values on race, difference, gender, sexuality, and disability with twenty-first-century values. As such, the activist adaptation re-interprets its source to redirect, contradict, and/or correct many social investments, thereby subverting the source's treatment of those traditional themes. In the end, *The Shape of Water* re-tells, re-locates, and re-positions *Creature from the Black Lagoon* in order to unwind reactionary twentieth-century American attitudes. With regard to unfinished cultural business, the adaptation's release into a post–Trump America suggests that those attitudes persist in the 21st century. An inspection of *Shape* as cultural adaptation accepts the text's invitation to flesh out and explore a set of twenty-first-century socio-political priorities in relief against a contrasting ideological backdrop.

Method: Reading Adaptations Through the Windshield

From the perspective of methodology and the critical discourse on adaptation, this study employs what I call the windshield approach to reading adaptations. The windshield approach prioritizes reading adaptations forward, thinking about the changes that occur as opportunities to consider the socio-political conditions out of which the text sprung and into which it was first received. It contrasts with the (fidelity-adjacent) rearview approach, which considers adaptive changes as invitations to look back at a source's decisions and investments. The rearview approach employs the adaptation as an opportunity to further investigate the source, the windshield approach as a chance to explore the adaptation's present.

The windshield approach is a twist on New Historicism. New Historicism (a term coined by Stephen Greenblatt, or, as Greenblatt renamed/adapted it, Cultural Poetics) argues, among other things, that imaginative texts are forged and shaped not merely in the singular minds of storytellers but also by the collective matrix of socio-historical contingencies that accompany the specific moment of their production. As such, texts like novels and films function as cultural artifacts, not merely in a personal or individual capacity but also in a macro-historical, reflective, rearview-mirror capacity. For example, Nancy Armstrong uses the lens of New Historicism to position the domestic novel of the eighteenth and nineteenth centuries as the (missing) political history of women. She challenges the assumption of "political history" as consisting only of officially sanctioned public political and economic events, because as most of the moment's public events excluded women, women's voices, choices, and fates would be necessarily left out of such a history. Armstrong and other New Historicists open their consideration to the historical capacity of creative output: "[W]e must read fiction not as literature but as the history of gender differences" (581). To the New Historicist, cultural artifacts such as literary texts and films function as historical incursions expressive of historical knowledge and perspective; the domestic becomes political, and the published becomes indistinguishable from the public.

Considered from a New Historicist angle, adaptations present an interesting critical opportunity in that they exert a sort of double presence, holding the capacity to reflect (at least) two historical moments, one traditional (source) and one innovative (adaptation). With that in mind, adaptations offer unique access to what I call Now Historicism, the critical ability to use adaptations to chart and explore, through the windshield, an immediate contemporary socio-political landscape. The fact that the adaptation exerts a double presence—that it occupies, in a sense, (at least) two moments—allows a focus on the specific changes as they concern not the source text but rather the moment in which the adaptation was produced and initially consumed. A film like *The Invisible Man* (2020) leaps to mind. It directly engages with tradition and innovation by using a previous work (or works) as a springboard to rehearse and process the concerns and anxieties of its (#MeToo) moment.[1] Many adaptive changes to Wells' short novel (1897) and/or Whale's movie (1933) relate directly to socio-political and economic issues, changes, anxieties, and principles present in 2020. Practicing adaptation criticism through the windshield and engaging with Now Historicism offers opportunities to tap into one of the most alluring aspects of adaptation (for practitioners and critics): its very structure allows (and inherently invites) the consideration and processing of the evolution of ideas through time, as they adapt themselves to an ever-changing world.

Viewing Creature's Features Through the Windshield

On one level, *Creature from the Black Lagoon* is a fun, Cold War sci-fi movie, perhaps the paradigmatic example of what 1960s television would dub the "creature feature." As Milton Luban put it in his 1954 *Hollywood Reporter* review of the film, "*The Creature from the Black Lagoon* is a good piece of sci-fi from the beauty and the beast school, the beast in this case being a monstrous combination of man and fish. It makes for solid horror-thrill entertainment" (Luban). Obviously though, even (especially?) fun creature features do work in the culture. So what work does *Creature* do? Specifically, how does the Creature and his story reflect the anxieties and concerns of the movie's moment of production and initial consumption?

The film's opening illustrates its investments. A voiceover from Genesis accompanies the Earth shrouded in mist: "In the beginning, God created the heaven and the earth. And the earth was without form and void." The planet then explodes, and the shot cuts to Earth amidst clouds. Now the voiceover pivots from biblical to scientific creation: "This is the planet Earth, newly born, and cooling rapidly from a temperature of 6,000 degrees to a few hundred in less than 5 billion years.... Now in the warm depths [of the sea] the miracle of life begins.... Living things appear and change and reach the land." The immediate rehearsal of tensions between science and religion signals that the film functions within the genre of sci-fi.

In 1950s sci-fi, the restoration of order tends to be driven by either the military (physical), science (intellectual), or some combination of the two. That is, military might comes to the rescue of impotent (and self-destructive) science, or science comes to the aid of out-of-control martial urges, or the two join forces in a balanced attack. As such, each restoration of order endorses a specific brand of masculinity.

These dynamics are manifest in *Creature*. Though no overt military aspect exists, we do have a face-off between the industrial capitalist, Dr. Mark Williams, played by Richard Denning and the scientist, Dr. David Reed, played by Richard Carlson. The two fight over the girl (Kay Lawrence, played by Julie Adams) *and* the Creature (Ricou Browning). Here the capitalist functions as the martial character, seeking to dominate and possess, while the scientist advocates an intellectual approach, to understand and do no harm. In the end, the intellectual posits an almost post-colonial approach to American incursions in places like the Amazon. Americans are outsiders in such places, and whether they have good (scientific) or exploitive (capitalist) intentions, the result is tragic. For the capitalist, everything is ours for the taking (girls, indigenous creatures, intellectual property), and if that taking need be violent, so be it. In the end, that version of masculinity is not sanctioned; the more sensitive version wins. And, of course, the Creature, representing the (tragic) Other in the film, is the big loser.

Many critics read *Creature* not through the lens of sci-fi but rather as a monster movie. Such criticism often refers to the Creature as the last of the Universal Classic Monsters, a loosely shared universe of creatures created by the studio in stand-alone films and then marketed in a series of crossovers. The cadre of iconic monsters includes Dracula, Frankenstein, the Mummy, the Invisible Man, the Bride of Frankenstein, and the Werewolf of London. Despite sharing a studio and subsequent iconic status with those monsters, the Creature remains an outlier for several reasons. The most obvious is periodization. While the Creature first appeared in 1954, all the other monsters named above were created by Universal by the mid–1930s. The 19-year gap saw the end of the Great Depression, the outbreak of World War II, the dropping of atomic bombs on Hiroshima and Nagasaki, the end of World War II, the revelation of the Nazi death camps, a cold war, a nuclear arms race, and a sustained economic boom in America. Which is to say, a lot had changed. James Neibaur points out that, with the Creature, Universal "responded to its past legacy of monster movies and adapted that perspective for another type of monster in another setting and a different era" (176). Indeed, the setting functions as another fundamental difference between *Creature from the Black Lagoon* and other Universal horror movies. Unlike those earlier films, *Creature* takes place exclusively in the remote jungles of South America. While *Werewolf of London* (1935) begins with a scientific expedition in the wilds of Tibet, the movie obviously brings its monster to London. This is also true of King Kong, who though not a Universal monster is perhaps the closest corollary to the Creature. But *Kong*, too, begins in the wilds but reaches its climax in a modern city. The Creature never threatens a metropolitan area, never menaces civilization—instead, his home is invaded by the group of scientists. These differences have caught the attention of recent critics: "[T]he film doesn't really belong among the Universal Monsters group at all. If anything it is a rather convenient line in the sand, marking the point where the more Gothic and atmospheric horror of the 1930s and 1940s gave way to the hideous monsters and mutants of the post-atomic 1950s" (Watson). In that way, he functions as a link from Depression-era horror monsters to atomic-age sci-fi monsters.

Indeed, as Neibaur asserts, the Creature is adapted not only to another setting but to another era—specifically, the 1950s. But in this way too, he proves an outlier. Melvin E. Matthews argues that "American terror films become popular entertainment during crisis moments" (3). For example, Hollywood's classic horror period (*Dracula* [1931], *Frankenstein* [1931], etc.) corresponded to the Great Depression. Similarly, Matthews points out, "science fiction was a Hollywood staple during the Cold War, when anxieties about Communist subversion and nuclear war gave rise to stories of extraterrestrials and radiation-sired mutants" (3). While Leonard Maltin refers to *Creature from the Black Lagoon* as the "archetypal 50s monster movie" (298), perhaps *Creature* isn't archetypical at all; perhaps it is a creature feature with a difference.

And that difference has to do with adaptation—in this case biological rather than cultural. In the movie, the Creature enacts a dynamic different from most post-atomic monster movies. In Matthews' terms, those movies posit a threat that is either extraterrestrial (*The Day the Earth Stood Still* [1951], *The Thing from Another World* [1951], *When Worlds Collide* [1951], *It Came from Outer Space* [1953], *The War of the Worlds* [1953], *The Quartermas Xperiment* [1955], *Invasion of the Body Snatchers* [1956], *It Conquered the World* [1956]), or a radiation-sired mutant (*The Magnetic Monster* [1953], *Godzilla* [1954], *Them!* [1954], *Tarantula* [1955], *World Without End* [1956], *X the Unknown* [1956], *Rodan* [1956], *Attack of the Crab Monsters* [1957], *The Amazing Colossal Man* [1957], *The Incredible Shrinking Man* [1957], *It Came from Beneath the Sea* [1957], *Beginning of the End* [1957]). *Creature* has more in common with *King Kong*, in which the "monster" is a naturally occurring species, living in harmony with a remote ecosystem outside of "civilized" human contact. Within the film, the Creature functions as a missing scientific link, an amphibious humanoid,

Figure 17. The Creature (Ben Chapman) menaces the camera in *Creature From the Black Lagoon* (1954). The creature was played by Chapman on land and by Ricou Browning underwater. The suit, which del Toro found "beautiful," was designed and created by a team of artists, including Milicent Patrick, Bud Westmore, Jack Kevan, and Chris Mueller, Jr. (Universal Pictures/Photofest).

a bridge between land and sea animals, unchanged since the Devonian period (419–358 million years ago). So in a way the movie amounts to an encounter with an animal that has never adapted.

In that way, the Creature parallels the less enlightened (evolved?) character of Dr. Mark Williams. Indeed, as indicative as it is with regard to many '50s conventions and tropes, *Creature* should be noted as a film that grapples with its own versions of toxic masculinity. Mark repeatedly makes inappropriate comments to Kay, seeks to undermine her relationship with David, bullies other scientists, and reflexively chooses violence to mediate conflicts with nature. He would rather kill and possess than study and understand. Thus he takes a position alongside the Creature as a threat/obstacle to the narrative's happy ending. Indeed, the coding of Mark's single-minded greed and violence as unacceptable goes a long way toward minimizing the Creature's monstrosity and making him sympathetic to the audience. Still, in the end, the Creature is, as the review cited earlier points out, a beast, a wild thing. And given the text's debt to '50s sci-fi/creature-feature tropes, the restoration of order depends upon him being driven out of the picture.

Adaptation Through the Windshield: Re-Shaping Monstrousness and Toxic Masculinity

But 63 years later, Guillermo del Toro will bring him back into the picture, front and center in *The Shape of Water*. Linda Hutcheon points out that "adapters must have their own personal reasons for deciding first to do an adaptation" (92). del Toro speaks of the genesis of the film in decidedly personal terms:

> I've had this movie in my head since I was 6, not as a story but as an idea. When I saw the creature swimming under Julie Adams, I thought three things: I thought, "Hubba-hubba." I thought, "This is the most poetic thing I'll ever see." I was overwhelmed by the beauty. And the third thing I thought is, "I hope they end up together" [Kit].

Indeed, the director related directly to the Creature: "I loved that the creature was in love with her, and I felt an almost existential desire for them to end up together. Of course, it didn't happen" (Kit). According to Hutcheon, adapters "not only interpret [the source] but in doing so they also take a position on it" (92). When Universal hired del Toro to head a remake of *Creature*, he pitched a revised version: "I said, 'Can we do the movie from the point of view of the creature?' They didn't go for it. I said, 'I think they should end up together.' They didn't go for that, either" (Rottenberg). He left the production in 2002, due to creative differences and scheduling conflicts, and the studio scuttled the entire project in 2012.

But *The Shape of Water*, for del Toro, is a clear return to *Creature from the Black Lagoon*. Just as clearly, it bears out Hutcheon's claim that an adaptation "can obviously be used to engage in a larger social or cultural critique" (94). While many critics immediately seized on the concept of *Shape* as an uncredited adaptation of *Creature*, much of the attention focused on del Toro's obvious shifting of—and playing with—the love story, which actualizes the six-year-old del Toro's fantasy: Elisa (Sally Hawkins) and Gill-man (Doug Jones) end up together. The critical focus on the film's adaptation of the love story is to be expected—the director himself framed it in such terms, and Hollywood loves a love story. But that centering of romance obscures the adaptation's larger ideological shifts, shifts that underpin but also potentially override the coming together of Elisa and Gill-man. Whereas the 1954 source can be read as rehearsing (and endorsing) the tragic fate of difference in post-war America, del Toro's adaptation clearly rehearses alternate fates for difference in twenty-first-century America.

The director refers to such ideological shifts as conscious: "If this was the 1950s … the hero would be Strickland. Strickland represents three things I find terrifying: order, certainty and perfection. He wants those three, which are impossible and they represent the torture of a life, because no human can have any of them" (Gray). While Colonel Strickland's dedication to "order, certainty and perfection" qualified him as a hero in the postwar '50s, they now position him as del Toro's stand-in for toxic masculinity and unchecked exploitive imperial urges (though the director does offer his audience the opportunity to see this new monster as exploited and marginalized by his military superior, General Hoyt [Nick Searcy]). In de-centering the traditional avatar of hegemony, *Shape* shifts toward centering the Other, freeing up the "alien" Gill-man to function as a hero. I use the article "a" instead of "the," because Gill-man functions as a contingent hero, working alongside a community of marginalized characters, each othered or forced to exist as outsiders for reasons of race (Zelda), sexuality (Giles), gender (Zelda, Elisa), disability (Eliza), and national origin/ideology (Hofstettler). And to fit even more snugly into its moment, *Shape* accents the intersectional nature of Elisa (and Zelda, Giles, and Hofstettler), marginalized for multiple facets of identity.

The Shape of Water works to rehearse social concepts and anxieties on issues of race, gender roles, sexuality, difference, otherness, and identity, and to process and renovate them in ways that reflect the priorities of its moment of production. del Toro points out that the movie's historical moment (1962) functions as a sort of ground-zero time in the making of the American psyche: "It's the time when the fantasy of America almost crystallized…. If you're white Anglo-Saxon and Protestant it was a great time to be alive. If you're not then it's pretty bad. The idea was to say, that was then—but it's also now" (Betancourt). The work of the movie, then, becomes to replace the exclusionary fantasy of America, re-inserted into the mainstream with a vengeance by Trump's MAGA candidacy and presidency, with an alternative inclusive fantasy. With regard to that genre and the ways that del Toro mutates it in his adaptation, the director says, "I think that fantasy is a very political genre. Fairy tales were born in times of great trouble. They were born in times of famine, pestilence and war" (Lawless). The debt to fantasy/fairy tale (Beauty and the Beast) floats right on the surface of the text. But critics quickly pointed out a good deal more generic complexity in the text: "Part monster movie, part noir thriller, part Hollywood musical, the film defies categorization" (Lawless). And that list doesn't even touch on del Toro's engagements with Greek mythology (Orpheus and Eurydice) and Sirk-ian social melodrama. In the end, the diverse genre engagements integrate with the parallel diversity of the category-defying characters on screen.

Interestingly, cracks in the façade (or in del Toro's terms, cracks in the crystal) of nostalgic American greatness actually began appearing in the 1950s in films such as those of Douglas Sirk, whom del Toro credits as a central influence for *Shape*, and even in more mainstream texts such as Billy Wilder's *The Seven Year Itch* (1955). That film is now best known for the shot of Marilyn Monroe straddling a subway grate, her dress blowing up. Just prior to that iconic moment, "The Girl" (Monroe) and Richard Sherman (Tom Ewell) emerge from seeing *Creature from the Black Lagoon*. The Girl muses on the movie: "Didn't you just love the picture? I did. But I just felt so sorry for the Creature…. He wasn't really all bad. I think he just craved a little affection—you know, a sense of being loved and needed and wanted." Here we see an immediate willingness to re-imagine the Other in American culture. Yet the diegetic joke is that The Girl, at least in Richard's imagination, will later compare Richard, itchy with out-of-control libidinous desire, to the Creature: "Then suddenly he turned at me. His eyes bulging. He was frothing at the mouth. Just like The Creature from the Black Lagoon!" Rather than employ the Creature to represent any number of traditional Others in need of recognition and acceptance, The Girl's empathic reading of Otherness posits his monstrousness as a stand-in for the White male lead's sexual rapacity. In an ironic twist, 1950s hegemonic masculinity is cast simultaneously as monster and victim, a boys-will-be-boys dynamic not to be scorned or feared but to be understood, pitied, accepted, and loved. Clearly, del Toro's interpretation of Gill-man moves directly away from associating him with hegemonic toxic masculinity and toward other Other considerations.

Still, *The Shape of Water* does engage centrally and directly with the boys-will-be-boys dynamic, not to sympathize with it but rather to completely un-wind it. After being rescued by Elisa and company, Gill-man is hidden in Elisa's tub. He wanders out of the tub and past a sleeping Giles, in order to explore his new environs. Next door, he encounters Giles's cat, Pandora. In a shot/reverse shot exchange, Pandora and Gill-man hiss at one another. By the time Giles bursts into the room, Gill-man is eating the cat. When explaining the situation to Elisa, Giles offers the boys-will-be-boys argument: "It wasn't his fault. He's a wild creature. We can't ask him to be anything else." Yet in the next scene, Gill-man is back in Giles's apartment, crouched in front of two more cats. He now seems to recognize and understand their domestic nature and they his, as they play quietly together. Thus, the film proposes and quickly rejects the concept of Gill-man as a "wild creature." In fact, Giles and Elisa don't have to ask Gill-man to be anything else—he just is. And the boys-will-be-boys argument, the idea that men are ruled by natural animalistic impulses, is dismissed in a mere three minutes of screen time.

The film presents Gill-man as an example of ideal masculinity. As such, he functions in direct contrast with Strickland's toxic masculinity. Indeed, *Shape* develops a spectrum of masculinity, with Gill-man and Strickland at the opposing poles. Giles and Hofstettler exist on the spectrum, as do several other traditional male obstacle-characters who serve as foils: the homophobic racist Pie Guy (Morgan Kelly) on whom Giles has an unrequited (fleeting) crush, and Zelda's chauvinist husband Brewster (Martin Roach). While Pie Guy and Brewster each tick a few undesirable boxes, Strickland does most of the ideological heavy lifting, specifically through his in-depth representation of toxic masculinity.

From the moment he enters the story, Strickland evidences an almost obsessive concern with defining masculinity. Elisa and Zelda (and the audience) first meet Strickland when he walks into the men's room that they are cleaning. Prior to his arrival, the women were lightly complaining about male urinary sloppiness. Strickland immediately washes his hands and then uses the urinal. After he finishes, Elisa offers him a towel, which he declines: "A man washes his hands before or after tending to his needs. It tells you a lot about a man. He does it both times, it points to a weakness in character." Later, as he walks through a dealership, with no intention of buying a car, the dealer sells him by appealing to shifting concepts of masculinity: "Four out of five successful men in America drive a Cadillac.... You're the man of the future." And even as his whole system unravels, Strickland still obsessively defines masculinity; in a conversation with General Hoyt, he offers more variables to his formula: "A man is faithful all his life. And he is useful," and finally, after he tracks down and shoots Gill-man and Elisa, he adds his claim to masculine avatar status: "I do not fail. I deliver."

But the moment that perfectly encapsulates Strickland's construction of a hegemonic toxic masculine identity comes during his first interview with Zelda and

Elisa. He has called the women to his office to warn them not to spend unnecessary time in the lab that houses Gill-man. After deeming Gill-man an "affront," Strickland wanders toward self-consideration: "You may think that thing looks human, stands on two legs, right? But we're created in the Lord's image. You don't think that's what the Lord looks like, do you?" When Zelda answers that she doesn't know what the Lord looks like, Strickland responds: "Well, human, Zelda, he looks like a human. Like me—or even you. Maybe a little more like me, I guess." Here we see the efficient construction of a hegemonic identity. Strickland manages to other both Gill-man and Zelda, directly denying the humanity of the one and implicitly denying the humanity of the other. Gill-man is an affront with only the posture of a human, while Zelda is made only roughly in God's image, or at least made less in God's image than Strickland himself. It is unclear whether Zelda's race or gender makes her less like God. But what is clear is the establishment and leveraging of a hegemonic identity: American, White, male. A phone call from General Hoyt leads Strickland to dismiss the women. Hoyt addresses the fact that Gill-man has bitten off two of Strickland's fingers, but Strickland brushes off the injury as minor: "I still got my thumb, my trigger, and my pussy finger." Strickland's inventory of his remaining fingers fully expresses his humanity as defined by toxic masculinity; he still retains everything it takes to be a dominant man: his thumb will allow him to manipulate technology, and he maintains the fingers associated (by him) with violence and sex. His toxic-masculinity bonafides are stellar: he is overtly concerned with avoiding any and all perception of indecision; displays material signifiers of success; eagerly serves and is useful to power; freely and frequently others those around him; presumes a god-like stature for himself, particularly in the presence of others; has a pronounced preference for voiceless women; readily threatens and resorts to violence; and makes impulsive, unwanted, and tone-deaf sexual advances on those over whom he has authority.

As Strickland represents a specifically twenty-first-century brand of toxic masculinity, Gill-man stands in for ideal masculinity in that shifting social landscape. Indeed, in Hofstettler's plea to study rather than vivisect him, he observes that Gill-man is not a mere biological freak but "is intelligent, capable of language and understanding emotions." That specific description positions him as the antithesis of Strickland. Indeed, while Gill-man quickly learns to communicate with Elisa through sign language, Strickland can't decipher Elisa's signing even as she curses him to his face. He also complains, as he tortures Gill-man, that he can't understand his cries. His fatal flaw seems to be an inability to recognize and understand others (Elisa, Gill-man, Zelda, Hofstettler) as subjects. He is a trained officer in charge of security for a top-secret American military operation, yet he works, unwittingly, with a Russian spy, and loses the "asset" he was charged to guard when he is outsmarted by two cleaning women and an out-of-work graphic artist.

Further, Strickland lacks the capacity to understand the emotions of others, or worse, fails to recognize the existence or validity of those emotions. Gill-man, as reflected through Elisa's gaze, possesses deep emotional range and intuition, as evidenced by her appeal for Giles's help in liberating Gill-man from the lab. Where Strickland looks at Gill-man and sees only difference, Elisa is struck by the

Figure 18. Elisa Esposito (Sally Hawkins) and the Gill-man (Doug Jones) gaze into each other's eyes through the glass of the tank where the creature is imprisoned in *The Shape of Water* (2017) (Fox Searchlight Pictures/Photofest).

similarities: "I move my mouth like him. I make no sound like him." After the rescue, Giles also recognizes an element of himself in Gill-man: "Maybe we're both just relics." But Eliza's recognition goes beyond similarities—she is also deeply impacted by her perception of Gill-man's recognition of her: "When he looks at me—the way he looks at me—he does not know what I lack or how I am incomplete. He sees me for what I am, as I am. He's happy to see me every time, every day." He sees her; he identifies her by her abilities rather than her disabilities. In other words, Gill-man's gaze subjectifies rather than objectifies Elisa, an inversion of the classic dynamic embodied by Laura Mulvey's theory of the male gaze in narrative cinema.

According to Mulvey, the male gaze is enabled "by sexual imbalance, pleasure in looking has been split between active/male and passive/female" (841). It objectifies the female, and in classic narrative cinema, her story-function is secondary to her function as a reward/trophy for the hero (and, by extension, the viewer): "The presence of woman is an indispensable element of spectacle ... yet her visual presence tends to work against the development of a storyline" (841). This is largely true of *Creature from the Black Lagoon*, where the character of Kay is primarily objectified—by the camera, as well as by the three principal male characters, the Creature, Mark, and David, all of whom compete for possession of her in some way. The moment that del Toro offers as his imaginary catalyst for *The Shape of Water* illustrates this triangulated male gaze: Kay swims in the Amazon River, her body on full display, both on screen for the spectator and inside the story for the Creature, who swims below, gazing up at her. In the end, after she has been dragged off twice by the Creature, David proves the most suitable of the gazers, his ultimate victory signified by his end-of-the-movie embrace of Kay. But *Shape* veers away from Mulvey's formula. Elisa's physical presence is not a matter of spectacle; it is un-objectified and works perpetually toward the development of storyline. Further, though she is subject to Strickland's gaze at times, it functions as clearly illicit, a gaze with which the audience is not complicit. While the movie engages with issues of sexual imbalance, the diegetic split between active/male and passive/female is blurred, complicated, and ultimately erased. Indeed, for most of the film, Elisa is the active character in her interactions with both Gill-man and Giles. And it is she who gazes at Gill-man throughout the film, as well as she who initiates the physical relationship and rescues him from imprisonment in the lab. Throughout the film, she rejects her passive/victim status, and her insistence on active subject status is contagious, spreading to Zelda, Giles, and Hofstettler.

As Elisa and the other Others rise to hero status, Strickland sinks deeper and deeper toward monstrousness. He becomes more unhinged psychologically and physically as the film builds to a climax, his eyes frantic and his body literally falling to pieces. Even he is disgusted by the stench of his rotting fingers, which he eventually tears off his hand. Strickland's bodily decomposition and his inability to heal contrasts directly with Giles's rejuvenated hair, delivered by Gill-man's mystical touch. In the end, after shooting Gill-man, Strickland is overpowered by Giles, and he watches impotently as Gill-man heals his own wounds and resurrects himself. His final words—"Fuck, you are a god"—directly contradict his own earlier hegemonic claim to Zelda that God looks not like Gill-man (or even like Zelda) but like him. Gill-man's coup de grace, a sharp swipe across the neck, sends Strickland to his knees, voiceless and unable to breathe in the world he once controlled. Thus, the mortal wound juxtaposes Elisa's scars, throughout the film thought to be the remnants of an injury that took her voice but which prove to be gills that will allow her to adapt to a new world and live a new life. Strickland, and his brand of masculinity, becomes the outsider, left behind. He is, in the words of General Hoyt, "unborn, unmade, and undone." This inversion of otherness and ideal masculinity represents some of the central work of the adaptation. Beyond (and alongside) that, *Shape* uses *Creature*'s basic dynamics and ingredients to specifically redefine a whole set of social concepts—monstrosity, masculinity, gender relations, difference, disability, heroism, and humanity. Viewed through the windshield, the adaptation does this work in ways that reflect and drive an emergent set of twenty-first-century values.

Conclusion: Re-Mapping Lines in the Sand

In his Oscar acceptance speech, del Toro called attention to his status as an immigrant, an outsider who, like Gill-man, had recently been made to feel his difference in America. But as an answer to the politics of resentment and division, he pointed to the power of culture: "I think the best thing our industry does is to erase the lines in the sand. We should continue doing *that* when the world tells us to make them deeper" (Pulver). His film, then, can be seen as working to erase a series of lines drawn in the sand by American society and the movies it produces and consumes. Further, when viewed through the windshield, the film does more than simply erase those lines in the sand—it positively remaps a set of boundaries, in order to make inclusion, diversity, and acceptance not only virtuous but productive, to the point of actively vanquishing intolerance and toxic masculinity and directly effecting a happy ending. Simply put, cultural adaptations erase and re-draw lines. As an adaptation of *Creature*, *Shape* revises consistently in the directions of acceptance of others and diversity. It also revises in the direction of moving away from traditional notions of masculinity to the point of making them monstrous. These adaptations don't merely represent alterations away from a source text—they use the status quo of elements of that source as a springboard to move toward representing the ethos of the adaptation's specific moment of construction.

When viewed through the windshield, *The Shape of Water* is an adaptation that centers the productive values of acceptance, diversity, and inclusion. And perhaps the productivity of diverse inclusion can also be seen in the act of adaptation itself—or at least adaptation as conceived and processed through that windshield reading strategy. The Creature of the source text is a tragic character; he represents an evolutionary dead end: unable to adapt to the encroaching future, he, like King Kong, does not survive modernity's invasion of his geographic isolation. But in the re-telling, Gill-man possesses the ability to change. In that way, he represents adaptation. It is his foil, Strickland, who finds himself stuck in place, unable to recognize shifts in the social landscape and move forward to change with the times. Thus he proves himself not the man of the future but a relic of the past. Interestingly, the word "adapted" can signify either mutability or suitability. To describe something as adapted to its surroundings can be to say that it has been either changed to fit or is already uniquely suited to those surroundings. In revision-ing *Creature from the Black Lagoon*, *The Shape of Water* adapts the past in order to adapt to the present. That is, it alters its cultural source in order to better suit its socio-political moment. In that way, a look at the adaptation's specific changes offers a critical opportunity to explore the socio-political priorities and anxieties of its moment of production, to explore the ways in which texts adapt themselves to the new world of their present.

Note

1. Other examples abound. Kate Hamill's #MeToo *Dracula* (2020) on Broadway, the BBC adaptation of *The Woman in White* (2018), Margaret Atwood's "Impatient Griselda," etc.

Works Cited

Armstrong, Nancy. "Some Call It Fiction: On the Politics of Domesticity." *Literary Theory: An Anthology*, 2nd Edition, edited by Julie Rivkin and Michael Ryan. Blackwell, 2004, pp. 567–83.
Betancourt, Manuel. "Review: Guillermo del Toro's Latin American Monster in *The Shape of Water* Is a Powerful Pro-Immigrant Statement." *ReMezcla*, 20 Dec. 2017, https://remezcla.com/features/film/guillermo-del-toro-shape-of-water-movie-review/. Accessed 27 Dec. 2021.
Bortolotti, Gary and Linda Hutcheon. "On the Origins of Adaptations: Rethinking Fidelity Discourse and 'Success': Biologically." *New Literary History*, Vol. 38, No. 3 (Summer 2007): 443–558.
Braudy, Leo. "Afterword: Rethinking Remakes." *Play It Again, Sam: Re-Takes on Remakes*. Edited by Andrew Horton and Stuart McDougal. University of California Press, pp. 327–33.
Gray, Tim. "Love and Danger on the Waterfront," *Variety*, 10, Jan. 2018. https://variety.com/2018/film/awards/shape-of-water-inspiration-from-monster-movie- 1202659976/. Accessed 27 Dec. 2021.
Hutcheon, Linda, *A Theory of Adaptation*, 2nd Edition. Routledge, 2013.

Kit, Borys. "How Guillermo del Toro's 'Black Lagoon' Fantasy Inspired *Shape of Water*." *The Hollywood Reporter*. 3 Nov. 2017, https://www.hollywoodreporter.com/news/general- news/how-guillermo-del-toros-black-lagoon-fantasy-inspired-shape-water-1053206/. Accessed 27 Dec. 2021.

Lawless, Jill. "Del Toro's 'The Shape of Water' Makes Waves in Venice." *AP*, 31 Aug. 2017, https://www.voanews.com/arts-culture/del-toros-shape-water-makes-waves-venice. Accessed 27 Dec. 2021.

Luban, Milton. "*Black Lagoon* Diverting Science-Fiction Meller." *The Hollywood Reporter*, 9 Feb. 1954, posted 15 Nov. 2014. https://www.hollywoodreporter.com/news/general-news/creature-black-lagoon read-thrs-749346/. Accessed 27 Dec. 2021.

Maltin, Leonard, *Leonard Maltin's 2014 Movie Guide*. Penguin, 298.

Matthews, Melvin. *Hostile Aliens, Hollywood and Today's News: 1950s Science Fiction Films and 9/11*. Algora, 2007.

Mulvey, Laura. "Visual Pleasure and Narrative Cinema." *Film Theory and Criticism*, 6th Edition, edited by Leo Braudy and Marshall Cohen. Oxford University Press, 2004.

Neibaur, James. *The Monster Movies of Universal Studios*. Rowman & Littlefield, 2017.

Pulver, Andrew. "Guillermo del Toro Wins Best Director Award for Shape of Water at Oscars 2018," *The Guardian*, 4 March 2018, https://www.theguardian.com/film/2018/mar/05/the-shape-of-water-wins-bestpicture-at oscars-2018. Accessed 27 Dec. 2021.

Rottenberg, Josh. "Guillermo del Toro's Highly Personal Monster Film 'The Shape of Water' Speaks to 'what I feel as an immigrant.'" *LA Times*, 5 Sept. 2017. https://www.latimes.com/entertainment/movies/la-et-mn-guillermo-del-toro-telluride-20170905htmlstory.html#:~:text=Q%26A%3A%20Guillermo%20del%20Toro's%20highly,%E2%80%9CThe%20Shape%20of%20Water.%E2%80%9D. Accessed 6 July 2021.

"The Shape of Water Press Conference with Guillermo del Toro, Sally Hawkins, Octavia Spencer, and Richard Jenkins." *Venice Film Festival*, 31 Aug. 2017, https://www.theupcoming.co.uk/2017/08/31/venice-film-festival-2017-the-shape-of- water-press-conference-with-guillermo-del-toro-sally-hawkins-octavia-spencer-and- richard-jenkins/. Accessed 27 Dec. 2021.

Watson, Grant. "*Creature from the Black Lagoon*." *Fiction Machine* (1954), 28 June 2017, https://fiction machine.com/2017/06/28/review-creature-from-the-black-lagoon-1954/. Accessed 27 Dec. 2021.

Filmography

The Amazing Colossal Man. Dir. Bert I. Gordon. American International Pictures, 1957. Film.

Attack of the Crab Monsters. Dir. Roger Corman. Allied Artists, 1957. Film.

The Beast from 20,000 Fathoms. Dir. Eugène Lourié. Warner Bros., 1954. Film.

Beginning of the End. Dir. Bert I. Gordon. Republic Pictures, 1957. Film.

Creature from the Black Lagoon. Dir. Jack Arnold. Universal Pictures, 1954. Film.

The Day the Earth Stood Still. Dir. Robert Wise. 20th Century Fox, 1951. Film.

Dracula. Dir. Tod Browning. Universal Pictures, 1931. Film.

Frankenstein. Dir. James Whale. Universal Pictures, 1931. Film.

Godzilla. Dir. Ishiro Honda. Toho Studios, 1954. Film.

The Incredible Shrinking Man. Dir. Jack Arnold. Universal Pictures, 1957. Film.

Invasion of the Body Snatchers. Dir. Don Siegel. Allied Artists Pictures, 1956. Film.

The Invisible Man. Dir. James Whale. Universal Pictures, 1933. Film.

The Invisible Man. Dir. Leigh Whannell. Universal Pictures, 2020. Film.

It Came from Beneath the Sea. Dir. Robert Gordon. Columbia Pictures, 1957. Film.

It Came from Outer Space. Dir. Jack Arnold. Universal-International, 1953. Film.

It Conquered the World. Dir. Roger Corman. American International Pictures, 1956. Film.

King Kong. Dir. Merian C. Cooper. Radio Pictures, 1933. Film.

The Magnetic Monster. Dir. Curt. Siodmak and Herbert L. Strock. United Artists, 1953. Film.

The Quartermas Xperiment. Dir. Val Guest. United Artists, 1955. Film.

Rodan. Dir. Ishiro Honda. Toho Studios, 1956. Film.

The Seven Year Itch. Dir. Billy Wilder. 20th Century Fox, 1955.

The Shape of Water. Dir. Guillermo del Toro. Fox Searchlight Pictures, 2017. Film.

Tarantula. Dir. Jack Arnold. Universal-International, 1955. Film.

Them! Dir. Gordon Douglas. Warner Bros., 1954. Film.

The Thing from Another World. Dir. Christian Nyby. RKO Radio Pictures, 1951. Film.

The War of the Worlds. Dir. Byron Haskin. Paramount Pictures, 1953. Film.

Werewolf of London. Dir. Stuart Walker. Universal Pictures, 1935. Film.

When Worlds Collide. Dir. Rudolph Maté. Paramount Pictures, 1951. Film.

World Without End. Dir. Edward Bernds. Allied Artists Pictures Corporation, 1956. Film.

X the Unknown. Dir. Leslie Norman and Joseph Losey. Warner Bros., 1956. Film.

PART III

Alien Invasions

The Day the Earth Stood Still, The Thing from Another World, and the Creation of Two Archetypes

DENNIS R. CUTCHINS

Nineteen fifty-one was a watershed moment in sci-fi filmmaking. *The Day the Earth Stood Still* (1951) set a pattern for cinematic contact with a benevolent alien working to save the people of Earth from their own savagery and ignorance. The alien in that film warns humans to change their ways or face destruction. *The Thing from Another World* (1951), on the other hand, set the mold for humans faced with an alien bent on destroying the human race. The only reasonable approach to this clever but vicious invader is swift and violent action. These two films, released within months of each other, created opposing patterns for the ways alien/human encounters would be portrayed in Hollywood for decades to come. Indeed, the patterns they established continue to be replicated in some of the most recent alien encounter films.

Despite their nearly opposite thematic content, the two films are strikingly similar in several ways. For instance, both were part of a small handful of high-budget sci-fi films produced in the early 1950s. Both were based on pulp sci-fi stories that had been published years earlier. *The Thing from Outer Space* was based on John W. Campbell, Jr.'s "Who Goes There" (1938), and *The Day the Earth Stood Still* was based on Harry Bates' "Farewell to the Master" (1940). The plots of both films center on the arrival of an alien on Earth. In both films the military takes quick action against the alien, while the scientific community is more sympathetic, seeking to understand the visitor, and perhaps even to help it. The press and the government also play important roles in both films, the first as it spreads word of the alien contact, and the second as an example of incompetence and bureaucratic red tape. Both of these films were also vehicles for Cold War era political and social statements, though their messages, as I will discuss in a moment, were quite different.

By 1951 the Cold War was in full swing. It had become a de facto part of American culture, and films about the Cold War were regularly finding their way onto the big screen. *The Third Man*, *The Red Danube*, and *The Red Menace* were all released in 1949, and *I Was a Communist for the FBI* came out in 1951. Nineteen fifty-two saw the release of a spate of Cold War films, including *Walk East on Beacon*, *Big Jim*

McLain, Atomic City, Hong Kong, and *Invasion USA.*[1] But *The Day the Earth Stood Still* and *The Thing from Another World* are a unique pair of Cold War films for a few reasons. First, they are sci-fi films in which an alien visitor/invader offers warnings about contemporary issues. As television shows like the original *Star Trek* (1966– 1969) later demonstrated, this allowed them a particular leeway in terms of their portrayal of current events. In the words of film scholar John Kenneth Muir, "The alien is a good dramatic tool for a filmmaker or television producer because this unique character permits the people behind the scenes to comment on society from an important perspective, a seemingly objective stance" (123). Second, the two films, taken together, represent much of the range of Hollywood's reaction to the Cold War military build-up, to the idea of the alien other, and to science.

The fact that both of these films were adapted from earlier short stories is particularly useful when we set out to analyze them, since adaptation, along with the character and narrative changes it always entails, provides an important vantage point. The source texts in both cases offer a kind of measuring stick that allows viewers to judge, insofar as that is possible, the intentions of the adaptors. Adaptation, particularly the adaptation of a short story to the big screen, always requires changes and, as I have argued elsewhere, we ought to celebrate those changes.[2] They represent the very essence of art. In fact, the way a particular story is adapted for the screen is often the most interesting part of studying a film. The way these two teams adapted the source stories for the screen reveals a great deal about their motives.

The Thing from Another World

John Campbell's "Who Goes There," the source for *The Thing from Another World*, is a long, complex, and sophisticated story. It concerns a group of American scientists working in the Antarctic. They discover a wrecked alien spaceship, apparently buried in glacial ice for millions of years. The scientists recover the body of an alien from just outside of the wreck; then, in an attempt to get to the ship itself, accidentally set the craft ablaze. The men return with the ice-encased body to their base, but once they get a chance to view the alien through the ice they are dismayed by its appearance. The alien is blue, has three red eyes, and is "angry" looking. Its head is covered by snake-like appendages and the men who come into contact with it complain of feeling sick or frightened afterward. Nevertheless, they decide to thaw the alien body in order to study it. The alien revives, however, and disappears. The men quickly find it but realize that it is in the process of "digesting" and simultaneously transforming itself into one of their sled dogs. They kill the half-transformed thing by electrocuting it but recognize the danger of a creature that can transform itself into anything it touches. They begin to worry that one of their own party already may have been taken over by the alien. The title of the story comes from the fact that the men have a great deal of difficulty distinguishing the real humans from the alien clones.[3] They eventually discover, however, that the alien clones are extremely selfish. That is, they are so bent on self-preservation that they will sacrifice each other in order to survive. McReady, one of the scientists, devises a test in which he places blood from each of the party members in test tubes and scalds them one by one with a hot wire. The blood from the monsters shrinks back from the wire, revealing the aliens. Fifteen men eventually are identified as monsters and destroyed, the last one as he is in the process of creating an anti-gravity device that will enable him to fly away from Antarctica and infect the rest of the world.[4]

The first film version of "Who Goes There," Howard Hawks' *The Thing from Another World*, has a bit of a campy feel for viewers today, but youngsters seeing it for the first time in 1951 found it genuinely frightening. Hawks later noted that Campbell's story "was an adult treatment of an often infantile subject" (Hawks, "Interview," Becker et al.,10). It featured a savage alien and a claustrophobic, haunted house aesthetic that several of my more senior colleagues have told me gave them nightmares for weeks. My father-in-law, who was 11 years old when the film was released, mentioned to me that it was the most frightening thing he had ever seen.

When the film began production, Howard Hawks, producer and unacknowledged director, along with nominal director Christian Nyby, and writer Charles Lederer, likely realized that they could not convincingly create Campbell's shape shifting monster on the screen. Their solution to this special effects problem was to create a seven-foot-tall plant monster that fed on humans, rather than transformed into them. Robert Cumbow notes that this threat of being absorbed "into a vegetative, unquestioning existence ... was widely understood as a metaphor for communism" (112). Hawks, himself, likely would have strenuously disagreed with this reading (Hawks, "A Private Interview," Lehman 175), but Todd McCarthy suggests that the unacknowledged screenwriter for the film, Ben Hecht, "realized that this modern-day horror story could serve as an effective allegorical vehicle with which to poke fun at growing Cold War paranoia about communism" (473). This, however, is not the most interesting adaptation Hawks and his team introduced. In what seems like a rather minor change they shifted the location of the action from Antarctica to the Arctic. This move is far from minor or accidental, however. The new locale allowed Hawks to place soldiers along with scientists on the base, something that would have been impossible on the neutral soil of Antarctica. This combination of soldiers and scientists allowed what was to become a familiar conflict to arise.

As the film begins, American scientists and soldiers rescue the frozen body of an alien from a recent, rather than ancient, flying saucer crash site, and accidentally destroy the ship. As in the short story, the alien (James Arness) soon revives and begins stalking the men and dogs of the base in order to drink their blood. The soldiers hunt for the alien, but Dr. Carrington, played by Robert Cornthwaite, and a few of the scientists, conceal the fact that the alien has broken into the greenhouse. They hope to communicate with the creature, but instead two of the scientists are killed and drained of blood. The monster loses its arm in a fight with the huskies, and the scientists realize that the severed hand contains seeds. These seeds are secretly collected and planted by Carrington in a garden of monster plants, which he feeds with blood from the medical supplies kept at the station. Musing over the alien's vegetable reproduction he praises "the superiority of its brain" and the fact that "its development was not hampered by emotional or sexual factors" and thus it has "no pain or pleasure as we know it, no emotions, no heart. Our superior. Our superior in every way." The soldiers, and one of the scientists, Dr. Redding (George Fenneman), led by Captain Patrick Hendry (Kenneth Tobey), eventually electrocute the monster, though in the film the soldiers take this step over the nearly insane protests of Carrington. The film ends as embedded reporter Ned Scott (Douglass Spencer) issues his famous warning, "Watch the skies, everywhere. Keep looking. Keep watching the skies."[5]

The Cold War implications of these narrative changes from the short story are probably obvious. From the moment it is discovered, the alien in *The Thing*, as it came to be known, is working to destroy the human race. It ignores attempts to communicate, and attacks at every opportunity. Captain Hendry and the other soldiers are quick to discern the threat, and work in a practical and sensible manner to isolate and destroy the creature. These soldiers, all veterans of World War II, are the clear heroes of the film. They protect the lives of the people on the base, and perhaps literally save the world. The value of their wartime experience and fighting skill is never seriously questioned. The scientists, on the other hand, are portrayed as impractical and naïve, at best. Cumbow calls them, "effete, idealistic crypto-commies" (132).

Figure 19. From left: Captain Patrick Hendry (Kenneth Tobey), Dr. Arthur Carrington (Robert Cornthwaite), Dr. Chapman (John Dierkes), Dr. Ambrose (Edmund Breon), and Lieutenant Dykes (James Young) examine Carrington's monster nursery in *The Thing from Another World* (1951) (RKO Radio Pictures/Photofest).

Redding, who eventually helps destroy the creature, even wears what appears to be his college sweater in several scenes, though he is a grown man. Rather than being naïve or foolish, Dr. Carrington's actions are downright subversive. His willingness to preserve the monster for scientific study is reckless and costs the lives of several of the men. Even his clothing and appearance suggests a specific Cold War context for his actions. His pointy beard and fur cap make him more than a little reminiscent of Vladimir Lenin. McCarthy notes that Hawks actually "took credit for introducing ... the critique of scientists and, by extension, intellectuals" into the film, though his intentions were likely more personal than political (476).

Though I am unaware of any memos acknowledging an attempt to establish an extended Cold War metaphor in *The Thing from Another World*, circumstantial evidence certainly suggests that is what the filmmakers were up to. The adapted changes, including the shift in the polar setting and the addition of the heroic soldiers all point in the direction of a reactionary Cold War message. Indeed, it seems a strong possibility that the filmmakers found Campbell's original shape-shifting monster with an agenda of world domination an apt, and frightening, stand-in for communist infiltration. Though they may have been forced to abandon the monster's abilities to shape shift for practical reasons, there's a strong chance this is what originally attracted them to this story. The pattern of the dangerous, destructive, and crafty alien foolishly welcomed by scientists and violently confronted by a handful of brave warriors established by *The Thing from Another World* is easily recognizable in dozens of mostly low-budget '50s and '60s films but may be most clearly recognized in the films of the *Alien* franchise (1979–2017), the *Predator* series (1987–2018),[6] and Roland Emmerich's *Independence Day* films (1996, 2016).

Alien (1979) embodies the archetypes established by *The Thing*, including the danger of unchecked scientific idealism and the need for violent action when facing aliens. Todd McCarthy goes as far as writing, "*The Thing* can be said to have directly spawned this entire subgenre, just as it stands as the unavoidable granddaddy of the more recent wave of *Alien*-style mutant beast shockers" (483). Based at least partly on A.E. van Vogt's "Black Destroyer" and "Discord in Scarlet," both published in 1939,[7] *Alien* begins on the *Nostromo*, a massive commercial spaceship towing an automated refinery across the galaxy. The civilian crew are awakened from "hypersleep" months early on their way back to Earth because a radio beacon of unknown origin has triggered emergency procedures. Obligated by law to respond to potential distress calls, the crew grudgingly disconnect the *Nostromo* from the refinery and prepare to land on the small planet where the signal originates. The planet is inhospitable, however, and the ship is damaged while landing. While engineers Parker (Yaphet Kotto) and Brett (Harry Dean Stanton) commence repairs, ship's captain Dallas (Tom Skerritt), Kane (John Hurt), and Lambert (Veronica Cartright) leave in environmental suits to explore the source of the signal. They discover an alien spaceship that has apparently crash-landed on the planet much earlier. The body of the gigantic pilot of the ship still sits in its command chair, but the Earthlings discover an apparent cause of death, a gaping hole in its chest.

In the meantime, Ripley (Sigourney Weaver) translates part of the message that has triggered the investigation and realizes that it is not a call for help but a warning beacon. She tries to warn Dallas's team, but it is too late. Back on the wrecked alien ship Kane has discovered a lower deck filled with hundreds of eggs. One of the eggs opens, and without warning a small creature attaches itself to Kane's helmet, and then to his face. Dallas and Lambert bring the unconscious Kane back to the *Nostromo*. Against Ripley's orders, as well as quarantine protocol, science officer Ash (Ian Holm) allows the landing party back aboard. Ash is unable to help the unconscious Kane, though, and the crew lift off to resume their journey to Earth, planning to place Kane, and themselves, in stasis for the ten-month trip. Shortly after leaving the planet's surface, however, Kane unexpectedly wakes up, and the crew members cheerfully plan a last meal before returning to hypersleep. During the meal, the film's most memorable scene takes place as Kane stops eating and begins to scream in pain. Seconds later a small alien bursts from his chest in a splash of gore and scurries from the dining room.

In the second half of the film the crew, with improvised weapons, search the ship and try to destroy the quickly growing alien while it picks them off, one by one. After Brett and Dallas have been killed, Ripley discovers a secret directive in the computer that reveals the company's knowledge of the alien lifeform, and identifies science officer Ash as a conspirator. She confronts him, and Ash tries to kill Ripley but is stopped by Parker and Lambert. In the ensuing fight, Ash is disabled and the crew discover that he is a robot. When they temporarily reestablish power to his severed head, Ash reveals the company's plan to acquire an alien, pities the doomed crew, and confesses his admiration for the alien's "purity." Ash's role as the science officer for the *Nostromo* follows the now familiar pattern of unchecked respect for logic, contempt for human life, and the reckless pursuit of scientific inquiry. Indeed, his admiration for the creature rivals that of Dr. Carrington in *The Thing*. In an echo of Carrington, Ash's final speech praises the alien whose survival instinct and reason is "unclouded by conscience, remorse, or delusions of morality."

There are no soldiers aboard the *Nostromo* to counterbalance Ash's worshipful reverence for the murderous creature, or to fight it, but the practical-minded Ripley serves well in their stead. She confronts Ash, and is able in the end to destroy the creature. It is worth noting that the second film in the franchise, *Aliens*, does feature "Colonial Marines" who heroically battle the Aliens, and eventually sacrifice themselves to save Ripley and a surviving colonist child.

A variation of the archetypes in *The Thing* is found in another unacknowledged adaptation, Roland Emmerich's *Independence Day* (1996). Based loosely on H.G. Wells' *War of the Worlds*, *Independence Day* tells the story not of a single alien bent on secretly conquering the world but of millions of bloodthirsty aliens in a fleet of ships methodically wiping out the human race. Emmerich's film also includes brave and heroic soldiers, willing to sacrifice themselves if necessary, naïve scientists who place themselves and others in danger, an overly bureaucratic (and even corrupt) government, and a press eager to spread word of the invasion.

The film begins as technicians at SETI discover a gigantic alien ship flying past the moon. The ship enters orbit, and dozens of smaller ships, each more than 15 miles across, slowly descend on the Earth and position themselves over population centers. Rioters and looters, along with panicked citizens, crowd the streets of the cities where the ships wait. David Levinson (Jeff Goldblum), a satellite expert for a cable company, intercepts and decodes an alien message being transmitted using Earth's own satellites.[8] He recognizes the signal as a countdown, and contacts his ex-wife, White House communications director Constance Spano (Margaret Colin). Despite misgivings, Spano alerts President Whitmore (Bill Pullman) and he, Spano, a handful of advisors, as well as Levinson and his father (Judd Hirsch, present mostly for comic relief), manage to get away seconds before the aliens attack and destroy Washington. The White House, where the alien attack is centered, is the first of many iconic buildings to be vaporized by the aliens; I can remember when the film was first released how shocked I was to see that kind of destruction on the big screen.

The film also intercuts scenes from characters in other parts of the country as they react to the invasion, and for the first half of the film there are several distinct storylines. In Los Angeles, Captain Steve Hiller (Will Smith) is ordered to report for duty at El Toro Air Force Base. He advises his girlfriend, Jasmine (Vivica A. Fox), and her young son, Dylan (Ross Bagley), to join him at the base after her shift as a dancer at a nightclub. During the first battle with the aliens, however, Hiller's whole squadron, along with the Air Force base, is destroyed by dozens of alien ships roughly the size of fighter planes. He manages to defeat one of the alien ships by his flying skill and by sacrificing his own plane. In one of the film's most iconic moments, he opens the hatch of the crashed alien ship and knocks out the alien pilot while quipping, "Welcome to Earth." Jasmine and Dylan survive the attack on Los Angeles by hiding in a tunnel, and slowly make their way, along with other survivors, to El Toro in a road maintenance truck. One of the survivors they pick up along the way is the president's wife, Marilyn Whitmore (Mary McDonnell), who has been gravely injured.

In a rural location, meanwhile, Russell Casse (Randy Quaid), an alcoholic Vietnam vet and crop duster, feels vindicated by the arrival of the invasion force. For years he has been ridiculed for his story of alien abduction and the trauma he suffered. He and his children leave in their motorhome to avoid the approaching alien ships.

All these storylines eventually come together as the various characters arrive at Area 51. There they discover the true nature of the aliens. When Hiller arrives with the alien pilot he has rendered unconscious Whitmore attempts to reason with it, asking, "We know there is much we can learn from each other if we can negotiate a truce. We can find a way to co-exist. Can there be peace between us?" When the alien responds, "Peace? No peace," Whitmore asks, "What is it you want us to do?" The alien's answer is simple and straightforward, "Die." This unambiguous animosity places the alien squarely in the camp of the creatures from *The Thing* or *Alien*. After the alien expresses its wish that humans will simply die, Whitmore begins to clutch his head and scream in pain, apparently the victim of alien mind control. The soldiers in the room draw their side arms and shoot the creature multiple times. These aliens are beyond reason, logic, or sympathy and can only be met with violence.

Science plays a mixed role in this film. Scientists in the secret labs at Area 51, for instance, follow the pattern established in *The Thing from Another World*. Though they have known about a potential alien invasion for years, they have kept the public, along with the President, in the dark as they conducted research on alien bodies and technology. Amidst all the destruction taking place around the world, Dr. Brakish Okun (Brent Spiner) is almost giddy. When President Whitmore asks what they know about the aliens and the wrecked ship they have repaired, he bubbles like a child in a candy shop; "We know tons about them, but the neatest stuff, the neatest stuff has only happened in the last few days ... since these guys started showing up all the little gizmos inside turned on. The last twenty-four hours have been really exciting." After this enthusiastic outburst Whitmore fires back, "Exciting? People are dying out there. I don't think 'exciting' is the word I'd use to describe it." Okun's adolescent word choice, disregard for human life, and general failure to connect with reality marks him as someone not to be trusted. At the same time, the scientific knowledge of communications engineer David Levinson is vital to the eventual defeat of the aliens. Levinson is the first person to discover that the aliens are preparing to attack the Earth, and in the film's conclusion, he creates the plan to defeat the invasion with a computer virus.[9]

While the film has both positive and negative portrayals of science and scientists, its treatment of the military is unambiguously positive. Captain Steven Hiller manages to destroy a superior alien fighter in his F/A-18, and eventually helps deliver Levinson's fatal computer virus to the alien mothership. Alcoholic Vietnam veteran Russell Casse heroically sacrifices himself to destroy the first of the large alien ships, and even the President of the United States proves his mettle not as a political leader but as a jet pilot.[10] This timely success of the military is a sharp departure from *The War of the Worlds*. In both Wells' novel and the 1953 adaptation, the military has some success but is clearly outmatched. The success of the military and practical-minded science in Emmerich's film is completely in line with the pattern established by *The Thing*, however, and gives an indication of the power of these archetypes. Emmerich's film may have been inspired by *War of the Worlds*, but *The Thing* is clearly a significant influence.

The Day the Earth Stood Still

The alien who appears in *The Day the Earth Stood Still* is almost antithetical to the violent, unreasoning creatures discussed so far. Thus, it should not be surprising that the proper human response to this alien, and to its Hollywood descendants, should be quite different from what we've seen so far. Like *The Thing from Another World*, *The Day the Earth Stood Still* is also based on a short story, but unlike Campbell's sophisticated "Who Goes There," the literary source for *The Day the Earth Stood Still*, Harry Bates' "Farewell to the Master" is a fairly contrived short story about Klaatu, a human-like alien, who lands on Earth with his robot. Upon their arrival, Klaatu is almost immediately shot and killed by a civilian lunatic. The robot, Gnut, quickly shuts down, apparently unable to function without his biological companion. A news reporter, however, hides one evening in the hastily erected museum built around the robot, and soon discovers that Gnut is quite functional. Indeed, the robot has been quietly and secretly conducting a series of experiments on animals each night aboard the spaceship. The story culminates as the reporter helps bring Klaatu back to life. The technology that allows this "resurrection" is imperfect, however, and the alien soon dies again in the reporter's arms. The story's "punchline" ending comes after this second death as the reporter explains to Gnut that his master's death was an accident. Gnut replies, "You misunderstand, I am the master."

As this rather simplistic story was adapted for the big screen it became a much more complex text. Joe Dante, in fact, observes that "there are very few science fiction pictures, certainly of the period, that are as literate and as intelligent and as carefully made" ("Making"). In the film, Klaatu (Michael Rennie) and the robot, renamed Gort (Lock Martin), land in Washington, D.C., and disembark. As happens in the short story, Klaatu is shot, this time by a trigger-happy U.S. soldier, though he is not killed. As with *The Thing from Another World*, the insertion of the army into the film narrative is far from accidental, but the army's role in this film is not as heroic and capable defenders of the Earth but as the single biggest threat to the survival of the human race.

Klaatu's wound heals quickly, to the surprise of the human doctors, and he requests a meeting with the president of the United States and leaders of the other countries of the earth. The president denies his request, however, as do the other leaders. Frustrated by what he perceives as bureaucratic red tape and petty, provincial politics, Klaatu escapes from his guards at the hospital. In order to get to know the people of Earth he disguises himself as an Earthling, adopting the name of

Figure 20. Klaatu (Michael Rennie) lies on the ground after being shot by a trigger-happy soldier (Warren Oates, just visible to the left) in *The Day the Earth Stood Still* (1951) (Twentieth Century–Fox Film Corporation/Photofest).

Carpenter.[11] After finding a room in a boarding house, Klaatu is befriended by two of the residents, young Bobby Benson (Billy Gray) and his widowed mother, Helen Benson (Patricia Neal).

During the first half of the film, news reports are constantly intercut with action scenes, and many of these reports are both inaccurate and incendiary. As Klaatu walks the streets after leaving custody, for instance, he overhears various radio accounts of his disappearance. One of the announcers declares, "There's no denying that there is a monster at large. We are dealing with forces beyond our knowledge and power." Other news reports are downright inflammatory. During breakfast at the boarding house the next day the residents listen as radio personality Gabriel Heatter asks,

> This creature, where is he? What is he up to? If he can build a spaceship that can fly to Earth and a robot that can destroy our tanks and guns what other terrors can he unleash at will? Obviously the monster must be found. He must be tracked down like a wild animal. He must be destroyed. But where would such a creature hide? Would he disappear into the North Woods? Would he crawl into the sewers of some great city? Everybody agrees there is grave danger, the question remains, what can we do to protect ourselves? What measures can we take to neutralize this menace from another world?

During this diatribe Klaatu smiles bemusedly at the radio, but the critique of media sensationalism is obvious. It is worth noting that most of the journalists featured in the film are real-life news reporters.[12]

Later that afternoon Bobby takes Klaatu on a tour of Washington, including visiting his father's grave in Arlington National Cemetery and stopping by the Lincoln Memorial. Recognizing the futility of his attempts to contact world leaders, the increasingly frustrated Klaatu, after discussing Abraham Lincoln with Bobby, is inspired to contact members of the scientific community. With Bobby's help, he manages to get in touch with eminent scientist Dr. Barnard (Sam Jaffe) and convinces him to bring the best scientists of the Earth together for a conference so that he may address them. Despite the efforts of Bobby and his mother to hide him until the conference, Klaatu's identity is eventually discovered and he is once again shot by soldiers, this time under orders. With his dying breath he gives Helen a message for Gort. She manages to repeat the message to the robot, and, as in the short story, Gort retrieves and resurrects Klaatu's body. Klaatu and Gort prepare to leave the Earth in their flying saucer, but the alien first delivers his message to the gathered scientists of the world. The message in the film is not an O. Henry–style twist ending, as in the story, but a stern warning to the people of the Earth. As the camera pans scientists of different races dressed in costumes from around the world, Klaatu advises them to control both their aggressive tendencies and their nuclear arsenal or face destruction by the "police" of the galaxy, Gort and other formidable robots like him.

The prototype established by *The Day the Earth Stood Still* begins with an alien arriving on Earth, and almost immediately being threatened by nervous, belligerent, or even murderous humans. Avoiding trouble, the alien often disguises himself[13] as a human and seeks to understand human culture and behavior more clearly by close contact with everyday people. Throughout the film, three basic "official" reactions to the alien presence are discernable. Scientists tend to meet him with tolerance and interest, military leaders with fear and distrust, and politicians with bureaucracy and ineptitude. Despite the official reception, or lack of it, interplanetary friendships with common people usually develop, and occasionally even a romantic relationship. In most cases, though not all, the alien eventually warns the people of Earth of their impending doom if they don't change some aspect of human nature or culture. Most of these alien visitors have the power of life and death, and actually bring someone, frequently themselves, back to life. Throughout the film, the alien is pursued and persecuted by the military, or by some kind of quasi-governmental organization. The model described above is surprisingly common, and part of its strength seems to be its flexibility. Since 1951 dozens of films have adopted the pattern established by *The Day the Earth Stood Still*, though the warnings issued to humanity in these films have varied widely.

The film's critique of the Cold War nuclear arms race, completely absent from the short story, is likely obvious, even from the short plot synopsis given above. The U.S. Army is the only real source of trouble in the film, and the fact that soldiers shoot Klaatu twice, once "accidentally," and once as he evades capture, suggests a real criticism of the military. This fact, by the way, was not lost on U.S. Army commanders. They had agreed in principle to furnish vehicles and extras for the film but after reading the script they quickly backed out of their commitment. Robert Wise, the film's director, wryly observes, "I guess they didn't like the message" ("Commentary"). The tanks and jeeps seen in the film were on loan from the apparently less choosy Virginia National Guard. Klaatu's final speech clarifies the real danger of the violence the army has committed against him. The police of the galaxy, he informs the men and women gathered to hear him, will not stand for the kind of violence he has suffered. The fact that Earthlings now control nuclear weapons and seem poised on the verge of space flight makes their aggression intolerable to the other inhabitants of the galaxy. Klaatu warns them that they'd better work out their petty differences before it is too late.

The film is not, however, a simple rejection of Cold War militarism. Rather it embodies a complex understanding of the problems that created the Cold War. Moreover, it offers an alternative to the arms race that preoccupied the American military through much of the second half of the twentieth century. This solution, embodied in the film by Gort in his role as one of the "galaxy police," is similar in many ways to the plan proposed by Bernard Baruch in June of 1946. Baruch suggested that the United States and other countries allow a strong United Nations committee, the Atomic Development Authority, to oversee nuclear arms production ("Baruch"). This committee would disseminate nuclear knowledge to all U.N. member countries, but it would also be empowered to enact quick and deadly reprisals against any country that dared to use nuclear weapons on its own. Nuclear arsenals, Baruch reasoned, would thereby remain small since they would offer no real advantage in any future war. Baruch's plan was rejected, however, and the much weaker U.N. International Atomic Energy Agency was formed instead of the powerful entity Baruch had imagined.

Julian Blaustein, the film's producer, later acknowledged this rather explicit connection to contemporary Cold War issues, arguing that "the screen has, maybe, a responsibility to advocate for peace" ("Making"). Indeed, Blaustein worked even before the beginning of the production to create a film that was anti-war as well as pro–United Nations. Although Blaustein did not have a story in mind when he decided to make *The Day the Earth Stood Still*, he did recognize that a sci-fi genre film could make the perfect vehicle for a commentary on militarism and war. He put the story department at Twentieth Century–Fox to work to find an appropriate tale, and read hundreds of stories and novels himself. He later confessed that he didn't like Harry Bates' "Farewell to the Master" much to begin with but notes that two things hooked him. The first was the idea of an alien being killed by Earthlings simply because he is different. The second thing that impressed him was that in the story, "peace in the universe had been achieved by sacrificing some sovereignty to a central agency, but irrevocably. So that the United Nations, for us, became the focal point of the way to go to world peace" ("Making").

In *The Thing from Another World* the scientists compound the danger of the alien, and cause most of the trouble faced by the film's military heroes. The opposite is the case in *The Day the Earth Stood Still*. Science and the scientists portrayed in the film are the only hope for Earth's long-term survival. Robert Cornthwaite may have been made to resemble Lenin in *The Thing*, but Sam Jaffe[14] as Dr. Barnard is made up to look like Albert Einstein (Keenan 74). He is portrayed as a well-meaning but essentially naïve soul who, while he may have helped develop the atomic bomb, has no real grasp of political realities. Despite their near-helplessness in the face of militarism and bureaucracy, the group of scientists gathered at the end of the film represent the only real hope for Earth in the kind of galaxy Klaatu has described. The clearly portrayed racial and cultural mix of the scientists in that final scene signifies scientific cooperation, toleration, and diversity in a not-so-subtle way.[15]

Like *The Thing from Another World*, *The Day the Earth Stood Still* was an "A" list sci-fi film. That was unusual in the 1950s. Cerebral, and full of high-minded ideals, high production values, and ground-breaking special effects, it showed viewers how serious sci-fi films could be. In addition to a big budget, it involved some well-known faces both in front of and behind the camera. Edmund North, the screenwriter, wrote dozens of films, including several war films. Director Robert Wise was a hard-working craftsman better known today for films like *West Side Story*, *The Sound of Music*, and *The Innocents*.[16] When asked how the film's somewhat controversial stance on the Cold War made it past studio heads, Wise suggests that Darryl Zanuck, "just thought it was a damn good piece of entertainment and that's what he was interested in. He wasn't concerned about the politics or the policy in it" ("Commentary"). Wise may have been right about Zanuck, but his own politics likely came into play in his decision to direct the film. "I've been an anti-militarist all my life," he later reported, and noted that his attraction to the film had to do with his feeling that it was "a marvelous way to get a message over to this world" to "start being sane" about nuclear war ("Commentary").

Dozens of films potentially fit this archetype,[17] including *The Man Who Fell to Earth* (1974), *Escape to Witch Mountain* (1975) and its two remakes, *Escape to Witch Mountain* (1995) and *Race to Witch Mountain* (2009), *Cocoon* (1985), and *Batteries*

Not Included (1987).[18] Arguably, *ET the Extra-Terrestrial* (1982) could be included in this list. It incorporates many of the tropes discussed here, including a single mother and a friendly alien who is menaced by the federal government and is able to resurrect himself. Each of these later films brings its own twist to the archetype.

One of the earliest reflections of the friendly alien archetype, *Stranger from Venus*, came out in 1954, just three years after *The Day the Earth Stood Still*, and also starred Patricia Neal, female lead of the earlier film, as the alien's love interest and sympathetic human contact.[19] The film begins as the unnamed alien (Helmut Dantine) is dropped off by his spacecraft in rural England. The approach of the spaceship causes Susan North's (Patricia Neal) car to crash as she drives to the train station to pick up her fiancé, a government official. She is gravely injured in the accident, but the alien rescues and heals her. The alien and Susan both make their separate ways to a small inn where her fiancé, Arthur Walker (Derek Bond), is waiting. Susan explains that the alien has healed her, but Walker, rather than expressing gratitude, leaves during the night to request that the army establish a cordon around the inn. Late in the evening the alien, known to the people at the inn as "The Stranger," breaks into the innkeeper's room and heals his injured leg.

The next morning Walker returns with a newspaper reporter and the chief of police. The Stranger's fingerprints are checked by the chief and declared to be non-human. The Stranger requests that Walker, who is now convinced of his authenticity, arrange for him to meet with world leaders. Susan, meanwhile, fearful of her growing attraction to The Stranger, asks that Walker find a way to get her out of his presence. Before that can happen, Walker arranges for The Stranger to meet with a half-dozen officials from the British government. Although the alien is hesitant to meet with representatives from only one government, he agrees, and warns the men present that their headlong development of nuclear weapons is endangering the entire solar system. "The scientific achievements of you men on earth are further developed than your emotional and intellectual powers," he explains. The Stranger then informs the men that within hours the ship that dropped him off will return so that his superiors can meet with world leaders to convey the same warning.

Soon afterward, The Stranger, because of his psychic ability, realizes that the government plans to capture the ship when it arrives. He warns Walker that everyone in the area will be killed instantly if they follow through with their plan. At the last minute, The Stranger is able to warn the ship not to land, though the failure to rendezvous with the ship costs him his life. In effect, he sacrifices himself to save the humans he has come to know. According to some sources, the plot of this film was close enough to that of *The Day the Earth Stood Still* that 20th Century–Fox threatened to sue when it arrived in the United States ("Stranger"). Certainly, the casting of Patricia Neal created a more or less direct connection between the two films.

In rather an odd historical coincidence, director John Carpenter has actually remade both *The Thing from Another World* and *The Day the Earth Stood Still*. Carpenter's remake of *The Thing* (1982), discussed briefly below, did not fare well at the box office, but his second remake, *Starman* (1984), did quite well. In fact, Carpenter calls *Starman* "a big apology for *The Thing*," and suggests that *Starman* got him back in the good graces of the studio heads. "The only way to do it was to make a little love story, a girl movie. So I did, and it was fun to make; I enjoyed it, and I have no regrets" (Carpenter, "An Interview," Borst 172). Though it was unacknowledged, this film bears a striking resemblance to *The Day the Earth Stood Still*. *Starman* begins with a point of view shot of Voyager, launched seven years earlier, hurtling through space. The point of view, it turns out, is an alien spacecraft heading toward Earth. As the alien ship enters the atmosphere it changes course and is shot down by U.S. defenses. It crashes near Jenny Hayden's cabin in the wilds of Wisconsin. Like Helen Benson of *The Day the Earth Stood Still*, Jenny is a widow, though, unlike Helen, she is childless. The alien entity, a kind of floating ball of light, enters the cabin and finds the drunken Jenny watching old 8 mm films of her dead husband, Scott. Finding strands of Scott's hair, the entity is able to use the DNA to reproduce and inhabit Scott's body. Jenny wakes and, fearing an intruder, retrieves a pistol to defend herself. When she sees the new "Scott," however, she drops the gun and faints. The alien Scott sends a message noting "Environment hostile," and agreeing to rendezvous in three days.

When Jenny wakes, Scott coerces her to help him make it to his rendezvous at Meteor Crater landmark in Arizona, but when they stop at a gas station she attempts to call the police. Scott, meanwhile, sees a dead deer strapped to the hood of a hunter's car. Using some kind of mysterious technology Scott resurrects and frees the deer. The belligerent redneck hunters catch and begin beating Scott, and Jenny abandons her plan to escape in order to help him. Similar to Helen Benson, Jenny apparently changes her mind about reporting the alien to authorities, and begins to assist him in earnest. Police, however, have been alerted to Jenny's identity and the car's description, and during a high-speed chase shoot Jenny, causing a spectacular crash. Scott pulls her from the wreckage, and resurrects her.

Abandoning the highway, Jenny and Scott sneak aboard a westbound freight car to continue their journey. They eventually make love as the car rolls west, and Scott reveals that Jenny is pregnant. With the help of a sympathetic government operative (Mark Shermin), Jenny and Scott eventually make it to the crater just in time for the rendezvous. In his last words before leaving the Earth, Scott explains that on his planet, "there is only one language, one law, one people. There is no war, no hunger, and the strong do not victimize the helpless. We are very civilized." Despite this idyllic description, however, he adds, "but we have lost something. You are all so much alive, all so different. I will miss the cooks and the singing and the dancing and eating." A moment later he concludes, "You are a strange species. Not like any other. And you'd be surprised how many there are. Intelligent but savage."

Perhaps the most successful recent incarnation of the archetype established by *The Day the Earth Stood Still*, and the real inheritor of the ideas that propelled the earlier film, is Denis Villeneuve's *Arrival* (2016). This film retains the thoroughgoing seriousness of Wise and Blaustein's film but identifies a completely new set of issues relevant to the early 21st century. The film begins with what appear to be confusing flashbacks in the mind of Dr. Louise Banks (Amy Adams), a linguist and college professor living alone. It appears that Banks' daughter has recently died, and she seems unable to get over her loss. In the midst of a lecture Banks' students are distracted by alarms on their phones, and Banks turns on the television in the classroom to find out what is going on. Fragmented news reports from around the world show twelve gigantic spaceships, shaped something like elongated satellite dishes, that have appeared and stationed themselves just above the ground in apparently random places. A state of emergency is declared, and soldiers from various countries are sent to confront the ships.

The aliens, who look something like large seven-armed octopuses or squids, show no signs of hostility, however, and seem eager to communicate. Banks, along with physicist Ian Donnelly (Jeremy Renner), is recruited by Colonel G.T. Weber (Forest Whitaker) to attempt to learn the alien language and converse with the aliens in one of the ships stationed in rural Montana. At first Banks, along with scientists from around the world, is mystified by the language. A wall of computer screens in the command center shows the network of scientists who lament their lack of progress. But against orders Banks removes her environmental suit during one session and approaches the transparent wall that separates the humans from the aliens. After pointing to herself and holding up a whiteboard that says, "Louise" she is answered by the two aliens who draw circular patterns with a kind of inky substance that disappears after a moment. Recognizing that these patterns are the alien names and that the similar-looking circles are each distinct words/sentences, Banks is able to start decoding the alien language. For the sake of convenience, she nicknames the two aliens "Abbott and Costello."

After Louise's linguistic breakthrough, translation work around the world progresses relatively quickly. The apparent flashbacks of her daughter's life and death become more frequent, however, and are almost crippling. More urgently, the message the various aliens around the world seem to be communicating is disconcerting. Under pressure from Weber, Banks asks their purpose, and the alien replies, "Offer weapon." The scientists in other countries seem to receive a similar message, and the CIA liaison to the command center (Michael Stuhlbarg) notes, "We have to consider the idea that our visitors are prodding us to fight among ourselves until only one faction prevails." When Banks suggests that there is no evidence of that, the CIA man quips, "Sure there is. Just grab a history book. The British with India, the Germans with Rwanda."

The film's crisis occurs as China issues a nuclear ultimatum for the spacecraft above their country to leave, and stops all communication with other countries. The wall of monitors from around the world quickly go blank, and Donnelly and Banks realize that the worldwide cooperation they have been experiencing is over. In desperation they return to the alien ship to attempt to understand what "offer weapon" means. In answer to their question, they are shown hundreds of circular symbols simultaneously. Unbeknownst to them, however, rogue soldiers have smuggled explosives into the spaceship. Just before the explosives go off the alien known as Abbott sacrifices itself to get Banks and Donnelly to safety.

Banks is knocked unconscious in the explosion, and when she wakes Donnelly reveals that the message they have received is only 1/12th of a much larger missive. Banks and Donnelly realize that the aliens have purposefully broken the message into twelve parts in order to force the people of Earth to cooperate. At the same time, Banks realizes that the more she understands the alien language the less rigid her perception of time has become. She somehow "remembers" a conversation she will have with General Shang (Tzi Ma), the Chinese military leader, months in the future, and manages to contact him and stop the threatened Chinese attack on the spaceship. On a more personal level, we realize that the "flashbacks" Banks has been having are actually premonitions of her marriage to Donnelly and the birth and premature death of their daughter. Apparently, the alien language allows humans to have prescience.

Although the movie has several unexpected and interesting twists, the pattern set by *The Day the Earth Stood Still* is clearly at play here. Scientists are the heroes, and scientific inquiry and curiosity are valued commodities. The film also explicitly expresses the idea that scientific cooperation is necessary for human survival; something only implied in *The Day the Earth Stood Still*. At the same time, members of the military are once again the only real source of trouble. Shang's threatened military response to the aliens and the U.S. soldiers' attack on the Montana ship are both clear examples of military over-aggression. Although the attack that kills Abbot is not "official," it does seem somewhat predictable. Soldiers are trained to fight. That's their job. As Banks tells Colonel Weber, "If all I ever gave you was a hammer…," Weber concludes, "Everything's a nail."

The news media plays an interesting role in this film. Similar to *The Day the Earth Stood Still*, news reports, often vlogger-style, are frequently playing in the background. We hear one of these over the radio as Louise drives home from the university. The announcer mentions the alien ships and opines, "If this is some sort of peaceful first contact why send twelve? Why not just one?" Several times we see shots of the soldiers at the command center watching these commentators voice their opinions and catch glimpses of riots and shots of graffiti reading, "Save our species." At one point a vlogger announces, "We could be facing a full-scale invasion and our president is just willing to sit back and let them waltz in and take our country." He continues, "What if the smartest thing we could do right now would be to give them a show of force?" After the explosion, when Banks is being treated for her concussion, she asks the doctor who set the explosion. He replies, "Some soldiers. They'd been watching too much TV."

This essay has focused primarily on later films that were *influenced* by *The Thing from Another World* and *The Day the Earth Stood Still*, but it is worth noting that both these films have acknowledged remakes. *The Thing* (1982), directed by John Carpenter, was a box office flop, despite a substantial budget of fifteen-million dollars and amazing special effects by Rob Bottin. The film's nihilistic tone and the fact that it was released a few weeks after *E.T. The Extra-Terrestrial* likely contributed to its initial failure (Muir 27). Robert Cumbow points out that *Starman*, "about a benevolent alien who finds that humans can't be trusted is virtually the flip side of *The Thing*, whose malevolent alien becomes a walking metaphor for the same truth" (131). Nevertheless, Bottin's "thing" fully realized the shape-shifting creature imagined in John Campbell's short story. Indeed, as Cumbow observes, "Unlike the Hawks-Nyby film…. Carpenter's film is less interested in its characters' response to their situation than in the growing indistinguishability of the monstrous from the human" (111). Like the 1951 film, this remake also strays from the plot of the short story but in quite a different way. Where Hawks introduced soldiers who save the world, Carpenter's film ends as the only two survivors of the alien encounter, MacReady (Kurt Russell) and Childs (Keith David), meet in the rubble of the burning Antarctic base after MacReady has (perhaps) destroyed the creature, along with any chance of survival. Each man is profoundly distrustful of the other, since either could be a transformed creature. At one point Childs asks, "How will we make it?" and MacReady answers, "Maybe we shouldn't." Instead of trying to find a way to survive, they share a bottle of whisky and wait for each other to freeze.[20]

Despite its initial failure, Carpenter's remake has become something of a cult classic. In the words of Michelle Le Blanc and Colin Odell, "its reputation has grown, and it's now appreciated as a classic horror" (64). The same cannot be said for the remake of *The Day the Earth Stood Still*.

The Day the Earth Stood Still (2008) starring Keanu Reeves as Klaatu, Jennifer Connelly as Helen Benson, and Jaden Smith as Jacob Benson largely follows the plot of its revered predecessor but veers away from a critique of the Cold War. In this film, alien Klaatu and robot GORT have come to warn the inhabitants of Earth either to stop ruining the environment of the planet or face annihilation. His requests ignored by the government, Klaatu follows the pattern of his predecessor and attempts to get to know some common people, while GORT, 40 feet tall in this film, is imprisoned in an underground bunker. Klaatu is arrested and interrogated by the authorities but escapes. He kills, and then at Helen's request, resurrects a state

Figure 21. MacReady (Kurt Russell), armed with a makeshift flamethrower, examines the frozen and partially transformed remains of one of his colleagues in *The Thing* (1982) (Universal Pictures/Photofest).

trooper. Believing that humans will not change, he eventually begins the process of destroying all human life on the planet. At a command, GORT transforms into a vast cloud of nanobots that swarm the Earth, turning people into puffs of dust in the blink of an eye. Just as things look hopeless, Helen and Jacob manage to convince Klaatu that humans are worth saving, and he stops the destruction at the cost of his own life.

Like many remakes of acknowledged classics, this film met with a poor public and critical response. Reviewer Matthew Lucas summed up the gist of what many other reviewers felt when he wrote, "This remake doesn't have a single practical reason for its existence. Go rent the original instead" (Lucas).

Conclusions

There are several conclusions we can draw from the examples above. The first is that all of the films discussed have been adapted in one way or another, and the work of adaptation has left fingerprints. In many cases, the intentions of the filmmakers become obvious when viewed in the context of earlier iterations. While direct remakes of these films have not been successful, films that have followed the more general patterns they set have often been quite well-received. It is always a dicey prospect to remake a classic, but later filmmakers who have been willing to *adapt* the basic patterns of earlier success have done better at the box office. This willingness to adapt has also allowed filmmakers to capture and preserve the cultural fears or concerns of their different eras, like bugs in amber. That, alone, is worthy of further study.

The second, and I hope by this point obvious, conclusion we can draw is that the patterns or archetypes established by *The Thing from Another World* and *The Day the Earth Stood Still* are alive and well. Even films like *Independence Day*, which are ostensibly based on other texts, often adjust themselves to fit the patterns set by these two films. These patterns are durable in part because the alien threat or the alien warning are both flexible. Aliens can serve as cautionary tales about anything from the threat of nuclear war and communist invasion to the dangers of environmental degradation and corporate overreach. Moreover, both responses to the alien visitors/invaders portrayed in these films potentially make sense depending entirely upon the nature of the alien. A suspicious and, when needed, violent military is an absolute necessity in *The Thing from Another World* or *Independence Day* but only causes trouble in *The Day the Earth Stood Still* or *Arrival*. The opposite may be said of scientific curiosity. The question, then, is not the absolute rightness of militarism or science but rather the nature of aliens encountered. Government bureaucracy and red tape, however, are nearly universal targets of ridicule in these films, as is the incompetence of the press/media.

Perhaps most importantly, there's nothing like an alien to remind us what it means to be human and to bring the people of Earth together. As Le Blanc and Odell write of Carpenter's *Starman*, it is "less concerned with examining alien cultures than it is about using alien eyes to interpret the human condition" (70). *The Day the*

Earth Stood Still offers a basically progressive message that there are things about human culture (either personal or public) that need to be changed, and encourages us to change them. *The Thing from Another World* suggests a conservative message reminding us of the goodness and value of the earthly life that we often take for granted. We are typically urged in these films to be watchful and protective of what we have. In both cases, the fictional aliens in these films allow us, as humans, to examine ourselves more carefully, and to see ourselves from a new perspective.

Notes

1. Other notable films from this period include the pro-communist Randolph Scott film *Abilene Town* (1946), *The Iron Curtain* (1948), *The Big Lift* (1950), *Guilty of Treason* (1950), *Peking Express* (1951), *Man on a Tightrope* (1953), *Never Let Me Go* (1953), *Blood Alley* (1955), *Kiss Me Deadly* (1955), *Shack Out on 101* (1955), and the East German *The Call of the Sea* (1951). A later film, *The Lost Missile* (1958), is worth mentioning for its blending of apocalyptic sci-fi and Cold War intrigue.

2. See the Introduction to *Adaptation Studies: New Approaches* (2010).

3. It is tough to miss the similarity of this central plot device to that of Jack Finney's 1954 novel *Invasion of the Body Snatchers* and the subsequent 1956 film adaptation.

4. For more on this film, see Jessica Metzler's essay in this collection.

5. It is worth noting here that Scott has been desperately trying to contact his newspaper during the entire ordeal. At first magnetic storms prevent his radio call, but later he is ordered by the military to keep silent. Though he grumbles at this, he knows it is for the best.

6. Although I will not discuss the *Predator* franchise here, it is certainly worth noting. These films focus on savage hunter-aliens who, à la Richard Connell's "The Most Dangerous Game," travel to Earth to hunt and kill humans as trophies. Although they don't seem to have any interest in conquering the planet, in other ways they fit the violent stereotype described above. Perhaps it should not be surprising that two of the films in this series, *Alien Versus Predator* (2004) and *Alien Versus Predator: Requiem* (2007) serve as crossovers between the worlds of these two franchises.

7. David Ketterer notes that van Vogt charged the *Alien* filmmakers with plagiarism and was eventually paid $50,000 in an out-of-court settlement (47).

8. In a nod to Arthur C. Clark, Levinson later explains the principle of geosynchronous satellite communications pioneered by Clark.

9. The computer virus is a twist on the biological virus that kills the aliens in Wells' *War of the Worlds*.

10. For a longer discussion of this film, see Joan Ormrod's essay in this collection.

11. The Christian overtones of the name have long been noted by scholars.

12. Drew Pearson, particularly featured at the beginning of the film, was quite suspicious of Joseph McCarthy and HUAC. He was even involved in a tussle with the senator in a nightclub (Tye).

13. These aliens are almost always coded as male.

14. Jaffe's casting was controversial. Blaustein reports that before shooting started he was approached by a nervous casting director and asked to fire Jaffe and recast the part. Blaustein wanted Jaffe, however, for a number of reasons, not the least of which was his left-leaning political views ("Making"). He finally appealed to Darryl Zanuck, who supported Jaffe.

15. *The Day the Earth Stood Still* was not alone in its science-fiction–based criticism of America's Cold War military policies. *Rocketship X-M*, written in part by another blacklisted Hollywood writer, Dalton Trumbo, had been released a year earlier in 1950. It concerned a team of astronauts who accidentally wind up on Mars, only to discover that the inhabitants have literally bombed themselves back to the Stone Age. Atomic weapons have devastated the planet's surface, forcing the few survivors to seek refuge in caves. While *Rocketship X-M* is largely unknown today, *The Day the Earth Stood Still* has become one of the most well-known sci-fi films of all time and a genuine fixture of American culture. For more on *X-M*, see Christopher Love's essay in this collection.

16. Wise also directed several sci-fi films, including *The Andromeda Strain* (1971) and *Star Trek: The Motion Picture* (1979), but he suggests that *The Day the Earth Stood Still*, despite being based on Bates' short story, is the most "original" of his sci-fi films ("Commentary").

17. *Algol* (1920) foreshadows some of the elements of *The Day the Earth Stood Still*. The film traces the rise and fall of Robert Herne (Emil Jannings) after he meets an alien, Algol (John Gottowt), and is given a machine that generates unlimited electrical power. Algol's roles as both a "friendly" alien, and also as one who bears a warning, are questionable, however, and most of the film's plot focuses on Herne's corrupt capitalism and the plight of the workers both before and after the creation of the machine.

18. Other films worth mentioning here are Ian Softley's *Kpax* (2001) and Greg Mottola's *Paul* (2011). *Kpax* follows the earthly adventures of prot (Kevin Spacey), an erstwhile alien locked in a psychiatric facility and cared for by Dr. Mark Powell (Jeff Bridges). Prot gives evidence of his extra-terrestrial origin but eventually is identified as Robert Porter, a man who went insane after his wife and daughter were murdered years before. The film ends ambiguously as prot apparently returns to his home planet of Kpax leaving behind a message of hope and good will as well as the catatonic body of Robert Powell. Striking a much lighter note, *Paul* is one of a handful of films that parodies the basic plot of *The Day the Earth Stood Still*. It retains the idea of a "good" alien at odds with a corrupt and dangerous human world. Throughout the film alien Paul (Seth Rogen) is pursued by a quasi-governmental agency while his human friends Graeme (Simon Pegg), Clive (Nick Frost), and Ruth (Kristen Wiig) fight to save him.

19. Jack Arnold's *It Came From Outer Space* (1953) also reflects the idea of a friendly alien established by *The Day The Earth Stood Still*, but in this film the focus is more centrally on the human reaction to the aliens, and less on the other elements of the archetype, such as the alien's warning. Coincidentally, John Carpenter cites this film as an important influence (Cumbow 4).

20. A prequel, imaginatively titled *The Thing*, was also released in 2011 to abysmal box office returns.

Works Cited

Albrecht-Crane, Christa, and Dennis Cutchins. "Introduction." *Adaptation Studies: New Approaches*, edited by Christa Albrecht-Crane and Dennis Cutchins. Fairleigh Dickinson University Press, 2010, pp. 11–22.

"Baruch Plan." *Wikipedia*, 15 Dec. 2021, https://en.wikipedia.org/wiki/Baruch_Plan. Accessed 27 Dec. 2021.

Bates, Harry. "Farewell to the Master." *Prospero's Isle*, 13 April 2017, https://www.prosperosisle.org/spip.php?article875. Accessed 21 June 2021.

Campbell, John W., Jr. "Who Goes There." *Prospero's Isle*, 16 Jan. 2020, https://www.prosperosisle.org/spip.php?article975. Accessed 21 June 2021.

Carpenter, John. "An Interview with John Carpenter." Interview by Ronald V. Borst, *The Cinema of John Carpenter: The Technique of Terror*, edited by Ian Conrich and David Woods. Wallflower Press, 2004, pp. 167–79.

"Commentary." *The Day the Earth Stood Still*, directed by Robert Wise, 2002, DVD.

Cumbow, Robert. *Order in the Universe: The Films of John Carpenter*, Second edition. Scarecrow Press, 2000.

Hawks, Howard. "Interview." Interview by Jacques Becker, et al. *Howard Hawks Interviews*, edited by Scott Breivold. University Press of Mississippi, 2006, pp. 3–15.

Hawks, Howard. "A Private Interview." Interview by Peter Lehman and staff, *Howard Hawks Interviews*, edited by Scott Breivold. University Press of Mississippi, 2006, pp. 159–92.

Keenan, Richard C. *The Films of Robert Wise*. Scarecrow Press, 2007.

Ketterer, David. *Canadian Science Fiction and Fantasy*. Indiana University Press, 1992.

Le Blanc, Michelle, and Colin Odell. *John Carpenter*. Kamera Books, 2011.

Lucas, Matthew. "Why Remake a Sci-Fi Masterpiece?. *The Dispatch.com*, 17 Dec. 2008, https://www.the-dispatch.com/news/20081218/why-remake-a-sci-fi-masterpiece. Accessed 29 Oct. 2020.

"Making the Earth Stand Still." *Bonus Materials*. *The Day the Earth Stood Still*, directed by Robert Wise, 2002, DVD.

McCarthy, Todd. *Howard Hawks: The Grey Fox of Hollywood*. Grove Press, 1997.

Muir, John Kenneth. *The Films of John Carpenter*. McFarland, 2000.

"Stranger from Venus." *Wikipedia*, 21 Nov. 2021, https://en.wikipedia.org/wiki/Stranger_from_Venus. Accessed 27 Dec. 2021.

Tye, Larry. "Drew Pearson vs. Joe McCarthy: The Unmaking of the Modern American Demagogue." *Nieman Reports*, 9 July 2020, https://niemanreports.org/articles/drew-pearson-vs-joe-mccarthy-demagogue/. Accessed 19 June 2021.

Filmography

Algol: Tragedy of Power. Dir. Hans Werckmeister. UFA, 1920. Film.

Alien. Dir. Ridley Scott. 20th Century Fox, 1979. Film.

Aliens. Dir. James Cameron. 20th Century Fox, 1986. Film.

Arrival. Dir. Denis Villeneuve. Paramount Pictures, 2016. Film.

The Day the Earth Stood Still. Dir. Robert Wise, 20th Century Fox, 1951. Film.

The Day the Earth Stood Still. Dir Scott Derrickson, 20th Century Fox, 2008. Film.

Independence Day. Dir. Roland Emmerich, 20th Century Fox, 1996. Film.
Rocketship X-M. Dir. Kurt Neumann, Lippert Pictures, 1950. Film.
Starman. Dir. John Carpenter, Columbia Pictures, 1984. Film.
Stranger From Venus. Dir. Burt Balaban, Princess Pictures, 1954. Film.
The Thing. Dir. John Carpenter, Universal Pictures, 1982. Film.
The Thing from Another World. Dir. Christian Nyby (Howard Hawks), 1951. Film.
War of the Worlds. Dir. Byron Haskin, 1953. Film.

Queer Anxieties and Perverse Desires in the Alien Infiltration Film

Mica A. Hilson

The alien invasion movie, epitomized by films like *Invaders from Mars* (1953) and *Invasion of the Body Snatchers* (1956), was a staple of 1950s sci-fi. A generation later, filmmakers who grew up watching these movies created their own remakes, including Tobe Hooper's *Invaders from Mars* (1986) and Abel Ferrara's *Body Snatchers* (1993). During the same later period, there were numerous parodies of 1950s mind-controlling alien invasion tropes on television sitcoms and cartoons,[1] as well as film adaptations of books with similar themes, like *The Puppet Masters* (1994), an adaptation of Robert Heinlein's 1951 novel. As scholars like Nora Sayre, David Seed, and Vivian Sobchack have argued, the first wave of alien invasion films spoke to Cold War paranoia about America and its institutions being infiltrated by forces seeking to subvert American freedom and individualism. But with the era of McCarthyist witch hunts long gone by the time this remake cycle rolled around, what cultural anxieties did these 1980s and 1990s remakes harness to generate a sense of horror and suspense?

I suggest that two other "witch hunts" from the late 1980s and early 1990s provide an important cultural context for understanding the cycle of alien invasion movie remakes and adaptations from that period. Namely, I will focus on the panic about the sexual abuse of children epitomized by the McMartin preschool trial and the paranoid discourse about gay men in the military, which culminated in the Clinton era's "Don't Ask, Don't Tell" policy. While the paranoid discourse of the Red Scare may have relied on some abstract metaphors about communists infiltrating and infecting the body politic, these later panics were fueled by lurid details about actual bodies being penetrated or violated. As many media critics have since noted, the coverage of the McMartin preschool case from outlets like the *Los Angeles Times* was highly sensationalistic, full of graphic descriptions of small children being fondled or sodomized by their teachers in increasingly bizarre settings, including a hot air balloon (Butler et al.). The McMartin case was only one of many cases in the 1980s where day care centers were accused of mass child abuse (often in conjunction with the practice of satanic rituals); other examples included the Kern County child abuse cases in California (1982), the Fells Acres Day Care case in Massachusetts (1984), the Wee Care Nursery School case in New Jersey (1985), and the Little

Rascals Day Care case in North Carolina (1989). What these cases all had in common is that they relied very heavily on the testimony of small children who were coaxed and coerced by child psychologists hired to "recover" memories of their supposed sexual abuse, claims which have since been discredited. Based on the credulous initial media coverage of these cases, many Americans in the 1980s might have assumed that the nation was experiencing an epidemic of ritual child sexual abuse, a fear that all three films I will analyze play upon.

Each of the three films I will be examining in detail here—*Invaders from Mars* (1986), *Body Snatchers* (1993), and *The Puppet Masters* (1994)—also depicts members of the U.S. military coming under the control of alien invaders. Furthermore, the two later films actually suggest that the military is uniquely vulnerable to such infiltration. Aside from one female soldier who appears in several shots of Ferrara's film, these movies depict the military as an all-male institution, one in which men who have been "corrupted" by the controlling aliens can easily corrupt their fellows. I seek to contextualize these scenes in relation to contemporary discourses surrounding the U.S. military's "Don't Ask, Don't Tell" policy, which allowed gay men and lesbians to serve in the military insofar as they remained completely closeted about their sexual identities. As Dana Britton and Christine Williams wrote in their 1995 analysis of the popular discourses surrounding the policy, "no contemporary discussion [of DADT] is complete without the requisite 'shower scene' in which gay men ... gaze licentiously at unsuspecting heterosexuals" (9). Considering the large number of anxious jokes about men "dropping the soap" in the shower and having to bend over to pick it up, they conclude that "heterosexual men are most concerned about ... exposing themselves to the possibility of penetration" (10). Thus, the imagined threats of both anal penetration and the penetrating gaze of the gay man loomed large in the paranoid discourse surrounding DADT. In the later films—and *The Puppet Masters* in particular—we get a conflation of these two threats, with numerous close-up shots where alien-controlled soldiers stare at their comrades for an uncomfortably long time, before giving those men over to aliens who penetrate their bodies, usually from behind.

The two panics I am considering as cultural contexts for the 1980s and 1990s cycle of alien invasion remakes—over sexual abuse in daycares and gays in the military—might not seem to have much in common, but they are both related to anxieties about sexuality and the breakdown of the traditional family structure. It is no coincidence that the hysteria about child care centers came at a time when an unprecedented number of American women were working outside the home. For this reason, the alien invasion films from this period lend themselves exceptionally well to a Freudian analysis. According to Freudian theory, the human subject starts off in a state of polymorphous perversity, indiscriminately aroused by a variety of sensations; eventually, however, we are taught to channel our desires in socially normative ways. A key part of this psychosexual development is what Freud terms the Oedipal phase, a period in which the boy identifies with his father but also views him as a rival for the mother's affections; eventually, the boy keeps his identification with his father but transfers his desires to a more age-appropriate female love object, setting up conditions for the heterosexual family structure to reproduce itself to a further generation.

In all three of the movies I will consider, the heroes are the ones asserting an Oedipal and heteronormative family dynamic, whereas the aliens are seeking to subvert the Oedipus complex and implant other, more perverse desires in their hosts.

Invaders from Mars

Consider two versions of a climactic scene from *Invaders from Mars* (the 1953 original directed by William Cameron Menzies and the 1986 remake by Tobe Hooper). Both have the same basic premise: young David, who has alerted the authorities to an alien takeover of his town, gets sucked into a sandpit near his house. Underground he finds an alien flying saucer. With him is a caring medical professional—Dr. Patricia Blake (Helena Carter) in the original, and nurse Linda Magnuson (Karen Black) in the remake—who has taken on a maternal role ever since David's own mother got controlled by the aliens. As David and his surrogate mother figure are held captive by the aliens, who plan to implant them with mind-control crystals, military forces are converging on the underground alien base. However, one member of the military, Sergeant Rinaldi, has also been abducted and is being controlled by the aliens.

Figure 22. Dr. Pat Blake (Helena Carter) is menaced by the mind control implantation device in *Invaders from Mars* (1953) (Twentieth Century–Fox/Henry Fera/Photofest).

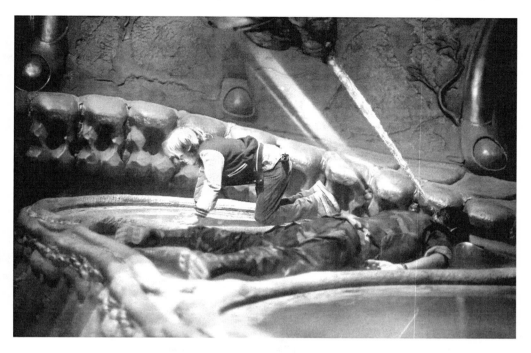

Figure 23. The alien implantation device looms over the unconscious Sergeant Major Rinaldi (Eric Pierpoint), as David Gardner (Hunter Carson) watches helplessly in *Invaders from Mars* (1986) (Cannon/Photofest).

Although they share this same basic premise, the two abduction scenes play very differently, and these divergences reveal quite a bit about how the 1986 remake is tapping into a different set of cultural anxieties than the 1953 original. In the 1953 version, we see two green humanoid aliens carrying a struggling David and Dr. Blake through the passageways of the alien ship, which appear similar to rock formations in a cave; only a few smooth, semi-transparent green bubbles on the walls convey that this is meant to be an alien space. As the film keeps intercutting to scenes of the military actions above ground, the aliens carry their captives into a cylindrical room with smooth metallic walls—apparently some kind of high-tech facility. We then get an oddly framed shot looking from the top of a device in this room: some kind of long metallic tube housed in a plastic cylinder. From this high-angled vantage point, we can just barely spy David and Dr. Blake being dragged beneath this device. Only later, the film reveals the significance of the device; it is what the aliens use to implant their mind control crystals in the necks of their human subjects. As David tries to rouse Dr. Blake, who has apparently fainted from the ordeal, Sergeant Rinaldi enters the room, his stiff gait and distant stare indicating that he is being mind controlled. David recognizes him and calls out his name, but Rinaldi ignores him, instead staring at the globe that houses the alien leader, a mute creature that has an enlarged humanoid head and tiny octopoid limbs. Under the orders of the creature—who he describes as "mankind, developed to its ultimate intelligence"—Rinaldi interrogates Dr. Blake, who is then hauled onto a smooth metallic operating table to be implanted with the device. We then get a number of shots, from a variety of different angles, of an unconscious Dr. Blake lying on the table; in one sequence, we get a close-up of the needle that is about to implant her, followed by a head-and-shoulders shot of her lying face down, her hand covering her forehead, the implantation device aimed at the back of her neck (Figure 22). This is, however, the closest we come to seeing one of the mind control devices being implanted; a minute later Dr. Blake is rescued by her love interest, Dr. Kelston.

Hooper's film, on the other hand, spares no details when showing us how the implantation process works. In his rendering of the scene, when David awakens on the alien ship, he is already in the same room as the device—a chamber that appears more organic, covered with soft pinkish membranes—and he witnesses the implantation of Sergeant Rinaldi. In Hooper's remake, Rinaldi is played by a younger, more handsome actor (Eric Pierpoint), and after David awakens, we get a shot of Rinaldi lying face down on one of these alien membranes, his legs splayed apart, the giant alien device in the foreground, looming over him, the needle at its tip pointed straight at the back of his neck, which is illuminated by a red laser pointer (see Figure 23). Unlike the high-tech metallic and plastic apparatus shown in the 1953 film, the device in the 1986 film appears organic and phallic, a brown bulbous shaft crisscrossed by veins. We see it close up from several different angles, including a low-angle shot with the long needle at the end of the device pointing down and the windows of the ship—which strongly resemble a pair of lungs—in the background, again giving us the sense that the alien ship is a living body.

As David watches in horror, we see the needle slowly start to descend, and then we get a close-up shot as it penetrates the back of Rinaldi's neck, screwing in deep so that not only the thin needle but also the thicker shaft of the device embeds itself at the base of his skull. Once David witnesses this, he immediately begins calling out Linda's name, fearful that his beloved mother figure will be the next to be implanted by the aliens. As he tries to awaken Linda, he is restrained by the Martians' servants, which this remake renders not as humanoids but rather as walking mouths with sharp fangs and veiny, gooey brown bodies. David, however, is not the only viewer of this penetration scene; we also get reaction shots from David's alien-controlled grade school teacher, Mrs. McKeltch, who is watching from one of the ship's lung-shaped windows. Played by Louise Fletcher, best known for her portrayal of sadistic Nurse Ratched in *One Flew Over the Cuckoo's Nest* (1975), Mrs. McKeltch views the process of Rinaldi's implantation with an expression of perverse delight.

On one level, the changes Hooper makes to this climactic scene are emblematic of the differences between sci-fi/horror films from the 1950s and those from the 1980s, when the relaxation of Hollywood production codes (and advancements in special effects makeup) led to more graphic onscreen gore, goo, and body horror. But the otherwise inexplicable presence of Fletcher's character in this scene points to another key difference: the 1986 version of *Invaders from Mars* is laden with psychosexual anxieties that are not present in the original film. Given Fletcher's screen persona, typecast as a castrating woman who enjoys watching the emasculation of men, the audience is invited to view Rinaldi's operation as a symbolic sodomization. Rinaldi, who earlier in the film appeared as a masculine role model for David, is shown to be vulnerable to rear penetration, and worse still—judging by the open-mouthed faces he makes immediately afterward—he seems to enjoy it.

In fact, the film is filled with images of anality. In another key scene set on the alien spaceship, the Martian leader—who resembles a huge swollen brain attached to the body of a tapeworm—slowly emerges through a circular hole in the wall that looks suspiciously like a giant sphincter. Both the aliens and the humans they control are also associated with perverse orality. Early in the film, David's father George is the first person shown to be under alien control, and we get an over-the-shoulder shot from David's perspective of the strange red mark on the back of his father's neck, the sign of his rear penetration by the aliens. As father and son sit down to breakfast, David gets an even clearer sign that something is wrong; staring silently at his son, George dumps an entire container of saccharine into his coffee cup, then gulps down the entire cup in a single sitting, coffee dripping down his chin as the film repeatedly cuts to shots of David's nauseated reactions. This is only one of several gratuitous scenes of gross orality that Hooper inserts without ever providing a logical explanation of why being under alien control would change the way people eat. In later scenes, we see David's mother Ellen—played, in another intertextual wink, by former *Saturday Night Live* Conehead Laraine Newman—eating a chunk of raw hamburger meat, then his evil teacher Mrs. McKeltch swallowing a live frog. The film's emphasis on orality culminates with the reveal of the alien mouth creatures, one of whom eventually swallows Mrs. McKeltch whole.

So why does Hooper place so much emphasis on mouths and the disgusting things people do with them? One practical reason is that it allows Hooper, best known for gory R-rated films like *The Texas Chain Saw Massacre* (1974) and *Lifeforce* (1985), an opportunity to sneak some body horror in a PG-rated picture. In fact, Hooper's *Invaders from Mars* is not the only remake of a 1950s alien invasion movie aimed at a juvenile audience that added gratuitous scenes of orality. A Halloween-themed 1990 episode of the family sitcom *Growing Pains*, which I vividly remember from my own childhood, includes a black-and-white parody of the genre, in which the teenage protagonist witnesses his friends and family members being replaced by alien doppelgangers who have the bizarre trait of craving coffee and wanting to pour it directly down the front of their pants, where their "mouths" are supposedly located. As in Hooper's movie, the young man panics when confronted with all this perverse behavior. He ends the story trying to resist the hordes (including his own mother and father) chanting "Join us!" while attempting to pour coffee down his mouth.

With its unsettling implication that the aliens have mouths where their genitals should be, the sitcom episode underscores something also seen in Hooper's *Invaders from Mars*; the aliens (and the humans under their control) are associated with what Freud termed the *pregenital phase* of psychosexual development, which is also part of the *pre–Oedipal phase*. As the name suggests, the pregenital phase predates the child's fascination with the genitals and the signs of sexual difference—to wit, in the *Growing Pains* episode, the boy's mother and father each have the same mouths where their different genitals should be. Instead, the small child in this phase of development is more interested in the pleasures of anality and orality. The entry into the genital phase is also the precursor into the Oedipal stage, wherein the boy identifies with the father and views him as a rival for the mother's affections. A Freudian reading of Hooper's film, then, might interpret it as a psychodrama about David's attempts to go through the Oedipal stage, resisting the "alien" forces trying to draw him back into pre–Oedipality.

As I have been arguing, the emphasis on bodies and perversity in Hooper's remake lends itself to a Freudian interpretation; however, although it has a much cleaner and technological aesthetic, the 1953 original is also highly Freudian in its own way. Each film focuses on different aspects of Freudian developmental psychology; the 1953 original is about the Freudian "family romance," whereas the 1986 remake offers an especially perverse take on the Freudian "primal scene." In the Freudian schema, the "family romance" is a fantasy that the child has when he realizes that his parents are flawed and begins to question their authority; as a result, he imagines that he must be adopted and his real parents are much better. This fantasy essentially plays out in the 1953 *Invaders from Mars*, as young David's loving parents suddenly become cold and angry, and he quickly acquires a pair of surrogate parents (Dr. Blake and Dr. Kelston) who respect him enough to act on his implausible stories about alien invaders. More specifically, it follows what Freud termed the "first (asexual) stage" of the family romance; unlike the 1986 remake, with its highly eroticized imagery, it is simply about the child fulfilling his desire for independence from his parents.

Hooper's remake of the film, however, might be best understood in terms of another Freudian concept, the "primal scene." This was Freud's term for the child's realization that his parents are having sexual intercourse, which the child initially misrecognizes as a scene of violence (often leading him to want to protect the mother from the father who is "hurting" her). To that end, Hooper makes some subtle but telling changes to an iconic scene from the original film, where David's alien-controlled father takes his wife on a walk "over the hill" (toward the sand dunes where the alien ship lies submerged). In the original scene, they are walking hand in hand in bright daylight; Hooper restages the scene from David's perspective, as he watches from out his bedroom window at night, wailing "Mommmm!" as he spies his father guiding his mother into this secluded make out spot with an arm draped around her shoulder. Although David is initially powerless to protect his mother, he is able to direct that protectiveness toward his mother-surrogate Linda; hence, after he sees Rinaldi being penetrated by the aliens, his first thought is to save Linda from a similar fate. Tellingly, the one key character absent in Hooper's remake is Dr. Kelston, the astronomer who serves as romantic male lead and rescues Dr. Blake (that film's Linda equivalent). A few of his plot functions are fulfilled by Bud Cort's scientist character, Mark Weinstein, but he is depicted as a buffoon who eventually gets eaten by one of the aliens. This gives David more room to assume his other plot functions as the male romantic hero, seeking to rescue his beloved Linda. Thus, in Hooper's remake, David's desires are highly Oedipal, and he is fighting against the pre–Oedipal erotics of orality and anality that the aliens represent.

The coldness of David's parents in the 1953 film also fits within the conventions of Cold War propaganda, which frequently represented Soviets and other communists as lacking the warmth that supposedly characterized typical Americans. Even though the Cold War was still an ongoing concern in 1986, Hooper's remake removes the alien invasion film from its Cold War contexts and instead situates its paranoia in relation to anxieties about secret perverts—a topic that would have been on the minds of contemporary audience members who were following the news about the McMartin Preschool trial or any of the other cases of alleged sexual abuse at daycare facilities. If the 1953 *Invaders from Mars* tapped into anti-communist propaganda about secret rings of conspirators trying to sabotage the U.S. government and its military operations, the 1986 remake devotes much less attention to the conspiracy thriller aspects of the story and much more to the queer behavior of the alien-controlled adults. Furthermore, whereas the original film emphasizes the sudden coldness and hostility of David's parents, in the remake they remain highly affectionate—perhaps even too affectionate, as we see David cringing a bit when his father strokes his cheek. Only five minutes earlier in the movie, similar gestures are used to signify that George and David have a healthy father-son relationship, as he tousles the boy's hair and tucks him into bed; the only difference in the later scene, aside from the ominous piano chords playing on the soundtrack, is that George's gestures appear slower and more deliberate.

Tellingly, the original film never shows David at school; this setting—and the character of evil teacher Mrs. McKeltch—are only added in the 1986 version, when the hysteria about child sexual abuse at schools and daycare centers was at its height. One of the most outrageous allegations from the McMartin Preschool trial came from children who—after being coaxed by child psychologists hoping to find evidence of mass abuse—claimed that they were taken to subterranean tunnels located beneath the school, where they were molested and forced to perform Satanic rituals. A group of parents was so determined to find evidence of these tunnels that, in 1990, they actually hired an archeologist to perform an excavation of the grounds beneath the preschool. Later analysis found that the school had simply been built on an old trash pit (Wyatt 33–34). In Hooper's film, Mrs. McKeltch is similarly determined to bring children to a lair of subterranean tunnels where their bodies will be penetrated. David even sees her driving a school bus of his classmates on an impromptu "field trip" to the sand pit near his house, which sucks unsuspecting victims down into the subterranean tunnels below.

Given how Hooper's film styles the alien ship as a living organism, we might say that the aliens' victims are ingested into the bowels of the earth. Whereas the original *Invaders from Mars* presented the alien ship as the technologically advanced product of a superior intelligence, the aliens in Hooper's remake barely seem associated with technology or intelligence at all; rather, they are all appetite, and the perversity of those appetites threatens both the nuclear family and the state.

The Puppet Masters

While not technically a remake, 1994's *The Puppet Masters* was the second attempt to adapt Robert Heinlein's eponymous 1951 novel into a film, the first being

1958's very loose adaptation *The Brain Eaters*. Although the 1994 film sticks more closely to the plot of Heinlein's novel—about mind-controlling alien parasites who attach to the necks and backs of their victims, quickly infesting a large segment of the U.S. population—it still omits some of Heinlein's more outlandish premises, like the twist that the remainder of the U.S. population quickly becomes nudists to demonstrate that they don't have parasitic aliens on their backs.

It does, however, preserve one of the novel's other strange plot points; one of the main signs that a man is under alien control is his lack of a heterosexual male gaze. Early on, the protagonists (a group of special agents) are investigating the strange flying saucer that landed in rural Iowa; in the film, a group of locals (a man and three teenage boys) are selling tickets to curiosity-seekers who want to go inside the craft. The curious tourists are unaware that this is a trap, as the people who walk inside the ship get infested by the parasites. After the special agents survey the situation but decide not to go inside the ship, the only woman in the group, Mary (Julie Warner) tells her male colleagues that "there was something odd about those boys, same with the man at the gate [...] A woman is used to a certain response from men when we meet them, and from those boys, I didn't get the automatic [...] based on what I was doing with my blouse, they should have tried to look down my top, something."

So what kinds of looks are the alien-controlled men giving instead? In the film, if not the original novel, they reserve their desiring, predatory gazes for other men, those who have yet to be taken over by the parasites. Later in the movie, when the main characters have returned to Washington, square-jawed protagonist Sam (Eric Thal) gets infested by a parasite; he then asks an apartment manager, Mr. Greenberg, to help him open a crate shipped from Iowa filled with alien pods. As Sam picks one up, it suddenly begins to open up before Greenberg's incredulous eyes, revealing a spiky tendril in the middle; we then cut to Sam's open-mouthed orgasmic face as he aims the tendril at Greenberg, then restrains the man, ripping his shirt open in the process. In the mirror of the apartment, we see the tendril shoot out of the alien pod and implant itself into the back of Greenberg's neck—a penetration that is then shown in extreme close-up, so we get a good look at the phallic grey tentacle taking him from behind. Then, as Sam continues his open-mouthed orgasmic expression, he looks at an open-shirted Greenberg twitch and spasm as the alien takes over his mind. With no words spoken, the two men then stand back to back so that their alien masters can communicate with each other; we see a string of alien tendrils crawling up the collar of Sam's suit, then interlace themselves with the tendrils extending from Greenberg's parasite, so that for a moment it looks like the two aliens are holding hands.

The film repeats variations on this scenario several times over, in all-male spaces where homosocial interactions quickly turn into homoeroticized scenes of violence. For instance, a few minutes after the scene described above, Sam and Greenberg meet with the leader of the security detail for the president of the United States, who agrees to go with them to a private room to hear confidential information about a threat to the president; once in the room, Sam resumes his orgasm face as he restrains the man, then Greenberg unbuttons his shirt to reveal two alien parasites clinging to his torso, their tentacles dangling just above his beltline. That these scenes depict a symbolic rape gets underscored in a later sequence after Sam has been captured by the protagonists who remove the parasite from his back. When Mary goes to visit Sam in the military hospital, she hears crying coming from the "Infirmary Shower Room"; then, as tinkling sad piano music plays on the soundtrack, she walks into the open shower to find a nude Sam frantically scrubbing his neck, then sobbing in a fetal position, muttering, "Get him off! Just get off of me!" The imagery here strongly resembles the cinematic cliché for depicting the aftermath of a woman's rape, as she sobs in the shower trying to wash away the unclean feeling of the rape. In *The Puppet Masters*, this scene also serves as an entry point into the re-heterosexualization of Sam, who only had eyes for other men when he had the parasite riding on his back; after Mary holds him and reassures him that "it's off you, it's not on you anymore," Sam leans in for an open-mouthed kiss (using roughly the same facial expression he made when penetrating other men under parasite control). It is a fascinatingly Oedipal moment, as Sam is first seen crying childishly and only makes sexual advances toward Mary once she cradles him in a maternal *Pieta* pose. This helps initiate a central plotline in the second half of the movie, where Sam takes on a more standard heterosexual action hero role, bravely venturing into alien-controlled territory to rescue his love interest Mary.

Tellingly, however, the first words we hear Sam sobbing in this shower scene have nothing to do with the parasite; in a childish voice he wails, "I won't! I'm not coming! I'm sorry, Dad," before eventually shouting, "Get him off!" Thus, there is some ambiguity whether the "him" refers to the parasite or to Sam's father, played by Donald Sutherland, who is also Sam's boss and goes by the codename "The Old Man." As Christopher Lockett argues, Heinlein's original novel follows a very Oedipal narrative trajectory, with Sam learning how to challenge his father's authority and ultimately taking over his father's job as national security czar (52). In the film, however, Sam does not challenge the Old Man until the very last action sequence; after it seems that the parasites have been defeated, they discover that the final parasite has hitched a ride on the Old Man's back, and Sam must physically fight him (and shoot him) to defeat it. Here, as in the shower scene dialogue, the parasite and the controlling father are represented as doubles, emasculating figures that the protagonist must overpower to assert his heterosexual manhood.

In the opening scenes of the movie, however, we get a perverse twist on Oedipality, with three teenage boys—the first to encounter the aliens and the ones we later see leading tourists into the parasite-infested flying saucer—defeating an older man. Inverting conventional tropes about sex predators and adolescents, here the boys take the predatory role, luring the man into the woods and knocking him over the head in order to mount a parasite on his back. Such imagery recurs throughout the movie, with children leading the hordes of parasite spreaders, preying on the vulnerability of adults who are afraid to fight them. In one memorable sequence, an army unit in full gear gets into position in an Iowa town, only to confront a wall of children and adolescents advancing toward them with parasites in hand. The film then cuts to a White House briefing room, where officials watch live footage of the raid shot through "a thermal image feed," which show the children's bodies outlined in halos of red, a sign of alien control; as the Old Man intones, "we cannot think of them any longer as children; they are the enemy." As the soldiers are ambushed, their video feed abruptly ends, and we cut to a shot of army jeeps entering a large military base; there, several National Guard troops ask to speak to the general, who has them escorted into his office—and there, behind closed doors, one of the troops takes off his shirt, and the familiar alien penetration scene happens once again. This whole sequence occurs immediately after the scenes where Sam recovers his heterosexual desires with Mary and thus serves as a counterpoint—an image of the contagious pre–Oedipal desires that can spread rapidly among children and in all-male institutions like the military (which, as depicted in this movie and Hooper's *Invaders from Mars*, contains no female soldiers).

Interestingly, if adolescents and children are prime vectors for the infection, a child also ultimately provides the cure. Near the end of the movie, Sam descends into the alien's underground lair (beneath the Des Moines city hall) to rescue Mary from alien control; as in *Invaders from Mars*, these perverse aliens seem most comfortable lurking in the bowels of the earth. There, they find a sick child whom the aliens have quarantined because he harbors a virus that is fatal to them. Taking turns cradling the sick child in their arms—and looking every bit like a nuclear family unit—Sam and Mary fight their way through the parasite-controlled hordes to safety, and before long, the aliens are defeated. Here we encounter what might seem like a paradox; at the start of the movie, minors are the initial vectors of the alien parasites' spread, but ultimately a child serves as a cure for this infestation. However, the key difference between them is that the boys at the start of the movie are represented as desiring subjects (with desires that, as Mary notes, diverge from the supposed heterosexual norm), whereas the child that inoculates humanity from this alien threat appears to have no desires, no dialogue, and no agency. It simply lies limp in Sam and Mary's arms, serving as a prop to illustrate their willingness to assume normative paternal and maternal roles.

Like Hooper's *Invaders from Mars* remake, then, the alien antagonists in *The Puppet Masters* implant their human hosts with desires that diverge from the (heterosexual, genital, Oedipal) norms of adult sexuality. Furthermore, even though one protagonist (David) is a child and the other (Sam) is an adult, they're both defined by their roles as sons and their desire to break out of that role by, in classic Oedipal fashion, heroically rescuing the women who show them affection. Of the two films, *Invaders from Mars* depicts a wider range of perverse acts, depicting scenes of orality and anality, whereas *The Puppet Masters* simply sticks to images of rear penetration, which get associated with the homoerotic male gaze.

Body Snatchers

In his four-star review of Abel Ferrara's *Body Snatchers*, Roger Ebert noted the clever ways that the film locates its horror within both a tense family dynamic and a military setting. The primary character, Marti (Gabrielle Anwar), is a military brat, who moves with her father, stepmother, and younger half-brother to a Southern military base, where they live in on-site housing. As Ebert observes, "Ferrara's key scenes mostly take place at night, on the Army base, where most of the other people are already pod-like in their similar uniforms, language and behavior. There is a crafty connection made between the Army's code of rigid conformity, and the behavior of the pod people, who seem like a logical extension of the same code."

In other words, Ferrara's film suggests that because of its existing culture of conformity and surveillance, the military base is uniquely vulnerable to an alien takeover. He even takes care to show how the military families' houses are spaced closely together, they can look into each other's windows, so that they have virtually no privacy. The base's daycare facility is no exception; Marti's little brother Andy briefly attends it, but he runs away after the teacher has all the children do finger painting and then gives him a hard stare when she discovers Andy is the only child who has not painted a red amorphous blob. As in *Invaders from Mars*, we see shades of the McMartin-era anxiety that daycares and schools might be unsafe spaces for children. Unlike *Invaders from Mars*, however, Andy is not the main hero (even though he is the first member of the family to intuit that something is wrong). Rather than giving Andy an Oedipal storyline (as Hooper's *Invaders from Mars* does for David), he becomes a prop in his sister Marti's Oedipal storyline. As soon as he runs away from the daycare, Andy is found by kindly young soldier Tim, who brings him back home, where Tim meets Marti and quickly becomes her love interest. By the climax of the film, Marti chooses Tim over her own father (who has become a pod person), and the two serve as surrogate parents for young Andy, trying to protect him from the pod people. Tim is shown to have pure intentions in a later scene, where he rescues Marti from an infirmary where the pods are converting humans en masse; he easily resists the seductions of Marti's sexy, topless double, whom he destroys in order to save Marti. Like *The Puppet Masters*, this film tries to have things both ways, by raising alarm about institutions like the military and the family becoming vectors for the alien takeover but also showing us that the best hope against the aliens is a strong-jawed military man, his beautiful female love interest, and the innocent child they protect—a tableau of patriotic family values.

While this hetero-romantic storyline takes center stage, the movie is also full of homoerotic moments, many of which play out silently through uncanny shots of lingering stares. In one scene, Marti and her new friend Jenn head to a bar near the base, where they flirt with Tim and his friend Pete. In the background of these heterosexual dyads, we see a drunken soldier dancing by himself. Before long, however, the camera zooms in on the lone soldier, who is now passed out with his head resting on the bar, and we can see several other soldiers in the background staring at him silently as two similarly stone-faced MPs enter and remove him from the bar. Here, then, the movie contrasts the familiar flirtatious gazes of the heterosexual couples with the menacing and unsettling homoerotic "penetrating gaze" the body-snatched soldiers are directing toward the vulnerable drunken man.

As I have suggested throughout this essay, this cycle of alien invasion remakes derived much of their horror from images of bodies (especially male bodies) being penetrated by aliens. However, they also depicted the penetrability of various spaces that might otherwise be assumed to be safe. The key body horror sequence in *Body Snatchers* is a good illustration of this. It depicts Marti sitting in a bubble bath, falling asleep

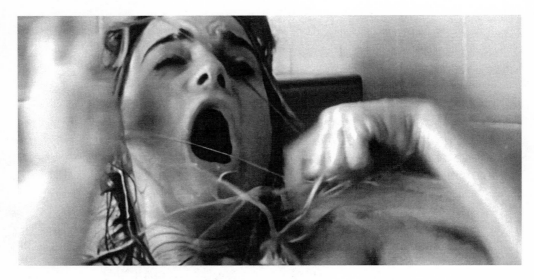

Figure 24. Alien tendrils cover Marti Malone (Gabrielle Anwar) as she bathes in *Body Snatchers* (1993) (Warner Bros. Pictures/Photofest).

as she listens to soothing music on her Walkman; it then cuts to a shot of the attic space above the bathroom, panning over to show a pod lying directly atop the bathroom's porous ceiling tiles. We see the pod's spaghetti-like tendrils snake their way down through those holes in the ceiling, then cut back to the bath, where the tendrils slowly drop down over Marti's head, eventually making their way up her chest and neck and into her mouth and nasal passages. As soon as the tendrils reach these penetrable membranes on Marti's body, the film cuts back to the attic crawlspace, showing an embryo begin to grow in the now-glowing pod, a grotesque version of the famous *Miracle of Life* documentary (1983). The intercutting in this scene helps to emphasize the porousness and vulnerability of both the body and the space Marti occupies. Remakes like Ferrara's *Body Snatchers* and Hooper's *Invaders from Mars* make visceral a notion that the original 1950s films only suggested abstractly: there is no safe space, because the alien can breach any cordon, penetrating anywhere and anyone.

These remakes and adaptations were the product of an era that saw much greater paranoia over the notion that spaces formerly considered safe (such as daycares and military bases) were actually hotbeds of perversity. By the late 1990s, there were still plenty of films and television series that used 1950s alien invasion films as sources of inspiration, but in these works, the aliens were no longer represented as forces of perversity that threatened the sanctity of the family, heteronormativity, and the Oedipus complex. Robert Rodriguez's irreverent *The Faculty* (1998), whose teen heroes defeat the mind-controlling aliens by snorting amphetamines, comes immediately to mind, as does the *Buffy the Vampire Slayer* episode "Bad Eggs" (1998). In that episode, the mind-controlling aliens hatch out of eggs that the show's teenaged protagonists have to care for as part of a home economics assignment preparing them to be parents. Thus, in keeping with *Buffy*'s generally progressive gender and sexual politics, the alien is associated with compulsory heterosexuality and reproduction, rather than with perverse impulses that might disrupt that.

In summary then, the alien invasion genre spawned by *Invaders from Mars* (1953) and *Invasion of the Body Snatchers* (1956) has proven remarkably malleable, capable of supporting allegories about a wide range of anxieties, from the political to the psychosexual. This essay focused on a specific time period (1986–1994) in which the genre moved away from geopolitical considerations (despite the strong military presence in all three films) to instead dwell on domestic sex panics. Further research is needed to fully consider the ways that alien invasion films have since morphed to reflect twenty-first-century fears.

NOTE

1. See, for instance, the "Happy Halloween" episode of the family sitcom *Growing Pains* (1990) or the Bugs Bunny cartoon "Invasion of the Bunny Snatchers" (1992).

WORKS CITED

Britton, Dana, and Christine Williams. "'Don't Ask, Don't Tell, Don't Pursue': Military Policy and the Construction of Heterosexual Masculinity." *Journal of Homosexuality*, vol. 30, no. 1, 1995, pp. 1–21.
Butler, Edgar W., et al. *Anatomy of the McMartin Child Molestation Case.* University Press of America, 2001.
Ebert, Roger. "Body Snatchers." *Chicago Sun-Times*, 25 Feb. 1994. https://www.rogerebert.com/reviews/body-snatchers-1994. Accessed 27 Dec. 2021.
Freud, Sigmund. *Three Essays on the Theory of Sexuality.* Translated by James Strachey. Basic Books, 2000.
Heinlein, Robert A. *The Puppet Masters.* Baen Books, 2010.
Lockett, Christopher. "Domesticity as Redemption in *The Puppet Masters*: Robert A. Heinlein's Model for Consensus." *Science Fiction Studies*, vol. 34, no. 1, 2007, pp. 42–58.
Sayre, Nora. *Running Time: Films of the Cold War.* Dial Press, 1982.
Seed, David. *American Science Fiction and the Cold War.* Routledge, 1999.
Sobchack, Vivian. *Screening Space: The American Science Fiction Film.* Rutgers University Press, 1997.
Wyatt, W. Joseph. "What Was Under the McMartin Preschool? A Review and Behavioral Analysis of the 'Tunnels' Find." *Behavior and Social Issues*, vol. 12, no. 1, 2002, pp. 29–39.

FILMOGRAPHY

Body Snatchers. Dir. Abel Ferrara. Warner Bros., 1993. Film.
The Brain Eaters. Dir. Bruno VeSota. American International Pictures, 1958. Film.
Buffy the Vampire Slayer. 20th Century Fox Television, 1997–2003. Television Series.
The Faculty. Dir. Robert Rodriguez. Miramax Films, 1998. Film.
Invaders from Mars. Dir. William Cameron Menzies. 20th Century Fox, 1953. Film.
Invaders from Mars. Dir. Tobe Hooper. Cannon Pictures, 1986. Film.
Invasion of the Body Snatchers. Dir. Don Siegel. Allied Artists Pictures, 1953. Film.
Lifeforce. Dir. Tobe Hooper. Cannon Films, 1985. Film.
Miracle of Life. Dir. Bo G. Erikson. Nova, 1983. Documentary.
One Flew Over the Cuckoo's Nest. Dir. Miloš Forman. United Artists, 1975. Film.
The Puppet Masters. Dir. Stuart Orme. Hollywood Pictures, 1994. Film.
The Texas Chainsaw Massacre. Dir. Tobe Hooper. Vortex, 1974. Film.

The War of the Worlds

Masculine Heroism and Symbolic Spaces in Invasion Narratives

Joan Ormrod

This essay maps out how masculine heroism operates in the different adaptations inspired by H.G. Wells' *The War of the Worlds* to reflect changing perceptions of heroism and the nation. In mapping the discursive construction of three eras' versions of *War of the Worlds* one can identify changing attitudes to American values underpinning politics, masculinity, religion and heroism from the 1953 film adaptation to Steven Spielberg's 2005 adaptation. H.G. Wells' novel became a paradigm for sci-fi alien invasion narratives, and it attracted a vast range of literature along with many cross-media reinventions. It also became the narrative paradigm for later alien invasion narratives.[1] Unlike many of the 1950s films treated in this edited collection, the 1953 film adaptation of *The War of the Worlds* has two precursors: the novel written by H.G. Wells and the radio adaptation by Orson Welles's Mercury Theater (1938). There are many more adaptations of media texts titled *War of the Worlds*, however; Wikipedia lists thirty-four that include "War of the Worlds" in the title. They include two theatrical release films, several television series, animations, comics, games, musicals and operas, mainly from the United States and the UK but also France, Poland and Malaysia. The alien invasion narrative is the model for many more tangential invasion narratives such as *Independence Day* (1996), sequels like *War of the Worlds* (1988), mockumentaries such as *War of the Worlds: The True Story* (2012), mashups like *Superman and the War of the Worlds* (1998), and parodies akin to *Mars Attacks!* (1996).

For this essay I mapped 40 narratives in films, television series and radio drama, mostly inspired by or featuring the title *War of the Worlds*, to identify the times when there were more adaptations or a surge in this sci-fi sub-genre.[2] These texts were predominantly produced in the United States. From this list, three eras emerged when there was a surge in alien invasion films and multimedia texts: the 1950s–1960s, 1987–1998, 2005 to the present. The latter era has more adaptations of the text than all the other eras. These eras roughly correspond to times of conflict that caused America to reconsider its place in the world.

The 1950s–1960s adaptations reflected an America confident in its power and future after World War II. Its future was constructed from a belief that science could answer all problems. Despite this confidence, the Cold War and the threat of nuclear annihilation and communism were constant concerns. Internally, America was wrought by concerns over threats to the American family and masculine power posed by women, homosexuality, and juvenile delinquency. It would be difficult to list the vast number of alien invasion narratives from the boom in their post–World War II production during the 1950s and 1960s. Most followed the model established by Susan Sontag: alien arrival, humanity's fruitless attempts to negotiate with them, a united defense, atrocities and humanity's panicked responses, and alien defeat (98). The films usually end with the warning that they are still out there. Most later alien invasion films follow this model.

The crisis in masculinity recurred in all three eras, and it corresponds with the assertion of Teresa Santerre Hobby that sci-fi films are often constructed from a heterosexual male perspective in which women are objects of desire. In the 1950s the fear for masculinity resided in the rigid heterosexual gender roles assigned to men and women within family life. Men were constructed as breadwinners, scientists and family men, women as housewives and mothers (13–36). In the late 1980s to late 1990s a backlash against second wave feminism reflected another crisis in masculinity (Faludi, *Backlash* 230). Externally the late 1980s to the late 1990s reflected *fin de siècle* fears of apocalypse and war in the Middle East. Yet this was a time when communism declined with the dismantling of the Berlin Wall and the USSR. This left America as the sole remaining world superpower. The alien invasion films of this era reflected fears of immigration, Middle Eastern conflict, and female power. *Independence Day* is a response to conflict within and outside of society that reflect war in the Middle East, gender conflicts and eschatological discourses of a *fin de siècle* narrative. These aliens are constructed as a plague of insects, their downfall orchestrated by reassertion of American masculine and global power.

The twenty-first century has been a time of cultural and global upheaval when peoples' lives have been rent by the rise in right-wing politics, global economic crashes, pandemics, and terrorism. The most significant event at the beginning of the century, 9/11, caused another crisis in masculinity according to Susan Faludi (*Terror Dream* 6–9) when the seats of American capitalism, the Twin Towers, were destroyed by an attack by Al-Qaeda. Faludi argues that the attack on the Twin Towers was regarded as a symbolic attack on capitalism and American masculinity. Part of America's cultural response was in the evocation of a 1950s mindset in which traditional values of family and gender roles were the foundation of a golden era. September 11 generated a paranoid mindset that was only exacerbated by later global crises, and it is significant that since 9/11 there have been several adaptations of *War of the Worlds* using the title or alluding to H.G. Wells in naming characters. I would attribute these closer alignments with the source text to *fin de siècle* sensibilities and to some of the apocalyptic, global events happening since the turn of the twenty-first century. The aliens of post–9/11 tend to be animalistic or utterly inhuman in their actions and the setting is usually localized. They arrive on Earth by accident as in *Monsters* (2010) and *Attack the Block!* (2011). Or else, in closer adaptations of the novel such as Spielberg's *War of the Worlds* (2005), Hine's

H.G. Wells' War of the Worlds (2005), and *War of the Worlds: The True Story* (2012), they attempt to appropriate Earth's resources. The main discourses evoked in this era are a postmodern skepticism of grand narratives in destabilizing realism, heroism, and truth.

In all three eras there was a crisis in masculinity and changes in notions of American heroism. The 1950–1960s scientist hero explored in other essays in this collection gives way to the maverick rag tag heroes of the 1980s–1990s and to the ordinary man, the bystander of the twenty-first century. These changes in heroism reflect fluid concepts of masculinity and hegemonic masculinity that Raewyn W. Connell argues, is variable. Connell argues that masculinity is linked with gendered, racial and ethnic power relations (30–34). Intersectionality, a concept identified by Pamela Hill Collins, suggests there are many masculinities, gay, heterosexual, racial, ethnic, each with its own constructions (Collins and Bilge 2). Each is as important as the others, and these notions inflect perceptions of what in the twenty-first century might be described as hegemonic masculinities. Nevertheless, certain characteristics define hegemonic masculinity in any one era. Hence, 1950s masculinity was embedded in the family in which the father was the head and the mother and children depended on him for the income and a regulating presence. In the 1980s into the 1990s, hegemonic masculinity was modelled on the hard, outdoor body as epitomized by President Reagan, Sylvester Stallone, or Superman (Jeffords 12).

These perceptions of masculinity affect perceptions of the American hero. The American hero has been discursively constructed based on American values and history, and so in identifying how heroism has changed, one can identify changing American ideals. Heroism, like masculinity, is a fluid concept. Mapping the changes in heroism in these three eras enables the identification of changing cultural values and the place of men in American culture. The model for America heroism was identified in a trilogy of books by Richard Slotkin (1972, 1985, 1992) in which he argued that the source of American heroism was the frontier and the hero's relationship with the land. The myth of the frontier as a space that forged heroism was a myth based on violence. The frontier formed the boundary between civilization and wilderness, and in European settlers' expansion into Native American lands violence was deemed necessary. The frontier formed the basis for the American monomyth of heroism in the hero who tames the wilderness and the corruption of society through violence.

The frontier wars between settlers and Native Americans, argues Slotkin, formed the narrative or the terms for later American conflicts. Vietnam and the space program, for example, were regarded as a means of expanding the American frontier. The frontier wars constructed American conflict through the binary savage-vs-civilized war. American conflicts were often predicated on America's construction as the blameless victim of aggression, and the alien invasion films are usually at great pains to illustrate how alien attack and the destruction of national monuments and places locates America as victim against a merciless foe.

Considering America's concept of heroism based on violence, masculinity and place, my analysis examines the symbolism America attaches to the places the aliens attack to determine what they mean to America at that specific time. These places often represent myths about masculine heroism; consequently, I examine gendered relationships at the beginning of the text and how they change by the end.

War of the Worlds *Three Ways*

The source text for *The War of the Worlds* is the *fin de siècle* novel by H.G. Wells (1898). The novel added an alien twist to the literary sub-genre of invasion narratives in the nineteenth century. It was written to reflect Wells' views on British colonialism in which Darwinism was frequently used as a rationale for the subjugation of other peoples, their lands, and their resources. Wells' novel showed how little it took to break down the civilized veneer of people under attack. The Martians attacked humanity to appropriate the earth's resources, much as European powers appropriated the resources from the lands they colonized. Wells described the Martian invaders using discourses constructing Mars in the nineteenth century as a dying, older planet inhabited by a race of superior beings. The Martians in Wells' *War of the Worlds* eschewed body over mind; their limbs were feeble and spindly and they possessed heads that were four feet in diameter, a nod to the Victorian pseudo-science of phrenology in which a large cranium denoted vast intellect (Gould). The Martians rely on technology to enable body movement and violence, and they attack using heavily armed tripods, heat rays, and poisonous black smoke to destroy humanity.

The protagonist of the novel is given no name. He is an ordinary man who is not always the focus of the narrative. Sometimes the narrative centers on his brother. Thus, Wells debunked notions of male heroism in favor of the hero as "one of us." This was not the only area in which Wells challenged traditional turn-of-the-century narratives. In his depiction of the Martians, Wells, an atheist, challenged notions of a protective God and a human-centered universe. The Martians seemed invulnerable and superior in most ways to humanity (Parrinder 16). A human deputation to parley with the Martians was incinerated by a heat ray, and the Martians set out on a destructive path across the globe, destroying humanity with heat rays and poisonous black smoke. The army proved nearly useless, and humanity was reduced to refugees, scavenging, hiding, and using violence against each other to survive. In one such scavenging trip made by the narrator and a curate, Martian cruelty and inhumanity is revealed; the men witness Martians draining human blood for food. Wells also challenged Western Cartesian philosophy that preferences mind over body. He showed that by ignoring the importance of the body, the Martians were as weak as humans for, by ingesting human blood, they also ingest and are defeated by viruses against which they have no immunity.

Joshua Gunn lists the influences on *War of the Worlds* adaptations starting with H.G. Wells' novel. He argues that the novel was a critique of British imperialism and relied on scientific evidence to convince readers of its authenticity. The first main adaptation of the novel set the scene for later revisions with an American setting. Orson Welles' radio play (1938) was written and performed in the style of news reportage. It inspired a host of its own literature[3] and spinoff adaptations.[4] In 1953 Byron Haskin and George Pal produced the first major film adaptation of *War of the*

Worlds, and it was infused with American values and heroism to reconcile fears of communism and the Cold War. The 2005 Steven Spielberg adaptation, on the other hand, responded to the horror of 9/11.

However, it was in the 1950s when sci-fi and alien invasion narratives became popular. Haskin's *The War of the Worlds* (1953) was one of the many alien invasion films produced in the 1950s and is regarded as a classic and influential film adaptation of the narrative. Like other alien invasion films of this era, it reflected Cold War fears of communism and the atomic bomb (Biskind 322–324; Jancovich 325). As such, according to Peter Hutchings, the film adjusted Wells' anti-imperialist position in favor of an examination of American cultural fears during the Cold War (33–36).

The War of the Worlds *(1953)*

Post–World War II America was affluent and optimistic, and its affluence was based on the growth of consumerism, the American project to expand their frontier, and the space industry. Although America superficially seemed invincible, it suffered from concerns about what it considered threats to the American way of life. Mark Jancovich describes American perceptions of itself as disempowered within a complicated and hostile outside world (325). Externally there was the threat of communism, internally there were threats to masculinity in terms of homosexuality, juvenile delinquency, crime, and violence. Jean-Paul Gabilliet argues that the rosy picture of the post-war American way of life was a response to the destabilization of American life during the Great Depression of the 1930s and World War II. After the War, newspaper reports raised domestic concerns with reports of a resurgence of mob crime but also in an increased reporting of alien visits that seemed to confirm Americans' perceptions of attack.

The first UFO sighting in America was on June 24, 1947, over Mt. Rainier, Washington State. Gabilliet argues that the American public at that time was disinterested in the claims of Soviet secret weapons or alien visitation, and preferred to believe that the sightings were of domestic origin. Fears of domestic subversion were garnered from Cold War rhetoric exacerbated by mass media narratives of invasions from Mars in comics, films and television shows. These fears were nurtured with the ending of the American nuclear monopoly (August 1949), the Korean War (1950), and the founding of the People's Republic of China (1949). Gabilliet ascribes the slow growth from the threat to public fears to "*culture lag:* the difference between the appearance of a true or false phenomenon and the time it takes for a society to catch up and deal with it" (6–7). Project Blue Book, stationed at Wright-Patterson Air Force Base, reported the number of U.S. UFO sightings 1947–1969 as 12,618 with 701 "Unidentified" (National Archives). Conspiracy theories surround many of these sightings, along with reports of alien encounters, the most prominent being an alleged cover-up of an alien spacecraft and its occupants at Roswell, New Mexico, in July 1947.

As noted above, American cinema embraced the alien invasion sub-genre whole-heartedly after World War II. The 1950s and 1960s films emphasized disaster and the apocalyptic breakdown of society in the wake of the alien

Figure 25. Movie poster from *The War of the Worlds* (1953) (Paramount Pictures/Photofest).

attack. Alien invasion films may be understood in part as the result of Hollywood moving away from vertically integrated studio systems to the rise of independent studios (Doherty 2). Independent studios, as Thomas Doherty argues, targeted teenage audiences, and they consisted of exploitative plots with lurid marketing that promised thrills, spectacle, and sex. Genres such as sci-fi that were previously regarded as Saturday Matinee fare became popular with these double feature B movies. Aliens represented the threat of communist invasion, often by stealth as in films such as *Invaders from Mars* (1953).[5] This film is set in the family as the ideal living arrangement. George MacLean is a scientist, shown in the beginning teaching his son, David, about space. On investigating a flying saucer landing site, George returns a changed man, and David soon realizes his father has been taken over by alien powers. The film aligns mindlessness with communism, and warns of the perils of falling prey to brainwashing. The Martians are ruled by a being with a large head who creates mutants to do the bidding of their master. In this way mind and body are separated, with intellect emphasized. According to Mark Jancovich, the aliens in alien invasion narratives are consistently aligned with science and technology. "They resist anthropomorphism and are little more than biological machines" (325). However, Jancovich points to the defeat of the aliens through humanity's access to emotions, intuition, and imagination, all of which, Jancovich claims, are female qualities discussed below.

The 1953 adaptation of *The War of the Worlds* is a paradigm of alien invasion films where the aliens make an overt rather than covert attack. It expresses American Cold War paranoia in the ways it represents aliens, and its use of stock footage from World War II to illustrate the utter devastation of Martian attack. It located itself in its marketing with H.G. Wells where his name and the novel featured prominently on posters with a logline, "At this very moment spaceships from the beyond may be on their way to destroy our planet!" The opening commentary, voiced by Sir Cecil Hardwicke, lays out the logic behind the Martian attack in the earth as the "Goldilocks planet" that presented the ideal conditions for life. Mars is a planet in the "last stages of exhaustion." The Martians consider the planets in the solar system that they might inhabit, but Earth is the only one that is not too hot nor cold and therefore the perfect place to colonize.

The film was produced by Paramount, one of the big five film studios, and it had a bigger budget ($2,000,000) than typical B-movie independent films. It was described in *Variety*, December 31, 1952, as "a socko science-fiction feature, as fearsome as a film as the Orson Welles 1938 radio interpretation of the H.G. Wells novel" (*Variety*, "The War of the Worlds"). This review makes particular mention of the special effects for which it achieved a glowing reputation that continues, even in this time of advanced CGI. The special effects were produced by George Pal who had made his name already in sci-fi films with *Destination Moon* (1950) and *When Worlds Collide* (1951). Pal was known for his Academy Award–winning Puppetoon animations, and he planned to use this technique on the war machines. Indeed, the special effects cost up to 70 percent of the budget, but they earned the film an Academy Award. They were also influential in later alien invasion films because of the sound effects. *IMBD* states that the Martian heat rays were produced by playing three guitars backwards, and these sounds were "widely used stock sound effects after the film was released" (*IMDB*, "The War of the Worlds"). The spectacular appeal of the special effects, as noted by Sontag, was one element that became a significant trope of later alien invasion and disaster movie sci-fi films (Bould 66). The special effects came to represent the spectacle that characterized sci-fi in later blockbusters in the genre.

The film was praised by the H.G. Wells estate as a faithful adaptation, despite changes made to the alien technology and to the representation of the aliens. These changes reflected Cold War politics, changes in the Hollywood studio system and changing audience demographics. In one important change, Wells' anonymous hero was replaced by Dr. Clayton Forrester (Gene Barry) an atomic scientist. Forrester is with USC library science instructor Sylvia Van Buren (Ann Robinson) in the small Californian town of Linda Rosa when a shooting star explodes nearby. Although the Martian cylinders land across the world, much of the action concentrates on this small town. This location suggests the significance of small-town America and the inhabitants' family-orientated lifestyles and close community. California in the 1950s and 1960s, too, had significance as the center of the American space industry, as well as a symbol of America as a youthful vibrant state. Consequently, an attack on California could be considered an attack on American values, consumerism, and scientific advancement.

The first indications of alien attack are similar to those from recent UFO sightings: failure of electrical equipment and watches. Major General Mann informs Forrester later in the film that the cylinders are coming down all over the world; "they're working to some kind of plan," he surmises. The first response of the townspeople is to reflect on the commercial implications as a tourist attraction for the landing site. However, when the townspeople find the vaporized remains of three of their neighbors, the shadow-like traces reminiscent of the incinerated bodies after the atomic bomb dropped on Hiroshima, the army is called. In the case of the film, footage of army maneuvers was shot. However, due to budget constraints, George Pal could not replicate the alien tripods from the novel. Instead, he designed spaceships described by Clayton Forrester as "probably some form of magnetic flux, like invisible legs. This is amazing. They must keep the opposing poles in balance and lift the machine." The spaceships were designed to look like manta rays with cobra heads. The Martians were designed and enacted by Charles Gamorra and his daughter, Diana. Their arms were worked with wires. They had huge heads, like the Martians in the novel, with three differently colored eyes like a television camera. The Martians are likened to insects; they live in nests and not family units, which were assumed as the common-sense grouping for people.

Steven Cohan points out the problems for masculine performance in this novel family arrangement. In the 1950s there was an assumption that masculinity could be regarded as a homogenous phenomenon which was explained in an article for *Women's Home Companion*, "The Paradox of the American Male" by Louis Lyndon. Lyndon argued that men who had been soldiers in the War were accustomed to violence, masculine company and constantly changing environments. However, "married men now have to adopt a docile persona that is fundamentally at odds with their inherent masculinity" (Cohan 34–35). As Cohan describes the contrary discourses constructing masculinity in the 1950s, he illustrates the socio-historic construction of masculinities; Lyndon proposes a specific type of masculinity, the soldier, as the ideal type. This, according to Cohan, is at odds with the various masculinities on display in 1950s cinema: playboy bachelors, spies, tough guys, delinquents. He does not mention scientists, another type of ideal masculinity proposed in sci-fi cinema of that period.

As mentioned above, the film departed from the anonymous protagonist in Wells' novel—an anonymity that showed the protagonist as ordinary, just like anyone else. Clayton Forrester is neither nameless nor ordinary. He is a physicist, and his name aligns him with the outdoors, an element reinforced in the opening of the film when we find him on a fishing trip. He values science and intellect, which, for him, can calculate a way to defeat the Martians. His companion, Sylvia, however, places her faith in God and the church. This juxtaposition of science and religion underpins ideas of gender and Cartesian philosophy in the film. Gender roles in *War of the Worlds* are influenced by religion and science, emotion and calculation. The men in the film tend to be aligned with science and intellect, and the women with religion, emotion and the body. One can see this in the male and female leads. Clayton Forrester is a physicist; Sylvia Van Buren is a librarian with a strong religious faith. However, the Martians are defeated only when Clayton realizes that there must be a balance between mind and body. As a scientist, Clayton calculates that they cannot defeat Martian technology so they must defeat the Martian fragile body. When Martian blood is analyzed in a laboratory, he states that the anemic blood might be a clue to defeating them: "We know now that we can't beat their machines," he reasons. "We've got to beat them." This is a tacit acknowledgment that intellect and mind cannot be isolated from the body, however, he does not have a solution for this quandary.

Forrester's lack of faith means he has no God on which to pin his hopes, but science cannot answer superior technology and cold Martian calculation. Sylvia tells Forrester that she received comfort as a child in the church. Sylvia's religious foundation is reinforced in her identification of the biblical apocalyptic theme. She comments that the Martians can destroy the earth in six days, "the same number of days it took to make it." At one point Sylvia's uncle, Pastor Collins, states he will "try to make them understand we mean them no harm. They are living creatures out there … they're more advanced than us, they should be nearer the creator for that reason." This evolutionary discourse places them with the angels and reinforces the religious discourses at play in the film. However, all the characters who attempt to communicate with or appeal to Martian empathy are killed. In what must, for the 1950s, be a shocking scene, Collins is disintegrated as he recites the 23rd Psalm. When Sylvia and Forrester are parted, he seeks and finds her in a ruined church. People inside are praying to God for help: "Grant us a miracle of thy divine intervention." Although not overtly connected, soon after this prayer, the aliens die of plague.

After the Cold War (1989–1999)

The next film I will discuss, *Independence Day* (1996), appeared at a critical moment in American history. The post–Cold War/*fin de siècle* adaptations

Figure 26. One of the gigantic alien ships literally overshadows both the Empire State Building and the Statue of Liberty in *Independence Day* (1996) (20th Century–Fox/Photofest).

(1987–1998) were produced at a time when America solidified its status of world power with the fall of the Berlin Wall and the collapse of the USSR after 1989. Yet Christine Cornea claims that the films of the 1980s and 1990s consistently referenced 1950s films of the Cold War era (32–33). Globally, the beginning of the 1990s saw the growth of the AIDS epidemic and the Gulf Wars (1990, 1992) and the overthrow of Middle Eastern leaders such as Saddam Hussein and Muammar Gaddafi. Despite successes on the world stage, America still burned at their defeat in the Vietnam War (Slotkin 613–24). Internally America also faced concerns over the attack on White masculine privilege with the rise of calls for equality for women, gay people, ethnic groups and immigrants. The films of this era reflected these concerns in what Susan Faludi described as a backlash against women.[6] Although not represented as monsters in *Independence Day*, female characters overrule and disobey male characters and, as Teresa Santerre Hobby argues, only when masculine assumption of power is reinstated can the aliens be defeated (52–53).

Independence Day, a blockbuster, delivered spectacle on a huge scale. By the mid–1990s CGI was becoming sophisticated, enabling cinematic special effects to become ever more realistic, but the most spectacular effects in *Independence Day* were created practically, as huge models of buildings, including the White House, were built and destroyed for the film. The film's stars, Will Smith and Jeff Goldblum, were both associated with sci-fi spectacle and multicultural appeal. It was produced on an estimated budget of $75,000,000 and made $817,400,891. It was the highest grossing film of 1996 with an appeal to all age groups. Like *War of the Worlds* (1953), its special effects contributed to the reputation of the film; it won an Academy Award and Saturn Award for best visual effects. The film's debt to 1950s invasion films is noted in Roger Ebert's review.

Independence Day is not just an inheritor of the 1950s flying saucer genre, it's a virtual retread—right down to the panic in the streets, as terrified extras flee toward the camera, and the skyscrapers frame a horrible sight behind them. Like those old B movies, the alien threat is intercut with lots of little stories involving colorful characters, who are chosen for their ethnic, occupational and sexual diversity.

Independence Day affirms the political reality of America as world power when aliens are defeated by the concerted efforts of the world under the president and a group of male heroes. The seemingly unbeatable odds of a small earth against gigantic and merciless foes are repeated throughout the film in images of the vast alien mother ship and the daughter ships with their colossal firepower. The opening shot of the moon at the Apollo Landing site reveals the vastness of the alien vessel as it flies overhead casting a shadow over the Apollo site. The heft of the vessel is signaled in the vibration it gives that quickly dissipates the human footprints on the moon as the aliens set their sights on distant, unprotected Earth.

Like H.G. Wells' novel, *Independence Day* was produced as a *fin de siècle* narrative and is informed by eschatological and biblical discourses in which time is counted down by alien technology, aligned with Earth's satellites,[7] and like other disaster and alien invasion films at this time, *Independence Day* is informed by 1950s rhetoric. The alien attack follows traditional American war narratives in which America is represented as the innocent victim of a merciless and unprovoked attack and the rationale for retaliation is established. *Independence Day* represented masculine power as aligned with American power. Like the films of the 1950s and '60s, the action centers around a group of (mainly men) at the center of the effort to defeat the aliens. Despina Kakoudaki states the men in this film are specialists, all pilots, although in different ways (134–35). U.S. president Thomas J. Whitmore (Bill Pullman) is elected on his record as a war hero but proves to be ineffectual. On learning that his ratings have plummeted, he notes that America "elected a warrior and got a wimp." Another "wimp," David Levinson (Jeff Goldblum), is a scientist whose jealousy and suspicion caused the breakup of his marriage three years previously. Even when he confronts Whitmore, whom he accuses of having an affair with his wife, his threat, "What I'm trying to say is—if you stay, I'll hurt you" is laughable. Russell Casse (Randy Quaid) is a Vietnam vet suffering PTSD whose life is blighted after he was abducted by aliens. He is now a joke, a crop duster, and in the film's opening, he is so drunk he dusts the wrong field. Air Force captain Steven Hiller (Will Smith) is no wimp, but he has been denied advancement because of his ethnicity and his partner's work as a pole dancer. The root of the failure of these men, according to Hobby, is their failure as fathers and partners. Even David's solution of infecting alien technology with a computer virus (in a nod to the Wells' defeat of the Martians by a biological virus) needs the assertion of masculine agency in aerial attack to insert the virus into the alien computers.

The film has strong religious themes running through it, and this can be seen in the representations of the aliens, of gender, and of symbolic space. The aliens in this film are aligned with the biblical ten plagues of Egypt, specifically the plague of locusts, and their devastation is influenced by the representations of apocalyptic devastation and panic in 1950s films. They do not attack to conquer but to strip the earth's resources and move on. Earth's invasion is random. It is in their path and ripe for attack. Unlike earlier biblical discourse, there is no benign god to save the earth. Only man's ingenuity will save humanity. But the alien technology seems invincible because of its superiority and its size; the mothership is described as a quarter the size of the moon from which it ejects smaller craft fifteen miles across. The danger of the alien arrival on Earth is signaled in a song playing on the space station which sights their arrival playing REM's "The End of the World as We Know It." The shadows of the smaller ships can be seen crawling across major American landmarks: the Lincoln Memorial; the Twin Towers; Central Park; and the Statue of Liberty (which is later toppled into the Hudson River).

The desert in this film becomes a kind of symbolic space in the narrative. An alien daughter-ship emerges from a cloud in the Iraqi desert (reputed to be the birthplace of humanity), and the scenes where Steven Hiller encounters and downs an alien in a dog fight occur in the American desert. This encounter evokes biblical myth in the temptation of Christ in the desert by the devil. The desert in this case was a place for contemplation and renewal. However, Hiller's encounter with the alien also evokes the American myth of heroism in Hiller's use of violence and masculine, brute strength to conquer. He downs the alien ship, punches the alien out, and then drags it across the desert to be examined by scientists in Area 51. Slotkin equates the desert with the notion of the reclamation of the wilderness from Native Americans by

White settlers and the spiritual "salvation in the wilderness of the human mind and soul" (39). However, the Great American Desert is also related to a more significant premise based on the fruitfulness of the land as exploited in agriculture.

Unlike the 1953 version of *The War of the Worlds*, *Independence Day* privileges masculine violence over female emotion. According to Hobby, women in this film are demonized or marginalized, punished when they disobey their male partners (52–53). Marilyn Whitmore, more popular than her president husband, dies. Constance Spano, David Levinson's ex-wife, ignores his warnings of imminent alien attack and her delay leads to millions of deaths. These infringements on male dominance can also be connected to biblical stories such as that of Adam and Eve. Eve's disobedience leads to the downfall of humanity. It is only when the men in *Independence Day* abandon their need to placate female power and resort to their power as military professionals that they defeat the aliens.

American confidence, in jeopardy at the turn of the twenty-first century, is also given a boost in the film. Eventually President Whitmore sends out a call for all men who can fly a plane to take part in an attack on the alien mothership.[8] In the pivotal moment of the film President Whitmore makes a rousing speech to initiate the attack on the alien invaders, finishing with:

> And should we win the day, the Fourth of July will no longer be known as an American holiday but as the day the world declared in one voice, "We will not go quietly into the night! We will not vanish without a fight! We're going to live on! We're going to survive!" Today we celebrate our Independence Day!

Thus, Whitmore assimilates humanity and the earth under America's leadership. The pilots also incorporate African American and Jewish ethnicities and this reflects the myth of American multiculturalism. The film ends with the alien spaceships crashing down over pre–European landmarks (Mt. Kilimanjaro and the Pyramids) and post-war Modernist buildings like the Sydney Opera House. Thus, it incorporates the pre-civilized natural features and "white settler culture" within one world order (Bould 160). This multicultural construction of the world as a homogenous American culture, according to Slavoj Žižek, "is the very form of asserting one's own superiority" (14).

Post–9/11

There have been three twenty-first-century spikes in *War of the Worlds*-inspired adaptations. The first, in 2005, consisted of several films, the best-known of which is Steven Spielberg's adaptation starring Tom Cruise. Spielberg's adaptation evokes evolutionary narratives and the will to survive. This is shown in the opening, a montage of the development of life from a single cell to complex organisms. The opening of the film also refers to the alien machines that are already present, buried in the earth for countless eons, waiting to be awakened. It also nods to the UFO narratives in earlier films and UFO sightings of the 1950s. The alien attack is signaled by biblical winds and vessels that emerge from clouds. The story centers on Ray (Tom Cruise), a divorced crane operator, caught up in the alien attack during his children's weekend custody visit. Unlike earlier films where the hero's aim is no less than the defeat of the aliens, Ray's aim is a road trip ending in Boston to deliver his children to their grandparents.

Like the men of *Independence Day*, Ray is a failed man, a feckless father and blue collar worker. But unlike the male protagonists of *Independence Day*, he does not care that he is a failure. His son Robbie does not respect him, and shouts at him at one point, "You never give a shit." Ray is not noble. He does not chew a cigar or punch out aliens. He ignores unpleasant facts in his own life, and continuously tells his daughter to look away rather than see the horror around her. This fear of seeing is connected to many of the images of aliens in invasion films. Granted, it serves to increase anticipation in the audience, but it also instils dread. Not looking is a constant theme in the film, and as Kirstin Moan Thompson argues, there is an aspect of the uncanny which should never be seen. Thompson describes this "scopic dread ... the act of see-

ing what one already knows (but has repressed), as closely tied to trauma and the horror of the visible" (25). Ray's fear of looking permeates the film. He shields his daughter's eyes from the sea of bodies and murders Ogilvy offstage so the audience cannot see. The aliens, as in many other alien invasion texts, are often concealed from view either in shadow or in clouds or darkness. The reflection of themes in the film do not end there, for the conclusion of the story replicates the evolutionary opening of the film with the aliens killed by a virus. It is a thing which the aliens do not see which, therefore, kills them.

There have been several traumatic global events since the beginning of the twenty-first century that have impacted alien invasion adaptations and overturned the optimism and confidence of late 1990s narratives. The attack on America on 9/11 led to revisions

Figure 27. Ray Ferrier (Tom Cruise) comforts his daughter, Rachel (Dakota Fanning), just before covering her eyes to prevent her from seeing an act of violence in *War of the Worlds* (2005) (Paramount Pictures/Photofest).

of the idea of heroism which are reflected in the films; the heroes of 9/11 were represented as firefighters, doctors, nurses, ordinary people rather than vainglorious heroes and superheroes. Where 1990s alien invasions promoted jingoism, post–9/11 narratives questioned the value of masculine heroism and the possibility of survival in an alien encounter. As Joshua Gunn argues, they are "not so much about aliens as about the behaviour of people when they are reduced to states of emergency or exception" (Gunn 4). Cultural traumas of this era have been treated metaphorically and tangentially in twenty-first-century alien invasion narratives.

Spielberg clearly aligns his aliens with terrorist cells, encapsulated in the marketing rhetoric, "They're already here!" Indeed, several of the adaptations from this period reflect the 9/11 attack on New York. Some of the imagery from the aftermath of 9/11 feature scenarios familiar to the American collective memory, including posters of the missing on walls, a river of dead bodies floating past, collapsing buildings, and grey dust, the remains of disintegrated bodies, raining down on characters. The first response of the protagonist Ray's son Robbie to the alien attack in Steven Spielberg's film is "Is it a terrorist?" Crystal Downing, however, argues that Ray is also aligned with the aliens (279). Ray's face is reflected in mirrors, windows, television screens. In a scene where Ray and his daughter hide behind a mirror as an alien prowls around the basement in which they hide, the screen is split with Ray on one side of the screen the alien on the other. Downing suggests that notion of the two polarized sides of the mirror show the close alignment of Ray and the alien. Ray's work as a crane driver also links him to the aliens. The crane is similar in size and shape to the alien Tripod exoskeleton.

The film does not replicate all the 1953 film elements, and in places seems more attuned to the novel. In the scenes at Athens Hudson Ferry, however, the panicking crowds riot, similar to crowds in the 1953 film. The alien attack, like earlier versions, is mysterious; bystanders see the results of the attack but not what causes it. The aliens do not look like George Pal's version of the Martians; however, like Pal's version, it is in the ruined basement of a building that Ray and his daughter encounter the aliens. Rather than the puppet aliens of Pal, these aliens are more closely aligned with those of the novel. They ride in tripod war machines. And the film alludes to the 1953 version by including Gene Barry and Ann Robinson as the grandparents to whom Ray delivers his children at the end.

In addition to Spielberg's film, there were also three short-lived television series released in 2005 (*Threshold*, *Surface*, *Invasion*), all of which referenced 9/11 (Hantke 149), and two straight-to-video films with the same title, *H.G. Wells' War of the Worlds*. The first, released by Pendragon Films, consisted of "found footage" and attracted a cult following. The second, *H.G. Wells' War of the Worlds*, released by Asylum, was a mockbuster, released a day before the Spielberg film and intended to capitalize on it. Like the novel, it told of George Herbert, an astronomer, separated from his wife and son and attempting to travel across America to meet them at the Lincoln Memorial. The opening reflected the opening of the two *Invaders from Mars* films in which Herbert and his son gaze through a telescope at the heavens. His son, tellingly, has a cold and the theme of infection threads through the film, culminating in the demise of the aliens, felled by Earth viruses. Like earlier films, the arrival of the aliens is signaled by the failure of electrical equipment and cars. The aliens in this film resemble huge crustaceans, and are often shown as crab-like legs trampling all in their path.

The second post–9/11 spike of *War of the Worlds* narratives were produced to commemorate the centenary of World War I. Both were docudrama narratives, referencing the Orson Welles' radioplay and authenticating the reality of an alien attack. Tim Hines' *War of the Worlds: The True Story* (2012) received a Cannes Award and was described by Shawn Frances on the *You Won Cannes* film review site as the best adaptation since the 1953 version. The second docudrama, *The Great Martian War* (2013), also purporting to be an account of a real event, was broadcast on the History Channel.

The third wave of *War of the Worlds* adaptations dates 2019–2020 and responds to the #MeToo movement, toxic masculinity, and upheavals in politics including the election of Donald Trump as American president in 2016 and the overturning of institutions like the European Union in a 2016 UK referendum. One BBC television series placed a female protagonist in the lead in 2019, and another 2019 series, released by Fox/Canal+, was a loose modern adaptation of the H.G. Wells novel.

As Crystal Downing noted, where the Wells' novel was constructed by a modernist attitude to science, the Spielberg film is constructed by a postmodern skepticism of science as the solution (277). Indeed, many of the alien attack narratives in this era are underpinned by a postmodern skepticism toward meta narratives (Lyotard, *The Postmodern Condition*); characters in these adaptations cannot be sure of truth, or of being saved by divine intervention, science, class, or even heroes, as in previous eras. Justice does not always prevail, good does not necessarily survive, and the bad are not always punished. Realism cannot be trusted. Such is the realism of CGI that it is now almost impossible to tell the real from the simulation. Acts of war and attack often feel random, with no intended purpose except to satiate appetite. This is reflected in films such as *Monsters* (2010) and *Attack the Block!* (2011) where aliens arrive by accident, drifting in on meteors. However, it is not the malignancy of the aliens that causes devastation in these films but their size and instinctive aggression. Thus, in *Monsters*, two aliens, unaware of the destruction they instigate, perform a mating ritual, killing several onlookers. The aliens in the UK film, *Attack the Block!* are driven by appetite and follow the pheromones of their dead colleague to feast.

Post–9/11 narratives do not tend to feature groups of heroes at the center of power battling an inhuman foe. Rather they are individuals on the margins, attempting to survive. Many protagonists in these films are not heroic, or even worthy, but are sometimes onlookers as in *Monsters, War of the Worlds: The True Story* (2012), and *The Martian War* (2013), only attempting to survive against a superior opponent. As one of the characters in Spielberg's *War of the Worlds* states, "This is an extermination" relegating humanity to an infestation to be eradicated.

Conclusions

There are several interconnected threads that recur in the three eras of *War of the Worlds* adaptations. These include gender, religion and family, all important in

American life. Alien invasion texts were produced as responses to imagined threats, and cultural confidence often aligned with these three issues. Hence the 1950s–1960s reflected fears of the Cold War, including communist infiltration and the atom bomb. The threat to the West in this case was from outside. The protagonists, often scientists, were located at the center of the conflict, tasked with saving humanity. Gene Barry, as the American hero, did not save humanity in the 1953 adaptation, but he was able to explain alien technology and how they might be defeated. In the post–Cold War *Independence Day* era, the threat to America came from emerging conflicts in the Middle East and internal threats, such as women's empowerment. The male protagonists were again at the center of the defense of humanity, and it was usually their expertise, intelligence and action that defeated the aliens. In the post–9/11 era the fictional alien threat was prompted by the real national trauma of an attack on American shores, something unheard of since Pearl Harbor in 1941. The emphasis in post–9/11 narratives has been on the powerless protagonist, the ordinary human attempting to survive in a world where death and injury are inflicted in seemingly random fashion.

In all three eras the concept of an ideal masculinity is in crisis. In the 1953 adaptation, Jancovich argues, although masculinity is represented as important, female qualities of emotion and empathy are also portrayed as necessary in order to balance out male strength. Small-town America and family life are represented as the status quo. Man must find his place in this model, despite a perception that it is not in the nature of masculinity to be contained and restrained. In *Independence Day*, when one might assume women were more equal, female qualities are undervalued and women are restrained in quasi-religious discourses that encourage them to obey male dictates. Family life is portrayed as important, but none of the families in this film are traditional. President Whitmore's wife and daughter do not respect him, and his wife dies because she ignores his advice. Steven Hiller is living with a pole dancer, but both of them are restrained through class and racial prejudice. His attempts to marry her are stymied by alien invasion. Russell Casse lives in a trailer park with his children. Nobody respects him at all, and he has no self-respect. David Levinson's ex-wife pursues a career, and she cannot bear his suspicion of her infidelity. All four men can only win their women or earn respect by acting as professional men and heading the mission to save the world. Casse can only achieve redemption by sacrificing himself for humanity. In Steven Spielberg's remake, women hold an invisible power. Ray's wife has abandoned him, but he is driven to return their children intact. Ray, however, is not a traditional male hero and often does unheroic things.

One can also map the decline in religion in these eras. There is tension between religion and science, God and man in the 1953 version. The film seems to conclude that it is necessary to balance the known with the unknown, logic with faith. The hero must acknowledge there is a greater power with humanity's interests at heart. In *Independence Day*, religion is metaphoric and connected with the *fin de siècle* and in rationalizing the gender binary. Men must be men and women must bow to their will. The postmodern sensibility of the twenty-first century adaptations is skeptical of any divine intervention, and in these adaptations there is no savior or hero to fight for humanity. It is biology that eventually provides the answer.

The cultural context for human defense in these films seems to reside in American confidence as a world superpower. The more heroic the protagonist, the more confidence there is in America's perception of its place in the world. In the 1953 and the 1998 versions of the story, the American mythic hero is confident there will be a world after alien attack. Their aims are great: to defeat the aliens and rebuild the world. In the 2005 version Ray's aims are modest, to return his children to their mother. Religion, too, changes over this period. In the 1953 version there is an acknowledgment that a divine hand may have contributed to alien defeat. This gives way to religious, symbolic, and apocalyptic discourses in *Independence Day*. In the post–9/11 versions the Martians were superior in kind to humanity, higher up the evolutionary ladder. They are defeated, it is inferred, by the will of God and, humiliatingly, by the smallest thing created: the virus.

At this point in the twenty-first-century humanity faces very real alien invasion with the Covid-19 pandemic and very real apocalypse with the ecological crisis. It is inevitable that *War of the Worlds* and alien invasion narratives will again spike, perhaps with a new type of hero that addresses the issues of disease and ecology. When new alien invasion stories are produced, who knows how they will allegorize the threat and the hero who can address it?

Notes

1. Sylvia Hardy, "H.G. Wells and British Silent Cinema: The War of the Worlds" in *Young and Innocent?*, edited by Andrew Higson (University of Exeter Press, 2002). P.J. Beck, *The War of the Worlds: From H.G. Wells to Orson Welles, Jeff Wayne, Steven Spielberg and Beyond* (Bloomsbury, 2016). J.R. di Leo, "Catastrophic Education Saving the World with H. G. Wells," *The Comparatist* 41 (2017), pp. 153–176. Peter J. Beck, "Wells' Strong Sense of Time: Contextualizing The War of the Worlds" in *The War of the Worlds: From H.G. Wells to Orson Welles, Jeff Wayne, Steven Spielberg and Beyond*, doi: 10.5040/9781474229913.ch-003. Peter J. Beck, "'The War of the Worlds' Multimedia Afterlife" in *The War of the Worlds: From H.G. Wells to Orson Welles, Jeff Wayne, Steven Spielberg and Beyond*. doi: 10.5040/9781474229913.ch-010.

2. It is worth noting that the threat to the West in alien invasion sci-fi was also felt in British post–World War II films and television series as discussed by Peter Biskind in "We're the Martians Now: British SF Invasion Fantasies of the 1950s and 1960s," *Liquid Metal: The Science Fiction Film Reader*, edited by Sean Redmond (Wallflower Press, 2004), pp. 337–346.

3. Peter J. Beck, "Wells' Martians Invade the USA Yet Again: Orson Welles's 1938 The War of the Worlds Broadcast" in *The War of the Worlds: From H.G. Wells to Orson Welles, Jeff Wayne, Steven Spielberg and Beyond*. doi: 10.5040/9781474229913.ch-012. Peter J. Beck, *The War of the Worlds: From H.G. Wells to Orson Welles, Jeff Wayne, Steven Spielberg and Beyond* (Bloomsbury, 2016). Peter J. Beck, "'The War of the Worlds' Multimedia Afterlife" in *The War of the Worlds: From H.G. Wells to Orson Welles, Jeff Wayne, Steven Spielberg and Beyond*. doi: 10.5040/9781474229913.ch-010. Peter J. Beck, "Wells' Strong Sense of Time: Contextualizing The War of the Worlds" in *The War of the Worlds: From H.G. Wells to Orson Welles, Jeff Wayne, Steven Spielberg and Beyond*, doi: 10.5040/9781474229913.ch-003.

4. There have been several films produced that recount the panic induced by Orson Welles's Mercury Theater broadcast of 1938. These include *The Night that Panicked America* (1975), *Bad Taste* (1987), *War of the Worlds: the True Story* (2012).

5. See the essays by Mica A. Hilson and Sam Umland in this collection.

6. One can identify this fear of the feminine in the female monsters of *The Faculty* (1998) whose beautiful exteriors, mimicking their human counterparts, conceal hideous squid-like creatures.

7. The illogic of this and many other elements of the film is noted by several commentators. Why do the aliens use Earth temporal measurements? Why do the aliens whose technology gets them across the vastness of space not have computer virus defenses in their technology?

8. Another gendered reference.

Works Cited

Beck, Peter J. *The War of the Worlds: From H.G. Wells to Orson Welles, Jeff Wayne, Steven Spielberg and Beyond*. Bloomsbury, 2016.

Biskind, Peter. "The Russians Are Coming, Aren't They? *Them!* and *The Thing*." *Liquid Metal: The Science Fiction Film Reader*. Wallflower Press, 2004, pp. 318–24.

Bould, Mark. *Science Fiction*. Routledge, 2012.

Carrasco, Rocio. "Alien Invasions and Identity Crisis: Steven Spielberg's *The War of the Worlds* (2005)." *Alicante Journal of English Studies*, vol. 29, 2016, pp. 7–23.

Cohan, Steven. *Masked Men: Masculinity and the Movies in the Fifties*. Indiana University Press, 1997.

Collins, Patricia H., and Sirma Bilge. "What is Intersectionality?" *Intersectionality*. Polity Press, 2016, pp. 1–30.

Connell, Robert W. "The Social Organization of Masculinity." *The Masculinities Reader*, edited by Stephen M. Whitehead and Frank J. Barrett. Polity, 2001, pp. 30–50.

Cornea, Christine. *Science Fiction Cinema: Between Fantasy and Reality*. Edinburgh University Press, 2007.

Crossley, Robert. *Imagining Mars: A Literary History*. Wesleyan University Press, 2011.

di Leo, Jeffrey R. "Catastrophic Education Saving the World with H.G. Wells." *The Comparatist*, vol. 41, 2017, pp. 153–176.

Doherty, Thomas. *Teenagers and Teenpics: The Juvenilization of American Movies in the 1950s*. Unwin Hyman, 1988.

Downing, Crystal. "Deconstructing Herbert: The War of the Worlds on Film." *Literature/Film Quarterly*, vol. 35, no. 4, 2007, pp. 274–81.

Ebert, Roger. "Independence Day." https://www.rogerebert.com/reviews/independence-day, 1996. Accessed 28 Dec. 2021.

Faludi, Susan. *Backlash: The Undeclared War Against American Women*. Crown, 1991.

_____. *Stiffed: The Betrayal of American Man*. Crown, 2000.

_____. *The Terror Dream: Fear and Fantasy in Post-9/11 America*. Metropolitan, 2007.

Gabilliet, J.-P. "Making a Homefront without a Battlefront: The Manufacturing of Domestic Enemies in the Early Cold War Culture." *European Journal of American Studies*, 2012, doi: https://doi.org/10.4000/ejas.9549. Accessed 28 Dec. 2021.

Gould, Stephen J. *Mismeasure of Man*. Pelican, 1992.

Grist, L. "Spielberg and Ideology: Nation, Class, Family, and *War of the Worlds*." *New Review of Film and Television Studies*, 2009. doi: 10.1080/17400300802602965. Accessed 28 Dec. 2021.

Gunn, Joshua. "Father Trouble: Staging Sovereignty in Spielberg's *War of the Worlds*." *Critical Studies in Media Communication*, 2008. doi: 10.1080/15295030701849332. Accessed 28 Dec. 2021.

Hantke, Stephen. "Bush's America and the Return of Cold War Science Fiction: Alien Invasion in *Invasion*, *Threshold*, and *Surface*." *Journal of Popular Film and Television*, vol. 38, no. 3, 2010, pp. 143–51.

Hardy, Sylvia. "H.G. Wells and British Silent Cinema: *The War of the Worlds*." *Young and Innocent? The Cinema in Britain, 1896–1930*, edited by Andrew Higson. University of Exeter Press, 2002, pp. 242–55.

Hendrix, Howard V., George Slusser, and Eric S. Rabkin. *Visions of Mars: Essays on the Red Planet in Fiction and Science*. McFarland, 2011.

Hobby, Teresa S. "*Independence Day*: Reinforcing Patriarchal Myths about Gender and Power." *Journal of Popular Culture*, vol. 34, no. 2, 2004, pp. 39–55.

Hutchings, Peter. "'We're the Martians Now': British SF Invasion Fantasies of the 1950s and 1960s." *British Science Fiction Cinema*, edited by I.Q. Hunter. Routledge, 1999, pp. 33–47.

Jancovich, Mark. "Re-Examining the 1950s Invasion Narratives." *Liquid Metal: The Science Fiction Film Reader*, edited by S. Redmond. Wallflower Press, 2004, pp. 325–36.

Jeffords, Susan. *Hard Bodies: Hollywood Masculinity in the Reagan Era*. Rutgers University Press, 1994.

Kakoudaki, Despina. "Spectacles of History: Race Relations, Melodrama, and the Science Fiction/Disaster Film." *Camera Obscura*, vol. 17, no. 2, 2002, pp. 1–153.

Lyotard, Jean-François. *The Postmodern Condition: A Report on Knowledge* (Theory & History of Literature). Translated by Geoff Bennington and Brian Massumi. University of Minneapolis Press, 1984.

May, Elaine Tyler. *Homeward Bound: American Families in the Cold War Era*. Basic Books, 1988.

May, Kirse Granat. *Golden State, Golden Youth: The California Image in Popular Culture, 1955–1966*. University of North Caroline Press, 2002.

Parrinder, Patrick. "How Far Can We Trust the Narrator of *The War of the Worlds*?" *Foundation*, vol. 77, 1999, pp. 15–24.

"Project Blue Book: Unidentified Flying Objects, Military Records." *National Archives*, https://www.archives.gov/research/military/air-force/ufos. Accessed 5 Aug. 2020.

Slotkin, Richard. *The Fatal Environment: The Myth of the Frontier in the Age of Industrialization, 1800–1890*. Atheneum, 1985.

_____. *Gunfighter Nation: The Myth of the Frontier in Twentieth-Century America*. Atheneum, 1992.

_____. *Regeneration through Violence: The Mythology of the American Frontier, 1600–1860*. Wesleyan University Press, 1973.

Sontag, Susan. "The Imagination of Disaster (1965)." *Science Fiction Film Reader,* edited by G. Rickman. Limelight Editions, 2004, pp. 98–113.

Thomas, Roy, and Michael Lark. *Superman: War of the Worlds.* DC Comics, 1998.

Thompson, Kirsten Moana. *Apocalyptic Dread: American Film at the Turn of the Millennium.* State University of New York Press, 2007.

"The War of the Worlds." *IMDB*, "Trivia," https://www.imdb.com/title/tt0046534/trivia?ref_=tt_ql_2 07/26/2020. Accessed 28 Dec. 2021.

"The War of the Worlds." *Variety*, 1 Jan. 1953, https://variety.com/1952/film/reviews/the-war-of-the-worlds-1200417345/. Accessed 28 Dec. 2021.

Žižek, Slavoj. "Multiculturalism, or, the Cultural Logic of Multinational Capitalism." *New Left Review*, vol. 225, 1997, pp. 28–51.

Filmography

Attack the Block! Dir. Joe Cornish, UK Film Council, 2011. Film.

Bad Taste. Dir. Peter Jackson, Wingnut Films, 1987. Film.

The Faculty. Dir. Robert Rodriguez, Miramax, 1998. Film.

The Great Martian War. Dir. Mike Slee, Entertainment One, 2013. Film.

HG Wells' War of the Worlds. Dir. David Michael Latt, The Asylum, 2005. Film.

Independence Day. Dir. Roland Emmerich, Twentieth Century Fox, 1996. Film.

Invaders from Mars. Dir. William Cameron Menzies, Twentieth Century Fox, 1953. Film.

Invasion of the Body Snatchers. Dir. Don Siegel, Allied Artists Pictures, 1956. Film.

Mars Attacks! Dir. Tim Burton, Warner Bros. Pictures, 1996. Film.

Monsters. Dir. Gareth Edwards, Vertigo Films, 2010. Film.

War of the Worlds. Dir. Orson Welles, CBS Radio, 1938.

War of the Worlds. Dir. Byron Haskin, Paramount Pictures, 1953. Film.

War of the Worlds, Dir. Stephen Spielberg, Paramount Pictures, 2005. Film.

War of the Worlds: The True Story. Dir. Timothy Hines, Pendragon Films, 2012. Film.

When Worlds Collide. Dir. Rudolph Maté, Paramount Pictures, 1951. Film.

Teleography

Invasion. Dir. Thomas Schlamme et al., Warner Bros. Television, 2005. TV Series.

The Night That Panicked America. Dir. Joseph Sargent, CBS Television Distribution, 1975. TV Series.

Surface. Dir. Josh Pate, Jonas Pate et al., Rock Fish Productions, 2005–2006. TV Series.

Threshold. Dir. David S. Goya et al., Paramount Network Television, 2005. TV Series.

War of the Worlds. Dir. Craig Viveiros, Mammoth Screen, BBC, 2019. TV Series.

War of the Worlds. Dir. Gilles Coulier, Richard Clark, Canal+, Fox Networks Group, Studio Canal, 2019. TV Series.

The Space Children and the Alien

Magic and Paranoia at World's End

Dennis R. Perry

The Space Children (1958) is a rare sci-fi film from the 1950s which features a group of children helping an alien visitor who comes to prevent their parents and others working with the military on a rocket project, code named "Thunderer," from inadvertently causing the destruction of the world. The first part of my title for this essay—"*The Space Children* and the Alien"—is purposely in the style of many '40s and '50s sci-fi adventure books, promising a story both scary and fun. The second part of the title—"Magic and Paranoia at World's End"—suggests the film's darker focus on the uptight, post–World War II paranoia haunting the major world powers. The title also denotes the distance between the more carefree children and their nervous parents who are working on an orbiting space weapon. Unbeknownst to the parents, other nations are simultaneously creating similar weapons.[1] The danger portrayed in the film then is that each nation, unaware of the similar plans in other countries, may develop dangerous international tensions and intensified paranoia that could lead to another world war.

As Victoria O'Donnell notes, most of the sci-fi films produced between 1948 and 1962 were "indirect expressions of anxiety about the possibility of a nuclear holocaust or communist invasion of America" (169). Phil Hardy put it this way: "Lurking behind every frame of fifties science fiction ... is fear of nuclear Armageddon" (O'Donnell 171). Susan Sontag refers to the world's "fear of collective incineration and extinction which could come at any time, virtually without warning" (Sontag 65). On another front, national paranoia was further encouraged by popular end-of-the-world sci-fi throughout the 1950s, including Nevil Shute's alarming 1957 novel *On the Beach* and its film adaptation of the same name (1959). In both texts an all-out nuclear war destroys the world. Many other films during the 1950s explore the same themes. These include *Five* (1951), *Robot Monster* (1953), *War of the Worlds* (1953), *Killers from Space* (1954), *Target Earth* (1954), *Day the World Ended* (1955), and *Invisible Invaders* (1959), among others.

In terms of paranoia, *Space Children* came to theaters during a particularly tense period in history. In 1957 Russia's Sputnik satellite put the international Space Race into high gear, and Senator Lyndon Johnson famously expressed the fears of many Americans: "Soon [the Soviets] will be dropping bombs on us from space like

182

kids dropping rocks onto cars from freeway overpasses" ("Editorial"). That, incidentally, is exactly what the fictional Thunderer Project is designed to do. To address what Harvard president James Conant famously called our "education gap" with the Soviets, the United States government went into a state of educational emergency. To play catch up, the government pumped federal funds into universities and made education a top priority. The national agenda included graduate fellowships to fund the sciences and foreign language study. Simultaneously, NASA was created and given the then whopping $500 million budget for space research. This was the historical context for the release of *The Space Children*.

A unique aspect of the film is that it portrays not merely the local fears of people associated with the Thunderer project but also emphasizes a more global paranoia. This was a giant step from the small-town paranoia seen in earlier sci-fi films, such as *Superman and the Mole Men* (1951) and *It Came from Outer Space* (1953). While several films released in the 1950s include paranoid characters, they rarely display the fear so pointedly and in so many worried conversations as in *Space Children*. Fear is clearly hovering over the film's bleak setting.

The film is also unusual in its somewhat leftist perspective—it does not present America as special and superior among the other world powers. That is a rarity among American sci-fi films of the period. There are, in fact, several worried conversations among the parents in the film about the ominous possibilities of another world war. As we learn by the end of the film, paranoia has infected the whole world as each of the major powers has built the same kind of orbiting weapon. Adding to the fears of the people in the film, the barren, desolate, rocky beach, where the Thunderer is in production, reflects the fearful imaginations of the people, whose paranoia suggests not the power and glory of America, but its fear and inability to work with other nations to live peacefully and safely together. As Cyndy Hendershot notes, cultural paranoia is a "delusion moved beyond individual psychosis into what was almost universally accepted in the postwar period as social reality" (1). In other words, "paranoia was … a background coloring for the whole life of the period, public and private" (2). She further notes that "there was a widespread feeling that 'You're next for something … alien invasion, communist takeover, nuclear war, dehumanization, or some other horror'" (2). Such fears are reflected in many of the characters in *Space Children*, including those in other countries, who share the same fear that they could be under attack at any time.

Despite its relatively realistic setting and gloomy subject matter, *Space Children* is notable for its fantasy elements and somewhat religious tone. Indeed, it is an unusual film for the period, and one that has had a significant influence on later sci-fi.

Adaptations

An often-overlooked distinction of this relatively obscure movie from the late 1950s is its central plot feature of kids working together in support of a visiting alien. This is a major element in such later films as *E.T. the Extra-Terrestrial* (1982), *Super*

8 (2011) and, most recently, the Netflix series *Stranger Things* (2016–). Children in all of these narratives learn from and help an alien either temporarily stranded on Earth, or on a helpful mission. *Space Children* was also part of a late 1950s avalanche of youth-centered sci-fi films popular in the heyday of drive-in movie theaters. During the same year that *Space Children* was released in 1958 several teen "classics," often with budding young stars, came on the scene. These include *The Blob* (Steve McQueen)*, Teenage Caveman* (Robert Vaughn), and *Monster on the Campus* (Troy Donahue). Even *Space Children* has a couple of minor kid "stars," including Johnny Crawford who began his stint on *The Rifleman* the same year *Space Children* hit the big screen. Many of these films featured groups of teens coming together to confront danger. Teens destroy the *Blob*, kill the *Giant Gila Monster* (1959), and in *Teenage Caveman*, another paranoid film, Vaughn's character mistakenly kills a human survivor of a late twentieth-century nuclear war. In a shock for the audience, the old man has revealing photos of the war that ended civilization—hence the film turns out to be about post-historic rather than pre-historic time.

Although ostensibly based on Tom Filer's short story "The Egg," *Space Children* may have been adapted from various paranoid scenarios in popular sci-fi novels from the 1950s. For example, Wilmarth Shiras' novel *Children of the Atom*[2] is about a hidden group of gifted children whose parents are workers at an atomic weapons facility. Because of an increasingly paranoid populous, their teacher works hard to protect them. John Wyndham's *The Midwich Cuckoos* features odd, genius children born to women fertilized by aliens. In both of these novels, as in *Space Children*, the youngsters have power over the troubled and angry parents, though the children in the novels are not so innocent. Finally, Jack Finney's 1955 novel *The Body Snatchers* is also about people, including children, being recruited by aliens. In all of these examples, groups of children render the society around them paranoid because they have power which gives them some control over their parents and the population in general. The same themes are present in films of the period. In fact, over twenty films of the 1950s era included children in key roles, including *The Day the Earth Stood Still* ('51), *Invaders from Mars* ('53), *Them!* ('54), *20 Million Miles to Earth* ('57), *The Monster that Challenged the World* ('57), *The Invisible Boy* ('57), *The Fly* ('58), *The Cosmic Man* ('59), and *Gorgo* ('61).

Also important in terms of adaptation is that *Space Children* was not only the product of a 1950s trend, but it was also the inspiration for sci-fi to come along later. Children had been a staple presence in many sci-fi films throughout the 1950s, and sci-fi featuring children resurged in a major way beginning in the 1980s. Films like *E.T.* and later *Super 8* both feature children confronting parents and military figures in order to help an alien. In the end of all of these films these authority figures watch in awe as the aliens return to their home planets. As with these later films, *Space Children* presents youth who are protecting an alien, and who are hiding their activities from parents.

Super 8 in particular has several similarities to *Space Children*. Both stories involve undermining the military's insensitive treatment of an alien creature stuck on Earth, and specifically in both stories, kids working to get around the military in order to save the alien. Viewing these films together suggests a common pattern:

1. The kids develop a relationship with the alien, helping it escape the earth;
2. the leader of the kids becomes able to communicate with the creature;
3. the alien hides out in a cave where it communicates with the kids;
4. the kids work together under the leadership of the wisest among them; and
5. the film ends with the kids, and the community, watching the alien ship ascend out of sight.

There are, however, some important differences between *Super 8* and *Space Children*. The kids in *Super 8* are a bit older, hence such issues as budding romance appear, and there are more relationship problems with each other in terms of minor irritations and jealousies. In one case some family issues between the kids' parents somewhat darken the story. *Super 8* also has close ties with the situation of the kids in *E.T.*, including a boy who makes friends with an alien. There are also several links between both *Super 8* and *Space Children* and the Netflix series *Stranger Things*. But because the latter text is a series, those children are gradually aging as they get further and further embroiled in the mysteries of alien abductions and the disappearance of friends and family members.

In short, *Space Children* both draws from popular 1950s sci-fi novels, and then becomes a model for later films which feature heroic children and their relationship to stranded aliens.

The Alien Arrives

The Space Children starts during the last leg of the Brewster family's trip to the base where the dad will continue his work as one of the engineers on the missile project at the center of the film. Upon arrival at the base the family find themselves in a desolate setting on a high bluff overlooking a bleak, rocky beach. At one end of the beach, scientists and military support are preparing to launch the Thunderer. Mrs. Brewster (Peggy Webber) begins to express her discomfort with their new home when they arrive at the stark row of trailers overlooking the rocky cliffs: "Everything is certainly strange and different here … the feeling of living so close to the end of the world maybe." Of course, her mention of the world's end has a double meaning, referring to the grim landscape as well as its relationship to the possible literal end of the world. The high cliff where the trailers are located certainly suggests a feeling of precipitous danger: the world, like the trailers, seem to be on the very brink. More striking still is how barren and dismal the entire area seems. As Vivian Sobchack aptly describes it, the "frightening limitlessness" of the setting is "desolate" and "terrifying," a part of the world that doesn't seem "a part of us … [that] does not even recognize us—[we know they have arrived at … 'the edge of an abyss']" (*Screening Space* 113).

Later that evening at a weenie roast to welcome project personnel, others express similar uneasiness about their grim situation. However, Hank (Jackie Coogan), a comical but hawkish engineer, starts the conversation by mentioning his enthusiasm for Thunderer, suggesting that once it is in orbit around the Earth the

United States should immediately begin using it. (Though unstated, his words and gestures clearly imply attacking the Soviet Union.) The more levelheaded but still worried Mrs. Brewster then asks, "When is it going to end? Year after year, racing, trying to find something bigger and better to blow ourselves off of the planet." Her fears about the significance of the Thunderer, together with her slightly more leftist perspective, give voice to the real fears of '50s film audiences as to the uncertain state of their world.

The paranoid conversation continues elsewhere on the beach the next day between Colonel Manley (Richard Shannon), who oversees the military aspect of the project, and the ominously named head scientist Dr. Wahrman (Raymond Bailey). Like everyone else, even these two leaders have questions and concerns. Happening upon Manley while walking on the beach, Wahrman notes what a "wonderful" day it is and how "innocent" the sky looks. Of course, he is inadvertently suggesting that it may soon not be so innocent once the Thunderer begins orbiting the Earth. The Colonel, too, has his own worries: "Doctor, will we succeed tomorrow?" He follows this up with a revealing comment, "I suppose people will get used to the Thunderer and its implications," suggesting that perhaps people may not get used to the horror of living in a world that could disappear at any moment. The men's teenage children briefly walk by after swimming off screen, but as they move on Manley says to Wahrman, "Life is a wonderful thing, Doctor," perhaps reflecting on its underlying fragility. Wahrman can only reply, "Let's hope we can preserve it for them," again interjecting the inescapable note of uncertainty that they may not be able to preserve it, or the world, given the uncertainties of a nuclear age.

Space Children is related to a string of 1950s films about misunderstood alien visitors, including *The Day the Earth Stood Still* (1951), *It Came from Outer Space* (1953), *The Cosmic Man* (1959), and a few others. In these films harmless aliens come to Earth—either to explore, fix their ships, or to deliver a dire warning to the misguided people of Earth. However, the alien in *Space Children* functions quite differently from its predecessors. In this case the alien comes down to save our violent, paranoid world, just as several countries, unaware of each other's plans, are about to launch space weapons simultaneously that will increase the danger and up the paranoid ante for everyone.

The alien in *Space Children* is clearly depicted as a savior figure who recruits children as its disciples to carry out its Earth-rescue program. The audience and the two main boys, Bud Brewster (Michel Ray) and Ken Brewster (Johnny Crawford), first see the alien as it descends from the sky via a shaft of light. The alien is about two feet long, and resembles a large, human brain. Later, when the kids find the alien near a cave on the beach, Bud—functioning as a kind of Peter-the-Disciple figure—is able to receive telepathic information from the alien, which he conveys to the other children as they also become the alien's disciples. Soon, the other children become, themselves, attuned to the alien's telepathic messages which enable them all to function as a unit (the audience never hears the alien's voice, effectively making the film more eerie). The alien is not only a Savior figure for Earth but an intergalactic Savior. In fact, the film concludes by quoting from the Bible: "Verily, I say unto you … except ye become as little children, ye shall not enter into the kingdom of heaven" (Matthew 18:3).

Figure 28. An original film poster for *The Space Children* (1958) (Paramount Pictures/ Photofest).

The alien's seemingly magical powers, together with its helpful child disciples, oddly anticipates the 1960s countercultural rebellion in San Francisco and elsewhere. As we know, the '60s were a time when many youth began to rebel against their parents' paranoid fears, finding appealing new peace-centered philosophies from hip gurus like Ken Kesey, Allen Ginsberg, and Timothy Leary who, like the alien, inspired rebellious actions from their loyal young followers. In essence, as a leftist film, *Space Children* is an anti-war protest by a rebellious youth underground movement. Like those of the 1960s, the kids in the film defy the military establishment in their own crusade to "save the world." In short, the alien uses the children to teach their parents what Walt Kelly famously observed in a Pogo comic strip on Earth Day, 1971: "we have met the enemy and it is us."

The Cave

Anciently caves were considered by some cultures to be sacred spaces. In *Space Children* the cave where the alien stays functions in various ways. First, it is where the children's initiations take place. Second, it is where instruction and warnings are issued by the alien. Finally, it is a place from which punishments can also be issued. The fact that the alien brain dwells in a cave suggests several relevant ancient concepts. First, the cave functions, as it did anciently, as *a site of initiation*. The children who enter the cave are mostly prepared to understand, while their parents seem unable to see the alien as anything but an enemy too powerful to cross. The brain's patience with his young "disciples" suggests Jesus's patience with his sometimes headstrong and very green apostles during their learning process. During the evening of the weenie roast the kids take off, following Bud down to the cave to meet with the alien and receive instruction. Once in the presence of the alien, one of the boys, Tim (Johnny Washbrook), panics because of the sheer weirdness of the alien creature, and he lifts up a rock to crush it. However, in doing so he finds himself unable move or bring his arms down. Bud, the silent alien's spokesperson, informs Tim when he can lower his arms. Apparently, all Tim needed was a minor display of the alien's power for him to understand both the supernatural abilities and tolerance of which the alien is capable. Tim then continues throughout the film as a faithful disciple.

The occasional adult interaction with the "thing" is handled by the alien with similar patience, though patience is not always enough. One horrendous case in point is that of Joe Gamble (Russell Johnson), a drunken beast of a man who follows the children to the beach, determined to beat his stepson, Tim, for not obeying his order to stay home. When Joe arrives at the cave, he menacingly picks up a large stick with which to beat the boy. However, the alien freezes Joe's arm and causes him to fall down; in a panic he drops the stick and runs back home. Upon later arriving at his trailer Tim finds Joe sitting in a chair—dead. While the alien is mostly kind and patient, using the least amount of force necessary to teach and control, it will not suffer anyone to hurt its "disciples" or to interrupt its plans to save the world. Unfortunately, Joe had to be sacrificed because he was beyond reclamation, and would have been a danger to the success of the alien's crucial mission.

In another experience with one of the kids' parents on the next day, Eadie (Sandy Descher—best known for her role as the traumatized young girl in *Them!*), the oldest of the female disciples, is seen by her father, Hank, coming out of the alien's cave. His insistent demands to know what she was doing in the cave make her nervous, mostly out of concern for him, but he is suspicious because of Eadie's unconvincing and nervous denials that anything was going on. Curious, and in the spirit of protecting his daughter, he walks into the cave to see for himself, only to come out a moment later white as a sheet, falling face-first in the sand as he tries to run away. He immediately gets up, looking like a zombie, and begins walking away. Later that day we see that he is more-or-less back to normal, though clearly somewhat chastened. Again, the brain uses its power depending on the person and the situation, inflicting no permanent harm except in a rare case like Joe Gamble's.

Science and Fairy Tale Magic

While the idea of mixing fantasy and fairytale tropes in a sci-fi film may seem an odd idea, writer Gene Wolfe notes that they "both address themes of human experience through the fantastic, and both bear the imprint of the culture of the time" (Chapman). As Arthur C. Clarke suggests, "any sufficiently advanced technology is indistinguishable from magic" (36). Finally, Bonnie Noonan writes that "in so many ways, these B science fiction films of the 50s are constructed like fairy tales" (121). In *Space Children*, the seeming "magic" of the alien is its more sophisticated mental powers compared to the relatively undeveloped science at the base. We understand by the end of the film that one aspect of the alien's magic is its incredible ability to communicate telepathically, not only directly with the children at the California base but also with other children on key military bases throughout the world where similar rocket projects are also being prepared for launch. The fact that the alien is continually growing—from two feet long to eight feet by the end of the film—suggests how it is gradually extending its influence worldwide.

Sci-fi, of course, often incorporates the miraculous. Examples of fairytale magic include such phenomenon as invisibility (*Phantom from Space*, 1953), the mental ability to open locked doors (*The Day the Earth Stood Still*, 1951), instant teleportation anywhere (*Cat-Women of the Moon*, 1953), making one's self look like other people instantaneously (*It Came from Outer Space*, 1953), reading others' thoughts (*Stranger from Venus*, 1954), growing to colossal heights like fairytale giants (*The Amazing Colossal Man*, 1957), shrinking to minuscule size (*The Incredible Shrinking Man*, 1957), going through walls (*4-D Man*, 1959), and healing a crippled child (*The Cosmic Man*, 1959).

Several sci-fi films of the 1950s include fairy-tale elements, most notably set designer and director William Cameron Menzies' *Invaders from Mars* (1953). Menzies creates the town's buildings and interior spaces with a fairytale minimalism, everything looking as the young protagonist David might have dreamed them. Examples include the minimalist police station, the extended path outside David's family's home, and the subterranean labyrinth where the aliens are hiding.

Additionally, like a child, David dreams of an astronomer who is his friend and who trusts the boy's strange story of the alien invaders he has seen. In a very dreamlike portrayal, the alien leader, itself, is something out of a nightmare, literally a little head with arms in a large jar from which it gives telepathic orders to its zombie minions by merely moving its eyes right and left.

As a later example of the continuing influence of fairy tales on 1950s sci-fi is Spielberg's *E.T. the Extra-Terrestrial* (1982), which, as in *Space Children*, involves the friendship of several children with a child-like alien. As the alien in *Space Children* is protected by its disciples, so *E.T.* is protected by the children in their room—which is messy enough to hide anything! Also, like *Space Children*, there are government officials who become aware of the alien's presence and try to capture it. Much as earlier kid-oriented sci-fi, the adults are mostly a sidelight to the goings-on between the children and the alien they hide and protect—as well as learn from. Similar to the alien in *Space Children,* the alien in *E.T.* accidently scares some of the kids at first but soon opens wonders to them. Like the men in *Space Children* who want to see the alien at the end, so do unidentified government agents wish to see *E.T.* and subject it to tests, etc. As the alien in *Space Children* can give the kids temporary magic powers, so *E.T.* can enable the children to fly on their bikes as the government agents get too close during the chase. As in *Space Children*, *E.T.* ends with a crowd of people watching the alien's departure. Just such a mixture of sci-fi and fairy tales is evident in *Space Children*, as the kids are given supernatural powers. Like many fantasy stories, the children's sympathetic loyalty to the alien dominates the film, while their parents are unable to see the alien as anything but a threat.

Finally, the alien functions in familiar magical fairytale ways: it reads minds, sends mental messages to other minds, wins the children's trust, and seems to have an omniscient global awareness. The alien sides with and seeks to protect the world's innocents and temporarily takes away normal functions from those who must be stopped from doing imprudent things. It shares its powers with the young and innocent, just as the fairy godmother shares some powers with Cinderella in order to help her overcome her menacing and cruel stepmother and "sisters." The military and the scientists in the film are the royalty and the magicians of the film's fairytale construction. While they are well meaning in working to protect their country and preparing to retaliate against potential enemy attacks, in fairytale terms their role in the world amounts to that of the beanstalk's angry Giant and Red Riding Hood's wolf. What the military do not understand is the fragility of the world situation. This danger will, however, only be revealed at the very end of the film, when the adults are finally somewhat prepared to understand, and perhaps, shed some of their collective paranoia.

Alien Saviors

The film concludes following the surprise destruction of the Thunderer. The final scenes take place just outside the alien's cave as angry parents and the military confront the children, demanding that they disperse so the authorities can "deal" with the alien which the children are guarding. The appearance of the military and the scientists at the cave is a reckoning. They want answers and revenge for the loss of the Thunderer. However, the children become a wall to block the adults from entering the cave. The alien, now having grown to about six-feet tall and eight feet long, begins to move out of the cave, suddenly rising skyward, leaving his "disciples" to explain what happened and why. The children explain to the flustered adults that other children throughout the world were also guided by the alien, sabotaging their various nations' weapons' projects, confirming that the trigger-happy, paranoid Earth was not ready to wield such dangerous power. Finally, the adults begin to understand the delicate nuclear situation that neither they, nor the other countries involved, realized. Hence, the lesson of the film finally becomes clear to the parents—the world powers must learn to communicate with and trust each other for their own sakes, and for that of their children.

Like many fantasy stories, the children's sympathetic perspective on the alien dominates the film, while the parents are at odds with their kids, and are unable to see the alien as anything but a threat. Coming near the end of the 1950s sci-fi craze, the left-leaning *Space Children* represents several other films of the decade that questioned the paranoid thinking of the period. If the film does not challenge America's superior weapons arsenal, it does challenge the fear that drives its motivation.

A film released the following year, *The Cosmic Man* (1959) has similarities to *Space Children* and seems to have borrowed a few ideas from it. For one thing,

Figure 29. The "space children" lock arms to protect the alien from belligerent adults (Paramount Pictures/Photofest).

Cosmic Man involves a friendly though mysterious alien that causes a panic among the local population and military establishment. Disguised in sunglasses and a hat, the alien makes friends with a crippled boy at the lodge where the scientists and military leaders are staying. While they seek the advice of famed scientist Dr. Karl Sorenson, who is not paranoid over the minor incidents the mysterious visitor causes by exploring the town, the temporary outages the alien creates makes the military brass and scientists increasingly angry and nervous. While the more liberal Sorenson is confident that the alien is not a threat, the increasingly paranoid general agrees with right-wing scientist Dr. Steinholtz, who concocts a plan to prevent the alien's departure so as to enable the military to torture the alien's scientific secrets out of him. Fortunately, the alien is able to escape, managing to cure a young boy's polio in the process. In *Cosmic Man*, as in *Space Children*, the right stands for paranoia, while the left stands for patience and not jumping to unsubstantiated, paranoid conclusions.

American sci-fi films were not the only ones questioning the wisdom of a military buildup. A British film featuring a friendly alien, *The Strange World of Planet X* (1957), came out the year before *Space Children*. The film involves a number of scientists who are working on a magnetic project which is generating an increasingly dangerous amount of power. Aware of this, an alien from "Planet X" comes to Earth to investigate, and it joins forces with a few of the more sensible scientists, explaining that these magnetic experiments are capable of penetrating the Earth's protective magnetic shield, thus causing insects to grow dangerously in size. Working together with Earth's scientists, the alien ends the danger, though this involves blowing up the lab where the magnetic experiments are taking place. As in *Space Children*, the alien's departure in *Planet X* is the happy climax of Earth's near disaster. Another British production, *Stranger from Venus* (1954), clearly borrowing much from *The Day the Earth Stood Still* (even including actress Patricia Neal), takes place at a country inn. Hawkish, right-wing British diplomats try to get as much information about the human-looking alien's planet as they can, hoping to trap the Venusian space ship that is coming to pick him up. In the end, the alien sacrifices himself to save his comrades whom he wards off from landing.

These films featuring alien saviors question the pro–American perspective of the 1950s, and demonstrate the unsuspected dangers underlying the arms race. In *Space Children* those supervising work on the Thunderer project are aware of some uncertainties and potential perils of their efforts, but administrators are unable to imagine the inevitable apocalyptic dangers which are linked to their project—potentially bringing the planet to the brink of another world war. The purposes of the alien are finally revealed at the end of the film as we learn that all the world's "Thunderer" rockets have been simultaneously disabled by the alien with the help of the children of the world.

The world of 1950s sci-fi, with its aliens, flying saucers, giants, tiny people, and awakened dinosaurs, are the twentieth-century's modern mythology. From the perspective of *Space Children*, it is the world's military establishments and their scientists, and not the dinosaurs and aliens, that are the real threat to the world. Of course, mad scientists have long played the real monsters, including Dr. Carrington in *The Thing from Another World* who tries to protect the dangerous alien monster from the military, and Mad Dr. Miers who tortures the visiting alien in *The Man from Planet X* (1951) to learn its secrets. In *Space Children* (as in *Day the Earth Stood Still* and other semi-radical sci-fi films), we learn that it is the Earth, itself, that is poised to endanger the other civilizations in space as its paranoid fears drive the world's powers to endlessly multiply their weaponry.

Notes

1. The 1980s Strategic Defense Initiative, during the Reagan era, actually considered creating such a weapon.
2. This novel, and the stories that preceded it, is something of a precursor to Marvel's *X-Men* franchise and Dr. Xavier's School for Gifted Youngsters.

Works Cited

Chapman, Jeff. "When Science Fiction Meets Fairy Tale." *Speculative Faith*, 28 Feb. 2013, https://speculativefaith.lorehaven.com/when-science-fiction-meets-fairy-tale/. Accessed 28 Dec. 2021.
Clark, Arthur C. *Profiles of the Future: An Inquiry Into the Limits of the Possible.* Holt, Rinehart and Winston, 1984.
Conant, James. *The Fifties Chronicle.* Legacy, 2008.
"Editorial: America's Impossible Mission to the Moon." *Chicagotribune.com*, 3 July 2019, https://www.chicagotribune.com/opinion/editorials/ct-editorial-moon-landing-apollo-20190702-tgcxa2xt5bhzvndtm6v2sfntim-story.html. Accessed 5 June 2021.
Hendershot, Cyndy. *Paranoia, the Bomb and 1950s Science Fiction Films.* Bowling Green State University Popular Press, 1999.
"Lyndon Johnson." *The Fifties Chronicle.* Legacy, 2008.
Noonan, Bonnie. *Women Scientists in Fifties Science Fiction Films.* McFarland, 2005.
O'Donnell, Victoria. "Science Fiction Films and Cold War Anxiety." *The Fifties: Transforming the Screen, 1950–1959*, edited by Peter Lev. University of California Press, 2003, pp. 169–96.
Sobchack, Vivian. *Screening Space: The American Science Fiction Film*, 2nd Edition. Rutgers University Press, 1999.
Sontag, Susan. "The Imagination of Disaster." *Commentary*, vol. 40, no. 4, 1965, pp. 42–48.

Filmography

The Amazing Colossal Man. Dir. Bert I. Gordon. Malibu Productions, 1957. Film.
The Blob. Dir. Irvin Yeaworth. Paramount Pictures, 1958. Film.
Cat-Women of the Moon. Dir. Arthur Hilton. Astor Pictures, 1953. Film.
The Cosmic Man. Dir. Herbert S. Greene. Allied Artists, 1959. Film.
The Day the Earth Stood Still. Dir. Robert Wise. 20th Century Fox, 1951. Film.
Day the World Ended. Dir. Roger Corman. Golden State Productions, 1955. Film.
E.T., the Extra Terrestrial. Dir. Steven Spielberg. Universal Pictures, 1982. Film.
Five. Dir. Arch Oboler. Columbia Pictures, 1951. Film.
The Fly. Dir. Kurt Neumann. 20th Century Fox, 1958. Film.
4-D Man. Dir. Irvin Yeaworth. Universal-International, 1959. Film.
The Giant Gila Monster. Dir. Ray Kellogg. McLendon-Radio Pictures, 1959. Film.
Gorgo. Dir. Eugène Lourié. MGM, 1961. Film.
The Incredible Shrinking Man. Dir. Jack Arnold. Universal Pictures, 1957. Film.
Invaders from Mars. Dir. William Cameron Menzies. 20th Century Fox, 1953. Film.
The Invisible Boy. Dir. Herman Hoffman. MGM, 1957. Film.
Invisible Invaders. Dir. Edward L. Cahn. United Artists, 1959. Film.
It Came from Outer Space. Dir. Jack Arnold. Universal Pictures, 1953. Film.
Killers from Space. Dir. W. Lee Wilder. RKO Radio Pictures, 1954. Film.
The Man from Planet X. Dir. Edgar G. Ulmer. United Artists, 1951. Film.

The Monster That Challenged the World. Dir. Arnold Laven. United Artists, 1957. Film.
Monster on the Campus. Dir. Jack Arnold. Universal-International, 1958. Film.
Phantom from Space. Dir. W. Lee Wilder. United Artists, 1951. Film.
The Rifleman. Four Star Productions, 1958–1963. TV Series.
Robot Monster. Dir. Phil Tucker. Astor Pictures, 1953. Film.
The Space Children. Dir. Jack Arnold. Paramount Pictures, 1958. Film.
Stranger from Venus. Burt Balaban. Princess Pictures Inc, 1954. Film.
Stranger Things. Netflix, 2016. TV Series.
The Strange World of Planet X. Dir. Gilbert Gunn. Eros Films, 1957. Film.
Super 8. Dir. J.J. Abrams. Paramount Pictures, 2011. Film.
Superman and the Mole Men. Dir. Lee Sholem. Warner Bros., 1951. Film.
Target Earth. Dir. Sherman A. Rose. Allied Artists Pictures Corporation, 1954. Film.
Teenage Caveman. Dir. Roger Corman. American International Pictures, 1958. Film.
Them! Dir. Gordon Douglas. Warner Bros., 1954. Film.
20 Million Miles to Earth. Dir. Nathan H. Juran. Columbia Pictures, 1957. Film.
War of the Worlds. Dir. Byron Haskin. Paramount Pictures, 1953. Film.

The Alien in the Graveyard

Extraterrestrial Reanimation in Ed Wood's Plan 9 from Outer Space *and Walter Mosley's* The Wave

PAUL PIATKOWSKI

Then and Now

It starts in a graveyard. Or just about.

Ed Wood's cult classic 1959 film *Plan 9 from Outer Space* opens at a cemetery, and though the horror genre component instantly comes into sight with this intrusion of the dead, it does not take long for the sci-fi elements to also enter the landscape literally as, within the first five minutes of the film, a UFO can be seen out of an airplane window by pilot Jeff Trent (Gregory Walcott) and his co-pilot Danny (David De Mering). Wood's *Plan 9 from Outer Space* incorporates several horror and sci-fi tropes, blurring alien invasion, vampires, ghouls, reanimation of the dead as well as detective-type story telling into a tangled crossroads of cinema. These intersections are one of the movie's unique elements, and one that separates *Plan 9* from a fellow 1959 film like *Invisible Invaders*, a more serious and better produced movie that otherwise shares key plot points like the reanimation of the dead and an alien invasion. Despite gaining its cult status primarily due to its notoriously low production value and, as Dennis Bingham states, the fact that "Wood's reputation […] had been as somebody to make fun of, with Wood himself as much the object of ridicule as his films" (157), recent work by scholars like Rodney Hill and Becky Bartlett make intriguing suggestions about the analytical potential of Wood's canon. Ernest Mathijs and Jamie Sexton try to explain that the cult appeal of a 1950s sci-fi film like *Plan 9 from Outer Space* is found in the attempts to "create an audiovisual world of the imagination [in] conflict with the financial realities of production, and in many films this gap between practical reality and imaginary fantasy is emphatically underscored by, in particular, cheap mise-en-scene and effects work" (208). Taking a new approach to the film, however, can reframe the familiar B movie and offer productive analysis amidst even such low budget, confusing and often ridiculous cinematic production. After all, *Plan 9 from Outer Space* has achieved a legacy few films can compete with, including a swath of documentaries highlighting the film, its director, and its key actors and actresses, adapted stage performances and

195

musicals, sequels, remakes, references in shows like *Seinfeld* and *The X-Files*, and even being featured as a backdrop for a full level of a video game.

Walter Mosley's *The Wave*, published in 2005, also opens in a graveyard, but it takes a little longer than the first few scenes for the alien dimension to come into focus, though the horror and sci-fi elements quickly merge as he constructs his novel's landscape. Unlike Wood, whose popularity rests on his ineptitude as a writer and director, Mosley has "cultivated an image of himself as a prolific writer and engaged public intellectual" (Larson 6). Known primarily for his detective novels, Mosley's sci-fi novels and stories share the nostalgic nods to earlier stalwarts of the genre, much like his hardboiled detective fiction references 1930s and 1940s era gumshoe detective stories. Because of those intertextual nods, one can see components of *Plan 9 from Outer Space* recycled in Mosley's novel, often with a touch of humor or irony. However, while he pulls material from, and gives homage to earlier examples from the genre, he also adapts the genre to fit his own "literary and political purposes." Writing about Mosley and the detective genre, Daylanne English suggests that "contemporary black writers" of detective fiction are "enacting a kind of literary-generic anachronism in order to comment on a distinct lack of progress regarding race" (English 773). Issues of race and social justice similarly rise to the surface in Mosley's adaptations of those earlier sci-fi tropes as he weaves them together with his own work. In his essay "Black to the Future," Mosley suggests that "[s]cience fiction and its relatives (fantasy, horror, speculative fiction, etc.) have been a main artery for recasting our [black] imagination" (Mosley, "Black" 405). Through refashioning these genres in his own work, Mosley colors his real-world commentary and reimagines it in ways that both break down and build up new sets of relations. Mark Rifkin has written on the social and political methodology in Mosley's sci-fi, finding metaphoric messaging coded into his sci-fi plots. It is one of Mosley's greatest skills to manipulate and tweak the components of literary genre in order to deliver his messaging.

My aim in this essay is to first bring to light the sci-fi and horror framework that draws both *Plan 9 from Outer Space* and *The Wave* together. In *Plan 9 from Outer Space*, Ed Wood ties the horror trope of reanimating the dead—creating zombie-like undead—to an external alien invasion. Wood's film is undergirded by the notion that the outsider presence is being ignored or hidden by those in power, and the idea that the habits of war are dangerous to both humans and more-than-human. Despite its reputation for having an incomprehensible plot, the film also urges an awareness of the effect dominant human cultural practices have on those outside of them and on the planet at large. In *The Wave*, Walter Mosley reframes this plot of alien reanimation of the dead, but the alien presence in his novel comes from within the Earth itself through a conscious mineral substance that has risen from deep within the planet. Wood's Others[1] decenter the normalized traits associated with human designations (including such qualities as gender, race, and disability) but not the imagined anthropomorphic superiority found in the hierarchy of animacy[2]; meanwhile, Mosely's separation does not just decenter the Westernized vision of the human, he also denaturalizes the centrity of the human to the narrative and to the audience's hierarchical approach to modes of narrative and levels of intelligence. He similarly draws attention to the repressive tactics of governmental policy and a lack of social justice for those outside Westernized visions of human life. In merging the sci-fi alien and the ghoulish undead, both Wood and Mosley negate what Peter Buse and Andrew Stott describe as a decline of interest in the revenant. These two suggest that "spectres, apparitions, phantoms and revenants have been eclipsed in the popular imagination by a rage for aliens, extra-terrestrials, conspiracy theories, Martian landings and all manner of paranormal occurrences apposite to millennial fever. In contrast, ghosts seem a little dated, paling in comparison with such sophisticated other-worldly phenomena" (Buse and Stott 1). However, the reanimated presences haunt both physically and metaphorically in Wood and Mosley's works and are as important as the sci-fi overtures. Jacques Derrida's "hauntology," explained in *Specters of Marx*, alludes to the inescapable and residual presence of history. Derrida's linchpin haunting in the text is that of the *Communist Manifesto* that is, after all, one of the most influential historical catalysts in the history of Western civilization.[3] Imaginative productions, therefore, continue to be haunted by the milieu that surrounded them in their creation, and those echoes continue into any analysis or reinterpretations that follow. I contend that the merging of the two seemingly disparate components of horror and sci-fi does much to advance more intriguing agendas as of a haunting of history and a decentering of both capitalist Western culture and the human itself. The use of genre, multiple genres, extracts a mélange of effects for the audience. Stuart Aitken states that "[t]he violence and horror of contemporary SF horror movies cannot be dismissed as evidence of a monolithic racism and unchanging misogyny. Their very existence and popularity hinges upon changes that take place in social relations and by changing notions of gender, sexuality and 'race'/ethnicity" (105). The fifty years then that separate the two works establishes different cultural and historical milieus, meaning a unique platform with deviations as to authorial messaging. In this way, *Plan 9 from Outer Space* and *The Wave* serve to unravel particular social and historical points with the animation of undead and alien Others entwined within that particular moment of production. Nick Bingham points out how specific the orientation must be for that certain convergence of components to occur as "the thing we call SF only ever emerges from the meetings of authors, texts and readers, meetings which always take place in particular forms, at particular times, and under particular circumstances" (181). From Wood to Mosley, the alien reanimation of the dead does more than entertain—instead it spotlights patterns of Othering as well as modes of human and cultural decentering. These works of sci-fi horror do much to discuss and reveal the environments in which they were created and to which they speak.

A Convergence of Kitsch

Ed Wood is often imagined to have had a grand conception of himself, an idea that is suggested in the biopic *Ed Wood* (1994). Though in the film Tim Burton took great liberties in depicting the title figure, most biographies agree that Wood was found to be charismatic, ambitious, and prolific. Wood, or at least the character of Edward D. Wood, Jr., as he has come to be seen by fans and biographers, has been described as a "sympathetic outsider" or a "unique auteur with a distinctive vision" (Bartlett 653). His work covered a wide and unpredictable range of genre and tone. Becky Bartlett explains that "Wood's movies include exploitation, horror, science-fiction, crime/noir, documentary, jungle adventures, prehistoric sex fantasies, westerns, comedies, and pornography." She goes on to state that "[t]hey vary in terms of genre, aesthetics, tone, narrative content, technical competence, and even the filmmaker's involvement, with Wood taking on various roles including director, writer, producer, editor, and actor" (655). Bartlett makes a point to illustrate the ways that Wood's life has been mythologized, with the great majority understanding his career only narrowly (usually just his three most famous films) and ignoring his decade of working primarily on pornographic features or really any of his work after *Plan 9 from Outer Space*. Bartlett makes a valid point and I do agree that the popular view of Wood is rather myopic, though it is his work with *Plan 9 from Outer Space* and that period of his career on which I am focused here. Writing on the cult status of *Plan 9 from Outer Space,* Mathijs and Sexton suggest that interest in Wood could come from "the idea of celebrating marginal products condemned by the mainstream" and that "it is, for example, common for such films to be celebrated in a generally condescending manner, as texts that can be laughed at as opposed to culturally 'worthy' objects." They go on to state that "*Plan 9 from Outer Space*, which marries its low-budget with emphatic incompetence, and by doing so has provided ironic pleasure for many" (208). Even Burton's biopic on Wood stresses the technical corner cutting and low-quality effects that saturate *Plan 9 from Outer Space*, but Burton also highlights a level of the visionary in the figure of Ed Wood. The films that Wood made are not always aesthetically pleasing or even intentional in their production, but they carry a certain gravity to them. After alluding to some critics' likening of Wood's works to Brechtian and absurdist traditions, Hill reminds the reader that these actions by Wood may or may not actually be "intentional." Wood was, in that light, likely an accidental film maker. Many of the potentially intriguing elements of his work were not even intended, but Wood was always willing to take a risk. Hill goes on to explain that "such innovative and experimental moves are primary aesthetic qualities of cult films" and he says that "the reputation of *Plan 9* as the 'worst movie ever made' (and, by extension, Wood as the 'worst director') is dubious at best" (186). According to Hill, such distinctions have created an "alternate canonization" and he connects this to Susan Sontag's linking of "bad art" to the concept of "camp" (186). While Wood's work has been critiqued for its B quality and low budget hijinks, recent scholarship has not only found in his work the appeal of such camp and cult qualities but also innovative, controversial, and queer components. *Plan 9 from Outer Space* pushes boundaries of understanding the human through its featuring of nonhuman Others. While the resurrection of the dead and alien invasion plotlines were already in vogue, the novelty of Wood's work comes from the increased intersectionality among these Others. Aliens penetrate both the manmade and natural ecologies, working between these systems in order to resurrect and control the undead and shape technological production to save other forms of life, reframing human-centered models of existence. The aliens animate the inanimate. Mel Y. Chen pivots his argument in *Animacies: Biopolitics, Racial Mattering, and Queer Affect* on the use of animacy within linguistic and theoretical fields as a method of defining life and liveliness, which suggests animacy itself is a site that is "relentlessly produced and policed" as it "maps" a topography of political distinctions (2). The idea of (re) animation then becomes interwoven into the task of defining personhood and positioning power dynamics within plays of differing social and cultural relations. *Plan 9 from Outer Space* questions human development and its relationship to existing ecologies, including the threats that humans are to established ecologies. Of course, it is only through his subversion (intentional or not) of norms in the cinematic tropes that Wood reframes or at least starts to rotate some of the generally unconscious animacy hierarchies embedded into popularized political and social constructions.

The opening monologue of *Plan 9 from Outer Space* sets the sensational tone for the film and informs the viewer how the story about to unfold ties in with their lives, stating that "[w]e are all interested in the future, for that is where you and I are going to spend the rest of our lives. And remember my friend, future events such as these will affect you in the future. You are interested in the unknown ... the mysterious. The unexplainable. That is why you are here." While the circular reasoning of this monologue fortifies such critiques of the film's poor or at least abrupt script (Wood, after all, was known for refusing to edit), it also builds up to a crescendo as the more surprising crossroads of genre are introduced in the closing lines: "My friend, can your heart stand the shocking facts of grave robbers from outer space?" (*Plan 9*). However, as Hill illustrates, the immediate introduction after this melodramatic opening speech is underscored by the depiction of Bela Lugosi's character, an "old man" whose wife has just died. After the funeral, the wife is the first of the alien reanimations. These significantly "human" scenes from the about-to-be zombies deviate from a traditional horror or sci-fi film which would "rely on the zombies as monstrous villains," whereas "*Plan 9* undercuts that strategy, letting us get to know two of the characters before their deaths and resurrections" (184). This kind of ambiguity is similar to the kind of confused understandings of the vampiric zombies seen in later films, like the 1964 *The Last Man on Earth*. Much like the characters in Wood's film, the "turned" characters are both monstrous in their transition and yet sympathetic due to their human origins. Wood's intentional or unintentional characterization in his film confuses the usual dichotomy of good and evil, right and wrong. The polarization one would expect between the clearly pegged heroes and apparent bad guys fades into a fog, at times literally as the undead seem to be particularly (re)animated at night in a misty graveyard. The "alien grave robbers," too, seem less villainous than is typical from a 1950s sci-fi plot. The motivation for the aliens is not world domination from power hunger or galactic imperialism but rather to stop humans from making war and the weapons of war that threaten to quench all the life in the universe. Because of this motive, "not even the aliens emerge as clear-cut villains and, indeed, Wood uses one of them, Eros (Dudley Manlove), as a mouthpiece for the film's pontifications against violence and military machismo" (Hill 184). Wood subverts norms of the genre even as he seemingly echoes the genre's most common characteristics. In one of his more didactic moments, Eros outlines the violent track record of humanity and moralizes about where the species is headed:

No, you hold on. First was your firecracker, a harmless explosive. Then your hand gre-nade: you began to kill your own people, a few at a time. Then the bomb. Then a larger bomb: many people are killed at one time. Then your scientists stumbled upon the atom bomb, split the atom. Then the hydrogen bomb, where you actually explode the air itself. Now you can arrange the total destruction of the entire universe served by our sun: The only explosion left is the Solaranite [*Plan 9*].

The alien grave robber introduced in the opening monologue, while he does plot to revive the dead so that the governments (who have ignored or kept secret the continued alien communications) will finally "notice" the aliens and their por-tentous claims, does so in the hopes of ultimately saving life. It is the war machine of Western civilization which is both haunted and haunting the Earthlings in *Plan 9 from Outer Space*. The embodiment of the undead army Eros threatens to resurrect constitutes a residual reminder of those prodigious acts of violence that continue to reoccur between and among many of the different social groups that make up the human species.

Hill links Wood's self-righteous alien, a literal Other in the film, to more met-aphorical Others. He points out that Wood's films "[*Plan 9 from Outer Space* and *Bride of the Monster*] share an added meaning perhaps more evident in *Glen or Glenda?* (1953), a film that Harry Medved sees as 'a plea for the world to understand' not only transgendered individuals, but anyone who falls outside the mainstream into the category of 'Other' (Flying Saucers over Hollywood)" and Hill, speaking of the link between Wood's three films—*Glen or Glenda?*,[4] *Plan 9 from Outer Space*, and *Night of the Ghouls* (1959)—makes the statement that "[t]his appeal for accep-tance of the 'Other' is probably the strongest link between these three films" (Hill 187). It is here in this uncovering of the Other that the film becomes possessed by the historical moment, an idea that Hill continues in his investigation of Wood. He suggests that in *Plan 9 from Outer Space*, Wood is not "simply calling for an accep-tance of his own way of life as a heterosexual cross-dresser; rather, he seems to be advocating for a much broader acceptance of diversity, years before the mainstream culture was ready to take on such matters" (184). It is this advocacy for acceptance that makes Wood's work influential then and still today. Hill deciphers a consider-able amount of coded messaging in Wood's film work. Using this hypothesis, Hill connects Eros' anger at the cognizant denial of his existence by the government and people in power with historical conditions of marginalization:

In this regard, Eros's frustration that the people of Earth refuse to acknowledge the existence of aliens also assumes a deeper significance, in such lines as: "We came to ask your aid; your government refused to accept our existence, even though you've seen us!" Combined with the aliens' stated plan of having an army of zombies march on Washington as "proof of our exis-tence," such dialogue takes on added symbolic and ideological weight, especially at a time in American history when minority groups of all stripes were denied fundamental rights and recognition, and were already staging their own marches [Hill 188].

Eros demands recognition and yet, even with his frequent UFO fly-by appear-ances and media coverage, the government continues to deny the extraterrestrial existence. This governmental erasure of Others is something that Walter Mosley similarly presents in *The Wave*, though for Mosley it is a more pointedly racialized

Other. In the late '50s, Wood is gesturing at the intentional erasure of non-normative groups by traditions of power. Not only does the government ignore these Others, but they demand that the rest of the population also ignore them. It is true that the fear of violence is seemingly the only means available for Eros and his claims to be taken seriously. In Mosley's *The Wave*, the alien presence learns and enacts violence in order to survive against the institutional genocide directed against it by the human government. Eros similarly finds that violent means are necessary to make survival possible for the Other. He must excavate the history of violence, bring back those undead, in order to be heard. The undead army is a reminder of Foucault's biopower and biopolitics, a "power that is not individualizing but, if you like, massifying, that is directed not at man-as-body, but at man-as-species" (Foucault 243) and, in this particular instance, the dehumanizing quality of such a body politic as the undead represent is simply a blunt, violent force materialized through the mass of bodies.[5] Eros states, "Those whom we're using cannot think. They are the dead, brought to a simulated life by our electrode guns. You know, it's an interesting thing when you consider: the Earth people, who can think, are so frightened by those who cannot—the dead" (*Plan 9*).

If the undead represent moments of history, they come to reflect a narrative of biopolitics at play and the use of bodies as power. The past, full of the dehumanization and deformation of what it means to be human, is literally dug up by Eros

Figure 30. Eros (Dudley Manlove, left), the Ruler (John Breckinridge, second from right), and Tanna (Joanna Lee, right) deal with the resurrected Inspector Clay (Tor Johnson, center) in *Plan 9 from Outer Space* (1959) (Photofest).

and used by him to gain some kind of recognition from these power structures. The fear felt toward the no-longer-alive (or no-longer-human) speaks to a greater disillusionment with the institutions which make up the strongholds of Western society. Reanimation in Eros' scenario exists as an embodiment of the historically marked and marginalized bodies of the past who are then given momentum to strike back against the very powers that made them invisible. However, the ultimate failure to be heard and recognized by dominant configurations of power suggests the great difficulty of any kind of real democratization in Wood's time. Revealing the markings of history that surround him and his immediate world, Wood alternates between the more traditional norms of 1950s sci-fi storytelling and his unusual aberrations of these trends. At times discordant and jarring, these moments of filmmaking formulate the very components that have made the work so endearing.

Speaking (Re)animatedly

In Ed Wood's *Plan 9 from Outer Space*, the alien Other claims recognition through a reanimation of the past, literally in the case of the undead ghouls that he unearths. Digging up history literally and metaphorically engages with the haunting presence of social and political injustice, as well as unveils the rampant bias and prejudice running the length of Western civilization. It is this long train of bias and prejudice that Walter Mosley begins to chisel away at in *The Wave*. Walter Mosley's best-known works are his detective novels and he has said that the "thing that I really like about the genre of mysteries is that they're exotic, and you can write about things which are unknown" (Davis and Mosley 54). His forays into sci-fi follow a similar pattern of delving into the unknown and using that mysterious site to politically (re)engage with his themes of social and political inequality. In *Understanding Walter Mosley*, Jennifer Larson states that "race remains ever dynamic and personal for [Mosley's] characters and their narratives. Mosley navigates the often-treacherous landscape of identity politics by asking audiences to connect with the characters' racial, cultural, and social realities through—rather than in addition to—engagement with the narrative" (3). Using the sci-fi and horror genres, Mosley resurrects the plot trope of reanimated dead in *The Wave* and invests it with this political agenda, though writing it in his usual and relatable narrative style. His books read as a story foremost, and the messaging is interwoven within the threads of the plot development. Larson recognizes this and points out that his "works are simultaneously artistic and political" (3). Assuming the iconic horror, sci-fi, and detective patterns of Wood's earlier film, Mosley's intersectionality both recalls and furthers Wood's ecological questions as his alien presence is not humanoid but rather a cognizant alien mineral pattern long entombed in the Earth. The presence, seeking to combine with a separate extraterrestrial entity, reanimates the dead as it works its way up and out of the Earth's core. Capturing the iconic images of graveyard undead and cosmic space travel, Mosley plays with the horror and sci-fi tropes and reframes these ecologies to decenter the human (and human-like) as the sole bearer of cognitive processes and allows for a reimagining of human and nonhuman relations.

Mosley believes in the power of sci-fi, and his social and political underlying meanings make an analysis of *The Wave,* as well as Mosley's other sci-fi books like *Blue Light* and *Futureland,* productive. In his essay on Black sci-fi writing Mosley expounds on the genre, saying that for Black writers, "[t]he last hurdle is science fiction. The power of science fiction is that it can tear down the walls and windows, the artifice and laws by changing the logic, empowering the disenfranchised, or simply by asking, What if?" Mosley goes on to explain that tackling the imaginative potential in sci-fi "is to break the chains of reality and go beyond into a world of your own creation" ("Black" 407). In *The Wave,* Mosley does just that, though this novel is set in a contemporary time and space more in tune with his book *Blue Light* rather than the dystopic *Futureland.* The setting ties the reader more closely to the here-and-now and makes potential readings of the political undertones more apparent while still recasting those lived realities through the sci-fi platform. Writing on *The Wave* as it concerns the handling of spatial and racial configurations in sociopolitical terms and connecting this to blackness and indigeneity, Mark Rifkin explores the notion that "*The Wave* builds on the social analysis offered in *Futureland,* retaining the sense of U.S. jurisdiction (and possibly all forms of state sovereignty) as carceral in its organization around geographies of racialization" (161). Rifkin's metaphoric reading of Mosley's novels highlights the real ground that Mosley is working with—the racial and social inequality systemically built into traditions of power. However, he also hints at Mosley's work recasting and restructuring that ground, which is the same method Mosley uses as he adapts and reframes the sci-fi and horror genres. Rifkin writes of the Wave, the alien Other of the novel, as a representation of blackness—it is, after all, a literal black tar, a cognizant mineral configuration. Identifying its historically marked location in Los Angeles and the racial undertones of that location, Rifkin correlates the geography to Mosley's political stance in the book. He suggests that, "[i]n offering a speculative redescription of how national space continues to be racialized in ways that cast blackness as an alien intrusion, Mosley explores the sociopolitical dynamics that produce ongoing experiences of Black alienation, but in response to such affects, he draws on the figure of the Wave" (157). The Wave reconfigures the space of the novel as it incorporates itself into and reanimates the human and nonhuman dead, moving through the landscape as an alien (yet not an invasive) presence—more in tune with the history of the land than its most recent occupants. The reanimation itself allows this Wave of blackness to embody and resurrect histories that have been forgotten through long established traditions of colonization and disempowerment. What seems to be evident here is the way that the reanimation of the dead along with the animation of the Wave work to reframe relations of the normalized Western conception of the human (White, male, abled, etc.) and the often-marginalized groups of humans as well as nonhumans.

While in his detective fiction, Mosley reveals an inescapable grasp of historical markings, he writes that Black sci-fi provides a platform from which to reframe history. He explains that "black people have been cut off from their African ancestry by the scythe of slavery and from an American heritage by being excluded from history." He continues, "For us, science fiction offers an alternative where that which deviates from the norm is the norm" (Mosley, "Black" 405). The novel gives Mosley the opportunity to estrange the familiar just enough to reconstruct an alternate world where blackness can continue to expand and be embodied, fooling the establishment and somehow finding a place in the universe. It allows Mosley the kind of power to normalize the alien when it continually appears that the programs and institutions in place actively work to disconnect and isolate blackness as a type of alien presence in the surrounding world. He says that "[t]his power to imagine is the first step in changing the world. It is a step taken every day by young, and not so young, black readers who crave a vision that will shout down the realism imprisoning us behind a wall of alienating culture" (406). The novel literalizes this racialized history with the Wave and through *animation* actuates the agency of blackness. Chen describes animacy as a "quality of agency, awareness, mobility, and liveliness" (2) and he explains that it is used consciously and subconsciously as a marker of humanness. Humanness as a qualifier and in this context often grants certain entities the privileges of personhood within the dominant cultural matrix. So animation gives life and power, while reanimation pulls histories to the surface and resurrects them. In discussing the film *Bamboozled* and the animation of certain objects in the film, namely the collection of Delcroix's racist toys, Bill Brown directs attention to the historical correlations of these objects brought to life through the animatedness they exhibit, explaining that "the point is not only that the inanimate comes to life but that the history of this ontological ambiguity—human or thing—is precisely what remains repressed within U.S. culture" (199). The manner in which histories are unearthed through animacy and reanimacy in the object is accelerated through Mosley's thinking black mineral presence. It seems then that "this act of reanimation congeals a history" (Brown 201), but it also challenges the notion of any kind of animacy hierarchy. Indeed, Mosley "challenge[s] readers to explore the philosophical debates that inform not only discourses of race, but also of morality in general" (Larson 4). This would push beyond a benchmark of blackness but also to everyone and everything that is marginalized in the Euro—and anthropocentric models of thinking.

Animal, Vegetable, Mineral, Alien

Throughout *The Wave*, Mosley does more than metaphorically look at issues of personhood as it deals with race: Mosley literally tackles issues of the democratization of all beings, human and nonhuman. In his novel *things* take on consciousness and spirit. They are literally more-than-human. As the novel progresses, the Wave as a character takes on narrative importance, and as it embodies humans, animals, and other forms, Mosley reframes the anthropocentric model of understanding complex sets of relations. Brian Willems, whose book ties the field of speculative realism and genre of sci-fi together, suggests that "when non-human things are taken to be equally as valid objects of investigations as humans, a more responsible and truthful view of the world can take place" (Willems 1). Mosley's decision to make his alien presence a conscious mineral alignment removes some of the anthropocentric privileging found in a great majority of imaginative representations. The issue takes on more relevance and timeliness when one considers the appearance of such fields as new materialism, speculative realism, posthumanism, thing theory, and object-oriented ontology in what has been called the nonhuman turn, nor are these considerations of the other-than-human new. In 1916, naturalist John Muir wrote "Man's Place in the Universe," an essay that problematizes assumptions regarding man's centricity to the universe as well as the privileging of man above all other minerals, plants, and animals. He asks, "why may not even a mineral arrangement of matter be endowed with sensation of a kind that we in our blind exclusive perfection can have no manner of communication with?" Muir imputes theology for this anthropocentricity, but human centrality can be found across a number of academic fields, theoretical lenses, and theologies, particularly as they appear in Western cultures. It is not all encompassing but very prevalent. Interestingly, it tends to be from extant belief systems and often indigenous ideologies as well as in more recent scientific and theoretical perspectives that these ideas of anthropocentricity are taken to task. Speculative literature has become one of the prime locations from which to probe notions of human placement in a universal scheme. In *The Wave*, Mosley works to dislodge human centricity through his problematization of human hierarchical assumptions regarding species superiority in realms such as intelligence, biology, and technology.

In *The Wave*, Mosley disorients the normative conception of what it means to actually *think*. Panpsychism, an often refuted yet stubbornly returning theory, suggests that "mind is a fundamental property of matter itself. This means that thinking happens everywhere; it extends all the way down (and also all the way up). There are differences of degree in the ways that entities think but no fundamental differences of kind" (Shaviro 86). At the center of Mosley's novel lies this rudimentary shift in the way we think of *thinking* itself. Of course, the relevance in using a method like panpsychism in an analysis of Walter Mosley's *The Wave* lies less in understanding how a godlike microorganism birthed from a meteor can be a thinking entity and more in the way the book dislodges a reading of humans and human processes of thought as central to being. It is this progression of thinking itself which defamiliarizes the reader in an active process of reorientation. While traditional sci-fi formulas would have the protagonist in some kind of ongoing battle with a violent and destructive alien enemy, Mosley reverses this concept and makes the alien—an entity not even humanoid—the victim of inhumane treatment and control. Mark Rifkin reveals the human-centered bias in the novel as he discusses the language of Dr. Wheeler, the doctor given the task of eliminating the Wave. The doctor terms the alien material entity "an 'invasion' and 'contagion,'" and he "refers to it as an 'infestation,' 'parasites' for which humans are the 'hosts,' and as an 'infection.'" Rifkin suggests that these names "oscillate between imagining the beings the Wave comprises as an immunological threat and a territorial one" (156). Mosley's light touch of humor in the stereotypical government scientist, Dr. Wheeler, a plastic surgeon bent on eradicating an "alien threat" and given the power to terminate anyone or thing along the way, underscores the evolving perceptions of protagonist Errol Porter on the essential nature of the Wave and the gradual shift in the reader, from cheering on the human species to rooting against the human xenophobic instinct and, in turn, the human domination of alien—and all Other—intelligence. Porter spends a majority of the book dislodging himself from human centricity as it comes to both thinking and the processes of identification as he partially merges with the mineral consciousness termed XTs, rewriting his coding processes in order to extend his cosmic view of life and for him to become part of the Wave.

Mosley exposes Dr. Wheeler's extremely reductive view of intelligence as Wheeler explains the XTs to a group of international visitors at his XT containment site, the Pit. He suggests that "[i]t wasn't until the colony had migrated to the DNA of simple creatures and maybe even the corpses of dead animals that they began to develop what we call intelligence" (110). Wheeler's definition of intelligence here remains problematically narrow. The only way that Wheeler can think to measure intelligence is on a human scale with accepted human perceptions, yet Porter's dreamlike insight into the Wave's origins suggests that this scale is disproportionate for grasping nonhuman beings. Following his tour of the underground facility where the government is holding (which means, of course, experimenting and torturing) the XTs, Porter has a vision that taps into the Wave's mind:

> In my dreams, I was floating in the earth, moving through stone as if were air. Sensations came from all around me: gravities and vibrations (not sounds) and other events that had no other correlation to my corporeal existence. I was immense, moving leisurely through solid stone at the rate of an inch a century. Time passed. Time stayed the same. But every micron was filled with the ecstasy of numbers and sameness and matchless difference. I was many and one. I was forever, remembering back before I was conceived, into the far reaches of the beginning [117].

Porter's integration into the Wave's awareness accents the cognitive evolution of the life form, a cognition based on "gravities and vibrations" which becomes "the ecstasy of numbers and sameness and matchless difference." This type of sensory awareness differs sharply from a human's cognitive self-awareness. This echoes what Porter's reanimated father, GT, earlier tries to describe as the Wave's origins, stating that its cognitive awareness began "[w]hile it was counting, [and] there came an awareness, a knowledge of the selves of numbers. One knew its own count, and so did Two and Three and Four. And when Four knew that it was also One, there was an ecstasy and a motion" (67). The focus on the mathematical logic of life as the cornerstone of awareness differs from a human mirror stage of development, yet the outline of identity construction can be clearly delineated. These steps away from human centrality open up new frames from which to reconfigure environmental issues and the entirety of the Anthropocene. Indeed, animal studies and plant theory challenge assumptions of human centricity, just as the Deep Ecology movement did when it began in the 1970s. In Mosely's words, "Yet if humans have become the new monsters, what happens when their dominance is removed? Are there other organizations of knowledge, time and space which could lead to a better future than the one now being created?" (Willems 1). Mosley's Wave perhaps offers some potential in confronting that question. After all, the Wave's instinctual and communal nature of identity sharing remains essentially alien to human understanding, and Mosley's speculation disrupts the human isolated assurance in difference which forms a keystone of traditional self-perception.

Isolation, while natural to humans, gets portrayed as alien through the Wave's perceptions as it rises. Describing the life forms that it came across on its ascent as having "experience, separate and alone," when the Wave finally "found myself a man," it describes the human species to have "made sounds rather than merging" (117). Reanimating the blueprint of the life forms, the Wave confusedly begins to grasp the nature of man, including the inclination of man to gradually want to efface all traces of the Wave from the planet. Counter to the Wave's gradual understanding of human thinking is Porter's incorporation into the Wave unity. GT tells him as they go on their search for the Wave's central point: "You've been floating in the granite, passing through stone toward the chorus of the infinite" (148). A few pages later, Porter connects with the XTs and extends outward into the various life and intelligences with whom the Wave merges. This does more than reveal the size of the Wave, it also taps into and equalizes multiple intelligences. It echoes GT's earlier statement that "there is something more than the single mind" (67). Porter describes what he sees while connecting with the Wave, saying, "[i]nside me, things were happening. The fingertips connected to nerve clusters. Pulsing energy began to chatter throughout my body" (152). He explains what it is like to look out from the Wave rather than into it: "Unity was a recurring theme. Onetwothree was another concept, a triangular form that interconnected in all directions, a three-dimensional counting system that somehow moved forward and backward through time" (152). This interconnection causes Porter's consciousness to body migrate, beginning as a human, then into a mackerel, followed by a sea gull, and finally a "larva burrowing into the flesh of the dead seabird" (153). These different life forms are experienced by Porter as more than bodily inhabitation but also in the form of the senses and intelligences of this multitude of life. This situates these beings in a horizontal relationship rather than a vertical one. When Porter finally reaches the cave of the Wave, there are ancient "russet-colored, prehistoric wolves" (154) and the Wave itself appears as a pit of tar, yet all of these life forms experience a sense of equality through the communal sharing of experience and, more importantly, *thinking* itself.

The human assumption of intelligence development and its workings suggests, more than anything, a bias in how intelligence is understood by a great portion of humanity. What humans perceive as creating intelligence—the use of tools or the ability to read—are distinguished as being limited and narrow. The Wave marks itself as exceptionally advanced, yet there are absences in its abilities that would be assumed to mark a lack of intelligence as Westernized humans understand it. For example, GT cannot read written language when he is first reanimated. He explains that "[r]eading is a complex, nonbiological system" (65). His point is that reading is not biologically natural or necessary. Meanwhile, the Wave "had the ability to *read* [italics mine] DNA and every other quantifiable thing about a human being. Thoughts, dreams, instincts, images, emotions—everything that made up life could be quantified and repeated" (110). GT is able to remember how to process reading as humans think of it, but Mosley makes it clear that this kind of intelligence barometer does not suffice as a measure of intelligence. Reading itself is not isolated to written alphabets but also to the signs and signifiers threaded into the very fabric of the cosmos.

Mosley digs into and disorients how humans understand such concepts as intelligence, biology, and technology. Through this dislodging of expectation, he shifts the way to understand the relationship of humans to nonhumans and reorient the understanding of intelligence itself. Like Steven Shaviro suggests in his discussion of panpsychism, "[t]here are differences of degree in the ways that entities think but no fundamental differences of kind" (86). The Wave and its completely alien mode of processing information is related to the reader in a very human form—funny and charming, whether it be GT or the "first man" reanimated, Veil Bonebreaker—to help integrate and naturalize this disorientation of the reader. Mosley speculates on the multifaceted ways intelligence can and should be understood and articulates reasonably why an anthropocentric method of measuring the mind and thinking itself is unreliable in a wider examination of the world and the universe beyond.

Back to the Start

Animation and reanimation from and of the nonhuman feature prominently in both Ed Wood's *Plan 9 from Outer Space* and Walter Mosley's *The Wave*. While Ed Wood's earlier cinematic feature is often used as an exemplar of low budget and ridiculously bad 1950s sci-fi, the film fits an intriguing pattern of Wood subverting conceptualizations of the Other. Critiquing the absence of recognition as well as the wartime machismo that seemingly justified such marginalization, the alien presence in the movie resurrects the dead, unearthing habits of violence and then mimicking those human traditions. The mass of bodies is used as literal biopower by the aliens. Walter Mosley's *The Wave* lifts the sci-fi and horror genre tropes of extraterrestrial reanimation of the dead from Ed Wood's iconic film, but his homage pushes the notions of Othering and the haunting of history to more distant ends. Mosley's racial reanimation reveals a complexity to issues of social and cultural inequity marked through time and facing the same threat of extermination by more recent manifestations of imperialistic impulses. While both Wood and Mosley reframe historic relations among groups of humans, Mosley gestures toward an even larger democratization between humans and nonhumans. In order to reach this point, Mosley decenters more than cultural positions in a human devised landscape. He goes so far as to suggest a reframed manner of *thinking* itself—a consciousness that does not have to be human in origin to be treated with personhood. Mosley's book breaks from anthropocentric and Eurocentric models of understanding in order to reorient relations between humans and other humans as well as humans and nonhumans in ways that work horizontally instead of in vertical hierarchies. While Wood's *Plan 9 from Outer Space* may have offered an alternative canon and a move toward greater equity with peoples who have been Othered, Mosley's novel suggests a move forward (or perhaps backward) to a point where there would be a democracy not just of people, but of people, animals, plants, and mineral.

Notes

1. I will continue to use the capital "O" Other tradition as I talk about the marginalized persons and entities whose placement on the fringes of dominant cultural practices Wood and Mosley's productions subvert.

2. I refer here to a hierarchy of animacy as explored by Mel Y. Chen in his book *Animacies: Biopolitics, Racial Mattering, and Queer Effect*.

3. Derrida's *hauntology* remains one of the most well-read pieces of "ghost theory" outside of, perhaps, mentions of the ghost in the field of psychoanalysis.

4. *Glen or Glenda?* deserves a bit more discussion when it comes to Wood's work to demystify society's Others. The film of course explores Wood's own cross-dressing habits, with Wood as the main writer, director, and actor.

5. Biopower has come to mean a great many things and to be integrated into numerous theoretical projects, including much of Giorgio Agamben and Alexander Weheliye's studies. I will later touch on more ways that biopower has been used in discussion, particularly in the animal studies field and in more recent plant theory.

Works Cited

Aitken, Stuart C. "Turning the Self: City Space and SF Horror Movies." *Lost in Space: Geographies of Science Fiction*, edited by Rob Kitchin, et al. Bloomsbury, 2005, pp 104–22.

Bartlett, Becky. "Madman, Genius, Hack, Auteur? Intertextuality, Extratextuality, and Intention in 'Ed Wood Films' After *Plan 9 from Outer Space*." *Continuum*, 33:6, pp. 653–65, DOI: 10.1080/10304312.2019.1677979. Accessed 28 Dec. 2021.

Bingham, Nick. "Frankenstein, Food, Factishes, and Fiction," *Lost in Space: Geographies of Science Fiction*, edited by Rob Kitchin, et al. Bloomsbury, 2005, pp. 180–92.

Brown, Bill. "Reification, Reanimation, and the American Uncanny." *Critical Inquiry*, 32:2, pp. 175–207. JSTOR, https://www.jstor.org/stable/10.1086/500700. Accessed 28 Dec. 2021.

Buse, Peter, and Andrew Stott. "Introduction: A Future for Haunting." *Ghosts: Deconstruction, Psychoanalysis, History*, edited by Peter Buse and Andrew Stott. Macmillan, 1999, pp. 1–20.

Chen, Mel T. *Animacies: Biopolitics, Racial Mattering, and Queer Effect.* Duke University Press, 2012.

Davis, Thulani, and Walter Mosley. "Walter Mosley." *BOMB*, no. 44, 1993, pp. 52–57, JSTOR, www.jstor.org/stable/40424633. Accessed 20 March 2020.

Derrida, Jacques. *The Specters of Marx: The State of the Debt, the Work of Mourning and the New International.* Translated by Peggy Kamuf. Routledge Classics, 1994.

English, Daylanne K. "The Modern in the Postmodern: Walter Mosley, Barbara Neely, and the Politics of Contemporary African-American Detective Fiction." *American Literary History*, 18:4, pp. 772–96, JSTOR, https://www.jstor.org/stable/4123621. Accessed on March 17, 2020.

Foucault, Michel. *Society Must Be Defended.* Translated by David Macey. Picador, 1997.

Hill, Rodney F. "Science Fiction and the Cult of Ed Wood: Glen or Glenda?, Bride of the Monster, and Plan 9 from Outer Space." *Science Fiction Double Feature: The Science Fiction Film As Cult Text*, edited by Gerald Duchovnay and J.P. Telotte. Liverpool University Press, 2015.

Larson, Jennifer. "Understanding Walter Mosley." *Understanding Walter Mosley.* University of South Carolina Press, 2016, pp. 1–7.

Mathijs, Ernest, and Jamie Sexton. *Cult Cinema: An Introduction.* John Wiley & Sons, 2011.

Mosley, Walter. "Black to the Future." *Dark Matter: A Century of Speculative Fiction from the African Diaspora*, edited by Sheree R. Thomas. Warner, 2000, pp. 405–07.

——. *The Wave.* Warner, 2005.

Muir, John. "Man's Place in the Universe." *A Thousand Mile Walk to the Gulf,* sierraclub.org, 1916, https://vault.sierraclub.org/john_muir_exhibit/writings/mans_place_in_the_universe.asp. Accessed 28 Dec. 2021.

Rifkin, Mark. *Fictions of Land and Flesh: Blackness, Indigeneity, Speculation.* Duke University Press, 2019.

Shaviro, Steven. "Consequences of Panpsychism." *The Universe of Things: On Speculative Realism.* University of Minnesota Press, 2014, pp. 85–107.

Willem, Brian. *Speculative Realism and Science Fiction.* Edinburgh University Press, 2017.

Filmography

Ed Wood. Dir. Tim Burton. Touchstone Pictures, 1994. Film.
Glen or Glenda? Dir. Ed Wood. Screen Classics, 1953. Film.
Invisible Invaders. Dir. Edward L. Cahn. Premium Pictures, 1959. Film.
The Last Man on Earth. Dir. Sidney Salkow. American International Pictures, 1964. Film.
Night of the Ghouls. Dir. Ed Wood. 1959. Film.
Plan 9 from Outer Space. Dir. Ed Wood. Reynolds Pictures, Inc., 1959. Film.
Seinfeld. Giggling Goose Productions, 1989–1998. TV Series.
The X-Files. 20th Century Fox, 1993–2002. TV Series.

Double Trouble

Martin Guerre, Invaders from Mars, *and the Body Snatchers Films*

SAM UMLAND

The popular cinema of the postwar period has been characterized as being pre-occupied with paranoid fantasies of Communist infiltration, frequently expressed in quasi-allegorical figurations of alien invasion, and yet the fear of enemy infiltration existed years before the Cold War. It is important to remember that the House Un-American Activities Committee was established as a special committee in 1938 to investigate alleged subversive activities against the United States government. A few years later, in 1945, it became a standing committee, and was not abolished until 1975. Indeed, the notion that a totalitarian regime could replace democracy in the United States had been so disquieting that movies on the theme took at face value the (ironic) title of Sinclair Lewis's novel about Fascist takeover, *It Can't Happen Here.*[1] Following Charles Chaplin's anti–Fascist *The Great Dictator* (1940) was Frank Capra's anti–Fascist fable, *Meet John Doe* (1941; re-released 1945), about Ann Mitchell (Barbara Stanwyck), a cynical, young newspaper columnist who writes a fraudulent column after being threatened with being fired. In order to save her job, she writes a letter to the newspaper using the name John Doe, "a disgruntled American citizen," who is threatening to commit suicide as a form of political protest. As a result of public interest—and increased newspaper sales—she needs someone to impersonate John Doe. A minor league baseball player and hobo named Long John Willoughby (Gary Cooper) agrees to play the role of the impostor, agreeing to impersonate the figurative Everyman. As it turns out, Ann's publisher, D.B. Norton (Edward Arnold) is an American fascist. While the film is concerned with public complacency as well as with the fear of take-over by fascist fifth columnists such as D.B. Norton, it is equally concerned with fakery. As Norton tells Willoughby, "*You're the fake. We believe in what we're doing.*" Insisting that his cause is greater than he is, Willoughby asserts, "This thing's bigger than whether I'm a fake."

Fakes, impostors, and dissemblers abounded in films and novels of the era. In 1941, the year *Meet John Doe* was released, Janet Lewis published *The Wife of Martin Guerre,* the story of an impostor.[2] The story is famous because it is so compelling: an impostor named Arnaud du Tilh posed as Martin Guerre, the husband who had abandoned his wife Bertrande eight years earlier. In the novel, du Tilh maintained the masquerade for more than three years, and in doing so gained a wife and property and fathered a child. Arnaud du Tilh was eventually exposed as an imposter just as he was on the verge of refuting those accusing him of deception—by the apparent return of Martin Guerre.[3] For historian Natalie Zemon Davis, in *The Return of Martin Guerre*, the story of Martin Guerre invokes the spirit of trickery, a compelling instance of imposture that is ultimately an exploration of the problem of truth and doubt. The catalog of themes associated with the Martin Guerre story include trickery and masquerade, duplicity, impersonation, verisimilitude, simulation, and dissimulation, all of which are general expressions of *subversion*, a fear that resonated deeply during in the years before World War II, during the war, and in the years after.

At least one sci-fi writer during the postwar period, Philip K. Dick, was aware of the Martin Guerre story, using it as the inspiration for the short story he completed in February 1953, "Human Is."[4] We know that he knew *The Wife of Martin Guerre* because "Human Is" hinges on the same moral problem facing Bertrande; should a woman, Jill Herrick, reveal her husband's true identity, or not? Arnaud du Tilh, masquerading as Martin Guerre, is a kind, solicitous, and generous husband to Bertrande, while the actual Martin Guerre, the one who abandoned her, was cold and distant. Dick tells his sci-fi story from Jill's point of view, just as Janet Lewis does in her novel. Dick's story hinges on Jill's dilemma when her actual husband returns. Should she denounce her present husband is an impostor, and return to her previous life in an unhappy marriage? Or should she lie, affirm her present husband's identity, and denounce the actual "Martin Guerre" as an impostor? Interestingly, Dick resolves the dilemma differently than Janet Lewis. In Lewis's novel, Bertrande tells the truth, admitting that her present husband is an impostor. In contrast, the wife in Dick's story lies to the authorities, averring that her husband is not possessed by an alien lifeform.

Deployed through narrative, subversion takes the form of oxymoronic substitution. In the tales by Lewis and Dick, a kind husband is substituted for an unkind one. Of course, this substitution is vulnerable to reversal (chiasmus), unkind for kind, as happens at the conclusion of *The Wife of Martin Guerre*, during which Bertrande acknowledges to the authorities that her present husband is actually an impostor. Oxymoronic substitution animates certain dystopian fantasies of the period as well. Arch Oboler's *Strange Holiday* (shot in 1942, revised and distributed 1946) is an example of how the narrative device can be deployed in the form of a frame story.[5] The film is about a middle-class American (Claude Rains) who returns from a fishing trip to discover a Nazi regime has taken power in his home town. In the end, though, it turns out to be a bad dream, but it inspires the formerly complacent Everyman to value his freedoms more and vow to fight to preserve them. The persistent themes of such cautionary fables are the fight against complacency and continual vigilance: "Eternal vigilance is the price of liberty."[6]

The war years saw films such as Fritz Lang's *Ministry of Fear* (1944), about a man who stumbles upon a Nazi spy ring, and William Cameron Menzies' anti–Nazi film *Address Unknown* (1944), but by 1951, Nazis had been replaced by Communists as the powerful enemy. William Cameron Menzies' film, *The Whip Hand* (1951), a sort of loose remake of Fritz Lang's *Ministry of Fear*, shows just how easily a different kind of menace could be substituted for Nazis. The original story of *The Whip Hand* featured a plot to hide the still-alive Adolf Hitler.[7] In late 1950, after viewing a rough cut of the completed film, RKO studio head Howard Hughes demanded retakes, ordering the Hitler plot line to be replaced with a Communist germ warfare story. Seeking medical help for an accidental injury to his forehead, a journalist on a fishing trip in Wisconsin comes across a small town where the locals are sullen and hostile. Puzzled by the suspicious behavior of the townspeople, the journalist begins an investigation into the town, and discovers that the Soviets are plotting to poison America's water supply.

Alfred E. Green's *Invasion U.S.A.* (1952) likewise uses the oxymoronic substitution device with a frame story, creating a dystopian fantasy. In Green's film, a group of complacent Americans sit around a New York bar, ignoring the dire headlines warning of a possible international crisis. The mysterious Mr. Ohman (Dan O'Herlihy) swirls a huge glass of brandy and eavesdrops on the grumblings of the group. After listening to their various complaints, Mr. Ohman, a hypnotist, swirls his brandy and puts the group members under his spell. A foreign invader, although never explicitly identified as the Soviet Union, mounts a nuclear attack on the United States. In the resulting attack, all of the members of the group die or commit suicide, after which Mr. Ohman awakens them from their delusional nightmare and lectures them on their complacency. As in *Strange Holiday*, the citizens awaken with a newfound sense of urgency and patriotism.

The didactic effectiveness of such cautionary fables is a consequence of the protagonist's *anagnorisis* and subsequent *dianoia* (the terms are Aristotle's).[8] As in a vision, the protagonist is shown some deep truth through a dream or a trance, and undergoes a conversion. George Bailey's (James Stewart's) dystopian vision is utterly essential to Frank Capra's *It's a Wonderful Life* (1946); he is given the chance to see what Bedford Falls would have been like if he had never been born. The oxymoronic substitution animating the simulation is that of a dark, noir-like urban landscape (Pottersville) displacing small town Bedford Falls. As Robert B. Ray points out, a typical feature in movies of the postwar period is "the interpenetration of the [*film*] *noir* and Andy Hardy worlds (Pottersville versus Bedford Falls)," which intimated an unsettling sense of the worlds' proximity.[9] Ray's reference to Andy Hardy's (Mickey Rooney's) small hometown of Carvel is an interesting connection given that *Love Laughs at Andy Hardy* (1946), the fifteenth Andy Hardy film produced by MGM, was released the same week in December 1946 as *It's a Wonderful Life*, meaning the two films were showing in theaters at the same time.

The lesson of George's vision is that he is the individual on whom Bedford Falls' very existence depended. He learns that if he had not been born, nothing would have prevented his brother Harry's death, and subsequently Harry would not have saved the men on the troop transport during the war. Upon further investigation George learns that the pharmacist Mr. Gower had gone to prison, Uncle Billy went mad, Ernie the taxi driver was divorced, and George's own wife, Mary, had become an "old maid." Only George Bailey had prevented these things from happening. If complacency can be understood as an unawareness of a real and present danger, then George Bailey is no different than the similarly complacent protagonists of *Strange Holiday* and *Invasion U.S.A.* While Bedford Falls has not been taken over by Nazis or Soviets, the narrative strategy of oxymoronic substitution is the same.

The interpenetration of *film noir* (Pottersville) and Bedford Falls/Carvel is an essential feature of *Invaders from Mars* (1953), a sci-fi dystopian fantasy of the postwar period. This is perhaps not surprising given that its director, William Cameron Menzies, worked extensively as an uncredited Art Director on *It's a Wonderful Life*, and was the uncredited co-director as well.[10] Following the arrival of the Martians, David MacLean's (Jimmy Hunt's) small town becomes defamiliarized, transformed into a sinister, threatening world. David MacLean's disorienting experience is not unlike George Bailey's upon his return to Pottersville. While David's parents do in fact recognize him—unlike the inhabitants of Pottersville who do not recognize George Bailey—they are cold, distant, and short-tempered, very unlike their previous selves. David notices a stigmatic mark at the base of his father's neck, which we learn is a Martian implant fitted to the base of the skull in order to control his behavior. *Invaders from Mars* features what Steven Zani and Kevin Meaux call "atomic age zombies," meaning zombies who have been created by extraterrestrials rather than occult ritual magic. Kevin Boon would go one step further and classify the zombies in *Invaders from Mars* (1953) as "tech zombies"—humans who have been "robbed of volition by technology"—but the film can be considered a forerunner of Jack Finney's *The Body Snatchers* in that human zombification is caused by creatures whose origins are extraterrestrial. Another important precursor was, of course, Robert Heinlein's *The Puppet Masters*, in which slugs from another planet attach themselves to humans' backs "and transform them into zombies."[11]

As in the dystopian fantasies described above using a frame story, the Martian invasion is revealed to be a bad dream, although because of the unexpected twist at the film's conclusion—the landing of yet another flying saucer—David, along with the audience, is left with an unsettling sense of the precariousness of the everyday world. It is as if the postwar substitution of Communist infiltrators for the fifth-column Fascists of the 1940s has become a loop, with one enemy replacing another in an endless cycle of repetition. Postwar cynicism in America was fueled by the perception that the long years of fighting Nazis had accomplished nothing.

It's a Wonderful Life revealed the uncomfortably close proximity of Pottersville to Bedford Falls or Carvel. In Jack Finney's foundational novel of the subgenre, *The Body Snatchers* (serial publication 1954, paperback publication 1955), the story is set in the small town of Santa Mira, California. As in the story of Martin Guerre, the initial oxymoronic substitution happens to a family member: husband, wife, son, daughter, and another relative, who have been replaced by impostors or simulacra. Critic David Seed has remarked on this feature as well, observing that the "first and most sustained impact of the pods in Finney's word [sic] is the division of family units" (159). In Finney's novel, the small-town doctor, Miles Bennell, is approached by his old flame, Becky Driscoll, who has sought him out to ask him for help. She tells Miles that her cousin Wilma emphatically believes that her Uncle Ira "*isn't*" her uncle" (emphasis in original, *The Body Snatchers*, 10). Wilma believes that

Uncle Ira is an "impostor, or something. Someone who only *looks* like Ira" (emphasis in original, 10). Becky persuades Miles to drive out and meet Uncle Ira. Upon his and Becky's arrival, Miles sees Uncle Ira mowing the lawn. He tells Wilma that the man he recognizes is Uncle Ira, to which she replies, "Miles, memories or not, appearances or not, possible or impossible, that is not my Uncle Ira" (19). Finney uses the term "impostor" five times in the novel's first seven chapters.

If oxymoronic substitution is fundamental to the body snatcher subgenre, the second fundamental feature, introduced in *Invaders from Mars*, might be considered metonymic substitution, or substitution by contiguity: impostors spread rapidly throughout the community, as if through contagious disease. The impostors disrupt quotidian normality and initiate the oxymoronic subversion of the familiar by the alien, which happens to serve as a succinct summary of the underlying thematic of Finney's novel.[12]

In his study, *Film Criticism, the Cold War, and the Blacklist*, Jeff Smith indicates that the term "brainwashing" had been introduced to the American public in 1951. He goes on to state that there arose a "loose association between Communist brainwashing and alien mind control," particularly as a consequence of the Korean War (260). As he points out, because brainwashed individuals lack will and self-control, "they are akin to persons in a vegetative state" (260). Subsequently, a key word in the discourse about the postwar science film emerged: "vegetable."

The idea of the extraterrestrial seed pods in Jack Finney's *The Body Snatchers*, which in order to survive reproduce their hosts through assimilation, seems to be taken, rather straightforwardly, from Howard Hawks' *The Thing from Another World* (1951). In *The Thing*, the scientist, Dr. Carrington, is quite favorably impressed that the Thing's evolutionary development "was not handicapped by emotional or sexual factors." He proudly exhibits to all present a "seed pod" he has removed from the Thing's detached forearm (torn off by one of the sled dogs), and announces that the seed pod is an example of the "neat and unconfused reproductive technique of vegetation. No pain or pleasure as we know it. No emotions, no heart. Far superior—far superior in every way." The asexual and unmarried scientist, who wants desperately to preserve this aggressive life-form that the others plot to destroy, ardently lectures the other members of the Arctic expedition on the virtues of being a vegetable, a being that is blissfully devoid of the strong emotions and unruly passions that plague sexual creatures such as human beings. During an interview with *Invasion of the Body Snatcher*'s director, Don Siegel, Stuart Kaminsky remarked upon the film's connection to *The Thing* as well, observing that the earlier film "dealt with an emotionless vegetable creature from outer space that lived off humans…" (LaValley 157). An "emotionless vegetable creature" is, by implication, one who is not handicapped by "sexual factors."

The producer of *Invasion of the Body Snatchers*, Walter Wanger, was well aware of the Cold War lexical significance of "vegetable." In a speech delivered at the American Booksellers Convention in 1955, Wanger made clear that he viewed *Invasion of the Body Snatchers* as a cautionary fable, saying that it was, among other things, about the fear of conformity. He said:

> Wisdom and reason based on education will allow us to have individual judgement and character like the founders of this nation hoped that we would have. I have just finished a picture

based on this subject of conformity. The film shows how easy it is for people to be taken over and to lose their souls if they are not alert and determined in their character to be free, otherwise they will become mere vegetables—just pods.... I know I am talking to somebody that is a *pod* and can be taken over by an enemy because there is no intelligent resistance [emphasis in original, LaValley 146].

Aside from his explicit statement that the film is about the fear of conformity, his insistence on vigilance and avoiding complacency ("how easy it is for people to be taken over and to lose their souls if they are not alert and determined") resonated with audiences in the mid–1950s just as it would have resonated with an audience in pre–World War II America, the audience of *Meet John Doe*. What distinguishes his rhetoric from the previous decade, though, is his use of the word "pod" to refer to someone who possesses "no intelligent resistance." Perhaps he is referring to someone who might be vulnerable to, for example, Communist indoctrination, or perhaps to someone who could be easily brainwashed, but he may also have had in mind someone who easily conforms, a conformist. In a letter addressed to film critic Bosley Crowther of the *New York Times*, Wanger described the film as a "plea against conformity" (LaValley 163). Hence, the use of the framing story, employed in previous cautionary fables and dystopian fantasies, would not have been unusual to audiences at the time.

By foregrounding the film's apparently important subject, Wanger was acknowledging the common Hollywood perception at the time that there was an audience for what might be called "serious" movies. By the mid–1950s, Hollywood had begun to merge the serious—socially conscious—movie with old-fashioned storytelling. These types of films are now referred to as a "problem pictures," movies "that explored disturbing areas of American life" which contain an "outward display of social concern" (Ray 144). Don Siegel's and Walter Wanger's earlier film, *Riot in Cell Block 11* (1954), about the abhorrent living conditions endured by prison inmates, was a problem picture, as was the film Siegel directed immediately after *Invasion of the Body Snatchers*, *Crime in the Streets* (1956), the subject of which was juvenile delinquency. Indeed, Al LaValley argues that the film's importance resides in its engagement with social problems, that is, that it was a problem picture. Moreover, given Don Siegel's previous experience using the *film noir* style, he easily transforms the small town of Santa Mira, with its *It's a Wonderful Life* setting, into a *noir* world of canted (or "Dutch tilt") camera angles, long, exaggerated shadows, back-lit characters visible only as silhouettes, extreme close-ups of desperate, anxious faces, and disorienting tracking shots. Which is to say, the world of sunny Santa Mira is transformed rather suddenly into Pottersville. Nora Sayre employs the term "subversion" in her discussion of the film's implications.[13]

Each age sees its own shape in previous eras. The concept which shaped Walter Wanger's film version of *Invasion of the Body Snatchers*—a "plea against conformity"—is still very much a part of Philip Kaufman's 1978 remake. However, given that Kaufman emerged from the Sixties counterculture which perceived individualism as dead due to the inevitable march of Modernity, his version sets out to "correct" the 1956 version. First, the remake removes the Americana of small-town Santa Mira. Kaufman's 1978 remake moves the action to the metropolis of San

Francisco, with its towering Transamerica Pyramid (completed in 1972) dominating the city's skyline, a looming, radical image of corporate-era Modernity representing the bureaucratic relentlessness that was out to destroy individualism and self-determination in America. Second, Kaufman's version includes a sequence in which Kevin McCarthy, who played Miles Bennell in the earlier film, is struck and killed by an automobile while running through the streets of San Francisco like a madman shouting, "Help, help! They're coming! You're next! You're next!" as he did at the conclusion of the 1956 version (before the sequence completing the frame story). Third, Kaufman's version features director Don Siegel in a cameo role as a duplicitous taxi driver whose body has already been snatched. Fourth, it cast *Star Trek*'s emotionless Mr. Spock, Leonard Nimoy, as the sinister psychiatrist, Dr. David Kibner.

The film's self-consciousness reveals the implied relationship between the movie and its audience. As Robert B. Ray has pointed out, Hollywood films designed for Sixties and Seventies countercultural audiences often displayed a noticeable self-consciousness about inherited myths and conventions (318). The casting of countercultural icon Donald Sutherland as Matthew Bennell also suggests the degree of the film's self-consciousness. Sutherland had been the star of *Klute* (1971) and the anti–Vietnam War satirical documentary *F.T.A.* (1972) with then partner Jane Fonda, as well as satirical anti-war films such as *M*A*S*H* (1970). In addition, Ray also points out that the heroes of countercultural films frequently confronted "depersonalized villains who came to represent the incessant advance of modernity" (303). The line frequently repeated in *Butch Cassidy and the Sundance Kid* (1969), "Who *are* those guys?" caught on as a countercultural tagline about the death of individualism in America and could have been used as the appropriate tagline for the 1978 *Invasion of the Body Snatchers* with its largely anonymous, depersonalized "pod people" villains. The "pod people" are those who figuratively have gone back to sleep, representing the death of individualism in America.

While Abel Ferrara's *Body Snatchers* (1993) is a more expensive production than Philip Kaufman's version, with elaborate special effects, Ferrara returned the story, as J. Hoberman observes, "to its B-movie roots" (142). Certain story elements have been retained, such as the horrific, banshee-like screech that the pod people use to identify an unconverted human, and the rigid, erect posture with one arm outstretched with a pointing finger (both films were produced by Robert H. Solo). However, the setting is neither small town America nor a major metropolis but a military base in Alabama where its tough-talking soldiers and civilian personnel are being replaced by impostors. Ferrara's *Body Snatchers* makes the identification of an impostor extraordinarily difficult given the military's demands for lock-step conformity and rigid discipline: as J. Hoberman writes, "the pod subversion is envisioned as a military coup" (144). The disruption of the family unit is, of course, central to the story, with the teenage protagonist's biological mother some time before having been replaced by an emotionally cold stepmother, who in turn becomes zombified, linking her to the transformed mother in *Invaders from Mars*.

Oliver Hirschbiegel's *The Invasion* (2007) is an awkward amalgam of sci-fi, horror, and action. A troubled production with extensive reshoots apparently overseen

Figure 31. Analyst/writer Dr. David Kibner (Leonard Nimoy) comforts a terrified housewife (Lelia Goldoni) in *Invasion of the Body Snatchers* (1978) (United Artists [1978]).

by the Wachowskis and (uncredited) director James McTeigue (*V For Vendetta*, 2006), the reshot material largely consists of action sequences, including a car chase, thus making director Hirschbiegel's original cut difficult to reconstruct. One possible source of inspiration for Hirschbiegel's and screenwriter David Kajganich's postmodern revision of Finney's fundamental story was Danny Boyle's *28 Days Later*

(2002), with its very real fear of a global pandemic. Apparently Hirschbiegel's original cut was shot in a sort of *cinéma vérité* style, giving the film a quasi-documentary look. Remnants of that approach remain, mostly in the film's somber and atmospheric first half hour.

The 2007 version employs very few elements drawn from Finney's novel. In this film a space shuttle disintegrates upon re-entry into the Earth's atmosphere, leaving a trail of debris that turns out to have been contaminated with highly contagious alien spores. Among those initially infected is, ironically, CDC official Tucker Kaufman (Jeremy Northam), who, given his position, enables the invading organism rather quickly to infect individuals within institutions of social control and regulation, especially those of the government. Once infected, these individuals are transformed into cold, unfeeling automatons whose sole purpose is to infect others. Kaufman's ex-wife is a Washington, D.C., psychiatrist, Dr. Carol Bennell (Nicole Kidman). She is understandably chagrined when, after long disinterest, her ex-husband suddenly requests that their young son, Oliver (Jackson Bond), be allowed a visit. Dr. Bennell drops off the boy at his father's home, then spends the evening at a dinner party with her friend, Dr. Ben Driscoll (Daniel Craig), with whom she is in the early stages of a romance.

Soon, however, the everyday reality of daily life begins to take on an unreal quality, and Dr. Bennell senses something is wrong. A patient tells her that "my husband is not my husband," again invoking the Martin Guerre story. When Dr. Bennell witnesses a woman struck by a car, but neither the driver nor the police do anything about it, her paranoia significantly increases. She soon forms an alliance with Ben Driscoll and his colleague, Dr. Stephen Galeano (Jeffrey Wright), in order to learn what is behind people's oddly altered behavior.

Like Philip Kaufman's version, *The Invasion* contains self-conscious references to the earlier versions. Just as Philip Kaufman's version had Kevin McCarthy and Don Siegel in cameo roles, *The Invasion* features Veronica Cartwright, one of the protagonists in Kaufman's version. Additionally, the last name of Nicole Kidman's ex-husband is "Kaufman." Beyond these sorts of contingent connections, however, Hirschbiegel's version is not so much metaphorically rich as it is commercially compromised, devoid of the intellectual depth that made the previous versions so memorable. If the pods of the Siegel, Kaufman, and Ferrara versions were rather clunky, the method of disease transmission in *The Invasion* is grossly juvenile: those infected vomit into liquids to be drank by others, or even into a potential victim's open mouth. However, *The Invasion* does, for the first time in an adaptation, employ the *deus ex machina* of Finney's novel, in which the invading organism is destroyed and order is re-established.

Trickery, imposture, masquerade, impersonation, simulation, and dissimulation are themes fundamental to the story of Martin Guerre, just as they are to the story made and remade about "body snatchers." Despite the era in which each of these films was made, there is a tendency to allegorize the story of the "body snatchers" consistently, as we have seen, as a dystopian fantasy. Perhaps it is important to remember Walter Benjamin's observation about the power of allegory: "Any person, any object, any relationship can mean absolutely anything else" (175). In other words, allegory completely eradicates detail, "it is ... a world in which the detail is of no great importance" (175). In other words, to allegorize is itself to perform an act of imposture: it is to replace a particular detail by another with a similar structure. The foundational myth at the root of the "body snatchers" story is that of Martin Guerre, about a man who abandoned his wife and allowed himself to be replaced by an impostor, an impostor so skilled at trickery, masquerade, and dissimulation that he fooled almost everyone. It is a story about the relationship between appearance and essence, truth and doubt. At its root is a Cartesian nightmare in which appearances provide no firm or reliable knowledge of the external world. A world so nightmarish, in fact, that we might be compelled to wonder, was the man who returned really Martin Guerre?

Notes

1. A couple of years before Lewis's novel, British author Thomas F. Tweed had published *Rinehard: A Melodrama of the Nineteen-Thirties* (London: Arthur Barker, 1933). Tweed's near future novel was adapted by future *Invasion of the Body Snatcher* producer Walter Wanger, as *Gabriel Over the White House* (MGM, 1933). Shot in two weeks, the film advocated dictatorial solutions to America's problems.

2. Janet Lewis's novel, *The Wife of Martin Guerre* (San Francisco: Colt Press, 1941), is short, at 152 pages.

3. If it was indeed Martin Guerre who returned. Natalie Zemon Davis raises the possibility in her study *The Return of Martin Guerre*.

4. Dick's story, although written in February 1953, was first published in *Startling Stories*, Winter 1955.

5. The source text for *Strange Holiday* was Oboler's own previous radio play, "This Precious Freedom," which aired December 30, 1939, starring Raymond Massey. In the film adaptation, Massey was replaced by Claude Rains.

6. This quotation, well-known in the nineteenth century, and known to be used by figures such as Frederick Douglass, James Buchanan, and William Henry Harrison, has been erroneously attributed to Thomas Jefferson. The quotation can be traced back to Irish orator John Philpot Curran's statement, "The condition upon which God hath given liberty to man is eternal vigilance; which condition if he break, servitude is at once the consequence of his crime and the punishment of his guilt." See Suzy Platt, ed., *Respectfully Quoted* (Washington, D.C.: Library of Congress, 1993), 200.

7. RKO production files, contained at the UCLA Arts—Special Collections Library, add the following information about the production: RKO purchased Roy Hamilton's original screen story in July 1949. In January 1950, Stanley Rubin was assigned to write and produce the picture. Stanley Rubin was replaced by Lewis J. Rachmil after Howard Hughes ordered retakes. According to the RKO production records, among the actors cut from the final film was Bobby Watson, a supporting actor whose who was frequently cast as Adolph Hitler.

8. In the *Poetics*, Aristotle defined *anagnorisis* as "a change from ignorance to knowledge" leading to *dianoia*, a change in thought or perception (1452a).

9. See Robert B. Ray, *A Certain Tendency in the Hollywood Cinema, 1930–1980* (Princeton: Princeton University Press, 1985), 203. Ray is also the author of *The Avant-Garde Finds Andy Hardy* (Cambridge: Harvard University Press, 1995), a work of film theory that is also a detailed study of MGM's highly successful Andy Hardy film series.

10. Frank Capra enlisted shortly after completing the filming of *Arsenic and Old Lace* in December 1941, and did not direct a motion picture for over four years. *Arsenic and Old Lace* was held from release until 1944 due to a contractual arrangement with the Broadway play's producers. William Cameron Menzies came onto the *It's a Wonderful Life* project (then titled *The Greatest Gift*) in late 1944, prior to Capra becoming involved. Menzies and Capra had worked together on *Meet John Joe*, and Menzies was once again brought onboard to design several sequences in *It's a Wonderful Life*. According to James Curtis, when *It's a Wonderful Life* went into production in April 1946, "Menzies was on the set, primarily to hold the veteran director's hand. By his own admission, Capra was nervous at the prospect of directing a $1.5 million production after such a lengthy hiatus." Suzie Menzies, daughter of the director, remembered her father working "on a lot" of *It's a Wonderful Life*. "Yet Menzies' name appears on none of the surviving production records, nor does the work he did on the movie appear to have been budgeted—raising the possibility his weekly salary was covered out of Capra's own pocket." See James Curtis, *William Cameron Menzies: The Shape of Films to Come* (New York: Pantheon Books, 2015), 286.

11. See David Seed, "Alien Invasions by Body Snatchers and Related Creatures," in *Modern Gothic: A*

Reader, Victor Sage and Allan Lloyd Smith, eds. (Manchester: Manchester University Press, 1996), 160. See also Kevin Boon, "The Zombie as Other: Mortality and the Monstrous in the Post-Nuclear Age" in *Better Off Dead: The Evolution of the Zombie as Post-Human*, Deborah Christie and Sarah Juliet Lauro, eds. (New York: Fordham University Press, 2011), 58, and Steven Zani and Kevin Meaux, "Lucio Fulci and the Decaying Definition of Zombie Narratives."

     12. The idea of contagion reveals the way body snatcher films share a family resemblance with zombie narratives such as *28 Days Later*, and why the 2007 remake of *Invasion of the Body Snatchers*, *The Invasion*, employs a disease of extraterrestrial origin.

     13. See Nora Sayre, *Running Time: Films of the Cold War* (New York: Dial Press, 1982), 199.

Works Cited

Benjamin, Walter. *The Origin of German Tragic Drama*. Trans. John Osborne. Verso, 2009.
Boon, Kevin. "The Zombie as Other: Mortality and the Monstrous in the Post-Nuclear Age." *Better Off Dead: The Evolution of the Zombie as Post-Human*, edited by Deborah Christie and Sarah Juliet Lauro. Fordham University Press, 2011.
Curtis, James. *William Cameron Menzies: The Shape of Films to Come*. Pantheon, 2015.
Davis, Natalie Zemon. *The Return of Martin Guerre*. Second Edition. Harvard University Press, 1983.
Dick, Philip K. "Human Is." *The Collected Stories of Philip K. Dick, Volume Two: Second Variety*. Underwood/Miller, 1987.
Finney, Jack. *The Body Snatchers*. Dell, 1955.
Hoberman, J. "Nearer My Pod to Thee." *The Science Film Reader*, edited by Gregg Rickman. Limelight Editions, 2004.
LaValley, Al, ed. *Invasion of the Body Snatchers*. Rutgers University Press, 1989.
Ray, Robert B. *A Certain Tendency of the Hollywood Cinema, 1930–1980*. Princeton University Press, 1985.
Seed, David. "Alien Invasions by Body Snatchers and Related Creatures." *Modern Gothic: A Reader*, edited by Victor Sage and Allan Lloyd Smith. Manchester University Press, 1996.
Smith, Jeff. *Film Criticism, the Cold War, and the Blacklist: Reading the Hollywood Reds*. University of California Press, 2014.
Zani, Steven, and Kevin Meaux. "Lucio Fulci and the Decaying Definition of Zombie Narratives." *Better Off Dead: The Evolution of the Zombie as Post-Human*, edited by Deborah Christie and Sarah Juliet Lauro. Fordham University Press, 2011.

Filmography

Address Unknown. Dir. William Cameron Menzies. Columbia Pictures, 1944. Film.
Butch Cassidy and the Sundance Kid. Dir. George Roy Hill. 20th Century Fox, 1969. Film.
Crime in the Streets. Dir. Don Siegel. Allied Artists, 1956. Film.
F.T.A. Dir. Francine Parker. American International Pictures, 1972. Documentary.
The Great Dictator. Dir. Charlie Chaplin. United Artists, 1940. Film.
Invaders from Mars. Dir. William Cameron Menzies. 20th Century Fox, 1953. Film.
The Invasion. Dir. Oliver Hirschbiegel. Warner Bros., 2007. Film.
Invasion of the Body Snatchers. Dir. Don Siegel. Allied Artists Pictures, 1956. Film.
Invasion of the Body Snatchers. Dir. Philip Kaufman. United Artists, 1978. Film.
Invasion U.S.A. Dir. Alfred E. Green. Columbia Pictures, 1952. Film.
It's a Wonderful Life. Dir. Frank Capra. RKO Radio Pictures, 1946. Film.
Klute. Dir. Alan J. Pakula. Warner Bros., 1971. Film.
Love Laughs at Andy Hardy. Dir. Willis Goldbeck. MGM, 1946. Film.
M*A*S*H. Dir. Robert Altman. 20th Century Fox, 1970. Film.
Meet John Doe. Dir. Frank Capra. Warner Bros., 1941. Film.
Ministry of Fear. Dir. Fritz Lang. Paramount Pictures, 1944. Film.
Riot in Cell Block 11. Dir. Don Siegel. Allied Artists Pictures, 1954. Film.
Star Trek. CBS Studios, 1966–1969. TV Series.
Strange Holiday. Dir. Arch Oboler. Producers Releasing Corporation, 1946. Film.
The Thing from Another World. Dir. Christian Nyby. RKO Radio Pictures, 1951. Film.
28 Days Later. Dir. Danny Boyle. Fox Searchlight Pictures, 2002. Film.
V for Vendetta. Dir. James McTeigue. Warners Bros., 2006. Film.
The Whip Hand. Dir. William Cameron Menzies. RKO Radio Pictures, 1951. Film.

PART IV

Other Worlds
and Dystopian Visions

Escaping Earth

The Uninhabitable Home in Rocketship X-M, Interstellar, and Ad Astra

CHRISTOPHER LOVE

In 1959, film scholar Richard Hodgens excoriated the genre of sci-fi film in the pages of *Film Quarterly* for its disjunctive, unrealistic, and unscientific portrayals of space travel. "The premise is always flatly impossible," Hodgens asserts, while admitting that there are exceptions to his rule. He particularly noted the films produced by George Pal, such as 1950's *Destination Moon* (31). In fairness to the quality of sci-fi films of the 1950s, they were often hampered by low budgets and rushed productions, which affected direction, acting, and scriptwriting; the genre, however, persisted. Therefore, what Hodgens and such scholars were criticizing about the state of the genre in the 1950s was a genre-in-the-making, one in search of itself and one lacking the support and resources needed to be fully realized in all its artistic potential.

Nineteen fifties sci-fi films, Hodgens and others complained, wavered between horror and science, with horror and Gothic-trappings overshadowing science (30). Later films, however, would eventually demonstrate the value of 1950s sci-fi by exhibiting the persistent and lasting influence of these early movies. Starting with *Rocketship X-M* (1950), science, horror, and the Gothic became inextricably intertwined as the genre developed into a mode of storytelling about humanity's fears about the limits, effects, unknown quantities, and consequences of scientific progress and space travel. But even more telling, *Rocketship X-M* and the films that it helped spawn provided obvious and subtle critiques of the world that had yet to solve its most threatening problems while dreaming about venturing into the great unknown of space.

Such films became the basis of Susan Sontag's landmark 1966 essay "The Imagination of Disaster," in which she argues that the genre provides an "inadequate response" to the issues that it raises (48). Specifically, Sontag argues for a portrayal of science as a product of social and political activity and collaboration rather than the genre's obsession with "the individual's psyche," especially as that psyche becomes warped by its obsession with individual and "collective incineration" because of fear from nuclear war (47).

As if in response to Hodgens' and Sontag's criticisms, subsequent sci-fi films have become so diverse and widespread that it is difficult for any critic to reduce the genre to a single formula. For example, future films would fulfill Sontag's wish by exploring the corporate and political ties to scientific exploration. But the push for absolute realism—whatever that means—is incompatible with creative fictional narrative, as demonstrated in the documentary-like *Destination Moon* (1950), a film widely criticized for its dullness. Literary and cinematic fiction, even manifestations of types of realist fictions, have always been a commentary on, engagement with, and means by which to reconstruct and imagine reality or possible realities. Furthermore, fiction is a moral endeavor, even if that endeavor is to question or shake the foundations of morality itself or to investigate the nature of morality or the sustainability of any given conventional morality. Thus, "sci-fi," by the very meaning of the combination of these words, is not about total commitment to scientific accuracy but is rather an allegorical meditation on how scientific progress and its possibilities force us to reconsider every aspect of what we believe to be moral and real.

In between Hodgens' and Sontag's criticisms came Hannah Arendt's 1963 essay, ironically titled "Man's Conquest of Space." While she does not discuss sci-fi, Arendt addresses problems which sci-fi films and literature had already been dramatizing. For one, she asserts that space travel and discoveries in physics shattered humanity's illusion that it has ever understood reality, or that there is a singular "true reality" (Arendt 533). Consequently, Arendt contends that in recognizing the complexity of science and the vastness space, humanity realizes its insignificance. Hence, Arendt suggests, the "conquest" comes at a great collective psychological cost as humanity seeks to find ways to reaffirm its importance by replicating its geocentric and anthropocentric views so that it might establish new settlements throughout the solar system (535). But in this, Arendt argues, humanity will fail because it must leave behind all that it once believed to be "natural," coupled with the realization that the vastness of space makes it unconquerable, even within the span of thousands of human lifetimes (535).

There, in a nutshell, are the problems films about space travel face. Because fiction primarily morally engages its subject, creators of sci-fi inherently approach their narratives from an anthropocentric position; they are among the humanists Arendt mentions, probing the meaning and consequence of scientific discoveries in terms of the human race. But the reality of space, the universe's vastness, makes it incompatible with humanistic storytelling—humans tell stories about themselves, their homes, and their significance—but what we have come to discover scientifically about the universe reflects its utter and complete indifference to our presence and its own lack of any meaning. Consequently, this puts creators of sci-fi in a conundrum. To be realistic, the inconsequential nature of human existence in relation to a conscienceless universe must be depicted and engaged in space travel films, but in order to be effective narratives these films must somehow maintain their humanity.

Many creators of sci-fi have tackled this problem in a time-honored manner. Like almost all fiction, sci-fi often incorporates the archetype of "the home," or at least the desire for or depiction of some degree of stable, peaceful, and fulfilling social relationships. In much sci-fi, this sense of home is sometimes represented by the Earth itself. Narrative tension is often driven by the image of "home" under threat, and sci-fi films frequently depict Earth as uninhabitable or under constant threat of atomic or biological warfare, or environmental destruction brought on by scientific and technological advancement. At the same time, films that portray space exploration force us to recognize our own and Earth's insignificance—and thus the insignificance of what humans have thought of as "home." Earth's portrayal as increasingly uninhabitable because scientific discoveries have diminished our geo-centric understanding of our place in the universe, which in turn, shatters our con-ception of Earth as a stable and permanent home.

In 1950, *Rocketship X-M* became the first postwar sci-fi film about space explo-ration, and therefore the first film of the 1950s sci-fi film renaissance (Warren 10). Although billed as a story about "man's conquest of space," *Rocketship X-M* belies this optimistic premise and instead tells a story of scientific miscalculation, lost time, and the haunting remnants of a Martian civilization. As a pioneering sci-fi film, *X-M* foregrounds the genre's portrayal of Earth's dismal destiny as later depicted in the 2014 film *Interstellar* and 2019's *Ad Astra*. *Interstellar* and *Ad Astra* continue a narrative line that had been well-established in the aftermath and under the influence of *Rocketship X-M*. Indeed, these films obfuscate problems on Earth and ironically reject technical and scientific advancements—outside of escape—as solutions to problems that forebode the end of humanity's home planet as a habitable space. Equally significant, though, is how these films dramatize the fear of losing Earth as a fixed meaning of "home" and the consequences of unraveling this nexus of human understanding, which binds, even if loosely, humans together. Indeed, the horrors that the characters discover are not just the physical threats that Earth is under. The deeper horror seems to be that Earth might lose its sociocultural mean-ing as a home for human beings.

Narratively, these three films, as well as many other sci-fi films, handle the dis-association of "Earth" from "home" in similar, paradoxical ways. Indeed, the tension of the narratives of these films arises from the narratives' as well as the characters' inability to grapple with the revolutionary yet disjunctive and destabilized meaning of Earth as a habitable space. As a result, the narratives and characters of the films retreat to the safe and familiar meanings of romantic love, family, and mysticism.

While *Rocketship X-M* was being written and hastily produced, its poten-tial economically damaging effect on the planned release of *Destination Moon* was anticipated. Plot details of *X-M* were leaked, and George Pal, *Moon*'s producer, went so far as to file a copyright lawsuit against *X-M*'s producers to prevent its release (Warren 10). It is not known what details were changed, but based on the original idea and title, it appears *X-M* went through a dramatic shift in its plot.[1]

Destination Moon was to be the first sincere attempt at realism in cinematic sci-fi, and with the threat of the lawsuit, the director and co-writer of *X-M*, Kurt Neumann, may have made alterations to create a more dramatic film than what *Moon* was expected to be. Nevertheless, *Rocketship X-M* attempts to establish real-ism by opening with a scientific explanation of the realistic viability of its intended moon-mission. In fact, in an opening monologue, Dr. Fleming (Morris Ankrum) addresses reporters asking them to recall "wild tales of the flying discs, flying sau-cers, and who knows what imaginative creations," before reminding them that this mission is purely scientific. Thus the film announces a departure from sci-fi films of the past (*Rocketship X-M*).

The crew for this mission consists of Dr. Karl Eckstrum, a physicist; chemist Dr. Lisa Van Horn; Colonel Floyd Graham, the pilot; Harry Chamberlain, an astronomer and the flight's navigator; and flight engineer Major William Corrigan. Thus, *Rocketship X-M* introduces a groundbreaking character in Dr. Lisa Van Horn, sci-fi film's first serious female scientist (played by Osa Massen). However, two of the men's treatment of Van Horn has harrowing consequences for the crew and crucial implications for the meaning of "home."

As the mission gets further from Earth, crew members view the planet as it recedes into the distance. Only now does the crew start to realize the profundity of their mission, not just for the world but for themselves. Major Corrigan and Colonel Graham (Lloyd Bridges) become nostalgic—and Graham begins his awkward romantic courtship of Dr. Van Horn. Although the film handles this comically, both intentionally and unintentionally, the scene conveys that characters are starting to recognize that their way of thinking of the Earth has forever been altered. They are the first to see the Earth as a dot in a window amid the vacuum of space. Nostalgia involves a sense of loss, a longing for a way of being that cannot be recovered, and for the crew of *X-M*, they have crossed that point as they move uneasily deeper into space.

Often in narrative, the farther from home, the more perilous the journey becomes, as conventional meaning and understanding break down and uncertainty takes over. And this certainly is the case with *X-M*; Eckstrum's calculations do not add up and are at odds with Van Horn's, but he dismisses her protests because she is "momentarily being a woman" (*Rocketship*). Van Horn, though, realizes the crew and the mission are in danger as they are running out of fuel. It is at this point the film awkwardly transitions toward what at first seems a distracting storyline but one that is integral to the direction of the film. Van Horn must endure Colonel Graham, who has seized the opportunity to woo her by ludicrously quoting Kipling and waxing on about night skies and convertibles. The film poses Van Horn as a woman who is too smart for her own good, although it is not her error that leads to the crew's impending demise. While fending off one of Graham's advances, she says to him, "I suppose you think that women should only cook and sew and bear children" to which Graham replies, "Isn't that enough?" (*Rocketship*). Van Horn, incredibly given their dire circumstances, indicates via a smile that she entertains Graham's notions that she, indeed, is a girl who works too hard and too much.

As absurd and sexist as the scene is, it is the film's attempt to reconcile the crew's fleeting sense of home as they drift deeper into outer space. Graham's romantic nostalgia for Earth makes him recall a family memory, and in his attraction to Van Horn he sees in her the possibility of "home." At this point, the music becomes eerie, for they are about to be bombarded by meteors, set off course, and hurled helplessly toward Mars.

After waking and realizing what has happened, Eckstrum, presented as a cold man of hard science, cannot explain their predicament and immediately declares that a divine force must have intervened and set them on a Martian destination.

Eckstrum goes on about how science cannot explain their new path: "There comes a time when a mere scientist has gone as far as he can. We must pause and observe respectfully while something infinitely greater assumes control. I believe that this is one of those times" (*Rocketship*). Unable to control the ship's drift farther from home, Eckstrum reverts to the familiarity of faith in mysticism for comfort. Consequently, the film begins to lose some of its scientific air. With the suggestion of some divine force guiding the crew, the film also changes course from scientific realism to scientific allegory.

When the unfortunate rocket ship lands on Mars, the film's underlying allegory becomes apparent. As the crew wanders the desolate Martian terrain, developed wonderfully using a red tint, they are attacked by rock-throwing, seemingly primitive human-like beings. Upon reading elevated radiation levels and encountering several of the Martians, Dr. Eckstrum concludes that these are the animalistic survivors of a nuclear holocaust, degenerated and mutated from radiation fallout. He muses, "Atomic age to stone age." Moments later Corrigan is killed by rocks thrown by the creatures, and Eckstrum is mortally wounded. He manages to make it back to Van Horn, Graham, and Chamberlain and tries to issue a warning but breathes his last before he fully explains his meaning. Despite Eckstrum's earlier obtuseness, he appears to realize that what they have encountered is Earth's destiny should the crew not find a way to warn Earth about what they have found.

For such a profound discovery, the scenes on Mars are short, accounting for about fifteen of the film's seventy-seven minutes. But the brevity creates an abrupt shift in the film's narrative direction and escalates its pace to a suspenseful and surprising end. In fact, the film's final minutes are the most thrilling and most innovative moments in the production. The startling revelation of the Martian nuclear holocaust forces viewers, who so far have been watching a rather pedestrian movie, to consider a disturbing question: How and why do advanced civilizations destroy themselves? And how far are we from such an end? With the recent onset of the Cold War in 1950, and the Korean War soon to follow the film's initial release, *X-M* forced viewers to confront a terrifying possibility.

Two concepts are juxtaposed in this short film. One is that space travel exposes the possibility that humans *can* leave Earth, forcing us to reconsider Earth as a permanent home, and the other is that we actually *may be forced* to leave in order to survive its destruction by our own hands. Only three members of the crew escape Mars, though Chamberlain is unconscious, wounded by a Martian, as the ship leaves. Van Horn and Graham begin the return voyage, for the journey away from home in narrative typically foreshadows a return. But the film ends tragically; they are not welcomed safely into Earth's bosom but instead die in a fiery crash when the ship runs out of fuel just before it could safely reach Earth. As they realize their doomed fate, Graham and Van Horn embrace and share their feelings for one another. Van Horn regrets that she neglected her romantic life, wishing that she and Graham could have met earlier and been together creating their "home." As they hurl to their deaths, Van Horn declares that she is no longer afraid, that "something" has intervened and removed her fear—another allusion to divine forces at work in the voyage (*Rocketship*).

Figure 32. Lisa Van Horn (Osa Massen) and Colonel Floyd Graham (Lloyd Bridges) discuss their future in *Rocketship X-M* (1950) (Lippert Pictures Inc./Photofest).

Although Van Horn and Graham deliver their warning via radio before they perish, science and human nature make an incompatible at best—and flat-out bad at worst—combination in *Rocketship X-M*. After all, the once-scientifically advanced Martians, allegorical humans, have destroyed themselves except for their degenerate remnants. Solace in love and hope of divine intervention provide two-thirds of the solution for human salvation. The third part of humanity's hope is uttered by Dr. Fleming at the conclusion of film. The crew has proven that "interspace travel is not only possible but practical," Fleming declares, before concluding the film by announcing the construction of a new rocket ship, the R X-M 2 (*Rocketship*).

Escape of Earth and space exploration have become the third part of the equation. But the sum does not add up, and the film's lack of engagement with the practical realities of Cold War politics and nuclear proliferation are never addressed specifically. In reality, the Space Age of the 1950s and 1960s was largely a product of American-Soviet military and technological rivalry that led to the looming threat of nuclear war. The film's cynicism toward the possibility of totally benign science is well-founded considering that the major technological and scientific leaps of the era sprang from war and escalating American-Soviet tensions. The crew's warning, in fact, proves cryptic, just like the divine intervention represented in the film. The only practical solution provided by the film is further development of space technology. Earth's time is waning, the film seems to suggest, and our best hope lies elsewhere.

Sixty-four years later Christopher Nolan's acclaimed *Interstellar* echoed much of *Rocketship X-M*'s convoluted narrative as well as many of its thematic problems. In a 2015 interview, Nolan admitted that with *Interstellar* he wanted the drama of the narrative to derive from the emotional elements of the film, rather than strictly from the plot. In short, he hoped that the crux of the film's themes would rest not in the science but in familial and romantic relationships (Nolan). Indeed, like *X-M*, *Interstellar* complicates the idea of science uncorrupted by human nature. At the opening of the film, Earth, as the home of humans, is dying. Failing food supplies and massive droughts plague the planet. But the science of the film is not used to find solutions to save it, because, we are told, that time has passed. Instead, the science becomes a narrative means used to fuel the real purpose of the film: finding meaningful existence through human relationships.

Interstellar is built on the premise that in 2067, climate change, pollution, and disease are in the final stages of making the Earth uninhabitable. Former astronaut Tom Cooper (Matthew McConaughey) has devoted his post–NASA life to his daughter, Murph (Mackenzie Foy/Jessica Chastain), and to farming, a career that has become more urgent in a time of failing harvests. Through a series of seemingly miraculous events, Cooper and Murph are led to a secret base where Cooper's old NASA mentor, John Brand (Michael Caine), has hatched a plan to save humanity. In a nod to Arthur C. Clark's *2001: A Space Odyssey*, astronomers have discovered a stable wormhole near Saturn that offers access to a distant galaxy with potentially habitable planets. Twelve volunteers have been sent through the wormhole to these locations to search for an alternative human home. The explorers were sent knowing that if their assigned planet was uninhabitable, they would be marooned and forced to accept their fate alone.

Brand recruits Cooper to command a spaceship christened *Endurance* on a mission through the wormhole. They are instructed to contact each of the twelve earlier explorers and make a judgement on which planet holds the most promise. The *Endurance* can visit perhaps two of these planets before running out of fuel. Romilly (David Gyasi), Doyle (Wes Bentley), and Amelia Brand, John Brand's daughter (Anne Hathaway), form the rest of the crew of the *Endurance*.

The mission of the *Endurance* seems doomed from the start, however. Upon exiting the wormhole in the new galaxy the crew receives positive signals from three of the twelve explorers: one from Miller, whose planet is relatively close by; one from Mann (Matt Damon), a well-respected astronaut; and one from Edmunds, with whom Amelia Brand fell in love before he left Earth. Because Miller's planet is relatively close, the crew of the *Endurance* decide to visit there first. But upon arrival at this planet they discover only ship wreckage and massive tidal waves. Miller is nowhere to be seen and Cooper orders an immediate retreat, but Brand insists on checking the wreckage. A tidal wave hits the crew before they can leave in their shuttle, however, washing Doyle away, and nearly stranding Cooper and Brand. To make matters worse, the proximity of Miller's planet to a black hole causes a time dilation, and the hour that the crew spends on the surface result in 23 years alone on the *Endurance* for Romilly.

Now the crew of the *Endurance* must make a decision. They must consider their fuel consumption (In another plot similarity to *X-M*, the lack of fuel is also a problem in *Interstellar*). With only enough fuel to reach one of the two destinations, the crew must decide between Edmunds' planet and Mann's planet. Brand argues emotionally for Edmunds, believing that his planet shows the most promise. Although Cooper is more tactful with Brand than Eckstrum is with Van Horn in *X-M*, he does accuse Brand of letting her emotions cloud her judgment. Brand, though, counters that it is because of love that the crew must be being guided to Edmunds's planet rather than Mann's. Cooper overrules her, trusting more Mann's reputation than Brand's theory of love as a guiding force. Like Lisa Van Horn, however, Brand proves to be correct.

The transparently named Dr. Mann (Matt Damon) has sent a false signal. He is the revelation of humanity's selfishness, derived from the individual's compulsion for self-preservation and companionship, even at the expense of the lives of others, and in this case, even at the expense of all humanity. Upon arriving on his icy planet, Mann immediately knew he was to die alone. Unable to overcome his fear of death and solitude, Mann falsely signals to the crew of the *Endurance* that he has found a habitable planet, hoping that the crew will rescue him. By sending his false signal, Mann knows that he dooms other explorers. More importantly, his selfishness may doom the entire human race. In his analysis of *Interstellar*, Pierre-Olivier St. Arnaud writes that "without society, without authority, without rules, without codes of conduct, left to himself, Dr. Mann has only one concern: his survival" (53).[2] Indeed, St. Arnaud concludes that the film demonstrates a Hobbesian conclusion of humanity's instinct (54). While not all characters are overcome as Dr. Mann, one conclusion is that the instinct is powerful enough to manifest itself predictably in each sample of human beings. In fact, twelve explorers had been sent to various intergalactic locations, and only Mann, and possibly Miller, transmitted in desperation to save themselves. Nevertheless, such was enough to endanger the entire project.

Perhaps more importantly, the narrative juxtaposes Cooper's faith in Mann's ethically scientific character versus Brand's romantic intuition—the belief that the mysterious force of love may be guiding them to reunite. The film then posits that either choice is a matter of faith. The basis for trusting that Mann has signaled honestly rests on his reputation, but there is no way of truly knowing. The crew's disastrous experience on Miller's planet, though, foreshadows the disaster on Mann's. The crew never considers that Miller may have transmitted a signal out of desperation to be rescued. Because Cooper's crew notices the enormous tidal waves within minutes of landing, it is reasonable to consider that Miller may have noticed them as well and had sent a false signal hoping to be saved. However, none of the scientists on Earth or on the *Endurance* ever factor in an individual's fear and desire to survive as an influence on the purpose of their signals; they trust the explorers wholeheartedly, perhaps out of desperation, but the factors of human nature or human psychology are not discussed until Brand concludes that the crew should go to Edmunds's planet.

Cooper, though, rejects this as evidence. Love, for him, is evidence of uncontrolled selfishness; it corrupts scientific reasoning. But the film subtly critiques

Cooper's faith in Mann's reputation. The entire mission relies on the faith that it puts into the explorers to transmit their signal honestly. Of the three explorers, however, Edmunds is the only one who seems to have communicated honestly about the conditions of his planet. Cooper and project directors, in their desperation, have overlooked the explorers' isolation and how it might complicate their trustworthiness.

Because Brand's choice of Edmunds's planet proves to have been the correct one, the film endorses her mystical reasoning—love and faith lie beyond science and should be considered as a guiding force, or at least factored into the equation. Thus, Brand echoes *X-M*'s Eckstrum who suggests when the rocket goes off-course that scientists must recognize their limits and put faith in something mystical—which, of course, is decidedly the antithesis of science.

Cooper, *Interstellar*'s protagonist, finally learns the film's lesson, though, and in all his interstellar travel he finds his meaning, and the narrative comes full circle. As noted earlier, at the onset of the film, the Earth is suffering from an inexplicable global crop failure. What is left of society is awash in conspiracy theories and alternate histories where space traveled is denied ever to have existed. Apparently, the conspiracy theorists have won out as they control the school curriculum. The film obfuscates the origins of the crop failure and how these fact-deniers seized control, especially while scientists and NASA can still build spaceships capable of intergalactic travel. If there is an allusion to current issues such as climate change denial as a source of humanity's inability to avoid agricultural failure, which might make sense in the historical context, the film understates such, and the question about the source of the catastrophe is left vague.

Even so, the film's foreboding premise indicates that most people have turned toward ignorance and fear: the denial of history provides a basis to deny the reality of Earth's apocalyptic fate. Because only a few have persisted in the face of ignorance, *Interstellar* underscores its grim view of human nature, and only the daring scientists and explorers can save humanity from itself.

In *Rocketship X-M*, Earth's habitability is threatened by advanced civilization—the ability of advanced people to create technology, nuclear weapons, to serve primitive instincts of tribalism and combat, the drive for one group to assure its survival at the expense of another. In *Interstellar*, Earth's habitability is threatened by ignorance and fear that drive human beings to comfort themselves with false narratives. Fear later drives Dr. Mann to betray his team and his scientific ethics. Thus, Earth is not so much a home but rather a space in which either Hobbesian or evolutionary drives play out, a zone that becomes used up or consumed by intertwining, inseparable aspects of human nature: where the differences and similarities among love, selfishness, faith, reason, and morality cannot be easily discerned. While this human drama plays out, Earth as a living space diminishes; its physical decay parallels the decay of civilization. The films are interested in science only insofar as it provides humanity with an out, a way to stave off destruction. With Earth's habitability used up, the only hope is to escape. Meanwhile, the extraordinary few cultivate meaning through individualistic, existential experience. This is the lesson that Cooper learns after his failure to have faith in Brand's and Edmunds's love for one another. As his journey continues, he comes to discover his own meaning.

Despite much of the scientific accuracy of *Interstellar*, the film relies on chance escapes and other action film trappings and takes great liberties by conjecturing the nature of black holes, tesseracts, and time travel. But these liberties help the film achieve not scientific ends but circularity that reinforces the film's ultimate sentimentalism. Indeed, the success of the film's narrative course decidedly depends on unknown rather than known science.

When Cooper, for example, asks Brand how it is possible for the "they"—the semi-mystical future beings providing plans and information—to travel back in time or to provide a mechanism for backward time travel, which Brand notes is counter to relativity, she can only conjecture that "they" somehow figured it out. But her conjecture also lends credence, within the narrative, to her suggestion that love is a real force in the universe that guides events as a form of destiny.

Indeed, one of the chief goals of the film is to provide meaning in human relationships through circularity and balance. Thus, the film needs to reconnect father and daughter; Cooper is like a space-age Odysseus set out on a great adventure, yet with the ultimate hope of returning home. Once this is achieved, the film balances the losses that Cooper and Brand have suffered and brings them together to begin anew. Consequently, the "science" of the film begins to lose its credibility as it stretches, conjectures, and serves as a *deus ex machina* to heal broken and estranged human relationships.

Before accepting the mission aboard the *Endurance*, Cooper promises his tearful daughter, Murphy, that he will one day return, although he knows it is very

Figure 33. Cooper (Matthew McConaughey) comforts his daughter, Murph (Mackenzie Foy), prior to leaving on his mission in *Interstellar* (2014) (Paramount Pictures/Photofest).

unlikely this will happen. The watch that he gives her establishes a central theme of the film: that time is circular, and the plot itself becomes a web of concentric circles. For example, at the climax of the film, Cooper encounters a black hole and travels through time. Sentimentally, the film has Cooper travel back in time to communicate with his daughter, completing one circle, to send her a cryptic message that she will only understand later.

The film suggests that future humans, part of the film's *deus ex machina* plot device, have inexplicably created a time traveling complex that allows Cooper to deliver to Murphy his message. Cooper's ability to return to this exact location in time and space is left unexplained, except for the hint that he has been guided there by the unseen, semi-mystical future beings through their time complex.

Murphy (now played by Jessica Chastain) grows up to become a scientist, in part because of the message Cooper has given her. Thus she completes another circle as she solves problems to save humanity and presumably allows people to develop time travel technology that helps Cooper to communicate to her the answers to the gravity problems. After coming through a black hole, Cooper finds that humanity had been saved and relocated to one of Saturn's moons. He is then reunited with an aged Murphy, though Cooper, having experienced time dilation, has not visibly aged.

As the film concludes, Cooper's journey within the film has not just been an "interstellar" journey but a journey to complete the promise to Murphy to one day return. Indeed, Murphy, on her deathbed, gets the opportunity to see her father once more, where he learns that she has used Cooper's message to solve a propulsion problem that enabled humanity's relocation to Saturn's habitable moon. In their sentimental reunion, Murphy is surrounded by her and Cooper's descendants when Murphy encourages Cooper to find Brand, who has found Edmunds's planet and is later shown having buried him there. Following Murphy's directive, Cooper flies off to reunite with Brand, completing another circle. Neither Cooper nor Brand have aged, and their alluded-to reunification on a lonely planet hints at a romantic, sexual union for regeneration.

Such an interpretation is buttressed by Cooper's widower status and is parallel to Brand's loss of her paramour, Edmunds. Cooper and Brand are a man and woman displaced from time, having no one else from their time but each other; Murphy dies and Brand's father, Professor Brand, has been long dead. Thus, Cooper and Brand, who have lost, will find hope and meaning again through a new relationship with each other, and on their implied new home: Brand's planet. The circles completed, the film ends.

But the film's circularity underscores a central problem: notwithstanding scientific progress, incurable human ignorance, fear, and savage instinct set the circle in motion. At the beginning of the film, Cooper lives with his family in a pastoral state of innocence; despite the blight, he is a farmer, like Odysseus, who gets called into action into the larger arc of human drama. Indeed, Cooper is chosen by the "they" as Earth's hero, and these beings are the guiding gods that provide human beings with signs and messages for them to interpret. They interpret some incorrectly and others correctly and die and suffer, yet persevere and survive. From innocence to destruction to regeneration, the cycle begins again. However, in *Interstellar*, the Earth is plagued incurably from the dysfunction of humanity; therefore, space travel can only provide us with the means to relocate to begin the cycle somewhere else.

The shock of losing Earth as home can be recouped by reuniting family, friends, and the continuation of a cyclic, epic journey. *Interstellar* is an epic allegory of humanism—not an admittance of space's hostility toward life. Within the film, we are told of the enormous odds that must be overcome, but we can be reassured that our interstellar Odysseus will complete his journey, though some may be lost along the way.

Released five years later, *Ad Astra* (2019) bears a striking thematic resemblance to *Interstellar*. The film centers on astronaut Roy McBride (Brad Pitt) and his relationship with his estranged father, Clifford (Tommy Lee Jones), who disappeared while on a mission to Neptune thirty years earlier. Detecting power surges and cryptic activity from the Neptune mission, Space Command secretly recruits McBride to untangle the mystery of what happened to the Neptune crew and mission. SpaceCom interprets the power surges to mean that Earth is in danger and perhaps McBride's father may hold the clues to solve the mystery and save the planet.

But what occurs is less a narrative about space than a comment on the icy state of human relationships and Clifford's total alienation from his earthly home. The film goes to great lengths to show McBride's stoic personality, which is a benefit to SpaceCom but a hindrance to his personal life. He is estranged from his wife, Eve (Liv Tyler), who only appears in McBride's thoughts. Moreover, the film establishes an atmosphere in which people have become emotionally distant and robotic, having been engineered by the protocols and training of SpaceCom.

But boiling beneath humanity's surface stoicism are steaming emotions and primal rage. The pace of the film builds toward violent scenes in which chaos threatens order. Humanity has established bases on the moon but cannot prevent terrorists and pirates from wreaking havoc across the lunar landscape. On his way to Mars, McBride and the crew stop to investigate a loitering ship that was used to house animals for experiments. Symbolically, escaped baboons have figuratively mutinied

Figure 34. Space pirates in lunar rovers attack Roy McBride (Brad Pitt) and his military escort on the far side of the moon in *Ad Astra* (2019) (© Twentieth Century–Fox/Photofest).

and savagely killed the crew. They kill McBride's crewmember before McBride can kill them and escape. Finally confessing his own rage in a psychological evaluation, McBride begins an emotional journey in which he reevaluates his relationships with his father and his wife. McBride learns that SpaceCom intends to kill Clifford, and realizes he must try to save his father. Like *Interstellar*'s Cooper and *X-M*'s Van Horn, McBride's ultimate mission is to return "home," in his case, to reconnect with his father and mend his relationship with Eve.

After SpaceCom tries to cancel McBride's mission, McBride secretly boards a spaceship, mutinies, and fights with the crew, recalling the foreshadowing scene of the uncontrolled baboons. Thus, the crew and all involved in SpaceCom's missions become the baboons who are simply subjects in an experiment. In the ensuing melee, everyone is killed but McBride. Upon reaching Neptune, McBride learns that his father's crew had mutinied against him to return to Earth. Clifford, McBride's father, murdered the crew so he could continue to search for intelligent life. Rage abounds as Clifford refuses to reconnect with his son, claiming he never cared for his family and refusing to return to Earth with McBride. Furthermore, Clifford tells McBride that he no longer considers Earth his home.

Fury, rage, and violence are eerily woven into a film with long stretches of calm and quiet. In an interview, James Gray, the film's director and co-writer, commented on humanity's fragile psychology, stating that he believes eventually a person would "unravel" during long space travel unless they become an "automaton" (Gray). Indeed, the film posits that the loss of one's humanity, characterized by emotional and social needs, is a necessary consequence of space exploration because, like all kinds of travel, it forces people away from their home—their sense of comfort, security, and society.

Ad Astra, much like *Interstellar*, identifies McBride's voyage as an allegorical journey home. But once again, "home" is not just the planet Earth but a comforting emotional space woven together by familial and romantic love. McBride through his training has suppressed his emotions, and SpaceCom, by administering frequent psychological evaluations, tries to ensure that such emotions remain contained. Through his journey, though, McBride learns to become human again. Just as *Interstellar* is about establishing loving relationships and reconnecting father and daughter, *Ad Astra* is about reestablishing loving relationships and reconnecting father and son. Although this reunion fails, it causes McBride to contemplate his emotional distance from Eve, and he longs to return to Earth, to his home, and to her. Despite the film's focus on coldness and isolation, it ends, like *Interstellar* and *Rocketship X-M*, on the sentimental chord of romantic love. Like Cooper's journey in *Interstellar*, McBride's quest is not about science, but it is a quest to get "home." As in the two earlier films, science fails McBride.

Like *X-M* and *Interstellar*, *Ad Astra* presents us with a fragile Earth, but, as Sontag predicted, it fails to imagine solutions to the problems that it raises. Instead it relies on sentimentality to provide an escape for the narrative. At the same time, the problems that these films confront are not limited to the physical threats facing Earth. They all posit threats to our concept of Earth as a permanent home. In *Ad Astra*, life on Earth is never depicted outside the confines of SpaceCom, which is like the limited Earth settings in *X-M* and *Interstellar*, and, therefore, like these films, the social and political problems on Earth are only alluded to rather than realized.

In *Rocketship X-M*, Earth's inhabitability stems from the threat of nuclear war; in *Interstellar*, environmental blight threatens the planet as people retreat into ignorance; in *Ad Astra*, Earth's plight is represented by the violence and mutiny aboard the Neptune mission. Even from more than two billion miles away, humanity's savage nature threatens the planet's existence. These three films also provide a frightening glimpse of the vast emptiness of the universe, its hostility to life, and the possibility of losing Earth as a signifier of home. Caught between our own destructiveness on our home planet and the perils of space, we are destined, the narratives reassure, to carry out our meaning familiar to us by some familiar means: romantic love, family, and hope in a mystical force that guides our destiny. This, though, is not science; instead, it is sci-fi's way of destabilizing Earth's fixed position as "home" in the human mind while simultaneously attempting to help us to recover or to create meaning when such is lost.

NOTES

1. The simultaneously celebrated and persecuted novelist and screenwriter Dalton Trumbo may have been brought on board to help revise the script, although he was not credited for any alleged contributions (asserted by J. Hoberman in *Army of Phantoms* [see works cited]).

2. Translated from French by the author of this essay.

WORKS CITED

Arendt, Hannah. "Man's Conquest of Space." *The American Scholar*, vol. 32, no. 4, 1963, pp. 527–40.
Gray, James. Interview by Joe Utichi. *Deadline*, 28 Aug. 2019, https://deadline.com/2019/08/ad-astra-james-gray-interview-sci-fi-future-fox-venice-1202705879/. Accessed 28 Dec. 2021.
Hoberman, J. *An Army of Phantoms: American Movies and the Making of the Cold War.* The New Press, 2011.
Hodgens, Richard. "A Brief, Tragical History of the Science Fiction Film." *Film Quarterly*, vol. 13, no. 2, 1959, pp. 30–39.
Nolan, Christopher. Interview by James Kleinmann. *Hey U Guys*, 5 Nov. 2014, https://www.youtube.com/watch?v=IlTfLREt9ko. Accessed 28 Dec. 2021.
St. Arnaud, Pierre-Olivier. "Un retour à l'état de nature pour l'être humain future? Analyse compare de *Les derniers rayons du soleil*, Pandorum et Interstellaire." *D'Asimov à Star Wars*, edited by Isabelle Lacroix and Karine Prémont. Presses de l'Université du Québec, 2016, pp. 37–56.
Sontag, Susan. "The Imagination of Disaster." *Commentary*, vol. 40, no. 4, 1965, pp. 42–48.
Warren, Bill. *Keep Watching the Skies: American Science Fiction Movies of the Fifties*. McFarland, 1997.

FILMOGRAPHY

Ad Astra. Dir. James Gray. 20th Century Fox, 2019. Film.
Destination Moon. Dir. Irving Pichel. Eagle Lion Classics, 1950. Film.
Interstellar. Dir. Christopher Nolan. Paramount Pictures, 2014. Film.
Rocketship X-M. Dir. Kurt Neumann. Lippert Pictures, 1950. Film.

From the Promise of the 1950s to the Uncertainty of the 1960s

The Surety of Forbidden Planet *Against the Empty Center of* Solaris

Robert Mayer

America's victory in World War II catapulted it into a role of world leadership as well as a period of economic growth that fuels political conversation even today. This boom was also fueled by technological advances, driven particularly through the advancement of the atomic age, and the potential of that position can be seen in its sci-fi films of the 1950s. Pictures such as *The Thing from Another World* (1951), *It Came from Outer Space* (1951), and *Them!* (1954) offered the theme of being ever vigilant against incursions from aliens as well as against our own hubris as a society. Those themes are usually countered by the idea that despite these fears, we can persist and thrive. As Andrew Huebner writes, "In both everyday and cinematic worlds, the message was clear: Science and technology held the potential to scare the planet and destroy its population, but they also offered the best hope for saving both" (17).

The years 1950 to 1954 feature many noteworthy sci-fi films that reflect this cautious yet optimistic side, but that theme begins to fade in 1956, with one notable exception. In *Forbidden Planet,* Captain Adams (Leslie Nielsen) lands on the planet Altair IV with his crew in an effort to find out what happened to a 20-year-old scientific expedition. There he meets the only survivors: Morbius—the representation of the pompous, hyperfocused scientist, played by Walter Pidgeon—and his daughter, Altaira, played by petite, blonde and blue-eyed, 26-year-old Anne Francis. The crew is both captivated by Altaira's beauty and fascinated with what Morbius has done with the technology of the extinct inhabitants of the planet, the Krell, including Morbius' use of Robby the Robot. Morbius issues warnings to the ship before it lands, and an invisible force later kills one officer while leaving tracks of a giant unseen creature. In the end, Adams convinces Morbius that use of Krell technology has also led to the embodiment of the professor's Id into a malevolent force. Morbius then convinces Adams to set the planet's power plants into overload and flee the planet with Altaira and his crew, leaving Morbius behind to die. The film ends with Adams, Altaira, and the crew watching the power plant overload and destroy the planet.

One could argue that the ending could be seen as an attempt to provoke questions about the dangers of unchecked science. However, the public and critical response suggests otherwise. Seth Lerer's description of the film years later summarizes the critics' reaction: "Few films have seemed as funny and as dark, as forward-looking and as retrograde, as richly textured and as hokey" (73). The movie did receive one Oscar nomination, for special effects, and its main achievement in the film world was that it was the first motion picture to feature a purely electronic soundtrack. The movie's most iconic character, Robby the Robot, epitomizes the movie's impact on culture. The robot would not only be featured as a prominent character in this film but in *The Invisible Boy* (1957), and its design appears in dozens of movies and television shows ranging from *Lost in Space* to four episodes of *Twilight Zone*. The robot appears in the cult 1980s animated film *Heavy Metal* and in the recent long-running television comedy *The Big Bang Theory*. Even one of the most famous film directors of our time, Steven Spielberg, puts both a poster and a toy of Robby in his 2018 film version of *Ready Player One*, a work itself considered by some critics to be a cultural homage to the 1980s.

Beyond the special effects, one factor in the positive response to *Forbidden Planet* are the stock characters. The film has the beauty in distress, the egocentric scientist, and the handsome hero. If one treats Morbius as a representation of Germanic/European intelligentsia, not just science generally, then the ending becomes far more pro–American. The darkness of Morbius' ideas and technologies represent a culture of skeptics who will get in the way of families, peace, and the American way of life. Thus *Forbidden Planet* fits the description Huebner gives of *The Thing from Another World*: "Technology is only good when married to level-headed, even militaristic realism" (14). Scholar Kevin Fisher sees Robby as "the domestication of the military industrial complex" and describes Morbius's "home as a microcosm of the state" (25). While Morbius "presents a cautionary figure for the rise of the technocratic elite in 1950s America" (Fisher 31), Nielsen's demeanor in this, one of his early films, is in strong contrast to his career reinvention into a comic actor starting in the late 1970s. Nielsen's Adams is stern but fair. He is respected by his crew, is willing to listen to his right-hand man, and gets the girl. Adams is the embodiment of the American coming to save the world from its overreliance on science, rescuing his crew and Altaira—both of whom symbolize the western world.

After *Forbidden Planet*, a darker, more fearful, and less optimistic view began to emerge in the sci-fi of the remainder of the decade as well as the start of the 1960s. Perhaps in tune with the arrival of Sputnik in space and the accompanying public reaction, the sci-fi films of the second half of the 1950s balance both a sweeping look at society and the in-depth examination of personal relationships. "Sci-fi films exhibited a new social consciousness," Lori Maguire notes. "Present day fears were still projected into the future with often devastating effects but the nature of these anxieties was more varied" (518). Two of the seminal films of the late 1950s, *The Incredible Shrinking Man* (1957) and *The Fly* (1958) focus on the dilemma of an

Opposite: **Figure 35. Robby the Robot (played by Frankie Darro and Frankie Carpenter) carries a scantily clad Altaira (Anne Francis) in one of the posters for *Forbidden Planet* (1956). The innovative design for Robby made him the face of the film (MGM/Photofest).**

individual and in the end offer very little hope of humanity saving itself from its foibles through science and technology. Perhaps the culminating sci-fi film of the decade, *On the Beach* (1959), is clearly the bleakest of these films, described by Mick Broderick as "the first truly pessimistic depiction of the short-term effects of nuclear war" (370). It is perhaps a perfect harbinger of the tone to come in the 1960s, as sci-fi films began to undergo a decline in popularity, for, as Maguire puts it, America "experienced a new vulnerability" (517).

This trend in film can be seen also in the printed word, in particular the works of Polish author Stanisław Lem (1921–2006). Lem holds a unique place in the field of sci-fi. Theodore Sturgeon has argued that Lem was likely the most-read sci-fi author in the world (Introduction, vii). Sturgeon's comments are curious and interesting in light of several facts. Just being a writer from behind the Iron Curtain, with limited access to the West, would be a good starting point, but one need only consider Lem's dissatisfaction with the translation of his foremost work, *Solaris*. The first English translation did not come to be until 1970, and that was based on a French translation of 1964, not a direct Polish-to-English translation. Lem, who also spoke English, expressed disappointment with that translation, and it would take more than 40 years after the first edition of the Polish original for a direct Polish-to-English translation to be completed. As of the date of this writing, the work is only available in Amazon Kindle format due to legal issues, although Lem's estate is on record regarding its satisfaction with the translation ("A New Translation").

Not only did the novel overcome translation issues, Lem's attitudes toward American sci-fi very well could have been an impediment to the public's reception to him. For example, in his positive 1975 review of Philip K. Dick, Lem said of American sci-fi, "One is annoyed by the pretentiousness of a genre which fends off accusation of primitivism by pleading its entertainment character and then, once such accusations have silenced, renews its overweening claims" ("Philip K. Dick" 54). Later that year, after comments in a Frankfurt journal again criticizing western sci-fi, Lem's status as an honorary member of the Science Fiction Writers of America was revoked (Tighe 761). In 1983, Lem offered a more direct assessment of sci-fi in film to an interviewer:

> Oh, it's so bad ... horrible. I used to be interested in such films, but then I stopped watching them. I am, of course, always ready to change my opinion if something good comes along. But so far, nothing like that has happened, and I do not see any signs that is going to change. The general rule seems to be that things that are of the least intellectual and artistic value are the most likely going to be made into a movie. The situation in Western cinema is that the film industry, the film producers, regard the public as a mass of fools who should not be disturbed, discouraged, surprised, frightened by anything new, original unconventional depiction of the future, or of anything. This is not only true of cinema, but of most SF [qtd. in Federman 9–10].

Lem also wasn't happy with how *Solaris* was treated on film. The 1972 adaptation by noted Russian director Andrei Tarkovsky drew critical acclaim and even won the Grand Prix Spécial du Jury prize at the Cannes Film Festival, while an adaptation by director Steven Soderbergh in 2002 received less favorable reviews. Because of the critical response to Tarkovsky's version, as well as Tarkovsky's status as an iconic director, it may be tempting to use it as the comparison piece to *Forbidden Planet*. However, Lem described Tarkovsky's version as "Crime in Punishment in Space," and was equally unkind in his assessment of Soderbergh's work: "to my best knowledge, the book was not dedicated to erotic problems of people in outer space.... As *Solaris'* author I shall allow myself to repeat that I only wanted to create a vision of a human encounter with something that certainly exists, in a mighty manner perhaps, but cannot be reduced to human concepts, ideas or images. This is why the book was entitled *Solaris* and not *Love in Outer Space*" (qtd. in Sfetcu 4). Lem argued that both films missed the point by using the setting as an opportunity to explore human relationships and human nature, eliminating a core Lem theme, that science and technology cannot solve everything, even with a warning.[1]

Lem's works suggest he saw what Wiesenfeldt observes, that scientists of the 1950s claimed to be stepping back out of the political and cultural spheres, with science to be "regarded as striving to transcend all worldly matters in search of objective truth," but in reality they "were becoming more and more involved in the military-industrial complex" (58–59). Lem himself has said he doubted science would provide the answers to the most important questions of life. For example, in a 1985 interview, he said, "the time of crafting seamless, unified philosophical systems is long past" (qtd. in Lem and Csiscery-Ronay Jr., 243). That attitude is seen in Rose's assessment of *Solaris* as a "highly self-conscious fiction that is as much a work of generic criticism as it is a new text in the genre" (qtd. in Klapcsik 143). By examining Lem's use of *Solaris* as the form of criticism Rose describes here, we can learn exactly why he felt that the cautiously triumphant hope present in sci-fi films of the first half of the 1950s, as represented by *Forbidden Planet*, is in reality a dangerous, empty path.

In both *Forbidden Planet* and *Solaris*, the impetus for action centers around human thoughts becoming a separate, animate force. In *Forbidden Planet*, it is Morbius' Id becoming an invisible monster; in *Solaris*, it is a planet whose ocean seems to be alive, generating both inanimate and animate creations to the point that some scientists in the book believe that there were "similarities between images of the electrical functioning of the [human] brain and certain discharges that occurred within the [planet's] plasma preceding the appearance of some of its formations" (loc. 2890).[2] Lem's story is set at the end of the research program focused on the planet. What was a large research contingent is now down to three, and their behavior is enough for the summons of a psychologist, Kris Kelvin. When Kelvin arrives at the orbiting Solaris Station, he learns that the only one of the three he knows, Gibarian, committed suicide at dawn just before Kelvin arrived. Of the other two, Sartorius stays hidden in his lab, leaving only Snaut[3] to greet Kelvin. Snaut is evasive but gives Kelvin a hint of the future trouble when he tries to justify what Kelvin is encountering: "If you should see anyone else, you understand, not me or Sartorius, you understand, then..." (loc. 162). Kelvin will soon learn that Snaut is referring to the way the planet appears to be connecting with its human visitors: lifelike recreations of people important to these researchers. For Snaut and Sartorius, these appear to be small children. For Gibarian, it is a mysterious tall, dark-skinned woman Kelvin encounters at the start of the novel but who is rarely mentioned again. For Kelvin, it is his late wife, Harey.[4] She appears after Kelvin's first night of sleep on the space station, and Kelvin, in a state of panic, tricks Harey into getting onto a small rocket and ships her to presumed destruction toward the planet's surface. When Kelvin and Snaut next meet, Snaut minimizes Kelvin's attempt to process what he had done, for Snaut and the other two had also attempted to eliminate their Solaris-produced "guests," as Snaut calls them, or "G-formations" (loc. 1628). As Kelvin learns the next day, the planet merely recreates the same "G-formation" after another night's sleep. Once Kelvin gives in to the idea that he cannot destroy his guest, he learns the guests are driven to be by their hosts' sides.

If we are to look at how Lem critiques science through *Solaris*, a good start would be to see how the fundamental piece of science, the hypothesis, is treated. *Forbidden Planet* follows a common theme in popular sci-fi film of the first half of the decade, in that its ending revolves around the development of the hypothesis to lead to a final solution. In *Solaris,* on the other hand, hypothesis after hypothesis crashes. In fact, science only begins to focus on the planet because one such hypothesis failed. The planet itself orbits around a double star, and "for over forty years no spaceship came near to it. In those days the Gamov-Shapley hypothesis, concerning the impossibility of life arising on planets around double stars, went unquestioned" (loc. 238). That is not the only theoretical supposition that is proven false: Original estimates suggested the planet's orbit would cause it to fall into one of those suns, but within 20 years of its discovery, that conclusion would be proven false as the orbit was unstable—something science could not solve or predict. In this case, hypotheses, assisted by a shortage of funding, actually get in the way of the one of the greatest goals of science, to find life: It would take almost 40 years after the initial prediction of the planet's doom before a full-blown, manned expedition would get to the planet (loc. 262).

While a single scientist, Morbius, causes the problems in *Forbidden Planet*, a forced unity between Adams and Morbius leads to the solution of those problems. In *Solaris*, the main obstacle could be seen as the scientists themselves and their discord, not the planet: Lem presents a multiplicity of angles, theories, and schisms that suggests the novel is more about humanity and its muddled interpretation of natural phenomena than it is about the nature of the planet. This quest is carried out by the scientists of Earth over years and is even the subject of a scholarly journal, *The Journal of Solaristics*. Early on in the novel, we learn there is also a *Yearbook of Solaristics* and a multi-volume academic *History of Solaris*. Those who have explored "the planet are known to every child on Earth" (loc. 1896), yet in the end, interest in the planet feels like a fad, as matters devolve into "an ever more entangled labyrinth full of blind alleys," also described as an "atmosphere of general indifference, stagnation, and discouragement" (loc. 2798). While a single scientist, a philologist, is able to open the immense world of the Krell in *Forbidden Planet,* research into Solaris results in ever more complex camps as the study of the planet developed into fields found only in the studies of *Solaris*. At one point, it is noted, "more than a thousand people took part in the research at the same time" (loc. 2758). As that research progressed, scientists in those new fields remained at odds with each other, and even had a difficult time communicating, leading the director of the Earth-based *Solaris* institute during Kelvin's time of Earthbound studies to say, "How can you communicate with the ocean if you can't communicate with each other?" (loc. 339).

In Lem's *Solaris*, the half-century-long scientific stalemate over the "main character" of the story, the planet's ocean, is one of the two key threads of the novel. The biologists in the expedition argue its intelligence is primitive, comparing it to a jellyfish, while astronomers and physicists argue that because the orbit of the planet is clearly irregular—because it does not move toward its suns as predicted—that its movement is influenced by the intelligence of the ocean (loc. 275). From here, "libraries filled, archives grew" (loc. 2013), but none of this research leads to unity of solution. Instead, there is a decided lack of unity, as Kelvin notes: "Some of the most venerable theories, universally regarded as correct, collapsed in ruins, the most heretical articles began to appear in the scientific literature, and the 'brilliant ocean' versus 'gravitational jelly' debate set every mind on fire" (loc. 301). While *Forbidden Planet* turns on one theory, Freud's notion of the Id, there is no such hope in *Solaris*. As researchers tried to figure out how the planet's surface and creations worked, "Too many phenomena were to be found in the giant's innards that could not be reconciled with such a simple (some said childishly naive) depiction" (loc. 1941).

Such growth leads to a trend that Lem describes in terms that seem applicable even today. Kelvin says, "Every science comes with its own pseudo-science, a bizarre distortion that comes from a certain kind of mind: astronomy has its caricaturist in astrology, chemistry used to have alchemy. So little wonder that the emergence of Solaristics was accompanied by a veritable explosion of the oddest notions" (loc. 1259). Pseudo-science, as Lem confirms, will go beyond these "oddest notions": The people involved in Solaristics, noted Kelvin, "often had nothing to do with science" and included "numbers of maniacal impostors from outside the scientific community, zealots whose fanaticism exceeded that of their distant predecessors," a situation "actually alarming many psychologists" (loc. 2810–14). From this we see that the line mainstream culture has established to separate the realm of myth, superstition, and even religion from that of science is not a solid one but is rather a fuzzy, perhaps even non-existent one, and that the culture surrounding science takes on the some of the traits of the former realm. The name of a work Kelvin regularly consults, *Minor Apocrypha* (loc. 589), evokes this idea, and Lem is even more explicit through his creation of a critique by one Muntius: "Solaristics […] is a substitute for religion in the space age. It is faith wrapped in the cloak of science; contact, the goal for which we are striving, is as vague and obscure as communion with the saints or the coming of the Messiah" (loc. 2854). Kelvin himself adds: "Solaristics, then, is the posthumous child of long-dead myths, the final flower of mystical yearnings that people no longer have the courage to utter aloud; while the cornerstone hidden deep in the foundations of this edifice is the hope of Redemption…" (loc. 2865). One need only note that the science of Solaristics is described more as a religion, as seen here as Muntius describes a phase of the science as "the splitting of the one solarian Church into a clutch of warring denominations" (loc. 2882). It is clear that Lem, in the guise of Kelvin, does not believe in the "can-do" science of *Forbidden Planet*.

What is left out or minimized in both film adaptations is actually a key tool in Lem's goal of portraying science as dysfunctional. Gone or reduced are the lengthy discussions among Kelvin, Snaut, and Sartorius about the planet, as well as Kelvin relaying the long history of research into the planet. While *Forbidden Planet* is a straight-forward linear account without any flashbacks, *Solaris* features lengthy interruptions by the narrator Kelvin as he recounts the history of Solaristics. These interruptions reflect our inability to access truth through science and resolve mysteries of life. For example, just as Sartorius begins to confirm one of Kelvin's theories, that the G-formations are made at the neutrino level, the videoconference is broken up and interrupted by Sartorius' guest. As Kelvin notes, "And so ended the discussion of the problem" (loc. 1710). Later in the text, after a seminal moment of action, instead of going right to dwelling on the potential impact, Lem interrupts the action by having Kelvin go to the station's library where he recounts additional theories of the planet's nature (loc. 2766).

The value of and the ability to reduce data and experience down into something coherent shows a remarkable difference as well. In *Forbidden Planet*, success occurs repeatedly, as Fisher points out when he refers to "Robby's ability to 'sample' any material object, reduce it to its essential molecular code, and reproduce it in any quantity" or how the Krell technology "extracts information from the brain and reproduces it in a technological medium" (22). Robby here is able to see something, objectively analyze it, and present an accurate duplicate, which fits the ideal for which science strives. The opposite is seen in *Solaris*, where Lem raises the specter of subjectivity by asking if the objectivity necessary for good science is even possible; seemingly legitimate eye-witness accounts and observations only deepen the mystery and fail to resolve the questions about the planet as well. Three weeks into the first manned expedition, two men get lost—Fechner, a physicist, and Carucci, a radiologist. A search party is sent out to find them, and in a moment befitting Lem's theme, radio contact is lost due to a sunspot. When their craft is finally found, only Carucci is left, and he reports passing out from a gas leak before Fechner disappears (loc. 622). The only clue to what happened to Fechner comes from Berton, the last member of the search party to return to base, and in this case, far overdue. Berton, a veteran of 17 years of flight experience, needs two days to recover, and his statement is deemed a product of "a mind poisoned by toxic gases of the atmosphere" (loc. 635). His account is not included in the rescuers' log but only in his medical report.

The fragmented structural approach is applied in the presentation and discussion of Berton's experience. While mention of Fechner's disappearance and Berton's meltdown occur within the first fifth of the book, the actual account is detailed when Kelvin reads Otto Ravinzter's work on Solaris, a work made suspect "by an introduction in which the editor distanced himself from this house of wonders" (loc. 1259). This is now more than a third of the way through the book, part of Lem's pattern of interspersing live scenes with lengthy summary. Berton's narrative starts with a scientific detachment—including a data log such as time, visibility, and altitude—and then he begins to describe a portion of the planet converting its ocean into a plastic replica of a garden of dwarf trees. There is no sense of panic, no emotion to his description, until the emergence of a facsimile of a 13-foot-tall naked newborn human. Even then Berton recovers to offer a description to suggest the planet is creating this simulation to communicate with or understand its visitors, saying the "baby" acted "as if someone were trying to find out what the child was capable of doing with its arms, what it could do with its torso and its mouth" (loc. 1350).

Lem, however, instead of giving us clarity, simply offers more of the report that rejects Berton, saying he suffered from "a hallucinatory syndrome resulting from poisoning by the atmosphere of the planet, a condition in which symptoms of confusion were accompanied by a stimulation of the associative regions of the cerebral cortex" (loc. 1387), and finishing with the damning statement "that these incidents had little or no correspondence in reality" (loc. 1387). A minority opinion offered by a physicist shows a hint of favor toward Berton, but the committee makes it clear that this opinion will have no influence. This physicist, named of all things, Messenger, attempts to get the board to reconsider. A rough draft of a letter by Messenger describes the committee's actions as "colossal obtuseness" (loc. 1409), but there is no indication that the letter had ever been sent, another example of both sides of a scientific argument being unsettled, disorganized, and incompetent.

The idea of competence goes to even below the microscopic level. In *Forbidden Planet* Fisher describes Robby the Robot's processes as "operating in a realm beyond and beneath the smallest known particles of matter" (23). However, while the robot of *Forbidden Planet* is successful in working at that level, Kelvin has just the opposite result in *Solaris* when he first runs into the idea of neutrino-level construction. When Kelvin tries to get some time away to study, Harey, who has been with him constantly, tears apart the stateroom door, leading to significant cuts to her hands and arms. Kelvin takes advantage of the wounds to analyze her blood. While his view in the neutrino microscope allows him to see that "the flattened shadow of a single molecule was filling the picture" and leads him to exclaim, "the mist was clearing now!" (loc. 1601), the mystery actually deepens. "But nothing happened," he continued, "I ought to have seen a trembling haze of atoms, like a quaking jelly, but it wasn't there. The screen glowed pure silver" (loc. 1605). Kelvin does try another angle, putting acid on the blood sample to confirm that decomposition can happen, but just as he is shocked to learn that the blood regenerates, he is interrupted with a conference call from Snaut and Satorius, the first lengthy conversation Kelvin will have with the latter. During the conversation, Kelvin speculates that the G-formations are built at the neutrino level, making the proteins, cells, cell nuclei, effectively a mask (loc. 1651). Kelvin, however, sees the pointlessness of these labors emerge again when he tells the others, "all we're doing is compiling a catalogue of behaviors of these ... these formations, nothing more. This is utterly futile" (loc. 1687).

Not only does *Solaris* counter the idea of unified competence in science such as those seen in *Forbidden Planet*, Lem also destroys the idea that science is objective, untainted by human bias and emotion. Lem uses the G-formations to reveal this, as reflected in Sartorius' description of the guests, "materialized projections of what our brain contains regarding a particular person" (loc. 1665). When discussing what to do when another version of Harey arrives Kelvin tells Snaut that he couldn't dispose of Harey a second time. Snaut defends his own heartlessness by calling Kelvin selfish: "If she vanished, you'd suffer terribly, right?" (loc. 2591). When Kelvin says he loves the replica of Harey, Snaut asks, perhaps rhetorically, "Who? Your memory" (loc. 2549). Coldly, he later adds, "she's basically a mirror reflecting part of your brain. If she's wonderful, it's because your memories are wonderful. You provided the recipe. A cyclical process" (loc. 2564).

Exploring a relationship with an alien lifeform demands scientists avoid both anthropomorphism as well as treating the alien as the Other, a task Lem is all too willing to tell us is impossible, no matter which lifeform is required to do that, for as Klapcsik concludes, "language inevitably humanizes the world with its tropes" (144). For example, as Kelvin discusses the catalog of 75 years of theories, we learn that some researchers call Solaris the "gelatinous machine" (loc. 2734) while others have been known to call it the "Rational Monster" (loc. 2742). This effort at describing the alien as the Other makes it clear that science is only an extension of the selfish nature of humanity. Just after Kelvin has sent his first Harey replicant into space, Snaut shares this thought: "We need mirrors. We don't know what to do with other worlds. One world is enough, even there we feel stifled. We desire to find our own idealized image; they're supposed to be globes, civilizations more perfect than ours; in other worlds we expect to find the image of our own primitive past" (loc. 1170). Even the experiments to get the planet to communicate reflect this selfishness. Kelvin notes "the administrative director of the Worldwide Cosmology Institute [...] stubbornly maintained that the living ocean wasn't ignoring human beings, but rather it simply didn't notice them, just as an elephant fails to see the ants crawling across its back; in order to call its attention to ourselves, then, what was needed were powerful stimuli" (loc. 2790). Instead of the reason and logic that led to escape and safety in *Forbidden Planet*, imagination and wild exaggeration tends to take place in *Solaris*, and, as Kelvin notes, "It may well be that imagination and the ability to formulate rapid hypotheses is nowhere more harmful" (loc. 1791).

All this tends to suggest immature behavior, the opposite of what science demands of its practitioners. For example, the director's analogy of an elephant is very similar to the self-centered child acting out to get the attention of the adult. A closer look at the director's term, "powerful stimuli," actually suggests a euphemism that could be used to describe an infant or young child throwing a tantrum to communicate, whether it be for hunger, sleep, or attention. Here, humans, unable to communicate with the larger lifeform, will use "powerful stimuli" such as X-rays to provoke the planet. If the analysis is expanded to not only include the idea of communication between the immature and the advanced being but to also take in the bickering and interplay among scientists in the field, then the immaturity could be seen as a juvenile acting out not only to get attention of adults but to also gain acceptance or status among peers.[5] Lem's description of the progress of research at one point suggests the melodrama we often see present in juvenile behavior: "impulsively optimistic romanticism" (loc. 2750). Such rash impulses lead to tragedy when one prominent researcher even commits suicide by flying into the ocean near the south pole, and for brief period, a handful of others follow suit (loc. 2762). In one of the greatest acts of immature impetuosity, after a particularly deadly crash that results in the deaths of 78, some think the accident was no accident, and push for a thermonuclear strike as retaliation. Fortunately, that vote failed (loc. 2028). Later research discards the subterfuge of altruism for something less mature. Instead, prizes are offered to find a way to use the planet for "the benefit of human beings" (loc. 2802), only to lead to discovering that the material of the ocean no longer lives or functions when it is delivered to Earth (loc. 2810).

Of the points Lem makes regarding science, the one that needs the closest inspection for its surface similarities to *Forbidden Planet* is how problems are started and resolved. Both the Krell and Morbius are destroyed because they attempted to use technology to turn thought into physical form. The Krell's advancements into telepathy lead to the violent collapse of its civilization, and Morbius' efforts to resume use of that technology leads to the magnification of his Id into a deadly presence. It is not until Adams hears the deathbed theory of his second-in-command, mortally exhausted in his own attempt to use Krell technology, that the captain realizes Morbius' Id is to blame.

The guests' arrival in *Solaris* also comes through overreach. Gibarian changes the nature of experiments conducted by his predecessors regarding the bombardment of the planet with X-Rays in an attempt to provoke a reaction. Snaut describes Gibarian's change as "the hard stuff; they packed everything they had into the ocean, the whole nine yards" (loc. 2077), which Kelvin notes is a violation of restrictions set by the United Nations. Soon after this type of bombardment, the guests begin appearing on mornings after—apparently, the planet is now able to probe the memories of researchers while they sleep. In a recording uncovered after his death, Gibarian describes the experiment, called Polytheria, and that description is telling: "All Polytheria did was apply a kind of selective amplifier to our thoughts. Seeking a motivation for this is anthropomorphism. Where there are no humans, there are none of the motives available to humans" (loc. 2195). In other words, the experiment wasn't intended to connect or bridge two intelligences but is merely a selfish act. Gibarian suggests he killed himself because he realized, "To continue the projected research we'd have had to destroy either our own thoughts or their material realization. The former is beyond our powers. The latter looks too much like murder" (loc. 2199).

Just as in *Forbidden Planet*, the problem caused by invocation of science will be solved by destruction. However, there is a significant difference in the two situations. While Morbius' Id is clearly violent and destructive, the guests in *Solaris* are merely clingy. In fact, one of the concerns that arise with the guests is not the damage they do but how to keep them from bothering their hosts. In this case, preserving life is not priority: eliminating inconvenience is. It is possible that Sartorius and Snaut see this as euthanasia, but Kelvin sees it as violence on a whim. This is evident in the names for the activity: Sartorius calls it "Project Freedom," while Kelvin retorts mockingly with "Project Butchery" (loc. 2109). There is even a difference in the execution of the plan. While Morbius and Adams are decisive about the final solution in *Forbidden Planet*, Kelvin provides Snaut with a variety of contradicting theories that muddy the water. Sartorius, it should be noted, is not present at the conversation.

The true ending for *Solaris* is in stark contrast to that of *Forbidden Planet*. In the earlier film one massive burst in a matter of hours destroyed the old world of the long gone Krell; in *Solaris*, changes on the planet's surface take about a month for the planet to die down, and yet the guests still remain. Harey then approaches Sartorius and Snaut and the three come up with a solution: Sartorius creates a hand-held anni-hilator that works on individual cases. While Harey, like Morbius, sees her destruc-tion as the only way out, her death is not seen as a noble sacrifice: Kelvin becomes irrational, calling for the destruction of the ocean of *Solaris*. When Snaut asks Kel-vin to help him prepare a report against Sartorius for the X-rays that started the affair, the psychologist starts into a rant of refusal, then digresses to philosophical musing: "Can a person be responsible for his own subconscious? If I'm not responsi-ble for it, then who could be…?" (loc. 2591).

And while Adams and his crew takes Altaira back to Earth after the evil is conquered and the matter resolved, the questions that drove the conflict of *Solaris* continue. In fact, the ending of the book features waffling and changing of minds frequently as Kelvin and Snaut continue the argument over whether the final act of the planet and of Harey demonstrate a highly evolved intelligence that sees humans as evil, or something far more primitive. Kelvin initially refuses to help Snaut write the final report, but when the narrative resumes five days later, we learn that Kelvin and Snaut have finished the report. Kelvin will also state that he planned on stay-ing at the station but changes his mind "several months later" (loc. 3231). Kelvin's thoughts are clearly unscientific as he engages in an unexpected philosophical dis-cussion with Snaut, taking on the idea of a "deficient god," "a God whose deficien-cies don't arise from the simplemindedness of his human creators, but constitute his most essential, immanent character." This, Kelvin continues, "would be a God lim-ited in his omniscience and omnipotence, one who can make mistakes in foreseeing the future of his works, who can find himself horrified by the course of events he has set in motion" (loc. 3265). Even then, it's a conversation that goes nowhere, ending with Kelvin saying, "I don't know. It seemed to me very, very authentic, you know? It would be the only God I'd be inclined to believe in, one whose suffering wasn't redemption, didn't save anyone, didn't serve any purpose, it just was" (loc. 3286).

Kelvin's last act is to fly down to the planet's surface, where he has discovered an island has arisen, and there he finds a scene similar to "an ancient city half in ruins, to an exotic Moroccan settlement from centuries ago that had been brought down by earthquake or other natural disaster," where one could see "the still intact battlements and bastions, their rounded foundations; and, in the bulging or con-cave walls, the dark openings like broken windows or defensive slits" (loc. 3341). After taking a look around, he goes back to the island's shore, and attempts to pro-voke a response from the ocean. A black wave approaches him and transforms into a plant-like structure, then fades away. This process of provocation and dismissal is carried out a few times, but Kelvin admits he doesn't have the patience or the interest to apply a more rigorous scientific experiment to what he was seeing.

Unlike *Forbidden Planet* and other sci-fi films of the 1950s that offer a wrapped-up cautionary tale that encourages progress, this 1960s novel ends on a hollow note. Kelvin takes down foundational principles such as love and time, and offers no comforting, cautionary ending. While Adams and Altaira hold each other close as the final spark of the destruction of Altair IV fades, there is no such com-forting reunion in *Solaris*. In Kelvin's words: "I didn't believe for a minute that this liquid colossus, which had brought about the death of hundreds of humans within itself, with which my entire race had for decades been trying in vain to establish at least a thread of communication—that this ocean, lifting me up unwittingly like a speck of dust, could be moved by the tragedy of two human beings" (loc. 3385). In fact, there is no closure in the final words of the novel as Kelvin waits for a ship to arrive to take him back to Earth: "What further consummations, mockeries, torments did I still anticipate? I had no idea, as I abided in the unshaken belief that the time of cruel wonders was not yet over" (loc. 3391).

Perhaps the best way to sum up Lem's critique of science—and, implicitly, the world of *Forbidden Planet*—is to look at Lem's creation of the writer Grattenstrom a few pages earlier, "a self-taught scholar," whose critique is described as "a kind of lampoon of our species, furious in its mathematical coldness," a "satire against the entire species." Kelvin tells us Grattenstrom "reached the conclusion that there cannot now, nor in the future could there ever be, talk of 'contact' between human beings and any non-humanoid civilization" (loc. 2818). Even then, Grattenstrom commits the error he rails against, as Kelvin points out that the ocean is never specifically mentioned in the seminal work. The question, he continues, was whether humanity had the courage to continue, and Kelvin has his doubts. He will offer similar comments to Harey: "It's about contact. [...] Contact means an exchange of experiences, concepts, or at least results, conditions. But what if there's nothing to exchange?" (loc. 2407–12).

Notes

1. For more on this tendency to explore human relationships in science fiction, see Christopher Love's essay in this collection.

2. All references here are to the Kindle version of the novel. Due to the nature of the Amazon Kindle format, some readers may find location markers in their versions of the text slightly different.

3. In the 1970 English translation from the French, Kilmartin and Cox used "Snow," as did Soderbergh in his 2002 film. Both Johnson's 2017 translation and Tarkovsky's film version used "Snaut."

4. Again, the Kilmartin-Cox translation as well as Soderbergh's film adaptation have a different name for Kelvin's late wife, that of "Rheya," an anagram of "Harey," the name Tarkovsky went with.

5. Thank you to Shannan Mayer for pointing out the distinction between childish and juvenile motives for such behaviors.

Works Cited

Broderick, Mick. "Surviving Armageddon: Beyond the Imagination of Disaster." *Science Fiction Studies*, vol. 20, no. 3, Nov. 1993, p. 362. MasterFILE Premier, search.ebscohost.com/login.aspx?direct=true&db=f5h&AN=9402234710&site=ehost-live. Accessed 28 Dec. 2021.

Csicsery-Ronay, Istvan, Jr. "Twenty-Two Answers and Two Postscript: An Interview with Stanislaw Lem." *Science Fiction Studies*, vol. 13, no. 3, Nov. 1986, pp. 242–60. Literary Reference Center, search.ebscohost.com/login.aspx?direct=true&db=lfh&AN=23547989&site=eds-live. Accessed 28 Dec. 2021.

Federman, Raymond. "An Interview with Stanislaw Lem." *Science Fiction Studies*, vol. 10, no. 1, March 1983, pp. 2–14. Literary Reference Center, search.ebscohost.com/login.aspx?direct=true&db=lfh&AN=23538585&site=ehost-live. Accessed 28 Dec. 2021.

Fisher, Kevin. "Information Feedback Loops and Two Tales of the Posthuman in Forbidden Planet." *Science Fiction Film and Television*, vol. 3, no. 1, 2010, p. 19+. Gale Academic OneFile, https://link.gale.com/apps/doc/A243358110/AONE?u=idaho_a_colsil&sid=AONE&xid=52f97dcb.

Huebner, Andrew J. "Lost in Space: Technology and Turbulence in Futuristic Cinema of the 1950s." *Film & History*, vol. 40, no. 2, Fall 2010, pp. 6–26. Communication & Mass Media Complete, doi:10.1353/flm.2010.0013. Accessed 28 Dec. 2021.

Klapcsik, Sandor. "*Solaris* as Metacommentary: Meta-Science Fiction and Meta-Science-Fiction." *Extrapolation*, vol. 49, no. 1, 2008, pp. 142–58. Gale Literature Resource Center, https://link.gale.com/apps/doc/A179987883/LitRC?u=idaho_a_colsil&sid=LitRC&xid=ed3a215b. Accessed 28 Dec. 2021.

Lem, Stanisław. "Philip K. Dick: A Visionary Among the Charlatans." Translated by Robert Abernathy. *Science Fiction Studies*, vol. 2, no. 1, March 1975, pp. 54–67. Literary Reference Center, search.ebscohost.com/login.aspx?direct=true&db=lfh&AN=22969889&site=eds-live. Accessed 28 Dec. 2021.

_____. *Solaris*. Translated by Bill Johnston. 2nd edition, Pro Auctore Wojciech Zemek, 2017. Kindle.

Lem, Stanisław, and Istvan Csicsery-Ronay, Jr. "Twenty-Two Answers and Two Postscripts: An Interview with Stanisław Lem." *Contemporary Literary Criticism*, edited by Jeffrey W. Hunter, vol. 149, Gale, 2002. Gale Literature Resource Center, https://link.gale.com/apps/doc/H1100039127/LitRC?u=idaho_a_colsil&sid=LitRC&xid=f51ed0b7. Originally published in *Science-Fiction Studies*, vol. 13, no. 3, Nov. 1986, pp. 242–60. Accessed 28 Dec. 2021.

Lerer, Seth. "Forbidden Planet and the Terrors of Philology." *Raritan: A Quarterly Review*, vol. 19, no. 3, 2000, pp. 73–86. MasterFile Premier, search.ebscohost.com/login.aspx?direct=true&db=edsgao&AN=edsgcl.60577875&site=eds-live. Accessed 28 Dec. 2021.

Maguire, Lori. "The Destruction of New York City: A Recurrent Nightmare of American Cold War Cinema." *Cold War History*, vol. 9, no. 4, Nov. 2009, pp. 513–24. Academic Search Premier, doi: 10.1081/1468274090319 8247. Accessed 2021.

"A New Translation of Solaris." Stanisław Lem: The Official Site, 2011, https://english.lem.pl/works/novels/solaris/196-a-new-translation-of-solaris. Accessed 28 Dec. 2021.

Sfetcu, Nicolae. Solaris, *Directed By Andrei Tarkovsky: Psychological and Philosophical Aspects*. Lulu Press, 7 May 2019. https://play.google.com/store/books/details?id=IrSYDwAAQBAJ&rdid=book-IrSYDwAAQBAJ&rdot=1&source=gbs_vpt_read&pcampaignid=books_booksearch_viewport. Google Scholar E-book. Accessed 28 Dec. 2021.

Sturgeon, Theodore. "Introduction." *Roadside Picnic/Tale of the Troika*, by Arkady and Boris Strugatsky, translated by Antonina W. Bouis, Macmillan, 1977.

Tighe, Carl. "Stanisław Lem: Socio-Political Sci-Fi." *Modern Language Review*, vol. 94, no. 3, July 1999, pp. 758–74. Academic Search Premier, doi:10.2307/3737000. Accessed 28 Dec. 2021.

Wiesenfeldt, Gerhard. "Dystopian Genesis: The Scientist's Role in Society, According to Jack Arnold." *Film & History*, vol. 40, no. 1, 2010, p. 58+. Gale Literature Resource Center, https://link.gale.com/apps/doc/A308598860/LitRC?u=idaho_a_colsil&sid=LitRC&xid=0bad21da. Accessed 28 Dec. 2021.

FILMOGRAPHY

The Big Bang Theory. Dir. Mark Cendrowski. Warner Bros., 2007–2019. TV Series.
The Fly. Dir. Kurt Neumann. 20th Century Fox, 1958. Film.
Forbidden Planet. Screenplay by Cyril Hume. Dir. Fred McLeod Wilcox. Prod. MGM, 1956. Film.
Heavy Metal. Dir. Gerald Potterton. Columbia Pictures, 1981. Film.
The Incredible Shrinking Man. Dir. Jack Arnold. Universal Pictures, 1957. Film.
It Came from Outer Space. Dir. Jack Arnold. Universal Pictures, 1951. Film.
On the Beach. Dir. Stanley Kramer. United Artists, 1959. Film.
Ready Player One. Dir. Steven Spielberg. Warner Bros., 2018. Film.
Solaris. Dir. Andrei Tarkovsky. Mosfilm, 1972. Film.
Them! Dir. Gordon Douglas. Warner Bros., 1954. Film.
The Thing from Another World. Dir. Christian Nyby. RKO Radio Pictures, 1951. Film.
The Twilight Zone. CBS, 1959–1964. TV Series.

New Maps of Hell

Racebending and Fahrenheit 451

WILLIAM HART

> In him, perhaps, we see the general ogre
> Who rode our ancestors to nightmare,
> And in his habitat their maps of hell.
> —Kingsley Amis

At the end of the 1950s, British novelist and critic Kingsley Amis asked in his poem "Science Fiction" why we write, read, watch or even study sci-fi. Why do we have an interest in the "ten-clawed monster" of sci-fi? As Amis posits, perhaps it is an attempt to better understand ourselves, all of ourselves, our vices and our follies. The poem opens his book *New Maps of Hell: A Survey of Science Fiction* in which he offers some predictions and proclamations. Somewhat famously, he expressed concern that sci-fi did not have a future in television and film.[1] He stated in 1959 that "it appears the boom of science-fiction film has passed" (40). Regardless of Amis' obviously failed prediction, his other observations shared in *Maps of Hell* carry more merit.

Writing specifically about the dystopian novel *Fahrenheit 451*, Amis notes that "Bradbury's is the most skillfully drawn of all sci-fi's conformist hells" (80). Banning and burning books, along with authoritarianism and oppression, are some of the "science-fiction hells" found in *Fahrenheit 451*. More to the point, Amis also saw the sci-fi of the '50s "as an instrument of social diagnosis and warning" and *Fahrenheit* as exemplary of that definition. He saw sci-fi moving beyond the futuristic, techno-logical aspects of the genre to a genre that also addressed social and political hells. He also covered issues of gender and colonialism in the sci-fi of the 1950s. He was seeing the beginnings of a sci-fi which would later be described as new wave sci-fi, the more socially conscious sci-fi of the 1960s and '70s. Both in content and in style, Bradbury was the beginning of this genre evolution.

One of the social and political hells, only briefly addressed by Amis, is racial oppression, but clearly, it is one of the "science-fiction hells" that should be well explored and plainly mapped out. There are at least three narrative spaces within which racial oppression and sci-fi intersect, and they can be demarcated thusly:

Area 1: A group of people who have been oppressed in the past also face oppression in the future of a sci-fi story. For example, Bradbury, in two short stories, discussed later, explored the exodus of African Americans from the Earth to Mars in order to escape racial oppression.

Area 2: A group of oppressed people are depicted allegorically as interplanetary aliens. For example, in the sci-fi film *Enemy Mine* (1985), Louis Gossett Jr., a Black actor hidden under extensive makeup, plays the role of an alien which Dennis Quaid, a white actor, learns to trust in order to survive on an alien planet. Also, in Area 2, can be found the original of *Planet of the Apes* (1968–1972) films with their clear allegory of race relations in the U.S. (Green).

Area 3: The race of a character is changed in a later adaptation of the sci-fi story. The Will Smith racebending, sci-fi film, *I Am Legend* (2007), based on the original novella of the same name, falls into this area[2] [Hart, "Race, Adaptation" 207].

The first two areas are intra-story, i.e., issues of race and racial oppression are happening within the story. Area 3 is extra-story; its politics exist in the space between stories, in the adaptation process. How and why does the racebending happen and with what effect? It is this last area which is the focus of this essay.

Of the approximately 250 sci-fi films made in the United States in the 1950s, only about 30 have been remade (Warren). In the sci-fi films remade, examples of racebending are very limited. The only film that seems, to some degree, applicable is *The Manchurian Candidate* (1962), which Bill Warren includes in his *Keep Watching the Skies! American Science Fiction Movies of the Fifties* along with its Frank Sinatra to Denzel Washington racebending remake. However, this film is on the edges of the sci-fi genre and was actually released in 1962. Some remakes of 1950s films may have been promising as racebending sci-fi adaptations (e.g., *The Fly* [1958] [1986]; *Journey to the Center of the Earth* [1959] [2008]; *War of the Worlds* [1953] [2005]). However, the casting of Jeff Goldblum, Brandon Fraser, and Tom Cruise in the main roles maintained the status quo.

To better explore the concept of racebending in the context of the 1950s sci-fi remakes, one has to consult the ur-texts of many 1950s sci-fi films and the 1950s sci-fi novels upon which they were based. When the novel/ur-text avenue is opened, there is a richer space to explore. This essay analyzes briefly the novel-to-film adaptations of *I, Robot* (1950, 2004) and *I Am Legend* (1954, 1964, 1971, 2007) as a means of setting up a deeper analysis of *Fahrenheit 451* (1953, 1966, 2018). I draw upon the previous sci-fi racebending literature to study the racebending of the 2018 HBO adaptation of *Fahrenheit 451* by using the theoretical frameworks of adaptation, ideological criticism, and Afrofuturism.

Adaptation, Ideological Criticism and Afrofuturism

One of the first key works in the study of adaptation, George Bluestone's *Novel into Film* set the paradigm for the field with its perhaps unintentional focus on fidelity. The chief question asked in such studies is: How faithful is the film to the original details of the novel? In this form of adaptation study, the critic might, for example, note that the main character wore glasses in the novel but not in the film. Adaptation studies, to a great degree, eventually shifted away from fidelity studies because such studies, for one, privileged the novel over the film. However, in the case of racebending, there is still value in applying a fidelity paradigm. Without recognizing racial choices in earlier texts, later racial changes, along with the weight they carry, can be effaced. Fidelity studies can only be seen as a first step, however. Once the differences between the source and the adaptation are identified, one should ask: Why the difference? What purpose does it serve? What are the results of the change?[3] If, for example, an interracial romance which appears in a novel goes missing in the film adaptation, then one should ask why (Hart, "Interracial Romance").

Ideological criticism provides a means to answer such questions. According to Stuart Hall, in a general sense an ideology is a

mental framework—the languages, the concepts, categories, imagery of thought, and the systems of representation—which different classes and social groups deploy in order to make sense of, define, figure out and render intelligible the way society works [20].

Ideologies are useful, but they are problematic when they become hegemonic, that is, when there is a "privileging of the ideology of one group over the ideologies of other groups.... [It is] a form of domination by more powerful groups over the ideologies of those with less power" (Foss 9). A colorblind ideology, for example, privileges those who have such a mental framework, chiefly Whites, and disadvantages oppressed people of color who face systemic oppression.

According to Hall and Foss, the task of the ideological critique is to make visible the underlying ideology of a text (novel, film, etc.), identify what groups benefit from the dominant ideology and which groups do not, and to ask what the implications are for building a better world. Bonilla-Silva identifies colorblind ideology as especially relevant. In his book *Racism Without Racists* (2017), Bonilla-Silva argues that regardless of the claim that we live in a "post-racial" or "colorblind" world, institutional racism still exists and is reinforced by an underlying colorblind, racist ideology. Essentially, Bonilla-Silva asks, "How is it possible to have this tremendous degree of racial inequality in a country where most whites claim that race is no longer relevant?" He argues that a colorblind way of thinking ("I don't see color"; "Racism is a thing of the past") is one of the things that keeps people of color oppressed. Some Blacks, Bonilla-Silvia suggests, do not see or seem to be aware of the systemic discrimination described in his book. A colorblind ideology reinforces systemic racism and thus allows racism to exist without individual racists.

Armed with an understanding of the kind of colorblind ideology described above, an ideological critic, for example, could study the integration of African American actors into U.S. films and interrogate such integration and in doing so become "suspicious of a naive integrationism, which simply inserts new heroes and heroines … drawn from the ranks of the oppressed" (Stam and Spense 9). As media scholar bell hooks notes, "merely putting black characters in a film does not assure that the work acts, whether covertly or overtly, to undermine racism. Those black characters can be constructed cinematically so that they become mouthpieces for racist assumptions and beliefs" (74). Putting a Black actor in a key role in a film should not stop others from questioning whether or not the appearance of the actor is "encouraging and promoting a counterhegemonic narrative challenging the conventional structures of domination that uphold and maintain White supremacist capitalist patriarchy" (hooks 3). The colorblind ideology ("I don't see race") suggests that interchanging the race of characters is a positive development, but the reality is more complex.

In the narrower case of racebending films, what is the purpose of the ideological critique? If racebending happens in a novel-to-film adaptation, then the task of the ideological critic would be first to identify the racebending changes and then to ask who benefits from such changes and what are the implications for a better, more equal world. There are thoughtful and provocative examples of racebending in sci-fi remakes, as discussed below, but if the act of racebending is found simply to reinforce a racist ideology, then what are the alternatives? A clear alternative simply to inserting a Black actor into a story previously written for a White character, is to tell a story of a Black experience from the beginning. In the realm of sci-fi, Afrofuturism is just that.

Afrofuturism is a movement, a perspective that places the Black experience in a future that has been devoid of Blackness. It is a means of allowing Black people to be seen prominently and positively in the future and in a genre of fiction that has a history of marginalizing Black people to secondary characters. Afrofuturism was first defined by Mark Dery as

> [s]peculative fiction that treats African-American themes and addresses African-American concerns in the context of twentieth-century technoculture—and, more generally, African-American signification that appropriates images of technology and a prosthetically enhanced future [180].

While defined by Dery as a genre of fiction, Afrofuturism crosses art forms from literature and fine art to dance and music.

In literature, Afrofuturism may be traced back to Edward Johnson's 1904 utopian novel *Light Ahead for the Negro* and to a recently discovered W.E.B. Du Bois short story "Princess Steel" from circa 1909 in which Du Bois weaves together speculative fiction, African mythology and issues of colonization (Carr, "W.E.B. Du Bois"). Ralph Ellison's 1952 novel *Invisible Man* can also be considered a precursor to modern Afrofuturism literature (Yazsek 298). The modern Afrofuturism movement in literature did not fully begin until the 1970s with the work of African American sci-fi authors, Samuel R. Delany and Octavia Butler (e.g., with her novel *Kindred* and later the *Xenogenesis* trilogy).

Well into the 1990s, however, Delany and Butler were still part of only a small handful of authors speaking to the Black experience in a sci-fi setting. So much so that in the early '90s Dery questioned: "Why do so few African Americans write science fiction, a genre whose close encounters with the Other—the stranger in a strange land—would seem uniquely suited to the concerns of African-American novelists?" (179–80). This was perplexing to Dery because, as he writes, African Americans, "in a very real sense, are the descendants of alien abductees; they inhabit a sci-fi nightmare in which unseen but no less impassable force fields of intolerance frustrate their movement…" (180). Today, thankfully, there are more voices, including the Afrofuturistic work of Nalo Hopkinson, Colson Whitehead, Ytasha Womack and the award-winning work of N.K. Jemisin. In their sci-fi and fantasy stories, these authors address the nightmares associated with the past, but they also write of a future which is free of the pain of the past.

As a movement and philosophy, Afrofuturism goes beyond literature to other artistic endeavors like music and film. Afrofuturism can be found in the jazz of Sun Ra, the funk of George Clinton and Parliament-Funkadelic, the guitar rock of Jimi Hendrix and, more recently, the Afrofuturism-inspired music of artists like Missy

Elliot and Janelle Monae. Sci-fi films with a strong Black perspective include the Sun Ra documentary, *Space Is the Place* (1974), *Brother from Another Planet* (1984), the *Blade* trilogy (1998, 2002, 2004) *Black Panther* (2018), Jordan Peele's *Us* (2019), or Matt Ruff and Misha Green's *Lovecraft Country* (2020).

As for scholarly work in Afrofuturism, early theorists include Greg Tate and Mark Sinker, and especially Dery and his defining article "Black to the Future." While there are earlier book-length studies of race in sci-fi in film and television, e.g., Daniel Bernardi's *Star Trek and History,* the first book on the specific study of African Americans in sci-fi film was *Black Space: Imagining Race in Science Fiction Film* (Nama). In this book, author Adilifu Nama notes an "absence/token presence" of African Americans in sci-fi film. Until the 2000s, Blacks were "absent or extremely marginal," and if there marginally, they "are certain to die prematurely in the second act" (Nama 2). This absence forces Nama to study the "narrative subtext or implicit allegorical subject" of some 30 films including *Star Wars* (1977), *Blade Runner* (1982) and *Minority Report* (2002) to find the presence of Blackness in the form of allegory (Nama). For example, Nama skillfully observes similarities between the treatment of the androids in *Blade Runner* to the Black experience with slavery in the United States, and noting this sub-textual comparison changes one's reading of *Blade Runner.*

Ytasha Womack's *Afrofuturism: The World of Black Sci-Fi and Fantasy Culture* (2013) gathers together in one book coverage of Afrofuturism authors like Butler and musicians like Sun Ra along with interviews with scholars in the field. Womack also includes coverage of Afrofuturism in films and discusses the Black experience as an "alien" experience. Reynaldo Anderson's *Afrofuturism 2.0: The Rise of Astro-Blackness* (2015) follows up on Womack's work and expands Afrofuturism to include broader coverage of related topics and moves Afrofuturism from a U.S./Western perspective to a more global Pan-African perspective. Afrofuturism, in short, demands a place for Blacks at the table of sci-fi, and highlights that absence where it exists. Perhaps more importantly, it questions why sci-fi is not more motivated by themes of color, race, and ethnicity.

In *Speculative Blackness: The Future of Race in Science Fiction* (2016) André Carrington analyzes the representation of Black Americans in sci-fi, especially looking at related fanfiction and the process of reception. Most notably Carrington writes that sci-fi "scholarship does not yet provide all of the tools required to articulate what sci-fi, fantasy, and utopia mean to Black Americans." The purpose of the present essay is to try to provide some of those missing tools. Armed with the philosophies of adaptation, ideological criticism and Afrofuturism, this essay works to provide methodological tools needed to better understand the Black experience in sci-fi, especially in terms of racebending

Racebending in I, Robot *and* I Am Legend

Until the 2000s, Blacks were "absent or extremely marginal" in U.S. sci-fi film (Nama). However, with the appearance of Will Smith in a series of blockbuster sci-fi films in the late 1990s and early 2000s, a shift started. But as the news site Vox notes in a 2016 YouTube video on Afrofuturism:

> When people envision a future in art most often it's seen through a white lens. Only 8% of the 100 top grossing sci-fi and fantasy films featured a protagonist of color. Half the time the protagonist was Will Smith (*Hancock* [2018], *I Am Legend* [2007], *Independence Day* [1996] and *Men in Black* [1997]). The future looks different if you look at it through the lens of black experiences. But we're not all white or Will Smith ["Sci-fi and Social Justice"].

Smith certainly looms large in this context of sci-fi blockbusters. *I, Robot* (2004) is based on the work of sci-fi writer Isaac Asimov. It is not an adaptation of a single work, however, but a pastiche, a mixture of some stories in Asimov's short story collection *I, Robot* and Asimov's 1953 novel *The Caves of Steel* (Hart, "Race, Adaptation" 207). *I Am Legend* (2008), on the other hand, is a direct adaptation of Richard Matheson's 1954 novella of the same name. In both films, a key theme is overcoming prejudice. In *I, Robot*, Smith's character has a prejudice toward robots, and believes that a robot killed a person who once saved his life. In *I Am Legend*, Smith's character is apparently the sole survivor of a pandemic who must survive alongside the zombie-like "nightseekers," people who are infected with a virus. As a virologist, Smith's character is looking for a cure and experiments on the nightseekers to help him accomplish his goal. In doing so he kills the nightseekers. At the end of the film, or at least, in the alternate Blu-ray version of the ending—an ending much closer to that of the novel—Smith's character comes to the realization that his prejudice led to the killing of dozens of nightseekers. To them, he has become a legend, the kind of story you might tell a misbehaving child.

In both *I, Robot* and *I Am Legend*, Will Smith plays the main character, but along with the integration of a Black actor into the films, there are also other signifiers of Blackness included. In *I, Robot*, it is the mention of sweet potato pies and Stevie Wonder music, for example. In *I Am Legend* it is Bob Marley music and more Bob Marley music.[4] But considered as a case of novel to film adaptation, is this racebending simply colorblind casting that actually recreates a racist hegemony? That is, can one simply insert elements of Blackness into a film based on a novel about a White character, especially a White character who must overcome prejudice as a key theme to the story?

In her analysis of *I, Robot*, Alexis Harley concludes that Will Smith's "blackness is a reminder of slavery, its human and historical reality, and that works in the logic of this film as an argument for freedom" (228). What is not clear is what it means to say it works. Both original stories and the subsequent films can be read as allegories for the oppression of African Americans in the United States (Palumbo 48; Hart, "Race, Adaptation" 207). And if the original stories from the 1950s were allegory, then what does it mean for Will Smith to take the role of the oppressor in the adaptation? One should be reminded of the warning of hooks, Hart, and Spence and Stam: simply inserting elements of Blackness into a film does not guarantee that that film does not reinforce a racist ideology. In both of these colorblind, racebending adaptations, the oppressed becomes the oppressor. Counterintuitively, it may have been better, more meaningful, and still relevant today to have a White actor as the oppressor, the one who overcomes prejudice to see the wrongs of his past actions.

Does the ideology found in *I, Robot* and *I Am Legend* continue in more current racebending films? Although limited, since 2016 there have been additional sci-fi and fantasy films featuring protagonists of color. Michael B. Jordan seems to have taken up the Black sci-fi mantle from Smith with his featured appearance in 2018's blockbuster *Black Panther* and in the racebending adaptation of *Fahrenheit 451*, also released in 2018. Does the potentially problematic ideology of Smith's earlier films carry on in *Fahrenheit 451*?

Fahrenheit 451: *Bradbury's 1953 Novel*

The 2018 film *Fahrenheit 451* is based on Ray Bradbury's 1953 novel of the same name, and the novel does hint at questions of racial oppression. Bradbury often looked to the past for his visions of the future. He once had an experience with a police officer who questioned him about why he was on a walk and he turned that experience into his short story "The Pedestrian" which in turn inspired *Fahrenheit 451* (Eller). Bradbury questioned authority figures and had a history of questioning injustices in his writing. In one of his non-sci-fi stories, "The Big Black and White Game" (1945), for example, Bradbury tells a heart-felt story from the perspective of a young White boy named Douglas[5] who is watching an annual baseball game between Blacks and Whites. Douglas admires the players on the Black team, even as the game turns to interracial violence. In "Way Up in the Middle of the Air" (1950) Bradbury writes of the exodus of African Americans from Earth to Mars to escape racial oppression. After the Martian colony is established "The Other Foot" (1951) describes how these Black colonists receive the first White man on Mars. While Bradbury was growing up, "[t]he racial biases of the times were all around him, but he had not bought into the ideology at all, and as he matured he managed to maintain the distance needed to write objectively about issues of race" (Eller). Bradbury and his agent had difficulty getting his two Mars exodus stories published in mainstream publications, but they did find publication in lesser known outlets. "Way Up" was first published in Bradbury's *The Martian Chronicles* in the spring of 1950 and then in *Other Worlds Science Stories* later that summer. "The Other Foot" was published in Bradbury's *The Illustrated Man* in 1951 and in *New-Story* magazine at about the same time. Bradbury wrote other similar stories, though they were not published (Eller).

As with *I, Robot* and *I Am Legend*, one way of avoiding the problems Bradbury had getting these two stories of oppression into print is to use allegory. Critics and scholars have pointed to obvious allegorical readings of *Fahrenheit 451*, including the parallel book burnings of the Nazis in World War II and the red-scare rhetoric of Joseph McCarthy in the 1950s. One can, however, also read it as allegory for other forms of oppression. On the surface the novel is the story of Guy Montag, a fireman, who does not put out fires but starts them. He and other firemen burn books. In the novel, books are banned. Montag begins the story happy with his job as a fireman but encounters a 17-year-old girl, Clarisse, who sparks in him a different perspective. She makes him question his purpose. Montag comes to realize the value of books.

After Montag begins to collect and read books, Montag's wife, Mildred, turns him in, and he goes on the run to escape the other firemen. The story ends with Montag finding a group of people who have memorized and can recite whole books. He becomes one of them as he learns to recite the Book of Ecclesiastes from the Bible.

With its references to banning books and to the value of orality, Bradbury's novel can be also read as allegory for the African American experience. During slavery in the United States Southern states established laws banning slaves from learning to read. A Virginia law, for example, stated that "every assemblage of negroes for the purpose of instruction in reading or writing, or in the nighttime for any purpose, shall be an unlawful assembly. Any justice ... may order such negro to be punished with stripes" ("Offences against..."). *Fahrenheit 451* is about oppression and more specifically it is about the banning of reading. As such it reflects the past experiences of slaves in the United States. In a similar fashion, Bradbury's novel stresses the value of orality. Orality, the emphasis on the spoken word, is part of several cultures, e.g., Greek culture, but it is also "well-established as part of Black culture" (Turner 7). It is part of African tradition, but it is also a result of slavery and anti-education laws. Without a means to read or write, oral literature, oral history, spoken folk tales, and folk songs became a means of maintaining culture. *Fahrenheit 451* is about the value of orality in maintaining a culture, and as such, the novel reflects past experiences of slaves in the United States.

With the anti-literacy and orality aspects of the novel, one has to read into the story. However, one key scene in Bradbury's novel more overtly shows views related to race, specifically with regards to political correctness. Early in the novel, when Montag begins to question his purpose as a fireman, his supervisor, Captain Beatty, lectures him on why books are banned. Beatty, the antagonist of the story, tells Montag that "the minorities" were "upset and stirred" by the offensive materials in books and, as a result, it was not the government who first "banned" books but the people. He continues, "Colored people don't like *Little Black Sambo*. Burn it. White people don't feel good about *Uncle Tom's Cabin*. Burn it. Someone's written a book on tobacco and cancer of the lungs? The cigarette people are weeping? Burn the book." The government in the form of firemen just took on the task of enforcing the banning in order to maintain happiness and equality. Beatty argues: "We must all be alike. Not everyone born free and equal, as the Constitution says, but everyone made equal. Each man the image of every other; then all are happy..." (Bradbury, *Fahrenheit*).

The context of this quotation begs the question, is this only Beatty's position, or does it also reflect Bradbury's own perspective? It is possible that the "lecture" in *Fahrenheit* may be a reaction to the censorship Bradbury himself faced in trying to get some of his race-related stories published. As mentioned previously, Bradbury had difficulty getting "Way Up in the Middle of the Air" published with a mainstream press. In the story, the antagonist uses the n-word multiple times. The publishers may have balked at this aspect and thus led Bradbury to his perspective on political correctness as it relates to censorship of fiction. Given Bradbury's stories related to race and his own views and experiences, there is reason for and value in reading *Fahrenheit 451* as racial allegory.

Figure 36. "Firemen" Captain Beatty (Cyril Cusack) and Montag (Oskar Werner) hard at work in *Fahrenheit 451* (1966) (Universal Pictures/Photofest).

Fahrenheit 451: *Truffaut's 1966 Film*

The 1966 film adaptation of *Fahrenheit 451* was directed by famed French director François Truffaut, known for his more intimate, relationship-based films and not for bigger budget sci-fi films. To this end, romantic relationships do get some attention in Truffaut's adaptation. Clarisse is aged slightly to 20 years old and kept as Montag's romantic interest throughout the whole film, whereas in the novel she was only in the first part. Montag's wife, named Linda in the film, gets more screen time as well, including a love scene with Montag. Truffaut has White, British actress Julie Christie play both roles, that of Clarisse and Linda. Montag is played by White, German actor Oskar Werner.

With the exception of the new scenes inserted for Clarisse's continued appearance, the overall plot of the film follows relatively close to the plot of the novel. The film tells the story of Guy Montag, a fireman who burns books. As in the novel, Clarisse sparks in Montag an interest in books. Montag is discovered to have books hidden away and is forced to run. This time, though, he finds Clarisse with the Book People in the woods. He becomes one of them and he learns to recite a book by Edgar Allan Poe as he walks with Clarisse in the woods.

As for allegory in the 1966 film version, Truffaut biographer Annette Insdorf notes the allegorical references to Nazis (Bouzereau). She mentions specifically the Nazi–like book burning, the German accent of Werner, the Nazi–like salutes early in the film, and the similarity of the firemen's uniforms to Nazi stormtrooper uniforms. Nama, in *Black Space*, also sees an allegorical comparison to the African American experience. As was noted above in relation to Bradbury's novel, Nama suggests that in the 1966 film the banning of books and the emphasis on the oral tradition may be seen as signs of the African American experience (125).

As for overt references to the African American experience, Nama finds in an early scene in the film that there are images of hooded KKK members in the comic-book–like newspaper that Montag is reading. "The virtually inconspicuous yet obviously intentional placement of such imagery, together with the structured absence of Black people in the film, signals a normalization of White supremacy in the future world of *Fahrenheit 451*" (125). Nama reads this as an indication that "virulent white racism is indicated as part and parcel of

Figure 37. Actor Michael B. Jordan (here seen in *Raising Dion*, 2019) (© Netflix/Photofest).

the high-tech alienation and systemic illiterate status of the citizenry depicted in the film" (125). This is likely true, despite the TV announcer, later in the film, who instructs the viewers, "do remember to tolerate your friends' friends, however alien and peculiar they may seem to you. Don't despise minorities…. Strangle violence. Suppress prejudice." Note that the "alien and peculiar" people viewers may encounter are likely to be "your friends' friends," not your own friends.

As in the novel, Captain Beatty lectures Montag on political correctness. In the 1966 film, the firemen find a library hidden in a home. Beatty points to a copy of *Robinson Crusoe* and says to Montag: "Ah, *Robinson Crusoe*. The negroes didn't like that because of his man, Friday. And Nietzsche. Ah, Nietzsche. The Jews didn't like Nietzsche. Now, here's a book about lung cancer. All the cigarette smokers got into a panic, so for everybody's peace of mind, we burn it." Like the character in the novel, Beatty argues that "we've all got to be alike. The only way to be happy is for everyone to be made equal. So, we must burn the books." In the *Fahrenheit* world, all people are made "equal" by banning books.

Fahrenheit 451: *Bahrani's 2018 Film*

In the 1990s and again in the 2000s there were two attempted remakes of *Fahrenheit* which went into "development hell" and eventually were canceled. From the mid–1990s to the late '90s Mel Gibson worked on the project with Warner Brothers, who had the film rights for the novel. Gibson initially planned both to direct and star as Montag but then moved to just the director's chair and considered younger actors like Brad Pitt and then Tom Cruise to play Montag ("Cruise Rumor Heats Up 'Fahrenheit 451'"). Scheduling conflicts with Cruise's other film projects led Cruise to drop out and then, too, did Gibson ("Ray Bradbury on Status of FAHRENHEIT 451 and Mel Gibson"). In the early 2000s Frank Darabont, who had screenwriting experience adapting Stephen King's *The Shawshank Redemption* (1994) and *The Green Mile* (1999), came in to rewrite the *Fahrenheit* script and to direct. Darabont reportedly had Tom Hanks interested in playing the role of Montag (Horowitz). After Hanks dropped out, however, the Darabont version also came to an end. In 2016, HBO won rights to the novel and director Rami Bahrani took over the director's chair.

Bahrani brought his adaptation into the current century. He integrated the Internet and social media into the *Fahrenheit* world and sought a diverse cast. In Bahrani's version, social media became a way for the society to view and participate in the book burnings that the firemen carried out. In terms of casting of the main roles, Clarisse is played by Algerian actress Sofia Boutella and Captain Beatty is played by White actor Michael Shannon. Other actors like Lilly Singh and Black actress Khandi Alexander both play minor roles. However, Bahrani's key racebending decision was to cast Black actor Michael B. Jordan as Montag.

Jordan was initially reluctant when Bahrani first asked him. In an interview Jordan says that he was reading the script and could not help but to "see brown and black faces" when the script mentioned the oppressed people in the story. "I didn't want to be an oppressor with what was going on in my community. The police brutality, the shootings and all that stuff. I didn't want to be seen as that" (Rourke). However, Bahrani convinced Jordan that the "movie can do more good than [Jordan's] perspective on the police brutality and the climate that was going on in the real world" (Kelsey). Jordan justified his choice to play Montag by saying that he "was so brainwashed in a way and traumatized by seeing police shootings in my community and police brutality" (Michael B.). The messages and themes of the *Fahrenheit* story outweighed, apparently, his initial concerns. Jordan agreed to star in and also be the executive producer of the film.

Bahrani and Jordan's 2018 adaptation does differ from Bradbury's novel. Apart from the role of Montag being played by Black actor and the inclusion of other Black actors, other signifiers of Blackness are included. In Truffaut's 1966 version the books that burned were very strongly Western, White literature. They included, for example, White American and French cultural references. In his adaptation Bahrani includes a more diverse selection of cultural artifacts in his book burning scenes. He includes visual references to Persian poetry and Chinese literature, for example. However, what is prominently included in his diversification of the cultural artifacts is the inclusion of African American artifacts. In the film the viewer is shown covers of books as they are being burned. In many cases they see references of Blackness including books like *Their Eyes Were Watching God*, *I Know Why the Caged Bird Sings*, *The Wretched of the Earth*, and *Things Fall Apart*. The viewer is also shown multiple photographs of Frederick Douglass and news photographs of Black men carrying "I am a man" posters. Near the end of the film, when Montag is brought to the rebel compound, he is introduced to some of the book people. Each of the members have memorized a book and are named after the book that they can recite from memory. Montag is introduced, for example, to *Song of Solomon*, *Half of a Yellow Sun* and *The Fire Next Time*.

In the novel, as well as its adaptations, the burning of the books symbolizes the erasing of culture, of history. The destroying of history and culture in the logic of the *Fahrenheit* world makes all people equal and happy. In this de-historized, homogenous world the citizens are colorblind. The viewer of the film may understand the references to Frederick Douglass, *Their Eyes* or *Caged Birds*, for instance, but the citizens of the *Fahrenheit* world do not. Even the book people seem only to be able to recite the words of the books without a deeper understanding of their meaning and implication. *Fahrenheit* citizens would not, for example, have a full understanding of the word "boy" in some contexts. Near the end of the film, soon after Montag is discovered to be a rebel by the other fireman, one White fireman calls him "boy." This slur will only have full meaning to the viewer, not to the "equal" and "happy" citizens of the *Fahrenheit* world.[6]

Apart from the different characters and story elements mentioned above, the plot differs significantly. Truffault's adaptation certainly was more faithful to the plot of Bradbury's novel. In the 2018 adaptation Montag is not married, but he is a fireman who burns books. Captain Beatty (Michael Shannon) is Montag's mentor and character model. However, when Montag meets Clarisse that changes. She opens his eyes to the oppressive nature of their society and the value of books and reading. Montag sides with Clarisse and joins a rebel group of book-readers. The rebel group has developed a way of encoding books into the DNA of a bird. As in the novel and 1966 film, Montag is found to have books in his home. When he is confronted, he fights back, kills a fireman, and escapes to the rebel group. As the film ends Montag sacrifices himself and releases the bird into the world with millions of books encoded into its DNA.[7]

Coda: Fade to Black

In February 2020 bookseller Barnes & Noble started a book campaign. The campaign was intended to raise awareness during Black History Month. On the covers of classic novels the booksellers recast the main characters as people of color. For example, the covers of Shelley's *Frankenstein*, Baum's *The Wonderful Wizard of Oz* and Melville's *Moby Dick* depict the main characters as Black. This racebending of the classic covers generated some harsh criticism on social media and mainstream media. It was referred to as "the classics in blackface" on social media and panned as "infuriating." "[I]f Barnes & Noble really wanted to honor black history, the company could promote books by black authors," like James Baldwin, Toni Morrison, or Maya Angelou (Frederick). Barnes and Noble did later acknowledge that the racebending covers were "not a substitute for black voices or writers of color, whose work and voices deserve to be heard" (Italie). In the context of this essay, another question arises: What is the difference between what Barnes and Noble did and what film directors do when they decide to racebend in their novel to film adaptations? Or to repeat an earlier question, can one simply insert elements of Blackness into a film based on a novel about a White character, especially a White character who must overcome prejudice as a key theme to the story?

The ideological critique of *I, Robot* and *I Am Legend* above concludes that these racebending adaptations are problematic because they support a colorblind ideology. In both cases the key theme of the novels and films is that of the main character overcoming prejudice. In a colorblind world where a person does not see color, this type of adaptation would not be problematic. However, in a world where there still exists racism (systemic and otherwise) "simply" inserting a Black character into such a story seems to put the onus of racism on the Black character. From a colorblind perspective it seems to suggest that we are all equal; when even Black people can be prejudiced too, we are even. However, such a perspective is blind to history and to the racism of the present. The ideological critique of *Fahrenheit 451* shared above does not fare any better. In this case, the theme is not prejudice per se but oppression. In this case the burden of oppression is placed on the back of a Black man, and he is the one who must see the rights and the wrongs of his ways. It is not a White character who has to do this.

In the end, there is limited value in the kind of colorblind racebending found in *I, Robot*, *I Am Legend* and *Fahrenheit 451*. But it might be more productive for filmmakers to consider the alternatives. Juxtaposing Michael B. Jordan's role in *Fahrenheit 451* with his role in *Black Panther* helps illustrate this point. Which more effectively questions racial stereotypes, Michael B. Jordan in a racebending role as an oppressor who comes to see the wrongs of his ways or Michael B. Jordan in *Black Panther*? For filmmakers, the better alternative likely is the telling of a story that, from the beginning, focuses on the Black experience, as suggested by the Afrofuturism movement. Instead of racebending individual stories, Afrofuturism suggests to adaptation scholars the idea of racebending or adaptation at the broader, genre level. The more interesting question may be, how does one adapt an entire genre, like science fiction. A study of relevant past stories in film and television may suggest some answers but so too would study of future Afrofuturistic stories like the upcoming installments of *Black Panther*, Ava DuVerney's adaptation of Octavia Butler's *Dawn* or N.K. Jemisin's TNT adaptation of her *Fifth Season* series. In the future the image of race in sci-fi will be forced to adapt, change, and mutate.

NOTES

1. In all fairness, Amis was speaking specifically of the issue of creating convincing special effects using 1950s technologies. As filmic technologies advanced, special effects make-up and CGI allowed for more convincing sci-fi special effects.

2. The racebending is particularly apropos in this film because of the emphasis placed on race in Matheson's novella.

3. It is worth pointing out that these questions are focused both on production (why did creators choose to do certain things) and reception (how have audiences received such things). Both are important avenues, worthy of exploration, but it is worth recognizing the distinction.

4. Smith's character spends significant time talking about the meaning of Marley's music.

5. It is worth noting that "Douglas" is Bradbury's middle name and the name of the protagonist in his semi-autobiographical *Dandelion Wine* (1957).

6. In Bahrani's storyworld, before the opening of the Montag story, a "Second Civil War" happens. There is little explanation, but the de-historized citizens would not have full understanding of the phrase.

7. It should be noted that while Montag's death may be noble, the White characters in the previous versions of the story lived and that there is a history to Black characters dying in sci-fi film (Nama).

WORKS CITED

Amis, Kingsley. *New Maps of Hell: A Survey of Science Fiction*. Penguin Classics, 2012.
Anderson, Reynaldo, and Charles E. Jones. *Afrofuturism 2.0: The Rise of Astro-Blackness*. Lexington, 2015.
Asimov, Isaac. *The Caves of Steel*. New American Library, 1955.
_____. *I, Robot*. Bantam, 1950.
Barton, Gina, et al. "Afrofuturism Mixes Sci-Fi and Social Justice. Here's How It Works." *YouTube*, https://youtu.be/jlPwTMMhGGI. Accessed 2 April 2020.
Bernardi, Daniel. *Star Trek and History: Race-Ing Toward a White Future*. Rutgers University Press, 1998.
Bluestone, George. *Novels into Film*. Johns Hopkins University Press, 1957.
Bonilla-Silva, Eduardo. *Racism Without Racists: Color-Blind Racism and the Persistence of Racial Inequality in the United States*. Rowman & Littlefield, 2010.
Bouzereau, Laurent. "The Making of *Fahrenheit 451*." Universal Studios Home Video.
Bradbury, Ray. "The Big Black and White Game." *The Golden Apples of the Sun and Other Stories*. HarperCollins, 1997, pp. 71–82.
_____. *Fahrenheit 451: A Novel*. Simon & Schuster, 2012. Kindle.
_____. *The Martian Chronicles*. HarperCollins, 2013.
_____. "Way in the Middle of the Air." *Other Worlds*, July 1950, https://drive.google.com/file/d/-1DLNo7vH8b8okRVUz-Z-vtk_EepCnyGmy/view. Accessed 21 Dec. 2021.
Butler, Octavia E. *Kindred*. Beacon Press, 1979.
Carr, Jane Greenway. "What a Recently Uncovered Story by W.E.B. Du Bois Tells Us About Afrofuturism." *Slate*, 1 Dec. 2015, https://slate.com/technology/2015/12/the-princess-steel-a-recently-uncovered-short-story-by-w-e-b-du-bois-and-afrofuturism.html. Accessed 27 Dec. 2021.

Carrington, André M. *Speculative Blackness: The Future of Race in Science Fiction.* University of Minnesota Press, 2016.

"Cruise Rumor Heats Up 'Fahrenheit 451.'" *Chicago Tribune,* 27 Feb. 1998, https://www.chicagotribune.com/news/ct-xpm-1998-02-27-9802270036-story.html. Accessed 4 Jan. 2020.

Dery, Mark. "Black to the Future: Interviews with Samuel R. Delany, Greg Tate, and Tricia Rose." *Flame Wars: The Discourse of Cyberculture,* edited by Mark Dery. Duke University Press, 1994, pp. 179–222.

Eller, Jonathan R. *Becoming Ray Bradbury.* University of Illinois Press, 2011.

Ellison, Ralph. *Invisible Man.* Random House, 1982.

Foss, Sonja K. *Rhetorical Criticism: Exploration and Practice, Fifth Edition.* Waveland Press, 2017.

Frederick, Candice. "Why Is Barnes & Noble Putting 'Literary Blackface' on Its Shelves?" *The Guardian,* 7 Feb. 2020, www.theguardian.com, https://www.theguardian.com/commentisfree/2020/feb/07/barnes-and-noble-diverse-editions-blackface. Accessed 27 Dec. 2021.

Greene, Eric. *"Planet of the Apes" as American Myth: Race, Politics, and Popular Culture.* Wesleyan University Press, 1998. Google Books, http://books.google.com/books?id=esgi9gn0qeEC&printsec=frontcover#v=onepage&q&f=false. Accessed 27 Dec. 2021.

Hall, Stuart. "The Rediscovery of 'Ideology': Return of the Repressed in Media Studies." *Culture, Society and the Media,* edited by Michael Gurevitch et al. Routledge, 2005, pp. 61–95.

Harley, Alexis. "The Slavery of the Machine." *Afterimages of Slavery: Essays on Appearances in Recent American Films, Literature, Television and Other Media,* edited by Marlene D. Allen and Seretha D. Williams. McFarland, 2012, pp. 218–32.

Hart, William B. "Race, Adaptation and the Films I, Robot and I Am Legend." *The Fantastic Made Visible: Essays on the Adaptation of Science Fiction and Fantasy from Page to Screen,* edited by Matthew Wilhelm Kapell and Ace G. Pilkington. McFarland, 2015, Kindle.

_____. "The Case of the Missing Interracial Romance: An Ideological Critique of *Kiss the Girls.*" *North Carolina Literary Review,* no. 21, 2012, pp. 59–76http://www.nclr.ecu.edu/issues/2012.html.

_____. "Racebending." *Encyclopedia of Racism in American Cinema,* edited by Salvador Jimenez Murguia. Rowman & Littlefield, pp. 692–97.

hooks, bell. *We Real Cool: Black Men and Masculinity.* Psychology Press, 2004.

Horowitz, Josh. "BREAKING: Tom Hanks Drops Out of *Fahrenheit 451.*" *MTV News,* 28 March 2008, http://www.mtv.com/news/2429887/breaking-tom-hanks-drops-out-of-fahrenheit-451/. Accessed 27 Dec. 2021.

Italie, Hillel. "Barnes & Noble Suspends Reissues of Classics with New Multicultural Cover Images." *Chicago Tribune,* 5 Feb. 2020, https://www.chicagotribune.com/entertainment/books/ct-ent-barnes-and-noble-dverse-classics-canceled-20200205-z32dg6gwbbetxbgxomo5ufjcwe-story.html. Accessed 27 Dec. 2021.

Johnson, Edward Austin. *Light Ahead for the Negro.* Grafton Press, 1904.

Kelsey, Eric. "Why Michael B. Jordan Thought Twice about 'Fahrenheit 451.'" *Reuters,* 16 May 2018, www.reuters.com, https://www.reuters.com/article/us-film-fahrenheit451-idUSKCN1IH1JZ. Accessed 27 Dec 2021.

Matheson, Richard. *I Am Legend.* Doherty (Tom) Associates, 1954.

"Michael B. Jordan, Spike Lee and LES CHATOUILLES." *YouTube,* https://www.youtube.com/watch?v=wmtGYcx3ZEY&list=PLehj-J7GtbVprUmtbg60Gjm51aPYpHlQ2&index=20. Accessed 23 Dec. 2019.

Nama, Adilifu. *Black Space: Imagining Race in Science Fiction Film.* University of Texas Press, 2010.

"Offences Against Public Policy," Title 54, Chapter 198; "Assembling of negroes. Trading by free negroes," Section 31. *The Code of Virginia.* William F. Ritchie, 1849, p. 747. Retrieved 22 Jan. 2020.

Palumbo, Donald. "Asimov's Crusade Against Bigotry: The Persistence of Prejudice as a Fractal Motif in the Robot/Empire Foundation Metaseries." *Journal of the Fantastic in the Arts,* vol. 10, 1998, pp. 43–63.

"Ray Bradbury on Status of FAHRENHEIT 451 and Mel Gibson." *YouTube,* https://www.youtube.com/watch?v=3LoyGErumO4&feature=emb_title. Accessed 4 Jan. 2020.

Rorke, Robert. "Michael B. Jordan Grappled with Racial Tension for 'Fahrenheit 451.'" *New York Post,* 17 May 2018, https://nypost.com/2018/05/17/michael-b-jordan-grappled-with-racial-tension-for-fahrenheit-451/.

Stam, Robert, and Louise Spence. "Colonialism, Racism and Representation." *Screen,* vol. 24, no. 2. Oxford University Press, 1983, pp. 2–20.

Turner, Darwin T. "African-American History and the Oral Tradition." *Books at Iowa,* vol. 53, Nov. 1990, pp. 7–12. *DOI.org (Crossref),* doi:10.17077/0006-7474.1186.

Warren, Bill. *Keep Watching the Skies! American Science Fiction Movies of the Fifties, The 21st Century Edition.* McFarland, 2017.

Womack, Ytasha. *Afrofuturism: The World of Black Sci-Fi and Fantasy Culture.* Chicago Review Press, 2013.

Yaszek, Lisa. "An Afrofuturist Reading of Ralph Ellison's Invisible Man." *Rethinking History,* vol. 9, no. 2–3, Routledge, June 2005, pp. 297–313. *Taylor and Francis+NEJM,* doi:10.1080/13642520500149202.

FILMOGRAPHY

Black Panther. Dir. Ryan Coogler. Marvel Studios, 2018. Film.
Blade Runner. Dir. Ridley Scott. Warner Bros, 1982. Film.
The Blade Trilogy. New Line Cinema, 1998–2004. Films.
Brother from Another Planet. Dir. John Sayles. Cinecom Pictures, 1984. Film.
Enemy Mine. Dir. Wolfgang Petersen. 20th Century Fox, 1985. Film.
Fahrenheit 451. Dir. François Truffaut. Universal Pictures, 1966. Film.
Fahrenheit 451. Dir. Ramin Bahrani. HBO Films, 2018. Film.
The Fly. Dir. Kurt Neumann. 20th Century Fox, 1958. Film.
The Fly. Dir. David Cronenberg. 20th Century Fox, 1986. Film.
The Green Mile. Dir. Frank Darabont. Warner Bros, 1999. Film.
Hancock. Dir. Peter Berg. Columbia Pictures, 2008. Film.
The Last Man on Earth. Dir. Sidney Salkow. American International Pictures, 1964. Film.
The Omega Man. Dir. Boris Sagal. Warner Bros, 1971. Film.
I Am Legend. Dir. Francis Lawrence. Warner Bros, 2007. Film.
I, Robot. Dir. Alex Proyas. 20th Century Fox, 2004. Film.
Independence Day. Dir. Roland Emmerich. 20th Century Fox, 1996. Film.
Journey to the Center of the Earth. Dir. Henry Levin. 20th Century Fox, 1959. Film.
Journey to the Center of the Earth. Dir. Eric Brevig. Warner Bros, 2008. Film.
The Manchurian Candidate. Dir. John Frankenheimer. United Artists, 1962. Film.
Men in Black. Dir. Barry Sonnenfeld. Columbia Pictures, 1997. Film.
Minority Report. Dir. Steven Spielberg. 20th Century Fox, 2002. Film.
Planet of the Apes. 20th Century Studios, 1968–1972. Films.
Ray Bradbury Theatre. First Choice Channel and HBO, 1985–1992. TV Series.
The Shawshank Redemption. Dir. Frank Darabont. Columbia Pictures, 1994. Film.
Space Is the Place. Dir. John Coney. 1974. Film.
Star Wars. Dir. George Lucas. 20th Century Fox, 1977. Film.
War of the Worlds. Dir. Byron Haskin. Paramount Pictures, 1953. Film.
War of the Worlds. Dir. Steven Spielberg. Paramount Pictures, 2005. Film.

Still Captive?

The Maternal Body in 1950s Science Fiction
Disaster Films and Mad Max: Fury Road

REBECCA JOHINKE

Introduction

Nineteen fifties American sci-fi disaster films serve as both thrilling entertainment and cautionary tales which warn about the perils of science and technology resulting in societal and environmental destruction (*Godzilla, Them! The Fly, Beginning of the End*). They continue to resonate in film and popular culture and serve as inspiration for direct and indirect adaptations which in turn elicit further sequels, prequels, and homages. Although there are some parallels with hot rodding films from the 1950s and with films like *The Creature Walks Among Us* (1956), *War of the Colossal Beast* (1958) or *The Giant Gila Monster* (1959) which feature car chases and monstrous creatures tossing cars and trucks around like toys, this essay positions Australian George Miller's *Mad Max: Fury Road* as an Antipodean response to themes first explored in 1950s sci-fi disaster films centered on women and the maternal body. These films include: *Five* (1951), *Captive Women* (1952), *World Without End* (1956), and *Last Woman on Earth* (1960). In these films, and others discussed below, nuclear destruction results in an environmentally devastated world where male survivors compete for access to resources like technology and fertile women. Like other forms of post-war political rhetoric, these films suggest that in a patriarchal society it is women's biological duty to ensure the survival of species. Miller clearly recognizes that these narratives are ripe for generational renewal and cultural reappropriation. Miller's *Mad Max* films provide a lens (or perhaps four snapshots) to examine filmic representations of patriarchal society and to observe the changing status of women on screen in the sci-fi genre from 1979 to 2015 (and now beyond).

The first *Mad Max* (1979) film was followed by *Mad Max 2* (aka *The Road Warrior*) (1982), *Mad Max: Beyond Thunderdome* (1985) and then thirty years later, *Mad Max: Fury Road* (2015). In April 2021, Miller announced that another instalment (a prequel to *Fury Road*), tentatively titled *Furiosa*, will soon be filmed in New South Wales, Australia. It will star Australian Chris Hemsworth (*Thor*) with Anya Taylor-Joy (*The Queen's Gambit*) in the title role as a young Furiosa. Given

267

their longevity, the *Mad Max* films offer a rich case study about intertextuality, pastiche, bricolage and the status of sequels and adaptations. Are the *Mad Max* films responses to 1950s sci-fi films, and are Miller's second, third, and fourth films sequels or adaptations of the original *Mad Max*? A case could be made that the latter *Mad Max* films are both sequels *and* adaptations which each speak to the ethos of the era in which they are made. The sequels function as adaptations of the earlier films in the cycle, with the first film an example of Australian Gothic and the later films transnational sci-fi action films and the type of spectacular disaster films famously discussed by Susan Sontag in her 1965 essay "The Imagination of Disaster" with its arguments about trauma and the aesthetics of destruction (Sontag 108). Following Sontag, and as Jeffrey Womack argues, sci-fi is uniquely positioned to explore (at a metaphorical level) and potentially exorcise that trauma (Womack 73).

1950s Sci-fi Disaster Films

In the 1950s, teenagers could indulge in two relatively new American loves—cars and movies—at the drive-in where they could marvel at the delicious horrors on the screen and scream and giggle with impunity. Despite the obvious attractions of spaceships, aliens, monsters, and giant spiders, 1950s sci-fi films were also popular because they addressed urgent social issues. Many of the films are extremely bleak and commence with an apocalyptic montage and a narrator intoning gravely that humanity is responsible for devastating environmental destruction. Accordingly, scholarship about 1950s sci-fi films typically clusters around three issues: Cold War ideology, fear of communism and potentially another world war (*Invasion of the Body Snatchers, The Brain Eaters, Invaders from Mars*); the military and research science resulting in the Atomic Age and nuclear destruction and long-lasting toxic fallout and contamination (*The Day the Earth Stood Still, Teenage Caveman, Beginning of the End, On the Beach*); and anxiety about reproduction, race, power, and gender roles in this new post–World War II or post-apocalyptic environment (*Five, The World, the Flesh and the Devil, Captive Women, Day the World Ended, Last Woman on Earth*). The latter two themes are most relevant in this essay.

One of the reasons that 1950s sci-fi and horror films like *The Incredible Shrinking Man* (1957), *The Fly* (1958) and *I Married a Monster from Outer Space* (1958) are of such interest to critics like Mark Jancovich (1996) is that they showcase culturally and historically embedded anxiety about threats to the family and traditional gender roles and marriage. In post-apocalyptic films like *Five, Day the World Ended, The World, the Flesh and the Devil,* and *Last Woman on Earth,* a recurring trope about the maternal body is revisited. Following a nuclear disaster, a limited number of young fertile women survive, and men compete for mating privileges in order to ensure the survival of the species. The aforementioned four very dark films do not feature monsters or aliens but instead explore post-apocalyptic scenarios where there is mass destruction, sickness and death following a nuclear accident or nuclear warfare. Society itself is monstrous.

Five (1951), produced, written, and directed by Arch Oboler, is "the first celluloid vision of an atomic apocalypse on Earth" (Stephens 131). It tells the story of "the day after tomorrow" and it is a pessimistic narrative haunted by the 1950s fear of a nuclear holocaust. Far bleaker and less optimistic than similar sci-fi films released soon after, the film is quite shocking in its representation of a desolate environment and desperate survivors. As the title suggests, five people survive the nuclear blast and subsequent fallout; a pregnant widow (Roseanne, played by Susan Douglas Rubeš) is at the center of the narrative. Michael (William Phipps), the first male survivor she encounters, is set up to play Adam to her Eve. Michael is not a particularly sympathetic character and at one point he tries to sexually assault Roseanne (a fact that is overlooked by critics like Stephens). The other three survivors include Eric (James Anderson), a racist, violent, selfish villain; Charles (Charles Lampkin), a kindly security guard; and Mr. Barnstaple (Earl Lee), an older, disorientated character and former assistant cashier in the bank where Charles was also employed. Although Michael, Charles and Roseanne work cooperatively, all of the characters are clearly haunted by their losses and suffering from trauma. Their numbers quickly dwindle as two of the men (Mr. Barnstaple and Eric) and Roseanne's baby subsequently die from radiation poisoning. The men fight over access to Roseanne, food, shelter, and resources, and this is further complicated by the issue of racism (Charles is African American and is murdered by Eric).[1] Roseanne is at the center of the narrative and her status as a pregnant recent widow signals that she is fertile and newly available. As Stephens notes, "The future of mankind depends on her procreative ability, so it makes sense that the de facto community would organize itself around her and the prospective birth of a child" (130). The scenes where Roseanne finds her husband's skeletal remains, escapes Eric and the city, and heads back to the house on foot are remarkably grim. The fact that her baby dies and that she carries the dead child back to bury it is harrowing to witness on the screen. Roseanne and Michael bury both Charles and the baby and survive to eke out an existence on the land in a desolated and isolated environment that is far from Edenic. The film closes with a final Biblical quotation from Revelation 21 signaling that there will be "no more sorrow" and "Behold! I make all things new!" but it is difficult to feel optimistic about their future.

In a similarly somber vein, in Roger Corman's *Day the World Ended* (1955), we are confronted by another "the day after" scenario. This time, Total Destruction day leaves Jim (Paul Birch) and his daughter Louise (Lori Nelson) alive with five other human survivors (and a mule). Jim has planned for this day but was not expecting to host non-family members and strangers (especially the gangster Tony and his girlfriend Ruby who Tony eventually murders). Issues such as xenophobia, racism, sexual violence, sacrifice and charity are some of the ethical topics addressed in the film. As Mortensen observes about a *Twilight Zone* episode titled "The Shelter," which explores a similar ethical scenario, "the 'fallout' of the nuclear arms race is not just radiation, but the threat of a dehumanising fear that unjustly places certain people above others" (74). The gangster Tony's violence and cruelty come to the fore when tested, whereas Rick (Richard Denning) soon establishes himself as the young hero and earns Louise's respect and love. Jim makes it clear to Louise that it is her obligation to have children to ensure the survival of the species, and Rick will make an ideal Adam to her Eve. In addition to dealing with Tony, the survivors are menaced by a "monster" who is a human with radiation sickness (presumably Louise's missing brother or fiancé). Most characters eventually kill each other or are killed by radiation with only Louise and Rick surviving. Jim manages to make contact by radio with others before he dies, and so Rick and Louise bravely venture out to start anew buoyed by the hope that there are other survivors. Corman ends the film on a positive note with the banner "The Beginning" rather than The End (he repeats this trope and many similar themes in *Last Woman on Earth* five years later). Louise's status as potential mother and savior of the human species (a new beginning) very clearly mirrors Roseanne's function in *Five*.

In *The World, the Flesh and the Devil* (1959), written and directed by Ranald MacDougall and starring Harry Belafonte (Ralph), we witness two male survivors of a nuclear blast (one White and one Black) competing for one (White) woman (Sarah, played by Inger Stevens). By 1959, this trope was well established, but this time the survivors head for the city (New York) rather than the country. Ralph is originally so lonely in the city that he "befriends" mannequins and role plays social interactions. After throwing a mannequin over a balcony, he is eventually joined by Sarah and then a second male, Ben (Mel Ferrer).[2] We learn little about Sarah, but she is presented as virginial, virtuous and kind. Sarah favors Ralph but the love triangle is complicated by Ralph's blackness. He struggles to consider a cross-racial relationship and racial anxiety permeates the relationships on screen. Prompted by Ben's aggression, it looks like the men will fight to the death for Sarah, but Ralph ultimately refuses to continue the fight and the film unpredictably ends with all three surviving and walking away hand in hand for a new "beginning" rather than an "end" (just as Corman concludes *Day the World Ended* several years earlier). The nature of the three-way relationship is left up in the air, but once again, it will be the surviving woman's role to ensure the survival of the species.

In Roger Corman's *Last Woman on Earth* (1960), he returns to the themes he explored several years earlier in *Day the World Ended*. This time, the plot is foreshadowed in the title with the appropriately named Evelyn (or Eve, played by Betsy Jones-Moreland) as the last woman on Earth, accompanied by her husband Harold (Antony Carbone) and their lawyer Martin (Robert Towne as Edward Wain). Rather than the usual mushroom cloud, the opening scene features a bloody cock fight, and this predicts the violence, jealousy and aggression that will develop between Harold and Martin. Even within this very bleak genre, this film is particularly pessimistic about human nature. All three unsympathetic characters survive a nuclear blast because they are under water scuba diving at the time the bomb drops. When they return to land, and to the life-saving oxygen generated by plants, the streets are full of the dead and the trio appear to be the last people on Earth. They load up a truck and another vehicle with supplies and head out of town where conflict and arguments about what best to do soon flare and then fester. The survival of the species clearly rests with Evelyn and she must choose between the two men, but Martin is pessimistic about the future and so reluctant to have children. Regardless, Martin and Evelyn plot to desert Harold, but he chases them down and the two men fight to the death in a church. Harold is victorious and emerges from the church

Figure 38. Riddon (Ron Randell) menaces a bound captive (Paula Dorety) in *Captive Women* (1952) (Everett Collection Inc./Alamy Stock Photo).

hand-in-hand with Evelyn with the clear message that they will continue life as man and wife to begin the task of continuing the human race. Although Evelyn is not presented as a virginial or even particularly likeable character, she survives and has value because she can reproduce.

This theme becomes more overt but less pessimistic in more fanciful films like *Captive Women* (1952) and *World Without End* (1956) where many of the survivors are "mutants" competing for undamaged women. Stuart Gilmore's *Captive Women*

Figure 39. Riddon (Ron Randell) subdues captives (Paula Dorety, left, and Chili Williams) in *Captive Women* (1952) (Everett Collection Inc./Alamy Stock Photo).

starts with a mushroom cloud and a bleak warning about what the world *might* look like in 3000 AD if they continue down a nuclear path. In this post-apocalyptic setting, survivors are divided into Norms (who live underground to protect themselves from radiation), the roaming Upriver Men led by Gordon (Stuart Randall), and the Mutates (those damaged by radiation). They have forgotten all of the old technologies and knowledge of "the ancients" and live a primitive life hunting and gathering (in the style of a sci-fi Robin Hood). The central story line is that Mutates capture and rape healthy and (conveniently) scantily dressed Norm women in an attempt to breed out the genetic abnormalities, but the children are always born with deformities and never survive. The narrative ends up being a more positive one as a Norm woman (Ruth played by Margaret Field) and a (marginally) deformed leader of the Mutates (Riddon played by Ron Randell) fall in love and the film ends with their marriage and the hope that their children, resulting from consensual sex rather than rape, will survive and lead to societal renewal. Again, the future rests with Ruth and other Norm women to ensure the survival of the species.

Edward Bernds' *World Without End*, starring Hugh Marlowe, Nancy Gates, Nelson Leigh and Rod Taylor, is similarly set in the future in a post-apocalyptic setting where a group of astronauts have accidentally found themselves two hundred years in the future on Earth due to a time dilation that occurs on their way back from Mars. Like the previous film, a small number of humans survive as mutates ("beasts" or "cavemen") who live in caves and roam above ground seeking unblemished women for breeding purposes (the children resulting from these unions do survive) and as slaves. The normal humans live entirely underground where, over generations, the men have become increasingly weak and less virile. The women, however, appear both nubile and robust (perhaps threateningly so). The astronauts

Figure 40. Deena (Lisa Montell) under threat in *World Without End* (1956) (Everett Collection Inc./Alamy Stock Photo).

go to battle with the mutates (and giant spiders) and eventually bring peace and reconciliation between the warring tribes. The women, once again, are valued for their healthy wombs and ability to produce viable children to repopulate Earth. The women are essentialized to their reproductive function and maternal role which means that they have no other skills to contribute to society. The women are not trained as soldiers, astronauts, engineers, pilots, doctors, or mechanics and so their sole value is their ability to give birth and ensure the survival of the species. An unblemished healthy body (the maternal body) is required in order for them to demonstrate their worth in the apocalyptic setting.

Looking ahead to sci-fi and horror films in later decades, a fascination with controlling reproduction is played out over and over again in films that feature robots, androids, and cyborgs. Critics like Donna Haraway and Mary Ann Doane are justifiably lauded for their scholarship in this area about gender and technology. As Telotte summarizes in *Science Fiction Film*, the films reflect "the dominant culture's efforts 'to control, supervise, regulate the maternal—to put limits on it'" (Doane in Telotte, 50). Similarly, a fascination with women's bodies as monstrous (abject and thus bloodied, messy, leaking) and with the vagina dentata in sci-fi and horror has been the subject of much feminist and psychological scholarship. Barbara Creed is also influential for her seminal work in *The Monstrous-Feminine* (1993) and *Phallic Panic* (2005) on later horror and sci-fi films. These earlier films from the 1950s, however, establish this trope about access to and ownership of women's bodies (wombs) and decades later Miller revisits and adapts that trope in *Fury Road*.

George Miller's Mad Max *Film Cycle*

The *Mad Max* films afford a rare opportunity to examine a sci-fi film cycle, created by a single director[3] and featuring the same protagonist (albeit one played by one actor [Mel Gibson] in the first three films and another actor [Tom Hardy] in the fourth) across almost half a century.[4] Like so many 1950s sci-fi films, the *Mad Max* sequels are all set in irradiated deserts. As Jeffrey Womack notes, the iconography of nuclear tests conducted in desert landscapes like New Mexico and Nevada have elided into an accepted film trope where a post-apocalyptic aesthetic is necessarily a desert aesthetic (81–82). The landscape of the *Mad Max* cycle is a wasteland that deteriorates across the forty-year cycle foretelling millennial fears of environmental collapse. The pall of nuclear destruction hangs over these films and Mick Broderick's filmography *Nuclear Movies* (1988) lists over 500 films dealing with the theme, dating from 1914 to 1988. Jerome Shapiro's *Atomic Bomb Cinema* (2002) builds on Broderick's work and notes that since 1945, over a thousand films have featured images of nuclear weapons and destruction (6). Shapiro calls this the "apocalyptic imagination," but it is also apocalyptic imitation with each adaptation creatively interpreting and extending the eschatological social imaginary (5). Filmmakers continue to remake and reuse atomic images and themes with most following a formula to set up and conclude the action. Accordingly, films like *Five, Captive Women, Day the World Ended*, and *Teenage Caveman* (1958) all start with the image of a mushroom cloud and a warning about military aggression. It is also commonplace to see the devastated ruins or empty streets of great cities like London, Paris and New York in the opening credits (*Captive Women, Five, The World, the Flesh the Devil*).[5] It is usually sufficient backstory for the narrator to warn about the devastation that is wrought by war, disease, waste and technology, and the *Mad Max* films set the scene very economically in this fashion. Thus, the *Mad Max* films increasingly tell a moral story about technology and the environment to the extent that *Fury Road* has been described as "eco-feminist" (Yates). However, can the films moralize about the environment while at the same time functioning as sci-fi car crash action films? As Sontag suggests, sci-fi films are "strongly moralistic" about the "proper or humane" use of science (105) and this is clearly Miller's intention, but the films convey a very mixed message about both gender and technology.

The *Mad Max* films are often described as sci-fi Westerns, but they are also examples of Australian Ozploitation "car crash" films (as defined by Dermody and Jacka 98). With their connection to early hot-rodding films like *Hot Rod Girl* (1956), *Hot Rod Gang* (1958), and *Dragstrip Riot* (1958), the indirect adaptations that emerged in the Antipodes several decades later center on cars crashing, smashing, exploding, and igniting. In addition to those films specifically focused on cars and "hot rodding," teenage culture and a rise in car ownership are explored in films like *Rebel Without a Cause* (1955) where cars play a pivotal role in the narrative and are associated with masculine rites of passage. Automobiles are not only signs of conspicuous consumption and technological advances but are also often featured prominently as a sign of adulthood, freedom, and masculinity. From that perspective, and within the context of sci-fi, the films interrogate men's relationship with other men and with technology. As Sontag asserts, "it is a question of scale" and there are "peculiar beauties to be found in wreaking havoc, making a mess" (102). Indeed, as Catherine Simpson observes, there are so many car crashes and stalled cars in Australian cinema, and in our car culture more generally, that car crashes are represented on film as normalized or routine, what she calls an "everyday and acceptable form of violence" and part of Australia's "social imaginary" (n.p.). We may be thrilled or horrified by the violence but we are not surprised by its ferocity or frequency as we have seen it on the big screen over and over. Thus, following Linda Hutcheon, we have "repetition without replication" (xvi) as each text references what comes before in acts of subtle homage or outright imitation.

Miller's aesthetics of destruction, however, have been indelibly imprinted in audiences' memories and, as Dan Hassler-Forest observes, so influential are the films that "the term '*Mad Max* future' instantly brings to mind a harsh landscape of ecological devastation, resource scarcity and the total breakdown of institutions" (301). The consequences of this environmental devastation are a celluloid environment where lives and livings must be scraped together by salvaging whatever tools and materials are at hand. As we see in films like *Captive Women* and *Teenage Caveman*, so-called "ancient" technologies like books, hi-tech engineering, architecture, electricity, radio, television, engines, and cars have all been lost, and society has regressed to a more atavistic state (conveniently allowing filmmakers to adorn their actors in loin cloths and scanty bikinis). Miller accentuates this loss of scientific knowledge and culture, and as the cycle progresses, society loses the ability to manufacture technology in cities and factories and instead citizens have become desert scavengers. In this context, those with access to motor vehicles and fuel are privileged and frequently cast as heroic. Miller picks up on these tropes and as the franchise matures, cars and technology survive but in smaller numbers, and roads gradually disappear and are covered by sand dunes.[6] In many Australian narratives there appears to be a validation of the use of technology at the expense of the environment, and as a means of marking the landscape as *terra nullia* or *tabula rasa*.[7] When characters attempt to walk, drive, or ride across the desert, they meet with disaster, and more often than not they are swallowed up by the sand. Indeed, this occurs in *Fury Road* where a spectacular dust storm creates its own weather system with destructive winds and terrifying lightening.[8]

Given that Miller's films are responses to 1950s tropes, what we witness across the cycle is the shift from Max as heteronormative family man with a wife, son, and a job as a police officer, to a loner confronted by queer bikers in the first and second films to a largely asexual existence in the third and fourth films.[9] We witness hostility toward women and traditional family structures in the first film as women are exterminated; to the situation in the fourth film where healthy women are scarce resources required for breeding. This signals a significant change in the status of women, and also speaks to the shift in genre from Gothic horror in the first film to sci-fi in the later films (Hassler-Forest 305). Miller's message about technology and the environment is a mixed one, the status of women across the cycle is perhaps more complex than it first appears.

Max is vulnerable in the first film when he is a married man and father but more stoic and lacking in affect as the series progresses, as he does not have a family to protect and nurture. It is clearly not Max's role to have any further children or to contribute to repopulation. Miller has been quoted as saying that in apocalyptic environments, heterosexual romance and family life would not be the norm when infants would be unlikely to survive (Martin 50). Max is increasingly dispassionate about women and indeed in the second (Warrior Woman), third (Aunty Entity, Savannah Nix), and fourth (Furiosa, the Valkyrie, the Five Wives) films he engages cooperatively with women, but he is not interested in them sexually.[10] In the first and second films, if Max is nervous or anxious about any characters sexually, it is the queer and camp male characters, not the women (Johinke, "Manifestations"). Over the course of the films, he is increasingly tortured and traumatized by loss and guilt and in search of redemption (as is Furiosa), but he is never intimidated by women or made to feel impotent, unlike characters from 1950s science films like *The Incredible Shrinking Man* and *I Married a Monster from Outer Space* (Wells). He is both the same and a different man. As Sontag suggests, in sci-fi disaster narratives "the lure of such generalised disaster as a fantasy is that it releases one from normal obligations and … the whole movie can be devoted to the fantasy of occupying the deserted metropolis and starting all over again" (103). In the later films, and indeed at the beginning of every sequel, Max starts again.

In *Mad Max 2*, with Warrior Woman eliminated, the role of the surviving female characters is familiar to viewers of 1950s sci-fi films. Curmudgeon informs

Max that the survivors' chief role will be performed in Queensland, where they will be required to "breeeeeed." This scenario again places women in the domestic sphere and inscribes them as sexual objects or mothers. Thirty years later, *Fury Road* picks up on this theme of women as breeders *and* warriors. It is notable that, until *Fury Road*, the female characters in this car-centered cycle rarely drive. At the beginning of the franchise in the 1970s, when Jessie gets behind the wheel, both episodes end in disaster. In the second film, Warrior Woman (Virginia Hey) is a respected combatant but not a driver. It is only when the roads disappear in the third film that women command more screen space, and we are introduced to Aunty Entity (Tina Turner) and Savannah Nix (Helen Buday).[11] In *Fury Road,* Max is played by Tom Hardy rather than Mel Gibson. This was a savvy but brave move on Miller's part as this enables the franchise and Max's status to endure without being potentially tarnished by associations with Gibson.[12] In this installment, Max plays the able sidekick with Imperator Furiosa (Charlize Theron) at the center of the film as an established driver, warrior, and leader. Thus, the focus shifts from an older and less marketable Mel Gibson to two younger, popular, and less polarizing actors. The fact that so many characters and viewers accept Furiosa as a worthy lead character in a franchise centering around the eponymous Max is perhaps the biggest surprise of the cycle. Indeed, even suspicious men's rights activists who were enraged by the prospect of Furiosa's dominance in *Fury Road* appear to have been won over (De Coning 174; Broderick and Ellis 54–55).

Unambiguously the best driver, Furiosa is entrusted to drive the War Rig on missions to places like Gas Town and the Bullet Farm and is revered as a capable "boss" by the War Boys. Thus, although heroism is still performed behind the wheel, our hero is a female driver, and she too is part machine (one arm is partially amputated and she wears a prosthetic). Indeed, much in the way that Max has typically been conflated with his car, Broderick and Ellis go as far as to say that "Furiosa *is* the Interceptor as her amputated arm merges with machines to render her the superior road warrior" (8). The characters recognize each other's skills and work cooperatively, and Max does not appear to be threatened by her competence, strength or her physical stature. In one scene Max hands a rifle to Furiosa and even permits her to use his shoulder as a prop as she is a better shot than him. As Yates observes: "Max is not reduced to a passive object as the women ascend to agency. Max's agency is both inspired by and supports the agency of the feminine" (360). Unlike Immortan Joe (played by Hugh Keays-Byrne who played Toecutter in *Mad Max*), Max is pragmatic enough to accept his status in relation to Furiosa who is a feted hero (albeit within Joe's regime). In this rescue narrative, it is another woman (Furiosa) who rescues the captive women (the Five Wives). Max not only shares the role of protagonist and heroic driver with Furiosa but most of the central characters are women: the Five Wives, the Valkyrie (Megan Gale) and the Many Mothers (wizened competent bikies) are members of the Vuvalini tribe from the Green Place. Apart from the first scene where Max is pursued and captured by the War Boys, almost every frame includes a woman as a central part of the action.

Thus, in *Fury Road* we see a shift in gender politics and the role of women on screen (albeit one written and directed by men), but a familiar commentary about the environment. Again, we see repetition without replication and a conscious revisitation of earlier themes. Despite an obvious wish to retell Max's story in a feminist context, Miller could be accused of both subverting and reinforcing gender stereotypes and a conservative social regime. In Sontag's terms, sci-fi "movies are in complicity with the abhorrent. They neutralize it" (113). Thus, despite Furiosa's tough, heroic role, and the competence of the motorcycle-riding Vuvalini, by the end of the film when women have seized control of the Citadel they are still typecast as Earth mothers who will heal the damaged environment. Before she dies, The Keeper of the Seeds hands over her legacy to one of the (pregnant) wives. Women, as is so often the case, are essentialized as nurturers and healers so much so that earlier in the film we see a room of corpulent naked women cradling dolls and hooked up to a milking machine to provide Mother's Milk for the chosen few in the Citadel. Although fuel is still a valuable commodity in *Fury Road*, water (dubbed "Aqua Cola" by Joe), blood, and milk are equally valuable liquid resources. Environmental politics and the politics of reproduction are showcased along with the car crashes. Rather than technology being required to "repair the damaged environment" (105) as Sontag predicted back in 1965, technology as it is employed across the expanse of the films, is the cause of the damage (just as it was in 1950s films). The social criticism is perhaps more compromised as Miller both succeeds and fails in this quest to tell a different story about Max, reproduction rights, and about patriarchal society.

Just like the characters in *Captive Women* and *World Without End*, in *Fury Road* most of the population suffer disabilities arising from accidents and environmental destruction (presumably radiation). Even the relatively able-bodied general populace

Figure 41. From left: The Dag (Abbey Lee), Cheedo the Fragile (Courtney Eaton), and Toast the Knowing (Zoë Kravitz), three of Immortan Joe's wives in *Mad Max: Fury Road* (2015) (Warner Bros./Photofest).

is emaciated and desperate for food and water. As Broderick and Ellis observe: "Max inhabits a post-catastrophe environment, one unnaturally contaminated by radiation and other toxins that have leached their way into the ecology and the very marrow of humanity, metastasising into diseases, mutation, scars, birth defects and tumours evident in the remnant population" (20). As Sontag enthuses, one of sci-fi film's "unique strengths" is "the immediate representation of the extraordinary: physical deformity and mutation" and "the undeniable pleasure we derive from looking at freaks" (101, 104). Enter the monstrous Immortan Joe, who has ulcerated flesh and wears a frightening breathing apparatus adorned with huge yellow teeth. Most of his offspring have disabilities or die prematurely. Similarly, the sickly War Boys have limited lifespans and are all fodder for Joe's battles, as he has indoctrinated them in the belief that their deaths are glorious sacrifices and that they will live again in the afterlife (another remake, perhaps?). In this environment, Max's body becomes a text that is branded with his "traumatic history" when his back is tattooed with a catalogue of his organs that might be utilized as spare parts (Broderick and Ellis 22). Although certainly battle weary and traumatized, he is still a useful commodity.[13] Max, however, cannot give birth.

Just as was the case in sci-fi from the 1950s, if most of the characters on screen are desperate, damaged or disabled, this makes any attractive and healthy inhabitants particularly valuable commodities (especially for reproductive purposes). Accordingly, Joe keeps his Five Wives captive in a chamber resembling a giant bank vault. Joe's treasures are normatively beautiful young women ("prize breeders") and are played by model/actresses Rosie Huntington-Whiteley, Riley Keough, Abbey Lee, Courtney Eaton, and Zoë Kravitz as the pneumatic wives. Joe's favorite wife, Splendid Angharad, is pregnant. When she is mortally wounded, Joe's concern is for his child, not his wife and hence her status as decorative breeder is emphasized. Rictus Erectus laments that the unborn baby was "perfect in every way" and it is clear that just like "norm" women who are abducted by "mutants" in *Captive Women*, Splendid's function is to provide "superior" healthy babies for society—to improve the blood line as a form of eugenics. Interestingly, Miller employed Eve Ensler (author of *The Vagina Monologues*) to coach the actors playing the wives about the gender politics of the film (Broderick and Ellis 65). To highlight the film's feminist credentials, the walls of the harem are daubed with slogans such as "Our babies will not be warlords," "Who killed the world?," "You cannot own a human being," and "We are not things." At various points in the action the wives repeat these mantras protesting their objectification and lack of agency in this toxic patriarchy (all the while offered up to the male gaze clad in bikinis and chastity belts as if straight out of a Victoria's Secret catwalk or the set of *Captive Women*). This, I suggest, is another example of the contradictions inherent in the films as they both critique and profit from popular culture and the exploitation of women.[14] Aesthetics are key.

Conclusion

Not only do George Miller's *Mad Max* films showcase a fascination with the car crash and with the spectacular aesthetics of destruction that Sontag explores, but they also increasingly fetishize women's bodies and reproductive capabilities. Given the longevity of the franchise, viewers witness how Miller interrogates and problematizes gender, sexuality, and power across the four-decade cycle of the films. The *Mad Max* films revisit, reinvent and retell the same story over and over about gender and technology and the aesthetics of violence and destruction. As he does at the end of every film, Max walks away from the community and goes it alone on the road (or off road, as it may be) and the story starts again where Max (as reluctant hero) will be called upon again to do battle against evil. There is both circularity and stasis, which is what viewers could logically expect of car crash films, and of sequels and adaptations. Each film acts as a time capsule capturing the zeitgeist about the gender and environmental politics of the time. By the (current) end to the cycle, we witness the empowerment of women with Furiosa as a strong, heroic woman respected by all, but we are also confronted with everyday sexism and routinised violence toward women like the Five Wives who are still only valued for their aesthetic value and their breeding potential. Despite some missteps, Miller is clearly headed backwards in the right direction in 2021 as he begins again with the production of *Furiosa*.

Disaster, as Sontag foretold in 1965, "is one of the oldest subjects of art" (101) which is why filmmakers keep remaking them and audiences keep returning to them. As this edited collection demonstrates, and as many scholars have argued previously, the same themes and anxieties are constantly reworked in remakes of 1950s sci-fi and horror films. Fans of these cult films return again and again to have their fantasies renewed and reinvigorated, to experience the visual and visceral pleasures of fast cars performing cinematic stunts. There is both pleasure and resignation in the familiar, in indulging in wish fulfilment, and ritualized social integration. Sometimes we do and do not want these stories to end and perhaps wish they had a different ending—one more like a 1950s sci-fi film—a beginning.

Acknowledgment

Thank you to Blythe Worthy for sourcing the images and thank you to Everett Collection Inc./Alamy Stock Photo for permitting them to be reproduced for this collection.

NOTES

1. The issue of race in sci-fi is not a focus of this essay but it receives scholarly attention in books like Isaiah Lavender, III, ed., *Black and Brown Planets: The Politics of Race in Science Fiction* (Jackson: University Press of Mississippi, 2014) and *Race in American Science Fiction* (Bloomington: Indiana University Press, 2011). See also William Hart's essay in this collection.

2. A female mannequin is executed in the first *Mad Max* film. Mannequins frequently appear in sci-fi narratives and serve to highlight characters' isolation and loneliness. See, for example, the *Twilight Zone* episode "Where Is Everybody?'" and Will Smith's interaction with mannequins in *I Am Legend* (2007) and Number Five's mannequin friend in *Umbrella Academy*. The liminal status of mannequins in the form of robots is obviously a theme explored frequently in sci-fi once technology has advanced enough to make life-like robots believable on screen.

3. For simplicity's sake, I will refer to Miller as the auteur of the *Mad Max* films. I acknowledge, however,

Byron Kennedy's role as producer of the first two films (he died in a helicopter crash in 1983) and the input of Terry Hayes and George Ogilvie in the second and third films.

4. The Ridley Scott *Alien* franchise starring Sigourney Weaver as Ripley is another example.

5. At the end of the third *Mad Max* film, *Mad Max Beyond Thunderdome* (1985), we see a band of survivors from the Lost Tribe heading for the bombed-out shell of Sydney.

6. Critics such as Falconer, Rummery, Broderick and Broderick and Ellis have all discussed the dominance of oil crisis or nuclear Armageddon tropes in the *Mad Max* films.

7. See Rummery, Falconer, and Haynes re: depictions of the landscape and desert in the first three films. Falconer and Gibson have written at some length about the disappearance of roads in *Beyond Thunderdome*.

8. More broadly, such images speak to typical nuclear firestorm tropes discussed by Toni Perrine and many others in their analysis of post-war disaster films (241). Aylish Wood's "*Mad Max: Fury Road* and the Toxic Storm: The Transcalar Possibilities of Digital Images" provides a comprehensive analysis of the technical and digital effects required to create that scene.

9. See Johinke ("Manifestations") for an extended argument about Max's interactions with the queer bikers.

10. As Meaghan Morris noted many years ago, heterosexual romances are remarkably absent from Australian films.

11. Savannah Nix is the leader of the Lost Tribe of children and, although an understated character, is perhaps the most powerful female character in the first three films. There are several parallels between *Beyond Thunderdome* and *Teenage Caveman*, with Nix a brave and curious young character like the Symbol Maker's son.

12. Notwithstanding his considerable success as an actor and director, for some years, Gibson has been embroiled in controversies relating to racism, homophobia, alcohol abuse, and domestic violence.

13. In car crash films more generally, stage-managed "accidents" are often the only way to garner parts. Indeed, the cars are often so central to the cultural and commercial economy in car crash films (like *The Cars That Ate Paris*) that they are responsible for births, deaths, and mechanical "marriages" (see, for example, Johinke, "Not Quite *Mad Max*" and "Uncanny Carnage").

14. Yates provides a helpful summary of some of the initial film reviews and debate about whether it is a feminist movie or whether it is a stereotypical "Edenic recovery narrative" (253–54).

WORKS CITED

Broderick, Mick. "Heroic Apocalypse: Mad Max, Mythology and the Millennium." *Crisis Cinema: The Apocalyptic Idea in Postmodern Narrative Film*. edited by Chris Sharrett. Maissoneuvre, 1993, pp. 250–72.

_____. *Nuclear Movies: A Filmography*. Post-Modem, 1988.

_____. "Surviving Armageddon: Beyond the Imagination of Disaster." *Science Fiction Studies* 20.3 (1993): pp. 362–382.

Broderick, Mick, and Katie Ellis. *Trauma and Disability in Mad Max: Beyond the Road Warrior's Fury*. Palgrave Pivot, 2019.

Corbett, Claire. "Nowhere to Run: Repetition Compulsion and Heterotopia in the Australian Post-Apocalypse—from 'Crabs' to *Mad Max Beyond Thunderdome*." *Science Fiction Film and Television* 10.3 (2017): 329–51.

Creed, Barbara. *The Monstrous-Feminine*. Routledge, 1993.

_____. *Phallic Panic*. Melbourne University Press, 2005.

De Coning, Alexis. "Recouping Masculinity: Men's Rights Activists' Responses to *Mad Max: Fury Road*." *Feminist Media Studies* 16.1 (2016): 174–76.

Dermody, Susan, and Elizabeth Jacka. *The Screening of Australia: Anatomy of a National Cinema*. Vol 2. Currency Press, 1988.

Doane, Mary Ann. "Technophilia: Technology, Representation, and the Feminine." *Body/Politics: Women and the Discourse of Science*, edited by Mary Jacobus, Evelyn Fox Keller, and Sally Shuttleworth. Routledge, 1990, 163–76.

Donovan, Barna William. *Blood, Guns, and Testosterone: Action Films, Audiences, and a Thirst for Violence*. Scarecrow Press, 2010.

Falconer, Delia. "Vanishing Points: Mapping the Road in Postwar American Culture." Diss., Melbourne University, 1995.

_____. "'We Don't Need to Know the Way Home': Selling Australian Space in the *Mad Max* Trilogy." *Southern Review* 27 (1994): 28–44.

Gibson, Ross. "Formative landscapes." *Australian Cinema*, edited by Scott Murray. Allen & Unwin, Australian Film Commission, 1994, pp. 45–59.

_____. "Yondering: A Reading of *Mad Max Beyond Thunderdome*." *South of the West*. Indiana University Press, 1992, pp. 158–77.

Haraway, Donna. *Simians, Cyborgs and Women: The Reinvention of Nature.* Routledge, 1991.

Hassler-Forest, Dan. "*Mad Max*: Between Apocalypse and Utopia." *Science Fiction Film and Television* 10.3 (2017): 301–06.

Haynes, Roslynn D. *Seeking the Centre: The Australian Desert in Literature, Art and Film.* Cambridge University Press, 1998.

Hendershot, Cyndy. *Paranoia, the Bomb, and 1950s Science Fiction Films.* Bowling Green State University Popular Press, 1999.

Hutcheon, Linda. *A Theory of Adaptation.* Routledge, 2005.

Jancovich, Mark. *Rational Fears. American Horror in the 1950s.* Manchester University Press, 1996.

Johinke, Rebecca. "Manifestations of Masculinities: *Mad Max* and the Lure of the Forbidden Zone." *Journal of Australian Studies*, 67 (2001): 118–11.

_____. "Misogyny, Muscles and Machines: Cars and Masculinity in Australian Literature." *Australian Studies* 15.2 (2000): 95–111.

_____. "Not Quite *Mad Max*: Brian Trenchard-Smith's *Dead End Drive-In*." *Studies in Australasian Cinema* 3.3 (2009): 309–20.

_____. "Uncanny Carnage in Peter Weir's *The Cars That Ate Paris*." *Sydney Studies in English*, 36 (2010), 108–26.

Jones, Nick. "The Perpetual Motion Aesthetic of Action Cinema." *A Companion to the Action Film*, edited by James Kendrick. Wiley Blackwell, 2019, pp. 99–117.

Lavender, Isiah III, ed. *Black and Brown Planets: The Politics of Race in Science Fiction.* University Press of Mississippi, 2014.

_____. *Race in American Science Fiction.* Indiana University Press, 2011.

Martin, Adrian. *The Mad Max Movies.* Currency Press, 2003.

Matthews, Sue. *35mm Dreams.* Penguin, 1984.

Morris, Meaghan. "Personal Relationships and Sexuality." *The New Australian Cinema*, edited by Scott Murray. Nelson, 1980, pp. 138–51.

Mortenson, Erik. "A Journey into the Shadows: *The Twilight Zone's* Visual Critique of the Cold War." *Science Fiction Film and Television* 7.1 (2014): 55–76.

Perrine, Toni A. *Film and the Nuclear Age: Representing Cultural Anxiety.* Garland, 1998.

Rummery, Ariane. "Oltre Nature—Landscape, Technology and Australian Films." *On the Beach* 13 (1988): 45–53.

Shapiro, Jerome R. *Atomic Bomb Cinema: The Apocalyptic Imagination on Film.* Routledge, 2002.

Simpson, Catherine. "Antipodean Automobility and Crash: Treachery, Trespass and Transportation of the Open Road." *Australian Humanities Review* (2006): 39–40, https://eprints.qut.edu.au/69244/1/simpson.html. Accessed 28 Dec. 2021.

Sontag, Susan. "The Imagination of Disaster." *The Science Fiction Film Reader*, edited by Gregg Rickman. Limelight, 2004, pp. 98–113.

Stephens, Bob. "D Is for Doomsday: *Five.*" *The Science Fiction Film Reader*, edited by Gregg Rickman. Limelight, 2004, pp. 114–31.

Telotte, J.P. *Science Fiction Film.* Cambridge University Press, 2001.

Wells, Paul. "The Invisible Man: Shrinking Masculinity in the 1950s Science Fiction B-Movie." *You Tarzan: Masculinity, Movies and Men*, edited by Pat Kirkham and Janet Thumin. Lawrence and Wishart, 1993.

Womack, Jeffrey. "Nuclear Weapons, Dystopian Deserts, and Science Fiction Cinema." *Vulcan* 1 (2013): 70–85.

Wood, Aylish. "*Mad Max: Fury Road* and the Toxic Storm: The Transcalar Possibilities of Digital Images." *Screen* 61.1 (2020): 75–97.

Yates, Michelle. "Re-Casting Nature as Feminist Space in *Mad Max: Fury Road*." *Science Fiction Film and Television* 10.3 (2017): 353–70.

Filmography

Beginning of the End. Dir. Bert I. Gordon. Republic Pictures, 1957. Film.

The Brain Eaters. Dir. Bruno VeSota. American International Pictures, 1958. Film.

Captive Women. Dir. Stuart Gilmore. RKO Radio Pictures, 1952. Film.

The Cars That Ate Paris. Dir. Peter Weir. British Empire Films, 1974. Film.

The Day the Earth Stood Still. Dir. Robert Wise. 20th Century Fox, 1951. Film.

Day the World Ended. Dir. Roger Corman. Golden State Productions, 1955. Film.

Five. Dir. Arch Oboler. Columbia Pictures, 1951. Film.

The Fly. Dir. Kurt Neumann. 20th Century Fox, 1958. Film.

The Giant Gila Monster. Dir. Ray Kellogg. McLendon-Radio Pictures Distributing Company, 1959. Film.

Godzilla. Dir. Ishiro Honda. Toho Studios, 1954. Film.

Hot Rod Gang. Dir. Lew Landers. American International Pictures, 1958. Film.

Hot Rod Girl. Dir. Leslie H. Martinson. American International Pictures, 1956. Film.

The Incredible Shrinking Man. Dir. Jack Arnold. Universal Pictures, 1957. Film.

I Married a Monster from Outer Space. Dir. Gene Fowler, Jr. Paramount Pictures, 1958. Film.

Invaders from Mars. Dir. William Cameron Menzies. 20th Century Fox, 1953. Film.

Invasion of the Body Snatchers. Dir. Don Siegel. Allied Artists Pictures, 1956. Film.

Last Woman on Earth. Dir. Roger Corman. Filmgroup, 1960. Film.

Mad Max. Dir. George Miller. Warner Bros, 1979. Film.

Mad Max 3: Beyond Thunderdome. Dir. George Miller and George Ogilvie. Warner Bros, 1985. Film.

Mad Max: Fury Road. Dir. George Miller. Warner Bros, 2015. Film.

Mad Max 2. Dir. George Miller. Warner Bros, 1981. Film.

On the Beach. Dir. Stanley Kramer. United Artists, 1959. Film.

Teenage Caveman. Dir. Robert Corman. American International Pictures, 1958. Film.

Them! Dir. Gordon Douglas. Warner Bros, 1954. Film.

The Twilight Zone. CBS, 1959–1964. TV Series.

The World, the Flesh and the Devil. Dir. Ranald MacDougall. MGM, 1959. Film.

World Without End. Dir. Edward Bernds. Allied Artists Pictures Corporation, 1956. Film.

Afterword

Yesterday's Tomorrows: The Double Consciousness of Science Fiction

Thomas Leitch

One of the questions that Dennis R. Cutchins, when he invited me to write an overview for this volume, left up in the air was whether it would be a Foreword or an Afterword. At the time I was puzzled by his apparent indecision, but once I read and reflected on his own Introduction and the seventeen essays that followed, it made perfect sense. For if there is one overriding takeaway from this rich assortment, it is that just as looking outside your familiar sphere inevitably encourages you to look inside it with fresh eyes, looking into the future is inseparable from looking into the past.

These apparent contradictions are effectively masked by the label "science fiction," which implies that the genre, like science itself, is progressive. But the genre's equivocations, which register as early as H.G. Wells' darkly imagined *The Time Machine*, *The Invisible Man*, and *The War of the Worlds*, would probably be equally obscured by alternative labels like "speculative fiction" or "futuristic fiction" or "prophecy." The first label, routinely applied to science fiction even though all fiction is in an obvious sense hypothetical or speculative, implies that the speculations of science fiction are different in degree but not in kind from those of historical fiction or what might as well be called present-day fiction. The second implies a report from the future, a best guess about where our world is heading based on a reading of present conditions. And of course the third is automatically assumed to be truthful; that is why "false prophecy" is assumed to be a deviation from "true prophecy," a label that is hardly ever used in place of "prophecy."

But science itself, as Wells was perhaps the first notable novelist to point out, is deeply equivocal, and the progressive narrative it claims for its discoveries and their impact on the world makes it all the more equivocal. So it is eminently logical for the essays collected here to revisit visions of the future rooted firmly in the past, looking forward as they look back. The utopian or dystopian landscapes of science fiction have always been designed to tell their audience at least as much about the present as the future, and since that audience continues to change as the futuristic stories, fading into the past, seek ever new audiences, they tell us a great deal about the past of their former audiences as well. Even more important, they invite us to make connections between the past, the present, and the future, and to consider the ways those connections are subject to change.

Behind their different interests and emphases, all the essays in this volume are united by the observation that science fiction encourages audiences to move both forward and backward in time and sensibility. In this regard, as several of them explicitly note, science fiction operates as a genre the same way that adaptation and remaking do as generic or meta-generic processes. Like the process of recognizing any adaptation as an adaptation, the creation, performance, and consumption of science fiction absolutely requires this movement at every moment. Whatever perspectives science fiction may present, its defining perspective, a future world presented to audiences living in a present world, is irreducibly multiple. Just as audiences who recognize adaptations as adaptations undertake "an interpretive doubling, a conceptual flipping back and forth between the work we know and the work we are experiencing" (Hutcheon 139), science fiction requires its audiences to "oscillate" (Hutcheon 121) between every new entry's speculative framework and their assumptions about what the world is, will be, and should be. More than any visionary or oppressive technologies, more than the characters' imagined freedom from physical or social limitations, more than any possible social critique of the past or present, this demand for a double consciousness of the sort that W.E.B. Du Bois ascribed to Black Americans compelled to see themselves both from within and without, as White Americans saw them, not only aligns science fiction with adaptation, on the one hand, and with interrogations of roles and identities rooted in race and gender, on the other, but also makes it unique among all popular genres.

Hence science fiction carries the potential to be both timely and timeless, ripped from tomorrow's headlines even as it appeals to universal assumptions and aspirations. A generation ago, Brian Henderson, writing about John Ford's 1956 Western *The Searchers*, proposed "to substitute black for red and read a film about red-white relations in 1868–1873 as a film about black-white relations in 1956" (19). Commentators influenced by Henderson went on to argue that a host of contemporaneous Westerns from *Broken Arrow* (1950) to *Two Rode Together* (1961) used nineteenth-century relationships between Euro-American settlers and indigenous peoples to dramatize mid-twentieth-century concerns about miscegenation and other fraught relations among members of different races that would be considerably more daunting if they were presented directly. In the same way, science-fiction movies from the 1950s invent futuristic scenarios to encourage audiences to ponder contemporaneous social problems that would be much less likely to serve as the basis for effective popular entertainment if they were presented in the present tense.

These scenarios may well be based in speculative hypotheses that are grounded in neither science nor the future, as Sam Umland points out: "The foundational myth at the root of the 'body snatchers' story is that of Martin Guerre, about a man who abandoned his wife and allowed himself to be replaced by an impostor, an impostor so skilled at trickery, masquerade, and dissimulation that he fooled almost everyone. It is a story about the relationship between appearance and essence, Truth and doubt. At its root is a Cartesian nightmare in which appearances provide no firm or reliable knowledge of the external world." Once scenarios like the story of Martin Guerre or the defense of a domestic, national, or global host culture against enemy aliens have been transplanted to the future, they can be recycled again and again to address emerging collective nightmares. Robin Jeremy Land observes that these new versions are often billed as updates of persistent fears: "Much like *Godzilla, Them!,* and *Beast from 20,000 Fathoms, Cloverfield's* creators believed the giant monster was an apt symbol for working through the concerns created by complex international problems." Alternatively or simultaneously, they can use their monsters to graft new fears onto old in Jessica Metzler's formulation: "*The X-Files* can be read as connecting a 1950s paranoia about not being able to trust one's family to a 1990s paranoia about not trusting the government." Land and Metzler agree that the keynote here is the genre's ability to accommodate its target audience's historically shifting anxieties, sometimes by updating old anxieties, sometimes by revealing the roots of new anxieties, sometimes by suggesting, as Umland does, that nothing has really changed: "It is as if the postwar substitution of Communist infiltrators for the fifth-column Fascists of the 1940s has become a loop, with one enemy replacing another in an endless cycle of repetition." Mica A. Hilson discerns a similarly evergreen pattern rooted in "two other 'witch-hunts' from the late 1980s and early 1990s": "the sexual abuse of children epitomized by the McMartin preschool trial, and the paranoid discourse about gay men in the military, which culminated in the Clinton era's 'Don't Ask, Don't Tell' policy." For Hilson, "[r]emakes like Ferrara's *Body Snatchers* and Hooper's *Invaders from Mars* make visceral a notion that the original 1950s films only suggested abstractly: there is no safe space, because the alien can breach any cordon, penetrating anywhere and anyone. [...] these remakes and adaptations were the product of an era that saw much greater paranoia over the notion that spaces formerly considered safe (such as daycares and military bases) were actually hotbeds of perversity." Although none of the contributors cites Julie Grossman's 2015 monograph *Literature, Film, and Their Hideous Progeny: Adaptation and ElasTEXTity,* they would likely all agree with her leading premise that the processes of adaptation, revisitation, and reinterpretation produce new versions of familiar beings that inevitably seem monstrous.

A further concern these essays share, therefore, is the complicated relationship between what future fictional versions of the present-day world change and what they don't—or, to be more precise, between what they indicate needs to change, what needs to stay the same, and what might go either way. Although they naturally differ in their emphases, several of them identify two targets that many others would probably agree need to change: toxic masculinity and systemic racism. These targets are naturally easier to identify in relatively recent films. Paul Piatkowski and Rebecca Johinke show, however, that these targets are deeply rooted not simply in earlier history but in earlier science fiction. Piatkowski reminds us that as early as "the late 50s, [Ed] Wood is gesturing at the intentional erasure of non-normative groups by traditions of power." Johinke reads *Mad Max: Fury Road* "as an Antipodean response to themes first explored in 1950s sci-fi disaster films centred on women and the maternal body." In retrospect, "Miller's *Mad Max* films provide a lens (or perhaps four snapshots) to examine filmic representations of patriarchal society and to observe the changing status of women on screen in the sci-fi genre from 1979 to 2015 (and now beyond)." Describing three eras "when there was a surge in alien invasion films and multimedia texts; the 1950s–1960s, 1987–1998, 2005 to the present," Joan Ormrod observes, "these eras roughly correspond to times of conflict that caused America to reconsider its place in the world," and later adds, "In all three eras the concept of an ideal masculinity is in crisis."

Piatkowski sees a direct line between Wood's notorious B features and Walter Mosley's visionary anti-racist parables: "In Ed Wood's *Plan 9 from Outer Space*, the alien Other claims recognition through a reanimation of the past, literally in the case of the undead ghouls that he unearths. Digging up history literally and metaphorically engages with the haunting presence of social and political injustice, as well as unveils the rampant bias and prejudice running the length of Western civilization. It is this long train of bias and prejudice that Walter Mosley begins to chisel away at in *The Wave*." William Hart sees racebending, the casting of actors of color in roles that were originally explicitly imagined or simply assumed to be White, as potentially both challenging and reinforcing racial stereotypes through minstrelsy, tokenism, and imperatives to assimilation: "If racebending happens in a novel to film adaptation, then the task of the ideological critic would be first to identify the racebending changes and then to ask who benefits from such changes, and what are the implications for a better, more equal world. If the act of racebending is found to still reinforce a racist ideology, then what are the alternatives? A clear alternative to simply inserting a Black actor into a story previously written for a White character, is to tell a story of a Black experience from the beginning. In the realm of science fiction, Afrofuturism is just that." Looking into the future inevitably requires us to return to look at the past through different eyes. In this connection, Piatkowski quotes Mosley, who says that "for black writers, '[t]he last hurdle is science fiction. The power of science fiction is that it can tear down the walls and windows, the artifice and laws by changing the logic, empowering the disenfranchised, or simply by asking, What if?'" Mosley's view of science fiction as the last frontier also makes it logically the first and most direct line of attack on the invidious and oppressive assumptions of the present, assumptions that can be best revealed through representatives of the oppressed, as in Rami Bahrani's racebending 2018 remake of *Fahrenheit 451*, whose theme, as Hart points out, "is not prejudice per se, but oppression. In this case the burden of oppression is placed on the back of a black man and he is the one who must see the rights and the wrongs of his ways. It is not a White character who has to do this." Richard Berger finds David Cronenberg's diagnosis in his 1986 remake of *The Fly* even more devastatingly intimate, for his "protagonist, Seth Brundle, is not here to warn us about a highly technologized future, where men can finally play God, but, as he puts it in the movie, 'society's deep fear of the flesh.'"

Joan Ormrod finds "[t]he model for America heroism" that underlies science fiction films in myths of "the frontier and the hero's relationship with the land" as set forth by Richard Slotkin: "The myth of the frontier as a space that forged heroism, was a myth based on violence. The frontier formed the boundary between civilisation and wilderness, and in European settlers' expansion into Native American lands violence was deemed necessary. The frontier formed the basis for the

American monomyth of heroism in the hero who tames the wilderness and the corruption of society through violence." Dennis R. Perry, looking forward rather than back, suggests: "The alien's seemingly magical powers, together with its helpful child disciples, oddly anticipates the 1960s countercultural rebellion in San Francisco and elsewhere. As we know, the '60s were a time when many youth began to rebel against their parents' paranoid fears, finding appealing new peace-centered philosophies from hip gurus like Ken Kesey, Allen Ginsberg, and Timothy Leary who, like the alien, inspired rebellious actions from their loyal young followers. In essence, as a leftist film, *Space Children* is an anti-war protest by a rebellious underground, younger youth movement. Like those of the 1960s, the kids in the film defy the military establishment in their own crusade to 'save the world.' In short, the alien uses the children to teach their parents what Walt Kelly famously observed in a Pogo comic strip on Earth Day, 1971: 'we have met the enemy and it is us.'"

If science fiction movies can reveal the deepest flaws in humanity, they can also celebrate humanity's greatest strengths, beginning with the importance of the traditional humanistic values of self-acceptance, compassion, and community. As Dennis R. Cutchins aptly says in his essay on *The Day the Earth Stood Still* and *The Thing from Another World*, "there's nothing like an alien to remind us what it means to be human, and to bring the people of earth together." Sometimes these values are joined by the progressive, empirical values of science itself, even if questionable advances in science and technology have played a leading role in unleashing the nightmares they are called on to put to rest. Zak Bronson explains: "By building on the tropes and conventions of 1950s sci-fi films, these recent prehistoric creature features return to the narratives of the atomic era to symbolize humanity's teleological placement over the natural world. Utilizing tales of prehistoric creatures that threaten humankind's evolutionary place on the earth, these films embody a fundamental faith in the power of techno-scientific and human progress—the same powers that contributed to the rise of the Anthropocene in the first place—to control nature and prevent the extinction threat." Just as often, however, scientists and science itself, like the military forces regularly summoned to defeat aliens, are cast as sadly inadequate or downright villainous. "What little optimism that accompanies the end of *Beast from 20,000 Fathoms* and *Them!* does not come from the American government or military's ability to kill the creatures, but from the human relationships forged in the efforts to understand and conquer the creatures," observes Robin Jeremy Land, who adds that "all that is certain in these anxiety-ridden films is the necessity of human connection. The government and military might fail us, but our love for each other will not."

It would be reassuring to see science fiction as offering enduringly universal, humanistic remedies for an ongoing barrage of historically based challenges like military conflict, the threat of alien invasion, the limiting myth of masculinity, and the oppression seen most clearly in systemic racism. And there are any number of science fiction films that seek to do precisely that. The essays in the present volume, however, are especially interested in films that refuse this bargain by questioning the very bases of humanism, baring its universal claims as favoring a single favored human species and an even more limited range of ways of defining what makes members of this species human. Robert Mayer notes the novelist Stanisław Lem's critique of science as it is represented by the writer Grattenstrom, "whose critique is described as 'a kind of lampoon of our species, furious in its mathematical coldness,' a 'satire against the entire species'" pivoting on Grattenstrom's pronouncement that "'there cannot now, nor in the future could there ever be, talk of 'contact' between human beings and any non-humanoid civilization.'" Grattenstrom's self-congratulatory dictum, challenged by *Forbidden Planet* and any number of other films, is precisely inverted, as Glenn Jellenik points out, in *The Shape of Water*'s revision of *Creature from the Black Lagoon*, by Elisa Esposito's scars, which are originally "thought to be the remnants of an injury that took her voice, but which prove to be gills that will allow her to adapt to a new world and live a new life. [Richard] Strickland, and his brand of masculinity, becomes the outsider, left behind. He is, in the words of General Hoyt, 'unborn, unmade, and undone.' This inversion of otherness and ideal masculinity represents some of the central work of the adaptation. Beyond (and alongside) that, *Shape* uses *Creature*'s basic dynamics and ingredients to specifically redefine a whole set of social concepts—monstrosity, masculinity, gender relations, difference, disability, heroism, and humanity. Viewed through the windshield, the adaptation does this work in ways that reflect and drive an emergent set of 21st-century values." In Guillermo del Toro's visionary film, the alien, more human than the self-justifying human beings who oppose him, offers a point-by-point refutation of their sorely inadequate humanity.

Science-fiction films rise to the challenge of confronting aliens who may be more deeply human than we are in several different ways. Noting "the declining popularity of [...] fantasies of humanity's dominion and mastery of nature," Bronson quotes Roy Scranton's *Learning to Die in the Anthropocene*—"In order for us to adapt to this strange new world [called the Anthropocene], we're going to need more than scientific reports and military policy. We're going to need ideas. We're going to need new myths and new stories [that will provide] a new way of thinking [about] our collective existence. We need a new vision of who 'we' are"—to point out a central irony: the best ideas about how to escape the predations of the Anthropocene Era, the period when human beings and their industries have had the most direct, far-reaching, and devastating impact on global ecology, may come from agents outside the human community who can teach us new, better ways to be human, beginning with the lesson that we need to make common cause with other species. Christopher Love uses the philosopher Hannah Arendt to identify a central contradiction of humanistic science fiction: "Because fiction primarily morally engages its subject, creators of science fiction inherently approach their narratives from an anthropocentric position; they are among the humanists Arendt mentions, probing the meaning and consequence of scientific discoveries in terms of the human race. But the reality of space, the universe's vastness, makes it incompatible with humanistic storytelling—humans tell stories about themselves, their homes, and their significance—but what we have come to discover scientifically about the universe reflects its utter and complete indifference to our presence and its own lack of any meaning. Consequently, this puts creators of science fiction in a conundrum. To be realistic, the inconsequential nature of human existence in relation to a conscienceless universe must be depicted and engaged in space travel films, but in order to be effective narratives these films must somehow maintain their humanity." Paul Piatkowski goes still further: "While both [Ed] Wood and [Walter] Mosley reframe historic relations among groups of humans, Mosley gestures toward an even larger democratization between humans and nonhumans. In order to reach this point, Mosley decenters more than cultural positions in a human devised landscape. He goes so far as to suggest a reframed manner of *thinking* itself—a consciousness that does not have to be human in origin to be treated with personhood. Mosley's book breaks from anthropocentric and Eurocentric models of understanding in order to reorient relations between humans and other humans as well as humans and nonhumans in ways that work horizontally instead of in vertical hierarchies."

Given the fact that many recent science-fiction films continue to invoke timeless humanistic and communitarian solutions to the timely threats they root in earlier films, while others hold the very ideas of timelessness, community, and the human up to critical scrutiny, a question inevitably arises: are these films more deeply invested in raising problems or solving them, scaring us or reassuring us, challenging us to think harder or to work harder? Land isolates a highly typical pattern when he observes that "audiences come to the kaiju film to see a gigantic representation of their fears and anxieties rampaging on the silver screen, but leave with a stronger sense of what is morally right for society." Bronson adds, "If human progress has made the planet vulnerable to destruction, it also provides the way out." Love quotes Susan Sontag's influential 1966 essay "The Imagination of Disaster" to make the opposite case: "the genre provides an 'inadequate response' to the issues that it raises." But this inadequacy, unlike the trademark double consciousness of sci-fi, is hardly specific to the genre; it is a foundational feature of genres from ritual tragedy to romantic comedies to superhero movies, which move from more or less sharply observed fictionalizations of widely recognized tribulations, from the mystery of death to the obstacles to romantic love to the difficulties in rallying allies of different minds and abilities together to fight powerfully single-minded enemies, before concluding that against all odds, a resolution can be achieved that either solves these insoluble problems or at least, in the stories about King Oedipus, King Lear, or King Kong, gives us greater and more consoling wisdom about them.

Some of this wisdom is frankly fictional, as Christopher Love acknowledges: "These three films [*Rocketship X-M, Interstellar,* and *Ad Astra*] also provide a frightening glimpse of the vast emptiness of the universe, its hostility to life, and the possibility of losing Earth as a signifier of home. Caught between our own destructiveness on our home planet and the perils of space, we are destined, the narratives reassure, to carry out our meaning familiar to us by some familiar means: romantic love, family, and hope in a mystical force that guides our destiny. This, though, is not science; instead, it is science fiction's way of destabilizing Earth's fixed position as 'home' in the human mind while simultaneously attempting to help us to recover or to create meaning when such is lost." And a good deal of it is shared with other popular genres that also retail the bromides that love conquers all, that crime does not pay, that people are strongest when they stand together, and that nothing can resist an idea whose time has come. But at least one kind of wisdom seems peculiar to, or at least peculiarly strong in, science-fiction films that look back to their predecessors in the 1950s, as Greg Semenza explains: "'50s sci-fi film references serve the story's most complex, and under-acknowledged, feature: its self-reflexive meditation on the sci-fi and horror genres—both literary and cinematic—as a kind of practical tool for managing social crisis." Science fiction may well be useful not only for imagining the unimaginable but for managing the unmanageable.

The double logic of adapting stories of yesterday's tomorrows to contemporary versions that are both the same and different as their precursors—hemimetabolic versions, as Berger calls them, that can take advantage of both yesterday's wisdom and the cutting-edge science that will become their most dated feature—shows once again how adaptation and science fiction, like a double star, depend on each other for their gloriously unstable stability. Cutchins notes, "It is always a dicey prospect to remake a classic, but later filmmakers who have been willing to *adapt* the basic patterns of earlier success have done better. The cultural fears or concerns of different eras are captured and preserved in these films, like bugs in amber." Mayer further illuminates the radical dependence of popular genres, and genre itself, on adaptation, even to authors like Lem who vocally disapprove of the film adaptations of their own fiction.

Adaptation scholars have long debated the question of whether adaptations should be interpreted and evaluated mainly in terms of their relations to the texts they adapt, as defenders of fidelity criticism from Colin MacCabe to Casie Hermansson have done, or mainly in terms of the functions they serve within their target cultures, as Gideon Toury's Descriptive Translation Studies and Patrick Cattrysse's Descriptive Adaptation Studies have done. Jellenik, whose version of this debate involves seeing adaptations in the rearview mirror or through the windshield, emphasizes the liberating power of target-based criticism for both futurist avatars and their present-day analysts: "When viewed through the windshield, *The Shape of Water* is an adaptation that centers the productive values of acceptance, diversity, and inclusion. And perhaps the productivity of diverse inclusion can also be seen in the act of adaptation itself—or at least adaptation as conceived and processed through that windshield reading strategy. The Creature of the source text is a tragic character; he represents an evolutionary dead end: unable to adapt to the encroaching future, he, like King Kong, does not survive modernity's invasion of his geographic isolation. But in the re-telling, Gill-man possesses the ability to change. In that way, he represents adaptation." And since, as Perry points out, it is undeniable that "the world of 1950s sci-fi, with its aliens, flying saucers, giants, tiny people, and awakened dinosaurs, has definite fantasy dimensions, functioning as the 20th-century's own modern mythology," it is clearly true, as Cutchins and Perry begin their Introduction by noting, that "science fiction films of the 1950s play a key role in understanding the present, and the future, of science fiction." However uncertainly science-fiction movies may prophesy the future, they are uncannily accurate in their prophecies about the future of science fiction, for as "Adapting a 1950s Sci-Fi Aesthetic," the title of Part I of this volume aptly indicates, they provide the enabling myths and images that later generations of science-fiction films will excavate, develop, or deconstruct.

Despite Cutchins and Perry's premise that "there isn't much difference between the future and the past, at least in terms of science fiction film," the single greatest reward of these essays may well be the impressively illuminating variety of ways in which they explore recent science fiction's revisitations of its 1950s roots. Berger takes David Cronenberg's remake of *The Fly* "as a metaphor for the process of adaptation/remaking itself; both films are biologically connected, rather like the twin brothers featured in the movie he would make next, *Dead Ringers* (1988)," so that in 1953 "Andre's experiments produce two new beings: a human with a fly head and hand/arm (fused with what was left of poor Dandelo) and a fly with a human head and hand. Both of these creatures (or versions) presciently predict the two filmed adaptation/remakes." Semenza glosses the continuing attachment of latter-day filmmakers like Frank Darabont to the black-and-white aesthetic of 1950s science fiction by contrasting "the 70s films' presentations of their sci-fi worlds as 'heightened recreations of reality'" with earlier films that "were powerful, according to Darabont, precisely because of their relative nonreferentiality: 'the only place you can see *that* representation of the world is in a black and white movie.'" The inevitable dependence of even the most state-of-the-art audio-visual representation on retro conventions their audience does not have to master on the fly complicates Jellenik's distinction between "reading adaptations forward, thinking about the changes that occur as opportunities to consider the socio-political conditions out of which the text sprung and into which it was first received," and "the (fidelity-adjacent) rearview approach, which considers adaptive changes as invitations to look back at a source's decisions and investments." Jellenik continues, the Janus-faced orientation of adaptations, looking both forward and back, provides "unique access to what I call Now Historicism, the critical ability to use adaptations to chart and explore, through the windshield, an immediate contemporary socio-political landscape. The fact that the adaptation exerts a double presence—that it occupies, in a sense, (at least) two moments—allows a focus on the specific changes as they concern not the source text but rather the moment in which the adaptation was produced and initially consumed." For Jellenik, science fiction offers the rare opportunity to foster the double consciousness that allows us to step back and recontextualize the present moment historically. When Cutchins and Perry argue that "Steven Spielberg's *War of the Worlds* (2005) and Tyler Bates' *The Day the Earth Stood Still* (2008) may not have eclipsed their originals […] but both updated the cultural and political contexts of the earlier films in creative and meaningful ways. This sampling of reimagined remakes attests to the continuing influence of 1950s science fiction," their argument, reduced to its most abstract terms, is that science-fiction films of the 1950s continue to be influential precisely because they provide a potential nexus of looking back and looking forward, inviting and even requiring updating. As Semenza puts it: "What the color version of *The Mist* may lose in its hyper-realistic, even nihilistic ending, the B&W version gains back through its reassuring reminder that it's only a movie. In such a way, the B&W version recreates an aesthetic experience closer to the one many 1950s sci-fi fans would have experienced at their local drive-ins." Indeed the goal of Darabont's black-and-white version of his own color film seems to be not to recreate the experience of watching such a film during the 1950s but to recreate a nostalgic simulacrum of that experience, along the lines of what Svetlana Boym has called restorative nostalgia, in which "the past is not a duration but a perfect snapshot" in which "the past is not supposed to reveal any signs of decay; it has to be freshly painted in its 'original image' and remain eternally young." At the same time, both versions of Darabont's film, which are clearly intended to disturb rather than reassure audiences, also appeal to the very different impulse Boym calls reflective nostalgia, which focuses "not on recovery of what is perceived to be the absolute truth but on the meditation on history and the passage of time" (Boym 49).

Just as Darabont's black-and-white version of his color film can invite audiences to both restorative and reflective nostalgia, the most glaring contradictions and limitations in all science fiction films may hint at their greatest strengths. Johinke aptly notes, "To highlight [*Mad Max: Fury Road*]'s feminist credentials, the walls of the harem are daubed with slogans such as: 'Our babies will not be warlords,' 'Who killed the world?,' 'You cannot own a human being,' and 'We are not things.' At various points in the action the wives repeat these mantras protesting their objectification and lack of agency in this toxic patriarchy (all the while offered up to the male gaze clad in bikinis and chastity belts as if straight out of a Victoria's Secret catwalk or the set of *Captive Women*)," offering "another example of the contradictions inherent in the films as they both critique and profit from popular culture and the exploitation of women." Hilson argues along similar lines: "Like *The Puppet Masters*, [Abel Ferrara's *Body Snatchers*] tries to have things both ways, by raising alarm about institutions like the military and the family becoming vectors for the alien takeover, but also showing us that the best hope against the aliens is a strong-jawed military man, his beautiful female love interest, and the innocent child they protect—a tableau of patriotic family values." But as Johinke notes, these contradictory appeals to both the liberation from and the endurance of conservative and even degrading attitudes are more than static or an error in an otherwise well-organized system, for they remind us that "[t]here is both pleasure and resignation in the familiar, in indulging in wish fulfilment, and ritualised social integration. Sometimes we do and do not want these stories to end and perhaps wish they had a different ending—one more like a 1950s sci-fi film—a beginning." As Daniel Singleton points out, the videogame *Fallout 3*'s "postmodern satire of '50s sci-fi belies its affinity for these films' binary conflicts between peace-loving Americans and aggressive aliens from Russia or outer space." The point is not to choose sides in any of these binary conflicts, or indeed to choose either blissful or troubled immersion in the simulacrum or critical distance from it; the point is to realize that there are myriad sides and to embrace them all, while acknowledging that the appeal of each one mandates a critical distance from all of them.

This both/and logic, which has become increasingly recognized as the primary appeal behind film adaptations and remakes, allows sci-fi films and their audiences the repeated indulgence of having their cake and eating it too, as in the sequences in *Fallout 3* that "eschew combat in favor of exploration [...] like Philip K. Dick by way of Norman Rockwell." As these essays' explorations of yesterday's tomorrows remind us, the double consciousness this both/and logic works to foster is equally foundational to reinterpretations, reframings, and fantasies of futures that are both alternatives to and projections of a present that are equally fraught but much more entertaining. To use the terms Piatkowski applies to Walter Mosley's novel *The Wave*, science fiction suggests "a move forward (or perhaps backward) to a point where there would be a democracy not just of people, but of people, animals, plants, and mineral." Unlike Wells' Time Traveler, who is freed from the tyrannical one-way march of time only to find himself shuttling forward and backward to one distant era at a time, revisiting 1950s science fiction films and their legacy not only allows but demands that we move at once forward and backward, placing ourselves inside and outside their worlds, surveying their mashups of past and future and adding our own in Forewords and Afterwords yet to be written.

Works Cited

Boym, Svetlana. *The Future of Nostalgia*. Basic, 2001.
Cattrysse, Patrick. *Descriptive Adaptation Studies: Epistemological and Methodological Issues*. Garant, 2014.
Du Bois, W.E.B. *The Souls of Black Folk: Essays and Sketches*. 1903. Yale University Press, 2015.
Grossman, Julie. *Literature, Film, and Their Hideous Progeny: Adaptation and ElasTEXTity*. Palgrave, 2015.
Henderson, Brian. "*The Searchers*: An American Dilemma." *Film Quarterly* 34.2 (1980): 9–23.
Hermansson, Casie. "Flogging Fidelity: In Defense of the (Un)Dead Horse." *Adaptation* 8.2 (Aug. 2015): 147–60.
Hutcheon, Linda, with Siobhan O'Flynn. *A Theory of Adaptation*, 2nd ed. Routledge, 2013.
MacCabe, Colin, Kathleen Murray, and Rick Warner, eds. *True to the Spirit: Film Adaptation and the Question of Fidelity*. Oxford University Press, 2011.
Scranton, Roy. *Learning to Die in the Anthropocene: Reflections on the End of a Civilization*. City Lights, 2015.
Slotkin, Richard. *The Fatal Environment: The Myth of the Frontier in the Age of Industrialization, 1800–1890*. Atheneum, 1985.
_____. *Gunfighter Nation: The Myth of the Frontier in Twentieth-Century America*. Atheneum, 1992.
_____. *Regeneration through Violence: The Mythology of the American Frontier, 1600–1860*. Wesleyan University Press, 1973.
Sontag, Susan. "The Imagination of Disaster." *Commentary* 40.4 (1 Oct. 1965): 42–48.
Toury, Gideon. *Descriptive Translation Studies—and Beyond*. John Benjamins, 1995.

About the Contributors

Richard **Berger** is a professor of media and education at Bournemouth University. His work has focused on the "fidelity approach" in the streaming era and ethical research with children and young people. He writes regularly for *The Conversation* and *CST Online*.

Zak **Bronson** is a PhD candidate in media studies at the University of Western Ontario. His research explores representations of climate change in contemporary science fiction cinema. He has published essays on the novels of China Miéville and the television show *Fringe*.

Dennis R. **Cutchins** is a professor of English at Brigham Young University. He is a co-editor of the *Routledge Companion to Adaptation* (2018) as well as *Adapting Frankenstein: The Monster's Eternal Lives in Popular Culture* (with Dennis R. Perry, 2018). He also researches ways to apply cognitive brain research to adaptation studies.

William **Hart** is the chair of Mass Communication and Journalism at Norfolk State University. His research interests include intercultural communication, global media, media research, and media theory. Publications include "A Rhetorical Vision of Tolerance: Teaching Tolerance through Post-9/11 TV Dramas" and "Racebending: Race, Adaptation and the Films *I, Robot* and *I Am Legend*."

Mica A. **Hilson** is an associate professor of English and communications at the American University of Armenia where he chairs the English & Communications program. His scholarship has appeared in *Pacific Coast Philology*, *The Comparatist*, and *The Harold Pinter Review*, among others.

Glenn **Jellenik** is an associate professor of English at the University of Central Arkansas where he teaches British literature, film, and adaptation. He has published essays on adaptation with Oxford, Routledge, and Palgrave.

Rebecca **Johinke** is an associate professor in the Department of English at the University of Sydney. Her work has a strong focus on gender and popular culture and her interests include writing and rhetoric, Australian literature, film and popular culture, and street narratives.

Robin Jeremy **Land** is an associate professor at McLennan Community College in Waco, Texas. His research interests are equally divided between nineteenth-century American literature and contemporary horror films. He also studies the impact of doubt on the development of Gothic and horror literature and films from the post–Enlightenment era to the twentieth century.

Thomas **Leitch** is a professor of English and Kirkpatrick Chair of Writing at the University of Delaware, where he teaches undergraduate courses in film and graduate courses in literary and cultural theory. His books include *The Oxford Handbook of Adaptation Studies* and *The History of American Literature on Film*.

Christopher **Love** teaches literature and writing at the University of Alabama. His scholarly expertise includes Gothic literature, African American literature, science fiction, and narrative theory. He has published and presented on William Wells Brown, Herman Melville, John Updike, Toni Morrison, and William Faulkner.

Robert **Mayer** is a professor of English at the College of Southern Idaho where he teaches subjects ranging from composition to film. His research interests include modern African and Eastern European literature, including the science fiction of Lem and the Strugatsky brothers.

Jessica **Metzler** is an academic program manager at the Minerva Project. Her academic writing has been published in edited collections from Palgrave Macmillan, Johns Hopkins University Press, and LIT Verlag, and has won awards from the Northeast MLA and the Society for Cinema and Media Studies.

Joan **Ormrod** has widely published in journals and edited collections. Her work focuses on fantasy, science fiction, audiences and comics. She edits Routledge's *The Journal of Graphic Novels and Comics* (2010–), published six times a year. She is on the organization committee of the annual international conference of graphic novels and comics.

Dennis R. **Perry** is a professor emeritus of English at Brigham Young University, specializing in American literature and film adaptation. He is the author, co-author, or co-editor of several publications on Hitchcock, Poe and Frankenstein.

Paul **Piatkowski** is a doctoral candidate at the University of North Carolina at Greensboro. His research interests include reading theory, postmodern and post-postmodern literature and theory, ecocriticism, speculative literature, Afrofuturism, and indigenous futurism.

Greg **Semenza** is a professor of English at the University of Connecticut where he teaches classes on adaptation, film, the Renaissance, and drama. He is the co-author or co-editor of books on the history of British literature on film, World War II propaganda, and Shakespeare on screen.

Daniel **Singleton** has taught at the University of Rochester, SUNY Brockport, St. John Fisher College, and the University of Iowa. His research interests include media convergence, fan/audience studies, and adaptation, and his work has appeared in *The Quarterly Review of Film & Video*, *Adaptation*, and *South Atlantic Review*.

Sam **Umland** is a professor and the chair of the English Department at the University of Nebraska at Kearney, where he has taught film and literature for the past thirty years. He has written books on Tim Burton, Donald Cammell, the Arthurian legend in Hollywood film, and Philip K. Dick.

Index

Ad Astra 4, 225, 234–236, 291
adaptation 12, 95–98, 100–101, 106–108, 110–112, 114, 116–117, 121–122, 128–129, 144, 165, 177, 184, 252–256, 263–264, 268, 286–287, 292, 292–294
Adaptation 96
Address Unknown 211
Afrofuturism 252, 254–256, 264, 288
Algol 145n17
Alien 26, 104, 131–132, 133, 145n6, 145n7, 281n4
Aliens 28
alternate history 35, 36, 39n20, 117, 204, 231
The Amazing Colossal Man 28
Amis, Kingsley 251
Antarctica 129
Anthropocene 61, 62, 67, 73, 203, 206, 289–290
Arctic 5, 52, 64, 79, 81, 129, 214
Area 51 133, 173
Arendt, Hannah 224, 290
Aristotle 219n8
Arrival 7n13, 140–142, 144
artificial intelligence 26, 32
Asimov, Isaac 33, 256
Atlas Shrugged 26
Atomic *see* nuclear
The Atomic Café 30
Australian Gothic 268

Baldur's Gate 30
Barnes & Noble 263
Batteries Not Included 139
The Beast from 20,000 Fathoms 3, 61, 64–66, 73n4, 75–77, 79, 80–82, 88, 92, 92n2, 92n5, 93n11, 287, 289
Benjamin, Walter 95, 97, 100, 218
Bethesda 29–30, 35
Beyond Castle Wolfenstein 34
The Big Combo 27
The Big Heat 27
Bioshock 25–26, 28–29, 32, 33, 35, 37
The Birds 17
Biskind, Peter 39n12, 45, 52, 56n15, 63, 179n2
black and white films 11–13, 20–21, 100, 106, 153, 293–294
"Black Destroyer" 131
Black Panther 255, 257, 263–264
The Black Sheep 27
"Black to the Future" 196, 255
blackface 263
blackness 203–204, 254–256, 263, 270; *see also* racism

Blade 255
Blade Runner 255
Blamire, Larry 5
Blaustein, Julian 137–138, 145n14
Bliss, Michael 3, 6, 100
The Blob 3, 184
Bluestone, George 252
Body Snatchers (film) 216
The Body Snatchers (novel) 184, 213
Bonneuil, Christophe 62
Booker, M. Keith 47
Boym, Svetlana 294
Bradbury, Ray 55n7, 79, 92n2, 251, 257–258, 264n5
brainwashing 45, 46–47, 168, 214–215, 262
Brave New World 25
Broken Arrow 286
Brother from Another Planet 255
Bucket of Blood 27
Buffy the Vampire Slayer 160
Burroughs, William S. 27, 96, 102
Butler, Octavia 254–255

Call of Duty 34
capitalism 25, 32, 38, 68, 97, 113, 145n17, 163, 197, 253
Captain Video 2
Captive Women 267, 272–273
Carpenter, John 4, 14, 56n14, 139–140, 142–143, 144, 146n19
Carrington, André 255
Carter, Chris 50
Castle Wolfenstein 34–35
children 17, 20, 47, 84, 133, 148–149, 155, 157–159, 175, 178, 182–193, 226, 241, 269–270, 273–274, 276, 281n11, 287, 289
Children of the Atom 184
City Under the Sea 26
Clark, Arthur C. 145n8, 189
climate change *see* environment
Closer Than We Think! 26
Cloverfield 87–90
Cocoon 102, 138
Cold War 2, 15, 20, 26, 28–30, 32–34, 38, 39n14, 45, 47, 49, 52, 75–77, 90, 92n5, 110, 112, 114, 127–131, 137–138, 143, 145n1, 148, 154–155, 163, 166, 168–169, 172, 178, 210, 214, 227–228, 268
The Colossus of New York 29
communism 22, 32, 43, 45, 47–49, 52, 55n8, 83,

100, 114, 129–131, 144, 145n1, 155, 163, 166, 168, 178, 182–183, 197, 212–215, 215, 268, 287
competence 245
computer hacker 51–52, 53–54
conformity 37, 159, 214–216
conspiracy theory 45, 47, 49, 53, 55n2, 55n9, 155, 166, 197, 231; *see also* paranoia
Corman, Roger 270
Corridors of Blood 27
The Cosmic Man 6, 186, 191
Counter Strike 34
counterculture 188, 215–216
Crash 96
Creature from the Black Lagoon 31, 110–117, 290
Crime in the Streets 215
Cronenberg, David 4, 11, 95–96, 101–102, 104–108, 288, 293
The Curse of the Fly 106
Cyberpunk 2077 29

Danse Macabre 14; *see also* King, Stephen
Darabont, Frank 11–12, 14, 17–19, 21, 23n4, 23n10, 261, 293–294
The Day After 30
The Day the Earth Stood Still (1951) 2, 4, 30, 114, 127–128, 134–139, 142, 144, 145n17, 184, 186, 189, 192, 268, 289
The Day the Earth Stood Still (2008) 143–144, 293
The Day the Sky Exploded 4
Day the World Ended 269–270
Dead Ringers 105
The Dead Zone 101
Demon Seed 105
Derrida, Jacques 197
Destination Moon 4, 168, 223–224, 225
detective fiction 195–196, 202–203
Deus Ex 26
Deus Ex: Human Revolution 29
Dick, Philip K. 211, 240, 294
The Dirty Dozen 34
"Discord in Scarlet" 131
Dishonored 29
Doctor Who 98, 99, 108n3
Du Bois, W.E.B. 254, 286

Earth vs. the Flying Saucers 31, 36
Einstein, Albert 27, 138
Elder Scrolls 30
encryption 49–50
Enemy Mine 252
environment 25, 33, 38, 61–63, 67–70, 72, 73n2, 76, 84–85, 87, 91, 92n9, 143–144, 206, 225, 229, 231, 236, 267–269, 274–276, 278, 280
Escape to Witch Mountain 138
ET the Extra Terrestrial 139, 183, 190
evolution 12, 63, 71–72, 106, 122, 170, 174–175, 179, 206, 214, 231, 289
extinction 61–64, 66–68, 70, 182, 237, 289

The Faculty 160
Fahrenheit 451 (1966 film) 259–261
Fahrenheit 451 (2018 film) 251–252, 261–263, 288
Fahrenheit 451 (novel) 251, 252, 257–259, 262
fairy tale 117, 189–190

Fallout 29
Fallout 3 29
family 49, 55n10, 133, 149–150, 153–155, 158–160, 163–164, 168–169, 175, 177–178, 185, 188, 191, 213, 216, 225–226, 233–236, 268, 276, 287, 291, 294; *see also* children
"Farewell to the Master" 127, 134–135, 138
fascism 25, 34, 35, 36, 38, 114, 210, 257; *see also* Nazi
Fiend Without a Face 6
film noir 117, 198, 212–213, 215
fin de siècle 163, 165, 170, 172, 178
Five 182, 267–270, 274–275
The Fly (1958 film) 29, 95, 98, 100–101, 184, 239, 252, 267–268
The Fly (1986 film) 4, 95–97, 101–106, 288, 293
The Fly (novella) 95, 108
The Fly: Outbreak 107
The Fly II 11, 106
The Fog 14
"The Fog horn" 79
Forbidden Planet 3, 6, 31, 237–239, 241–249, 290
Frankenstein (1931 film) 52, 114
Frankenstein or the Modern Promethesus 105, 263
Fressoz, Jean-Baptiste 62
Freud, Sigmund 149, 153–154, 157, 158, 237
Fukushima Daiichi nuclear power plant 68, 91

gender roles 7n1, 86, 111–112, 115–121, 156, 158, 159–160, 163–164, 169–170, 173, 177–178, 196–197, 226, 251, 268, 274–280, 286–288, 290; *see also* masculinity
George Clinton and Parliament-Funkadelic 254
Giant Gila Monster 184
Gibson, Mel 261, 274, 277
Godzilla (2014) 61–63, 67–68
Godzilla vs. Kong 4, 73
Gojira 4, 15, 27, 61, 66, 67, 70, 75–76, 84–86, 90–91, 92n7, 92n8, 114, 267, 287
Goldblum, Jeff 104, 107, 133, 172–173, 252
Gordon, Bert I. 11, 13, 15–16, 21–22
Gothic 106, 114, 223, 268, 276
Gray, Jonathan 102
The Great Martian War 177
Greenblatt, Stephen 112
Grossman, Julie 287
Growing Pains 153
Gulf War 88, 172
The Guns of Navarone 34

Halloween 71
Halo 28
Harryhausen, Ray 11–12, 15, 79
Hartwell, David 5
Hawks, Howard 4, 129, 131, 142–143, 214
Hedison, David 102
Hendershot, Cyndy 39n10, 39n14, 63, 66, 183
Hendrix, Jimi 254
Hiroshima 36, 63, 75–76, 80–81, 84–85, 87, 114, 169
HIV/AIDS 97, 172
home 114, 149, 185, 189, 224–227, 229, 231–236, 291
hooks, bell 253, 256
Hooper, Tobe 152
horror 5, 11, 13–16, 18–21, 66, 71, 75, 76–78, 87,

92*n*1, 95–98, 100–102, 104–105, 108, 111, 113–114, 129, 143, 148, 152–153, 158–159, 175, 186, 195–199, 202–203, 208, 216, 223, 225, 268, 274, 276, 280, 292

The Host 92*n*9

"Human Is" 211

Hutcheon, Linda 110, 116, 275, 286

hyperobject 67

hypnotism 212; *see also* mind control

I Am Legend 252, 255–257, 263, 280*n*2

I Married a Monster from Outer Space 28, 268, 276

I, Robot 252, 255–257, 263

I Was a Teenage Wereskunk 5

Icewind Dale 30

illegal immigration 88–89, 163

The Illustrated Man 257

"The Imagination of Disaster" 6, 92*n*3, 223, 268, 291; *see also* Sontag, Susan

The Incredible Shrinking Man 29, 114, 189, 239, 268, 276

Independence Day 37, 131–132, 144, 162–163, 170–175, 178–179, 256

Inglorious Basterds 35

internet 49–50, 52, 54, 261

Interstellar 4, 223, 225, 229–236, 291

intolerance 122, 254, 258

Invaders from Mars (1986) 150–153, 158–160, 176, 213

Invaders From Mars (1953) 43, 45–47, 52, 148, 150–155, 168, 176, 184, 189, 213–214, 268, 287

The Invasion 216, 218, 220*n*12

Invasion of the Body Snatchers (1956 film) 3, 14, 20, 27, 28, 37, 48, 114, 148, 161, 214–215, 268

Invasion of the Body Snatchers (1978 film) 216–217

Invasion U.S.A. 212

The Invisible Boy 239

Invisible Invaders 195

Invisible Man 254

The Invisible Man (2020 film) 112

It Came from Beneath the Sea 26

It Came from Outer Space 43, 45, 49, 186, 237

It's a Wonderful Life 212–213

Jordan, Michael B. 257, 260–264

kaiju 4, 61, 68–70, 75–81, 84–88, 91, 92*n*3, 291

King, Stephen 11, 13–18, 21, 101

King Kong 4, 15, 63, 75, 114, 122, 291–292

Kolbert, Elizabeth 61–62

Kpax 146*n*18

Langelaan, George 95, 97–98, 100, 105

Laserblast 4

The Last Man on Earth 31, 199

Last Woman on Earth 270–271

Leave It to Beaver 32

Leitch, Thomas 101

Lem, Stanisław 240–247, 292

Light Ahead for the Negro 254

The Lord of the Flies 19

The Lost Missile 145*n*1

The Lost Skeleton of Cadavra 5

"The Lottery" 19

Lovecraft Country 255

Lucky Dragon 84, 92*n*6

Lynch, David 100–101

Machine Games 35

Mad Max 267, 276

Mad Max: Beyond Thunderdome 267

Mad Max: Fury Road 267, 275–278, 287, 294

Mad Max 2/The Road Warrior 30, 267, 277

The Magnetic Monster 5

The Man in the High Castle 34–35

The Man Who Fell to Earth 138

The Man with X-Ray Eyes 27

"The Man Without a Body" 99

The Manchurian Candidate (1962) 19, 28, 252

The Martian Chronicles 257

masculinity 70, 111, 113, 115–119, 121–122, 162–164, 166, 169–170, 177–178, 275, 287–290; *see also* gender roles

McCarthyism 3, 39*n*14, 46, 145*n*12, 148, 210, 257

McLaughlin, Neal 5

McMartin preschool trial 148, 155, 159, 287

Meet John Doe 210

The Meg 61, 63, 67, 70–72

Méliès, Georges 1

Menzies, William Cameron 219*n*10

Metamorphosis 105

#MeToo 112, 122*n*1, 177

Metro 33

Metropolis 1

The Midnight Sky 4

Midwich Cuckoos 184

Mihm, Christopher 5

military 12, 14–15, 18–19, 43, 46, 53–54, 64–66, 73, 76, 79–80, 82–85, 88–91, 113, 116, 119, 127–129, 132, 133–134, 137, 138, 141–142, 144, 145*n*5, 145*n*15, 148–151, 155, 158–161, 173–174, 182–186, 188–193, 199, 216, 228, 239, 241, 268, 275, 287, 289–290, 294

Miller, George 267, 274–276, 278–280

mind control 45–48, 133, 150–152, 156, 214; *see also* hypnotism

Ministry of Fear 211

Minority Report 255

The Mist (film) 11–12, 17–18, 21–22

The Mist (novella) 12–17

Moby Dick 5, 16, 263

Monroe, Marilyn 117

Monster on the Campus 6, 184

Monsters 87–90, 92*n*9, 163, 177

"The Monsters Are Due on Maple Street" 32, 37

Mosley, Walter 196–197, 200, 202–208, 288, 291

mutant 5, 29–31, 34, 38, 114, 131, 168, 271, 279

mysticism 121, 231–233, 236, 243, 291

Nabokov, Vladimir 102

Nagasaki *see* Hiroshima

Naked Lunch 27, 96

The Naked Monster 5

Navajo code talkers 53–54

Nazi 34–38, 114, 211, 258, 260, 266; *see also* fascism

Neanderthal Man 6

Neumann, Kurt 96–97, 225

New Historicism 112
news media 20–21, 54, 87, 134, 136, 141–142, 144, 155, 165, 200, 262
Newsom, Ted 5
1984 27, 36
nuclear 1, 4–5, 25–31, 33, 36, 38, 43, 52, 63–67, 75–76, 79–81, 83–86, 92n7, 100, 114, 136–138, 166, 169, 182–184, 191, 212, 225, 227, 231, 236, 240, 246, 268–269, 274, 279
Nyby, Christian 5, 129, 142

Oblivion 30
O'Brien, Willis 15
Odysseus 232–234
On the Beach 5, 19, 29, 182, 240, 268
Oppenheimer, Robert 6, 27, 80, 92n4
"The Other Foot" 257
The Outer Limits 18
Ozploitation films 275

Pacific Rim 61, 63, 67–68, 70, 72–73
Pal, George 165, 168–169, 176, 223, 225
Palmer, R. Barton 96
pandemic 22, 97, 179, 218, 256
paranoia 2, 28, 45–49, 51, 54, 55n10, 63, 100, 129, 148–149, 155, 160, 163, 168, 182–184, 186, 188, 190–193, 210, 218, 287, 289
paratext 102, 104, 108
Paul 146n18
Plan 9 from Outer Space 5, 195–202, 208, 288
Planescape: Torment 30
Planet of the Apes 252
pod people 159–160, 215–216
post-apocalypse 6, 14, 29–30, 33, 35, 166, 173, 268, 272–274
posthumanism 205
Predator 131, 145n6
Prey 29
Price, Vincent 98, 104, 106–107
"Princess Steel" 254
privacy 43, 47–52, 54, 159
production code 152
Psycho 71, 98, 102
The Puppet Masters 148–149, 155–159, 213, 294

Quake III 34

Ra, Sun 254–255
racebending 252–267, 261, 263–264, 288
racism 96, 111, 118–119, 138, 196–197, 202–204, 251–256, 258, 260, 262–263, 269–270, 280n1, 287–289; *see also* blackness
reality TV 54
reanimation 195–197, 199, 202–204, 208, 288
Rebel Without a Cause 275
religion 6, 84, 113, 136, 162, 170, 173, 177–179, 183, 186, 188, 243, 258
remake 11, 18, 95–97, 101, 104, 107–108, 110, 139, 143–144, 148, 154–155, 172, 215, 252, 274, 279, 288, 292–293
The Return of the Fly 106
Rinehard: A Melodrama of the Nineteen-Thirties 219n1
Riot in Cell Block 11 215

Robbie the Robot 237, 239–240, 244
Robot Monster 5, 182
Rocketship X-M 1, 4–5, 145n15, 113, 225–228, 231, 236, 291
romantic love 78–79, 90–92, 116, 137, 154, 159, 218, 225–227, 229–230, 233, 235–236, 241, 253, 259, 276, 291

Sayre, Nora 47, 56n15, 148, 215, 220n13
science/scientist 1, 5–6, 12, 14–15, 26–27, 29, 32, 34, 36–37, 38, 39n3, 45, 47, 52, 56n15, 62–64, 66, 69–72, 79–81, 91, 96, 98, 102, 104–106, 113–114, 127–131, 132–134, 136, 138, 141–142, 144, 154, 163–164, 168–170, 177–178, 186, 189–191, 192, 200, 205, 214, 223–224, 226–229, 231–233, 235–236, 237, 239–247, 249, 268, 275, 285, 289
Scientist Movement *see* Oppenheimer, Robert
The Searchers 286
Seed, David 47
September 11 attacks 23n11, 36, 54, 87–88, 163, 174, 175–176; *see also* terrorism
SETI 132
The Seven Year Itch 117
sexual abuse 148–149, 155–156, 287
The Shape of Water 110–111, 116–122
shapeshifting 48–49
Siegel, Don 214–216, 218
Silent Spring 73n2
Slotkin, Richard 164, 172, 288
Smith, Will 133, 172–173, 252, 255–256
Sobchack, Vivian 48, 78, 148, 185
social media 38, 54, 106, 108, 261, 263
Soderbergh, Steven 240–241
Solaris (1972 film) 240–241
Solaris (novel) 240–249
Sontag, Susan 6, 78, 163, 169, 182, 198, 223, 235, 268, 275–276, 278–280, 291; *see also* "The "Imagination of Disaster"
The Sound of His Horn 35
Space Is the Place 255
Space Race 2, 76, 97, 182–183
space travel 2–4, 202, 223–224, 227, 234–235, 291
S.T.A.L.K.E.R. 33
Star Trek 33, 99, 128, 216
Star Wars 4, 17, 25, 38, 55n7, 255, 277
Starman 139–140
Starship Troopers 28
Strange Holiday 211
The Strange World of Planet X 192
Stranger from Venus 4, 139, 189, 192
Stranger Things 185
Super 8 183, 184–185
Superman and the Mole Men 2
Sutherland, Donald 157, 216
System Shock 26

Tarkovsky, Andrei 240
Teenage Caveman 184
Teenagers from Outer Space 3
Telotte, J.P. 5, 274
The Terminator 30
terrorism 33, 37, 45, 49, 54, 76, 87–90, 163, 176; *see also* September 11 attacks
The Texas Chainsaw Massacre 153

Them! 3, 6, 14–15, 19–22, 27, 31, 73*n*2, 75–77, 79–83, 86, 88, 92, 114, 184, 189, 237, 267, 287, 289
Thief: The Dark Project 26
The Thing 4, 17–18, 55*n*14, 139, 142–143
The Thing from Another World 4–6, 14, 43, 45, 52, 114, 127–131, 133, 138–139, 142, 144–145, 193, 214, 237, 239, 289
"Time Enough at Last" 31
The Time Machine 99
transgender 200
translation 95–96, 105, 141, 240, 292
The Trollenberg Terror 14
Trumbo, Dalton 145*n*15, 236*n*1
Tunnels and Trolls 30
28 Days Later 217
20 Million Miles to Earth 31, 39*n*14, 184
20,000 Leagues Under the Sea 26
The Twilight Zone 18, 30–32, 37, 239, 269, 280*n*2
Two Dooms 35
Two Rode Together 286
2001: A Space Odyssey 4

UFO sightings 166, 169, 174, 195, 200
United Nations 91, 137–138, 247
Us 255

Van Vogt, A.E. 131
The Vast of Night 5
vegetable 52, 129, 214
Le Voyage dans la Lune 1

Wanger, Walter 214–215
War Games 30

The War of the Worlds (1953 film) 4, 31, 134, 166–170, 172, 174
The War of the Worlds (novel) 132, 134, 145*n*9, 162, 165–166
The War of the Worlds (2005 film) 163, 174–176
War of the Worlds: The True Story 164, 177
Wasteland 30
The Wave 196–197, 200–208
"Way Up in the Middle of the Air" 257–258
Welles, Orson 162, 165, 168, 177, 179*n*4
Wells, H.G. 99, 112, 132, 134, 145*n*9, 162–166, 168–170, 172–173, 177, 179*n*1, 285, 295
Werewolf of London 114
"Who Goes There" 127, 128–129, 134
The Wife of Martin Guerre 210–211, 218–219
Wise, Robert 137–138, 140, 145*n*16
Wolfe, Gene 189
Wolfenstein: Enemy Territory 35
Wolfenstein: The New Order 33
Wolfenstein 3D 34
Wolfenstein II: The New Colossus 33, 36
Wood, Ed 195–202, 208, 209*n*4, 287, 291
The World, the Flesh and the Devil 36, 268, 270, 275
World War II 1, 33–36, 39*n*17, 53–54, 76, 84–85, 92*n*9, 114, 130, 163, 166, 168, 182, 211, 215, 237, 257, 268
World Without End 114, 267, 271, 273–274, 278

X-Files 43–55, 196, 287

"The Zanti Misfits" 18
ZeniMax Media 35
zombie 4, 189–190, 196, 213, 219*n*11, 256